Bill Cara has become the defacto spokesman for a growing group of finance and investment professionals who are speaking out on inequities in capital markets. He started blogging four years ago with perhaps 20 readers "tuning in" a day. His message for the investor was: "... what you need to know to compete against Wall Street". He has maintained his "day one" thinking through four years of daily writing and steadily built a large blog readership ranked as one of the more elite and enlightened among that of any media offering. His readers work with him as a community through lively discourse and help evolve and fine tune the focal point around which his views are anchored — capital markets and social equity. His unique ideas have now infused themselves into the commentary of broadcast, industry and political leaders such that *Lessons from the Trader Wizard* offers different things to various readers. Traders will be exposed to a way of looking at markets that can not be found in the classroom. Investors will find the clear basis for assessing the appropriateness of their portfolio with an increasingly global "trading floor". Scholars of the dynamics of groundswell movements and social change, will witness the direction cumulatively initiated by Bill Cara's writings, which mirror his transition from that of altruistic trader-statesman to Free Markets Patriot[sm]. There are many ways to yet develop and envision the core thinking as regards Free Markets Patriotism[sm] and the protection of trader rights that Bill Cara uniquely advocates. *Lessons from the Trader Wizard* embellishes and puts into perspective the appeal of the daily journalistic correspondence on free market dynamics that people, in growing numbers, have come to expect from the Bill Cara Blog.

Peter C. Simmons, Ph.D
Chief Market Sciences Executive
Enterprise Support Company/ESC

Lessons from the Trader Wizard

Bill Cara

ISI *publications*

Lessons from the Trader Wizard

ISBN: 978-1-897403-00-6
Copyright © 2008 Bill Cara
All rights reserved.

About the Publisher

This book is published by ISI Publications Limited. All enquiries should be directed to ISI Publications at info@isipublications.com or call:

UK
Tel: 44 1892 548881

Hong Kong
Tel: 852 2877 3417

Toronto
Tel: 416 849 1926

All ISI titles can be reviewed and purchased on-line at:

BOOKSonBIZ.com

THE ON-LINE BUSINESS BOOKSTORE

Printed in the United States of America

Dedication

To Pat, Will and Stef, for your love and understanding. And to my late parents John and Kay Ciccarelli, for your gift of values.

Acknowledgements

As this book probably took me 40 years to write, I have many teachers and industry associates to thank. After business schools at Waterloo Lutheran University and McMaster University, and a career in public accounting, a second career in systems consulting and a third career in the securities industry, I believe I learned a lot.

Along the way, I took notes and put them into files with the hope that one day I would write this book. You may spot a little of Graham & Dodd, Edwards & McGee, Warren Buffett and others. They all had a profound influence on me.

Unquestionably, the two people who had the biggest influence in my trading and my writing are Ian Notley, who has been described as "the world's finest technical analyst of capital markets," and Frank Kaplan, who I consider to be a business writer without equal. Ian taught me how to see the inter-related parts of the big picture, and Frank convinced me to write it simply.

As a first time author and close to 1,000 pages of notes, I probably wasn't the easiest client taken on by ISI Publications. But Sarah Barham, CEO and co-founder of ISI, Carol Bonnett, Editorial Director, and Eleanor Bramah, Editor, persisted for a year as I went through a series of re-writes, the likes of which I am sure they had never seen before.

I'd also like to thank Richard Zemnickis, Bud Wood and David Rosenblum for assisting with the graphics, and Ermanno Pascutto and William Woods for pointing me to ISI Publications.

Thanks!

Table of Contents

Table of Contents

Table of Contents

Part 1

What is the Market? What is Trading?

The point I have consistently made since I started blogging almost three years ago is that markets are not free. Markets are driven by forces that are related to interest rates, economic activity, commodity and forex prices and by vested interests.

Randomness occurs in a vacuum. We don't live or trade in a vacuum. I have never met a successful veteran trader who suffers from credulity syndrome and believes in Random Walk theory. In fact, the best of the lot are typically hard-ass skeptics.

Rule number 1, 2, 10 and everything in between is, "We trade prices (not stories)." In other words, success comes to those who don't care who is operating in a backroom to manipulate prices, just thankful they (whomever they are) do enough to create volatility.

March 31, 2007
from BillCara.com*

*All quotations opening chapters in this book are taken from the author's blog: BillCara.com.

1 Getting your head around

capital markets and your place in it

At the end of the day, you will come to see you are not investing (in products or companies), but you are trading prices, and that your motivation is to increase your financial wealth and lower your risk. You will look at trading as a process, a journey which has a right road and a wrong one, and with a few skills, some experience and a bit of determination, you can make it on your own, and that you should make every possible effort to do it on your own. It is, after all, your capital.

April 21, 2007

What is the market?

As complex as it might seem, the market is merely a case of "people acting like people" — with all their fears, enthusiasms, prejudices, stupidity and wisdom. Together, we create prices. The market is us.

Trading in securities and contracts is not investing. All of us invest in assets like homes and cars and personal computers and, just like Warren Buffett and Bill Gates, some of us even buy companies.

But for 99% of the rest of us in the market, we trade securities, which happen to be stocks and bonds, options, futures, commodities and forex, in what is called the capital market.

A security, by the way, is technically a financial instrument that has real value evidenced by underlying equity or debt. A commodity or financial future, on the other hand, includes all products and forward contracts linked to those products that trade on an exchange. These are physical goods, foreign currencies, financial instruments and market indexes, trading either at spot (ie, cash) or forward prices.

In the case of commodities and futures, there is no equity, debt or physical value. Instead there is time value.

When you trade time contracts, you engage in a zero-sum activity, which simply means that no new wealth is being created. The impact of futures trading, of course, helps establish a cash or spot price that reflects the sum total of knowledge of the underlying security, including projected price trends.

In terms of the principal value at the end of the contract, there is none. The expression "zero-sum" means that winners equal losers. Everybody, of course, pays transaction costs, including charges not fully disclosed in a net price.

While technically a capital market is one that involves only debt or equity securities, I refer to all matters relating to securities, currencies, futures and commodities as involving the capital markets. Let's not get stuck on semantics.

In this book, *Lessons from the Trader Wizard*, I'm not here to tell you that trading in any type of security is best or that trading securities is better or worse than trading time-based contracts. It's all just a process of finding a price that differs from the underlying value. I am here instead to tell you about the trading process and how you can become successful at it.

You see, in the market, we trade prices, and most traders — including you perhaps — have never thought about it in those terms.

By the way, if you do get stuck with terminology, it's helpful to look at the definitions provided by different library and Web services. Often one service will explain a word in a different way than another, perhaps in a way you can understand. Even I, the Trader Wizard, often refer to the glossaries of *Investopedia*, *Forbes* and *InvestorGuide* because I find the language of capital markets can be a challenge. Often the same thing is referred to by different names.

In this book, I'm not going to suggest any one approach to trading the markets. That will depend on you and your personality. But I will show you the disciplined approach I take, which works.

We all bring a different set of values, personalities and resources to the market. Having a conservative leaning, for example, you will usually tend to see danger in markets. If you are an enterprising sort, you will mostly see the lack of creativity of traditionalists. If you are speculative, you will soon see that most traders are predictably inactive and you'll wonder why.

The important point I want to make at the start of this book — the beginning of a journey, really — is that in this book I give what I think is sufficient information about a wide enough range of topics in capital markets in enough detail to help you become a successful trader. This information is based on my professional experience.

Lessons from the Trader Wizard

Unfortunately, of the ton of information I know is available from many sources, precious little content is qualified, independent and/or objective. You will soon see that you can, on the whole, trust and rely on the information here.

There are no absolutes in the market. With the Trader Wizard, you get a chance to see the markets as I see them — whether right or wrong — so bear with me. The axe I grind — the one we all carry — will be patently obvious.

You'll see that there are aspects of Wall Street that I don't much like. As the expression goes, I have been there and done that. Based on my many years experience, there are people and tricks and concepts I frankly don't trust at all, and neither should you.

If you do choose to go down the long road of high finance with me, it's good to keep in mind the basic guidelines I outline for you in this book, because they are timeless and boundless. They will apply tomorrow as much as they do today. They will apply in Europe or Asia-Pacific as much as they do in North America.

This knowledge of markets: my ability to execute and communicate to people, young and old, today and tomorrow, is why I'm called the Trader Wizard.

The road ahead

The premise of this book is that if you follow my market-proven guidelines, use common sense, set realistic goals and exercise a whole lot of self-discipline, you will find that trading in the capital markets is a journey anybody can make with considerable success.

Is the road a difficult one? Well, there is definitely sophisticated art and science involved in the trading process, but in my view, nothing people with a secondary school education can't handle.

We'll cover the material a bit at a time because there is a lot of content here. However, if you decide to become a student of the market — which is to say you intend to remain open-minded, always learning, always trying to get better — you will, in time, acquire a life skill, a skill you can pass along to family and friends.

At the end of the day, your success will even seem to have come naturally, because the capital markets are nothing more than a personification of human nature. You just have to find the natural rhythm. What occurs in

What is the Market? What is Trading?

San Francisco at this very moment in the capital market is the same thing going on in Sydney or Shanghai, Sao Paulo or Stockholm.

Is seeking financial success via trading the end goal? Well, without a destination, you'll never get there. Like your friends, you will probably measure your success at reaching your goals in money terms, but you should not forget that money by itself is never as important as peace of mind, which is merely another way of referring to happiness.

In addition to monetary capital, the market also contains what I refer to as social capital, which I'll also discuss in this book. Enjoy the journey!

To start with, I have a simple rule: Regardless of whether in personality and philosophy you happen to be conservative, aggressive or speculative, the first and simplest rule to trading is that if any trade ever causes you or your family to worry, do not make it.

I will repeat that statement, often. The market is chock-full of opportunity, but trading is mostly about avoiding aggravation and risk. If there is a single bottom line, that's it.

Yes, there is mystique in financial markets, but trading has always been simply a business of common sense, intuition, faith, courage, knowledge, patience and luck. Trading, as I like to state, is not rocket science, but life itself. And the capital market is just space we occupy for a moment. Attaining success should not be a mystery.

If you're just starting out in a career in finance or making important life decisions about your financial affairs, it's not going to be easy because Wall Street lays some pretty serious obstacles in your path to success. In any case, I like to think trading is like a long journey where everybody needs some help along the way.

So why take my lead? How did I become a Trader Wizard?

I believe that I qualify as an expert in many aspects of the capital markets. I have managed major broker-dealers as well as smaller ones. I have built them from scratch — in fact, I did that a couple of times, one full-service and one electronic. I've also worked in research, retail sales, institutional sales and corporate finance.

I've worked onshore and offshore. The firms I've worked for are names I'm sure you know and a few I believe you won't. I very much enjoyed my time as a professional money manager and a builder of automated decision systems.

Lessons from the Trader Wizard

I have been an expert witness for securities commissions and governments, worked on a government task force to re-organize securities markets and made presentations in Senate Banking Committee hearings. In the Far East I gave speeches side by side with Canada's Trade Commissioner. For many years I've been publishing investment articles in magazines and via the Internet and given many free seminars.

Before any of this started, I worked hard to earn two professional accounting designations (CA and CMA) as well as an MBA. By working 24/7 and at night school, I accomplished all three goals in just one year. I was even awarded the *Wall Street Journal* Student Achievement Medal in undergraduate school, which was the top business school award.

Although I valued highly my upbringing and my formal education, I always saw it as part of a process of making me the independent person I wanted to be. So, in wanting to put myself out into the world as "me" and not somebody's perception of me, I discarded the wrappings.

In 1972, I legally changed my name from Ciccarelli to Cara. This was a story that started a year earlier when my wife and I had discussed changing our name, possibly to Cecil, which my Uncle Joe had done in the 1940s to launch his business career.

On the final day of my professional accounting career, while being entertained at the Cara Inn by the General Manager of the Toronto Airport Cara Operations, I was talking of a name change that would help launch my next career in healthcare systems consulting. I was doodling letters of my surname on a napkin. I recall chopping the first and last three letters and my host simply looked at the four letters "c-a-r-e" and said, "Why not Cara?" My wife agreed.

Holding the designations Chartered Accountant and Registered Industrial Accountant (now Certified Management Accountant) along with a B.A. (Hon. Bus.) and an M.B.A., my calling card looked like alphabet soup.

Anyway, I stayed in that second career for eight years, built a business, did some writing (won a National Business Press Association Award) and ultimately got bored. In 4Q 1980, I decided I had the requisite business experience to venture into the securities industry, which I knew to be dominated by my peer group who had been raised in a "silver spoon" environment. A year into my third career, despite a gruelling Bear market and a crash in gold, I knew this was where I would spend the rest of my life. I also decided I no longer wanted to be branded CA and CMA, so, while working at the prestigious firm of Dominion Securities Investment Management Ltd. in Toronto, I made a change — just like changing my name 11 years earlier. I called the two professional accounting institutes that had bestowed their status on me and told them I was mailing back my papers. I then dropped all the fancy letters that followed my name.

You see; nobody brands me. I am what I am. Some people refer to me as eccentric; I call it independent. Other than my immediate family, I owe nobody. No mortgage debt, no credit card debt, no car loan — no financial obligation of any kind. I am beholden to no one, including those two accounting institutes that were demanding I pay "professional fees" for the rest of my life, for whatever reason I cannot imagine since I was no longer practising accounting.

Actually, I do have a debt — to society for giving me my independence.

Was this eccentric behavior? I don't think so, because as a young man I had discovered who I was and where I was going. I knew that I had considered every angle and planned every move in my life. I still do.

Within five and a half short years of joining the securities industry, I founded and built out the penthouse floor of the Toronto Stock Exchange Tower for Canada's largest full-service independent broker-dealer. I built their Eastern Canada operations from scratch. Twenty years later, I'm called the Trader Wizard. I am presently setting up to trade securities professionally in the Bahamas under the name Cara Trading Advisors (Bahamas) Ltd.

As well as giving back to others where I can, I take from life only what I think is fair and honest. Despite the criticism, I will continue to speak out on behalf of the interests of global owners and managers of capital against an industry too willing to exploit them.

Why I made my move to the Bahamas

The big decision, for me, came down to choice of lifestyle. I like the sun and the sea and the sand. I like the relaxed ambiance of the island nation and its friendly people.

The Bahamas is a jurisdiction with no income tax act, which frees me of being a nation's chattel and allows me to pay my fair share of the cost of government on the basis of my spending. More than anything, that represents my core values.

Over the years, I have travelled to and checked out many so-called tax havens: Cayman Islands, Barbados, Bermuda, Singapore and Hong Kong, among others. I became an expert in offshore legal structures like IBCs (international business companies), trusts and special-purpose vehicles. But the principal reason I chose the Bahamas was that I fell in love with the country, the people and their values.

Does that mean I'll stay forever? Possibly not. I'll remain a permanent resident here, but I would hope to spend lots of time with my family in Toronto and Vancouver and other parts of the world too.

Hopefully now you understand my motivation and my perspective. Understanding motive, more than anything, is the bridge to knowledge and from knowledge to action. It's the same thing in the market.

Let the journey begin!

Stop listening and talking; start reading and thinking, then doing

By now, you are no longer surprised that I feel so strongly that every person has a responsibility to look after their own affairs and not rely on others — in particular Wall Street or any form of government — to work in their interest.

That's not to say a person ought to do their own trading. That's not practical in many cases. They may need help. They may even need to decide to put their capital under the management of a professional. But if that must be the case, it is still a decision that requires knowledge, planning, execution and subsequent oversight.

A trader is the owner or manager of capital. That is clearly a buy-side role. Job number one, then, is to stop listening to the sell-side or talking to people who might mislead you.

Job number two is to start reading, discussing and thinking. Then acting. Traders are actors, not part of the audience.

At the end of the day, it is your capital and nobody — not even the participating organizations that make up the New York Stock Exchange (NYSE) — should be trusted with your capital unless you, an actor, are intimately involved in the process.

From direct experience, I believe that deceit in financial institutions is commonplace and could easily and frequently be discovered by legitimate independent audit. However, regardless of suspicions, the deceit that I believe exists on the sell-side is not often discovered, unless the wrongdoers are literally caught with their fingers in the cookie jar, because they are all "Humungous Banks and Brokers" (HB&B).

Call it what you wish — HB&B, the Club, the Firm, the Sell-side — but don't call it a place that works for you ahead of its own financial interests, goals and objectives. In the eyes of the HB&B, you are either their customer or their employee. To those (not me) who refer to the market as a casino, they are the owner-operator and the gaming commission combined, and you play by their rules or you don't play. That's a fact.

I will go further; it is also my belief that the HB&B controls (or at least materially impacts) the people's government in the United States and every important financial agency in it. And you are a chattel. You owe them. You see, HB&B and the government are in the business of credit and every person who has a debt is owned by them ... is beholden to them. You are not independent and they know it.

With respect to capital markets, you will discover that, burdened by debt, you are clearly disadvantaged and that when you complain loudly enough, there may be token examinations by one government agency or another and occasionally fines levied to keep up appearances.

Having risen to the penthouse in the HB&B structure, I think I've earned the right to say that the HB&B controls our markets and runs them in its own interests. It really is a closed society. The rest of us have been treated unfairly in the process. That has always stuck in my craw.

During my time in the HB&B, an insider like me got to experience first-hand human nature at its worst: 99% pure greed and gluttony. I discovered it's not that different from what was portrayed in the movies *Wall Street* and *Boiler Room*. Self-interest rules.

But I'm not at all sour today because my time in the HB&B was an education. It helped me to see the market as a place of fear, greed and ignorance, which I can exploit. It took me a long time to realize that with knowledge and skill I could become an independent Trader Wizard.

Harping at the HB&B is not a bandwagon I recently jumped on. I have always spoken out (including at the highest level of government and at industry public forums) opining that Joe Public would be best served if governments would force the financial services industry to eliminate their conflicts of interest and to act in a totally transparent manner. They say they do, but they don't.

Take, for instance, a broker-dealer. If brokers were separate from dealers, you wouldn't be giving your order to an organization that shows that order to their principal trading desk, which then trades in their interest, against your order.

If you think this sell-side and government-dominated market is not fundamentally sick, then ask yourself a couple of questions. Has the HB&B ever shown you their principal trading orders? In addition, these firms control the US Federal Reserve Bank. Has the "Fed" ever shown you its principal trading orders?

Yet these same companies demand to know your wealth and your trading instructions. They do that so they can trade against you. It's a flat-out conflict of interest.

I guess their "we-are-fair-and-transparent" charade will continue until the capital markets implode in a "financial armageddon", collapsed under the weight of debt and misguided credit. My friend Michael Panzner has published a book (2007) by that title. I hope you read it.

Too busy cutting down trees, people fail to see what's happening to the forest. Panzner, however, is one of the few people I know who can deal with day-to-day Wall Street action as a top-flight institutional salesman and yet have a big picture perspective — a picture he paints in *Financial Armageddon* as one that should terrify us.

Must this multi-trillion-dollar house of cards collapse and, if so, can society still protect itself? Time, Panzner says, is running out.

I happen to be more concerned about what happens before the financial system collapses. As I see it, until the financial services industry and government is restructured to a point where the owners of capital have equal opportunities for wealth enhancement, there will be a continuous transfer of wealth from the middle class to the HB&B and the government.

Our job as traders is to build and retain wealth, not to give it to others.

Here's a case in point: At the peak of the equity prices in 2000, the sell-side was advising 97.5% Strong Buy, Buy or Hold positions in stocks. Then when the market started to look shaky, Wall Street started a story of monumentally mythic proportions in order to cause independent traders to take their eye off the ball.

The sell-side was telling us that "public day traders" had caused a bubble in the market. So blame day traders for the catastrophe that happened to be unfolding, Wall Street said.

But it wasn't true. All day traders — including the thousands of day traders working on the HB&B's principal trading desks — in fact, hold open positions for hours, minutes or sometimes a second or two.

An HB&B spokesperson going on a financial TV network program like CNBC to decry the practices of "day traders" showed me the true nature of these scoundrels.

What is the Market? What is Trading?

The truth was simply that central bankers and commercial bankers had feared that when 1999 came to a close, computers would crash, throwing the banking system into worldwide chaos. So, to avoid a liquidity crisis, excessive money printing went on all around the world.

But money printing is simply done by credit expansion, which creates an imbalance between global debt and equity if done too quickly. Independent commentators and analysts who chose to warn you of the certain and looming collapse of market prices were ridiculed.

I can think of many critics who decried buying a General Electric (GE) at 50 times earnings (its normalized PE ratio is in the 13-to-19 range) who encountered unjustified personal attacks on their character and judgment.

It's not enough for the financial services industry to say they failed us. They knew precisely what they were doing when they sold you GE at up to 60 and later bought it back from you under 25 when valuations returned to long-term norms.

The extent of the over-bought market in 1999 and the 2000-02 crash would never have happened but for a steady stream of characters from Wall Street "advising" the public how good a deal was GE with a 50 PE.

As it turned out, the bubble was nothing more than an opportunity for the HB&B to transfer probably trillions of dollars of wealth from the general public to a relatively few market insiders, many of whom earned multi-million-dollar bonuses for their efforts. This self-serving conduct was despicable and ought to be the basis of huge class-action lawsuits.

At the end of the day, you and I are just average people trying to get ahead. We are told that a HB&B is in place to serve us, but I happen to know better. I know that if you are well down the pecking order (which starts with HB&B executives and then travels down through their families, friends, biggest clients, church and charities and so on) and you listen to and rely on these HB&Bs, you'll be sorry.

How did the public get sucked in? That should be easy to figure out.

The sell-side are, first and foremost, storytellers. In 1999 and 2000 even the Madison Avenue storytellers — the advertising kids — got into the game, producing television commercials for the online discount brokers to suck you in with stories of truck drivers using their stock market winnings to buy tropical islands. One old lady even supposedly bought a country! Right up to the market crash in mid-year 2000, we were supposed to be laughing at this stuff. But the public got sucked right in, which was a substantial cost to pay.

Lessons from the Trader Wizard

All seems to be fine on Wall Street until a bull market ends. Then reality sets in. It's a fate worse than death for the buy-side. You know what I say is true when your portfolio falls to a third of its previous value. Yes, the suicide rate jumps and unfortunate families are left holding the bag.

Oh yes, there are investigations. When Wall Street helped its biggest clients participate in a front-running scam against mutual funds owned by "Mom & Pop", do you know what the SEC regulator called it? The crooked practice was called "market timing"!

Almost everybody in the securities industry is against the client who takes control of decision making via market timing expertise, so the height of industry deceit was to label their own fraud by the name of a legal and valuable trading practice they detest. Talk about killing two birds with one stone! But really, that is the type of people who lead and regulate this industry.

Market timing exists for a legitimate reason. There are always pullbacks in equity markets because ultimately, market price and real value must match up.

Whether the landing is short and hard, like it was in 1987, or lengthy but no less painful, like 2000-02, the buy-side customer always pays. But do you think the salesperson really cares? They soon get over the hardships of bear markets and hope that you do too.

In a bear market, business is slow, so they simply take an extended vacation, change employers or start new businesses.

They want to start afresh with the next bull market so that they can show a baseline performance from bear market lows. This makes them appear to be smart traders and effective advisors. In fact, they are neither. They simply know that the public soon forgets the passing of a bear market, which is something very basic that Wall Street and shareholder-owned corporations count on.

In conclusion, there is one person on this earth who should be responsible for your assets — you. If you hand over that responsibility to others, you are putting yourself into an institution in more ways than one.

With my background described here, the Trader Wizard is going to try helping you along the way to independence — to an understanding of what the market really is — and teach you what you need to know in order to be a successful trader. That process will be complete as soon as you understand who you are and why and how you're intending to go forward in search of your financial goals.

What is the Market? What is Trading?

Remember, the market is just about average people like you and me, on a life-long journey. Every journey needs a map and a plan and a starting point. Decisions have to be made. I am here to show the way.

2 Deciding to self-trade securities, get help or do a little in between

When you understand how markets work, you see that it is like a dance. There is an undulating price motion as market drivers go through an ebb and flow. Occasionally, you get poked in the ribs or have your foot stepped on and you call that the work of an interventionist. All I am saying, at a time like that, is there are participants in the market who do not share the values and the mission of independent buy-side traders who have a need to protect and to grow capital. So the market is a place of conflict, and unfortunately for you and me, the rules are not the same for the major interventionists (central bankers, finance ministers, bankers and so-called private equity). The game is slanted in their favor, which is a fact.

June 14, 2007

Do you really want to be a professional trader?

Some people can make a good living as a work-from-home, full-time trader. They can even incorporate as a business and enjoy all the usual write-offs and perks of other businesses. But unfortunately they may still be deemed by tax authorities as an amateur trader.

Several court cases addressing this issue have led to some general guidelines, but this may be a matter for tax counsel. What we can say is that the smart approach is to handle so-called "trader" activity differently to "investor" activity. That can be done by keeping separate long-term holdings (Investor Status) from short-term holdings (Trader Status), by recording them as such in your accounts on the day you buy the position.

Is a full-time trader always a day trader?

First, let's clear up a misconception about day traders. The sell-side likes to say that day trading is flat-out speculating, but that happens to be a self-serving misrepresentation. In fact, day trading is very different to speculating.

While speculating is a strategic approach to trading, day trading is simply a tactic that involves more frequent decisions and actions.

What is the Market? What is Trading?

Unlike speculative traders, who seek a return on capital commensurate with their risk, day traders seek to achieve the greatest percentage of winning trades over a short period of time.

If they can make gains on two-thirds of trades (even gains of half a percent or 1%) and keep the average percentage gain larger than the average percentage loss, they will achieve success — and lots of it, if they have deep pockets for trading.

In fact, all the major broker-dealers and banks employ huge trading floors full of day traders. But these — maybe 20,000 day traders from the financial services industries — are in the minority. In the entire world today, there are probably 50 to 100 times as many full-time day traders in the public, mostly working from home. And the number is rapidly increasing.

While both types might work from home as easily as from an office, I think there is a difference between a day trader and a pro. A pro trader is any individual who earns the majority of income from trading in securities. As a sub-set of pro trading, I define a day trader as one who makes between 20 and 1,000 daily buy and sell trades. If a trader exceeds 50 daily trades, I categorize that person as a "hyper-trader".

From an endurance perspective, very few professionals could make a living doing trades at the rate of about once every eight minutes (ie, 50 trades a day). However, I know someone who never worked as a registered trader, but who completes at least 700 trades every day — about one every 35 seconds — and about 75% are winners.

With commission costs now under $10 per 1,000 shares, he's paying less than 1 cent per share to the broker to buy and under 1 cent to sell. Let's say he'll buy ABC at say $3.30 and sell at $3.35, possibly in less than 15 seconds. He'll earn over 3 cents a share, net of commission. That's a 1% net gain on the exposed capital in less than a minute. There are people who wait half a year for that kind of return on their savings account at the bank.

Do I recommend hyper-trading? With advanced technology and very low commission costs, it could be a success. But for the public to do so there must be a reality check — some basic understanding of the nature of trading, and a lot of skills training.

Consider the case of my friend who averages 700 transactions a day, which is really 350 round trades. Can you see yourself taking losses in 25% of them? That's about 90 losing trades a day. Most of you are far too competitive to accept it. You have been trained to win at all costs, at all times. You believe that losing is failing and that being a loser is bad. You simply can't take it.

Anybody can take a risk, but few — perhaps one in 100 of those of you reading this book — are likely to succeed at hyper-trading. But if you think you can, I encourage you.

You should know that day trading is not an easy life. In one trading room, I observed a young man leave the trading floor at least once every hour. I discovered he was visiting the washroom to throw up. He couldn't accept losing. And many of these traders get hooked on drugs or alcohol to calm their nerves. Later they realize they don't have the requisite day trader personality.

I think, more than anything, a full-time trader has to have an ability to laugh at life. You can't internalize life's misfortune or else pro trading would eat you up.

I am guessing there are probably fewer than 10 million people out of the 6.5 billion in the world who would remotely qualify as professional traders, and maybe one-tenth of them as day traders. The fact is, only a small percentage of them work for an HB&B, thank goodness!

Many people have a misconception about traders — they see people on TV standing or running around exchange floors and think that's what it's all about. Most of these people, interspersed with a few independent traders, are basically brokerage house administrative clerks who execute trades from the orders received by their offices as and when the owners and managers of capital (perhaps you?) call them in.

Most of these traders are like the mechanics and pit crew for a racing team, whereas the principal trader (called a liability trader or a proprietary trader) is the race car driver; the one who takes the risk and makes profits (and takes losses). Sometimes the "prop trader", as they are called, works for an HB&B and sometimes they are independent.

Although you may have heard awful things about day traders and pro traders, the best ones are smart and successful. Honest, too, because they're putting their own capital at risk. They are in fact running a business enterprise. They belong to what I call the enterprising trader group, not the speculative trader group, which I describe later.

Most full-time traders work away from the exchange floor or broker-dealer or money manager's office. They work mostly at home or at order-entry trading offices, where they are surrounded by the best technology and information they need to succeed.

What is the Market? What is Trading?

Just like doctors or lawyers, full-time traders have carefully trained for their vocation. Many day traders, in fact, even think of themselves as the capital market's version of fighter jet pilots and pro race car drivers because of the high levels of experience, skill, teamwork, technology and competitiveness needed to win.

The pro race car driver analogy is actually a good one because people in both groups require superior sensory and reactive proficiency to win (or survive), and they need a team to win. The speculator, on the other hand, is a loner and needs time and good judgment to succeed. It's just a different skill set and obviously suits a different personality type.

I have often said that millions of motor sport spectators would love to race a sophisticated open-wheel Formula One car at 250 miles per hour, but the reality is that there are probably only a thousand or so who are qualified to race at this speed. And only a few dozen to whom corporate sponsors actually provide the necessary team support.

Regrettably, most full-time traders are, in fact, independent work-at-home risk-takers who don't have the benefit of such support — inside information, for example. Despite their lack of organization, they still have to bear the slings and arrows of Wall Street, being looked down upon as "day traders" because, as a group, they represent skilled competition.

3 Choosing your advisor carefully

When it comes to money, I have a simple rule: trust no one but yourself. I learned that rule after spending five years as an independent auditor. Follow the money; ask the questions. Give no one — and I mean no one — the benefit of the doubt. BTW, I am accusing nobody. I'm just pointing to the charts.

March 21, 2007

Choosing advice and administration from the sell-side

They don't care to admit it, but registered stockbrokers and mutual fund advisors are licensed as salespersons. They are not licensed traders or investment/securities advisors. They are not paid to be independent and objective. They are paid to sell; they represent the sell-side.

Some of the ideas of a sell-side stockbroker or registered representative (RR) actually do make money for the client, which keeps the client returning for more ideas. The successful commission-paid brokers (ie, the big producers) — and there are many good ones — sell good ideas on a continuous basis in order to earn a living. I respect that; I used to do it.

That's how the capital markets work. Or at least how they once worked. But, as the separate pillars of the financial services industry collapsed over the past 25 years, giant banks gobbled up the smaller brokers. Giant brokers became giant banks. The Humungous Banks & Brokers were born. The trouble is, everybody forgot about the customer's man, the independent RR.

The client had always counted on his RR for objective market advice in the challenging pursuit of profit. When I started in the business as a rookie RR, it was a matter of "here's your desk, phone and phonebook; now go build your book". I was employed by the country's largest broker-dealer, and our job was to build a book of business, not make money for clients.

We RRs referred to our broker-dealer firms as "the umbrella" because we were free to take our business wherever we wanted, as long as we didn't step on somebody else's toes in the firm. Working for major firms, that was always a problem, but the system worked back then. When the banking institutions moved in to supplant brokerage firm management, they brought with them a different culture. It was an institutionally oriented dealer distribution culture. In spite of their advertising and promotion to the contrary, these banks weren't interested in working with clients one at a time.

The executives in charge were too busy thinking about themselves. The big producers called these people "floaters". To keep up with the firm's internal profit expectations — and the obscene personal bonuses of executive management (most of whom wouldn't recognize a bond if it was stuck to the end of their nose, as a former partner of mine was widely quoted as saying) — they set up systems that sold products, not ideas, to thousands of customers at a time.

Yes, even the once-valued client was now called a "customer" and referred to as a number. As you know, customers come and go. So, in order to hoodwink the public, the old brokerage RRs were dressed up in banker's clothes and called "advisors". Never mind the fact they were principally not advising, but selling. They had become part of a distribution channel.

But the clients still expected the retail brokers (the "customer's men") to provide opinions, and they paid them to provide counsel. They wanted independent and objective advice, not a stream of products crafted and packaged by the bank, many of which, like tax shelters for the rich such as Enron, the client didn't understand.

In order to help clients make the right decisions, registered representatives need to be objective, which is a tough game, especially when the sales manager is shouting from his corner office to make this or that quota or to push this or that product.

The age-old conflict between a broker and a dealer really did get worse during the 1990s. The banks, who are dealers, bought up all the stock of the major brokerage companies. As much as they don't like to admit it, the formerly independent RRs and analysts who stayed with their new employer have been bought and paid for.

More than once or twice a retail broker in a dealership has simply wanted to tell his client to avoid his bank's products like the plague. The same goes for the professional analysts who work for these monolithic product-distributing banks, which, as you know, I refer to as Humungous Banks & Brokers, or HB&B for short.

In the securities industry, legitimate (registered) investment advisors require a separate license that prohibits them from selling, but who's to quibble with the facts. When an HB&B can print the money, they own the game, so they can call their sales people "advisors" or whatever else they choose to call them. And believe me, their "advisors" are told what to say and what to sell.

Of course, there exists many unhappy buyers of products who thought they were actually being "advised" and not having the products of these banks stuffed down their throats. Yes, there have been a few lawsuits, and the banks have paid damages into the billions. Just goes to show how big the dealers' product distribution game is.

Independent traders, however, can still find a first-rate retail sales "advisor" where the commissions paid are worth the good advice you get. If you look hard enough, there are many out there and the good ones are worth every dime you pay them.

Having risen to a position of importance in the securities industry, I am concerned that it is failing to meet the needs of the public. My main concern is not with advisors or commission structures at all, but with the form and integrity of the industry structure itself. Every securities firm you deal with that has administrative or management control over your capital is required to be licensed as a broker-dealer, which is essentially a conflicted structure.

I made a presentation to the securities commissions of all the provincial jurisdictions of Canada in which I questioned the definition of broker-dealer. "Is it a broker, which is an agent, or is it a dealer, which is a principal?"

Yes, I'm sure you see the obvious conflict I'd like to see it addressed. Why can't they? Better still, why won't they?

The bottom line is that the securities industry is founded on the ridiculous notion that the public can be well represented by insiders who have a personal interest in the transactions they are conducting for their clients. Furthermore, these people set the rules of the game and put in place their own people to regulate it (which is a way of saying "to enforce compliance to their rules").

So, I approached the nine chairmen of all the securities commissions of Canada, sitting like the Supreme Court up on a long bench in a formal hearing room and posed this question: "Isn't that rather like a divorce fought in court where lawyers representing the opposing litigants plus the presiding judge all work for the same law firm?"

As much as I like regulators, I didn't expect an answer. Too many are lawyers, so if the answer is not already in the book, these regulators can't grasp the concept of change. What the world needs is more wealth creators, not administrators of rules and regulations.

Legislators, on the other hand, are supposed to be concerned about the public's interest in the securities industry, but due to the power of lobbyists, they mostly appear to see just the symptoms and not the problem itself. Over the years legislators have poured a lot of taxpayers' money into the regulatory process rather than examining the structure of the financial services marketplace, which is the only proper place to start.

I personally have also acted as an expert witness on this subject in formal Government of Canada Senate Banking Committee hearings, so I know first-hand the political concern for the stability of the capital market system.

The reality is, however, that the intertwined interests of corporate executive officers and directors, stock exchanges and broker-dealers will take a long time to set aside so that independent and objective experts can re-structure a global capital markets system that is fair and true to the interests of the owners and managers of capital.

Is it any wonder that the public takes out their frustrations on their front-line sales advisor? Just like a dead and rotting fish stinks from the head, I assure you that the problem is much higher up in the system. As I see it, a good customer's man (or woman) is worth his (or her) weight in gold and more, depending on the extent of their independence and the size of your portfolio.

So, don't stop looking if you haven't found one.

Licensed buy-side portfolio managers

Wealth managers who charge success fees are more to my liking than salaried advisors, because they are focused on the end result of successful trading, rather than the process.

I find nothing wrong with the asset manager who earns a success fee for beating the market adjusted for inflation. In fact, clients ought to insist on the formula of "no success, no pay".

Maybe I'm partial due to my wealth manager background. I only left a nice job in portfolio management with the country's largest bank because I found the job boring. The bank was interested in employing hand-holding relationship managers, not wealth managers. Besides, the firm's policy would not permit me to split the profits I made for clients.

Lessons from the Trader Wizard

Most wealth managers that serve retail traders today are individuals or groups that are associated with brokerage firms, bank holding organizations or financial services companies. As a matter of principle, however, I feel they must be operating independently or be charging success-based fees so that I know they are working for me and not against me.

In any event, I would check them out thoroughly. I'd want to look them in the eye before doing business, and hopefully this book will help the average person attain a level of understanding where that can happen.

To avoid conflict of interest, many firms in recent years say they became independent. But that's not the main issue in my view. "Independence" may be marketed as a feature of the service because the service provider knows he has to be independent in the current environment in order to get new clients. Who's checking to see if he's really and truly independent?

The operative word in the wealth manager's role is the word "professional".

According to the SEC and the State of New York Prosecutor (2003), it seems that many of these licensed investment advisors and portfolio managers have been acting somewhat less than professionally. Having worked in the industry for years, it has long been a concern of mine too.

Suppose I see a 28-year-old money manager running a fund or a portfolio for a wealthy family trust and the results are pathetic in a generally rising market. Then suppose I see that young person living well beyond his (or her) means. What am I to think?

There is an expression in the capital markets, "when it comes to money, people are funny". I have to think the worst because too often in my career I have seen the effects of discretionary authority on young (and not-so-young) "professionals".

In fact, the president of the investment management arm of a major investment bank I know apparently went off the deep end. In a large global operation, he ran the firm's second most profitable division out of 17.

But, that was not enough.

A couple of years later, that head man was fired. Acting on complaints from 85- to 95-year-old clients that over $1 million dollars was missing from their accounts, securities regulators worked with the police to arrest the man. It seems he was having a tough time paying his million-dollar mortgage, so he dipped into the client money.

Yes, these idiotic things happen even in the largest financial firms.

Without getting into a litany of potential issues, there are two operating practices of portfolio managers that frequently happen and are destructive to capital markets not to mention highly illegal:

(1)   purchasing securities where the money manager obtains a secret benefit; and
(2)   front-running, which is a case of using one's knowledge to enter personal orders ahead of the client.

The problem is that these practices have gone on for years. I watched them from the inside.

Con artists don't have the word "CROOK" stamped on their forehead like on the Sprint TV commercials. As securities regulators like to say: "Sunlight is the best disinfectant".

When seeking a professional asset manager, first look at their whole track record, including regulatory filings. If this individual has ever been the subject of a regulatory investigation, you ought to have pretty good reasons for not starting a professional relationship with this person.

During the first interview, you'll want to see that there is an effective match-up with your personality and philosophy, but it's more important that the potential account manager has a track record in specific areas that match up with your needs.

Earlier I stated, "Regardless of whether you are conservative, aggressive or speculative, in personality or philosophy, the first and simplest rule to trading is that if any trade causes you, or your spouse, to worry, do not make it. Or if you have already done so and you worry about it, then sell it". When you are interviewing a prospective manager of your assets, recall this "gut feel" rule. You may soon be investing huge trust and confidence in that person.

Roughly, the asset manager's fees are 1% or more of portfolio value with an annual fee minimum of $1,000 or more a year in the smaller firms, so to make your fees worthwhile you'll need to put a sizable portfolio with them. Instead of $100,000, however, most require $500,000 or more. Above $1 million, the fees are scaled down. Under $250,000, smaller fees can be gotten through standard portfolios designed for various investment objectives such as commodity pools.

Lessons from the Trader Wizard

Generally, their performance will be average at best, but your money is probably safe, fees are relatively low, reports are detailed and all you have to do is give them money.

If you can agree to a written statement of deliverables with people you respect and have checked out, and they offer you a success-fee arrangement and low administrative charges and allow you a chance to regularly interact with your portfolio manager, I'd say jump at it.

Then watch that portfolio very closely, electronically if possible.

Choosing a fee-based financial planner

If you happen to believe a person will be conflicted by earning commissions on the products you buy, then you could seek out the fee-based services of an independent financial planner.

You see, I don't trust a system that is not built on the concept of accountability. Success fees and commissions are linked to accountability. A salary doesn't buy accountability.

In my career, I have seen more than a few 20-somethings who have never successfully managed a client portfolio in their brief careers but who nonetheless are driving expensive automobiles (even Rolls Royce and Ferrari cars) around town. In many cases, we're not talking about having rich fathers either. Based on experience, I immediately think the worst and so should you.

Now, if you think I'm a bit harsh with the broad brush, listen to a true story about how a salaried "professional" made money off a client without earning it. I was a broker-dealer's RR selling a residential condominium security to a wealthy individual and his spouse. The client said to me that because it was a tax shelter I had to run the final details by his accountant. Expecting to pick up a large commission check, I confidently faxed the paperwork. Was I surprised when the accountant soon called back to ask what would be his split of the commission. He then said in all seriousness that his client had many other buying opportunities, all of which would result in a secret commission split. Horrified, I hung up the phone and then called the principal to inform him he was dealing with a crooked advisor. I lost the sale, but I knew I had done the right thing. Sometimes there is not enough money to satisfy people — even your most trusted advisors.

Bank managers, as well, have on occasion proven themselves to be deceitful. Once, a group of doctors I had known for many years struck it rich on an oil-drilling venture. As I was a portfolio manager with the country's largest investment bank at the time, I had to follow KYC (know-your-client) protocol. I called the group's commercial banker to discuss the sizeable account transfer that was to be made to me. Lo and behold, this man of presumed integrity, manager of the main branch of the country's largest bank, subsequently broke confidences and called an obscure money management firm (by whom he was obviously being paid secretly) and helped switch the money to them. All I could do was make a formal report and hope the bank manager was terminated.

Another time, two managers in the technology group of another major bank advised that they personally could provide me (for a substantial business I owned) better service directly rather than via their employer. The catch was that if I didn't agree to their scheme the bank was going to double my transaction costs. That was flat-out extortion, so on the weekend I invited them to my home where I secretly recorded the pitch for their sideline business. On Monday morning I called the Executive VP responsible for all banking operations in the country. He invited me for tea, where I handed him the tape. I believe he fired those scoundrels. So I have seen crooks at the top level of our banking system, and my experience has taught me, when it comes to your money, to trust no one without good reason.

There are salaried fee-based advisors in the financial services industry who are completely honest. I am even willing to admit I know many. But the next question is, are they useful? Can they make money for you?

The trouble is, I have never found a trustworthy fee-based financial planner who could successfully trade securities that would interest me, like say exchange traded funds (ETFs). These advisors are out there, but I haven't encountered a single one who gets paid by salary.

Adopting a published portfolio:
A case of the blind leading the blind

Most of you will come across a trader's model portfolio in a magazine article or a market guru's newsletter. Beware! Think hard about its real value. You are dealing with the publishing industry and not a personal advisor.

Mainstream media is paid by somebody other than you to publish material to catch the attention of a broad audience, not work in your interest.

In some cases, the magazine writer, usually a person not registered to provide specific trading advice or trained for it, is just a parrot. Often he regurgitates the advice of a market guru (whom I label, more appropriately, "a market personality"). By definition, a "guru" is supposedly a spiritual leader. If you are looking for that kind of support in the capital markets, then you've gone to the wrong place if you're applying their model portfolios to your needs.

A couple years ago, I kept and followed up a special investment issue of a world-leading magazine, which was published specifically to help readers make informed trades for retirement. The results of their retirement issue were an unmitigated disaster. I keep that issue handy to this day to remind me mainstream magazines are not the answer to one's personal desire to build and retain wealth.

More qualified to help, arguably, are the model portfolios of the broker-dealers and the wealth management firms. If you do a thorough search of these, you may find a style of professional management that matches yours.

But should you decide to follow their recommendations, you are, in effect, turning over control of the management of your money to people you've probably never met. Again, buyer beware.

The best support I've found in this area, for the new trader, has been the model portfolios created by independent, competent analysts at Value Line and displayed on their website (http://valueline.com). Over the long run, they do as good (or better) a job as anyone. In fact, they have a solid track record over many years.

If you are a young student of the market with time to learn, why not keep your own hypothetical model portfolio using top-rated Value Line picks? You should also seriously consider joining a securities trading club where you can contribute to the analysis, discussions and decisions. Then you can use this information to see if your hypothetical portfolio comes close to meeting your own goals.

In the interest of education and research, the information I post at http://BillCara.com can help anyone get started with a high-quality company watchlist that would appeal to various age levels and general interests (eg, ethical investing). But in no case do I advise subscribers of the free blog to invest in any particular security at any point in time. I try to teach people how to trade on their own or at the least to be able to freely communicate with their advisor.

Furthermore, I believe everybody must continually do their own homework and feel comfortable with their personal decisions. That is my fundamental belief.

What is the Market? What is Trading?

Market advisory letters: A few things to know

The market is about marketing. Market letters are about marketing letters. Enough said. Despite their outlandish claims, over 80% of market advisory letters fail to beat the major market indexes over the long term. If a market letter service goes to perhaps a hundred thousand people, its comments will, at best, be general and useful primarily as background. If it's directed exclusively to a small segment of traders, it's possibly too expensive and too limited for your needs.

An authority who for years has given good advice with respect to trading newsletters is Mark Hulbert. I've taken the liberty of reprinting one of his old advertisements:

> First and foremost, *The Hulbert Financial Digest* is not an investment adviser. It's a completely independent, impartial and authoritative rating service that arms you with the facts about stock and mutual fund investment letter performance.
>
> Nobody cares more about your wealth and the future it promises than you do. That's why you might subscribe to a stock or mutual fund advisory newsletter. Mark Hulbert started his newsletter to help you choose yours. Based on proven performance, not unproven claims.
>
> In 1979, Mark attended an investment seminar and heard dozens of newsletter editors promise to double, triple or quadruple investors' money each year — with complete safety. Out of curiosity — and disbelief — Mark Hulbert followed many of the advisors' recommended portfolios on paper and found their claims to be wildly exaggerated. The same gurus who promised to perform miracles were actually being beaten by the market averages.
>
> From that eye-opening experience, *The Hulbert Financial Digest* (HFD) was born. Today, the firm computers track the performance of over 160 stock and mutual fund letters with more than 500 recommended portfolios, so that HFD can give you the true picture.
>
> With performance records going back as far as 1980 you can choose the newsletters that have consistently made the most money ... and are likely to make the most money for you. Because, believe it or not, over 80% of advisory letters fail to beat the market over the long term. Yes, 80%, in spite of their extravagant claims.

Knowing which newsletter to trust depends on choosing the right one for your investment goals and current market conditions, and which has a successful long-term track record. That's why you'll find *The Hulbert Financial Digest* indispensable.

I think Hulbert does provide an excellent information service, but in my view if you work at it, you can do as well for yourself as the best performing market advisory letters.

That Hulbert ad also states: If you followed the advice of the top five best performing advisory letters over the last 10 years, you would have profited between 241% and 514%".

However, if you look at General Electric (GE), Wal-Mart (WMT), 3M (MMM), Microsoft (MSFT), Johnson & Johnson (JNJ), Procter & Gamble (PG) and a few other components of the blue-chip Dow 30 index, you'll see pretty much the same picture over the past 20 years.

If you feel the need to purchase a market advisory letter, I recommend the best way to check them out is by short-term discounted trial subscription to several at once, as offered in *Investor's Business Daily*, *Barron's* and other respected financial periodicals.

With these letters, you would be looking for counsel with investment objectives that match yours. If you are looking specifically for long-term growth, don't subscribe to a technically oriented chart-based service, and so forth.

Also, you should look for advice that's easy to understand and implement. Beware of obfuscations, complex language and, my worst complaint, general statements such as "buy on weakness", "sell on strength", without accompanying supporting detail. I found more than one long-running, top-selling editor particularly unhelpful in this regard. In subsequent issues of their publications, however, they take credit for specific advice the reader never got. But that's the publishing industry and why Mark Hulbert became indispensable.

Learning to trade is the first step, however, you need more than background data to enable you to improve your trading returns. You require specific buy prices, target points and logical reasons why actions should be taken. There are people who would try to do that with fancy charts but, as I see it, they are so wrong so often that they need to continuously re-draw the charts in order to look competent.

The bottom line is that I haven't, in 40 years, found in any one market letter what I believe most of you need. I expect you'll be entertained and not much more.

What is the Market? What is Trading?

4

Purchasing investment products called mutual funds

Remember, it's the best traders in the world who are right about 65% of the time; the worst about 35%. When there is a string of losses, which happens to the best, you reduce your order size and try to limit the average percentage loss. If you don't you lose your confidence.

August 14, 2007.

Many individuals do not have the time, skills or personality to manage their own capital. In that case, there is a ten-trillion-dollar mutual funds industry waiting with bated breath. There is a whole system in place, from registered portfolio managers to registered sales persons who work for mutual fund distributors.

The question is, what is it that these people do to earn annual fees totalling hundreds of billions?

The case for mutual funds

Although I do not usually advocate them, there is a case for mutual funds and there are people who need them. I'll give you the best case I can make for funds.

Mutual funds were designed for the general public. If you qualify as a wealthy or sophisticated trader, you qualify for a type of fund called a hedge fund. Nevertheless, the basic features of any type of fund today are similar: diversification and performance.

Diversification

It's costly to buy in odd lots (ie, less than 100 shares) and if you buy round-lot shares of quality corporations, your average stock will cost over $50. To buy just 100 shares of each of the 30 stocks that make up the Dow Jones Industrial Average (DJIA) today would cost over $150,000 plus commissions. But if you buy the Dow 30, you still would not be well diversified across industries, countries and types of financial objectives.

What is the Market? What is Trading?

Unless you have $100,000 or more, it is almost impossible to create a properly designed stock portfolio by buying individual stocks. Alternatively, with a relatively small amount of capital (say $10,000, preferably supplemented by regular savings), you can buy wide diversification in professionally managed mutual fund products or in securities called exchange traded funds (ETFs).

Fund managers are well paid to be aware of the conditions and drivers that affect capital market prices, including:

(a)   price and volume data and other stock market activity, such as insider purchases or sales and unusual transactions;
(b)   money supply, interest rates, gross national product, industrial capacity, productivity, tax laws and other economic details;
(c)   developments in new technology, manufacturing processes, labor contracts and other business matters that could influence or materially change a company's or industry's future; and
(d)   corporate news releases and the up-to-date news reports of the international wire services.

Then they have to meet company management, attend quarterly company conference calls and industry meeting presentations.

The distributor is responsible for providing administration and research, which is often well done.

Unless you have the time to spend many hours studying the global and domestic economy, interest rates and currencies, the stock markets in various countries and specific industries and stocks, you might wish to consider using the products or services of investment companies.

Performance

Many mutual funds that lose money shut down, which over time makes the fund group performance seem better than it actually is. The performance results of some others look as if their money had been managed by someone's daily horoscope, but it is true that the majority of investment companies are well managed and their positions thoroughly researched.

Most mutual funds did not do well in the bear markets of 1973-74, 1981-82, 1987 and 2000-03; but over the years, when compared to the continuously top quartile funds ranked by Morningstar (http://morningstar.com), which is arguably the best mutual fund rating service in the market, very few individuals have done as well.

Lessons from the Trader Wizard

See for yourself. Pit your average annual total returns (dividends and interest and capital gains) for the past 10 years against the leading funds. All funds provide detailed information and while you may have to read some boring material, the facts are there.

To find one that might appeal to you, it might seem obvious to look for consistency rather than erratically brilliant performance, but these funds are sold, not bought, so all too often the buyer — that's you Mr. or Ms. Investor — buys a fund just as it starts to under-perform.

The case against mutual funds

While I certainly agree that for many traders, the mutual fund concept is sound and wise, a case can be made against using them. And I'm not referring to the many investigations by market regulators in recent years where it has been alleged, and occasionally proven, that customers have been cheated. Most funds are honest; they just under-perform.

The downside of funds is mostly due to problems within the funds themselves. Units of mutual funds are like all pooled investments. The most important factor is the caliber and competency of management. Just as with corporations, there are able, mediocre and poor asset managers.

There are also crooks. Every few months there seem to be major investigations into fraudulent funds or illegal trading in funds. Even your favorite highly regulated mutual fund might not be working so hard for you, but against you. When does the nonsense stop?

In my view, with the availability today on the Internet of all kinds of corporate and financial markets information, particularly with a recent type of security called the exchange traded fund, you can basically do the same job as those professional fund managers. Possibly. Some of you just have to learn a few market-timing skills.

If you do want to buy them, the ones to be most wary of are the highly publicized, aggressively promoted funds. If you are intending to speculate in an aggressive fund, you must realize that market risks do not vanish just because there's professional management.

Some operational disadvantages can be avoided by wise planning. For example, if you are an American you can postpone but not avoid all taxes on gains. When periodic capital gains distributions are made, you must pay a tax on that gain even if you immediately reinvest the proceeds. If you do not reinvest this money, you not only have the tax to pay but you also must face the problem and cost of reinvestment elsewhere.

33

What is the Market? What is Trading?

When you decide to buy fund shares, do so soon after the capital gains distribution. If you do it before, you will be getting back part of your own money on which you will have to pay a tax.

This distribution policy works against older people and long-term traders who plan to hold fund shares indefinitely. If, on the other hand, they had bought good quality growth stocks and held onto them for the long-run, those holdings would become part of their estate, so there would be no capital gains taxes during their lifetime. With mutual fund units, however, capital gains tax will have to be paid when distributions are made.

Watch out for penalties. Some funds penalize heavily for failure to maintain contractual accumulation plans, under which half or more of the first year's payment is used for sales commissions and expenses. If you should be unable to continue payments, such a plan can be very expensive. It is better to have a voluntary accumulation plan or, if possible, a non-penalty program.

Fund promoters argue that a front-end load helps to prevent lapses in the early years of the plan. But it also serves to cut down long-term trading results because there's much less money available for trading.

What I dislike most about mutual funds is the high management expense ratio (MER), which is a percentage of managed assets fee-based arrangement, particularly when 80% of these managers don't even produce results equal to the market index. It's worse than paying something for nothing. You're often paying money for losing. Same thing goes for the financial planner who puts you into 3rd and 4th quartile funds. Why pay a fee for that kind of advice?

Open-end load funds

All open-end funds, which are officially termed mutual funds, stand ready to sell new units or redeem old ones at net asset value (NAV). NAV is the current worth of the underlying securities. The load is the sales commission an agent will charge if you don't buy the fund directly from the company.

What differentiates an open-end fund from a closed-end fund is that the open-end fund sells you units of a pooled holding and the closed-end fund is a regular financial corporation whose shares are bought and sold, with traders like you, on the securities market. When you wish to sell your mutual fund units, you redeem them directly with the fund management company.

As an aside, a rising market favors the open-end mutual fund company over the closed-end fund because there are few redemptions. However, in a falling market, redemptions hurt the fund management company because it has to then sell its underlying stock holdings into the market to raise the cash needed to meet redemptions. That selling further pushes down the price of stocks.

Commission costs for trading in open-end funds are much higher than for closed-end funds. You may pay from 5% up to 8% commission for the open-end load fund versus a fraction of 1% for the closed-end funds.

Load versus no-load

As I explained, the open-end fund may be either a no-load fund or a load fund. In the case of a no-load fund, the management company sells you the units directly, whereas in the case of the load fund an authorized sales agent of a distributor offers the units for sale.

You may buy an open-end load fund from a broker-dealer's registered representative or from a salesperson employed by the mutual fund distributor company or independent sales company registered to sell funds.

A sales charge or "load", which is typically up to 8% (but could be lower), is deducted from the amount of the capital available for trading. If you commit $10,000 and the broker/salesman keeps say $800, the trader's money at work is only $9,200. In that case, the true charge is 8.7%, which is $800 divided by $9,200.

All traders pay annual fees for client services, custody, asset management, reports and administrative expenses. So, even after two years, after all charges have been paid in a load fund, less than 90% of the trader's original capital may be working for him in many cases.

But the possible upside is that the sales representative may be giving wise continuous counsel on the most appropriate fund and handling all details of the investment. To some traders, that service may very well be worth the cost.

Open-end no-load funds

In the case of a no-load fund, the mutual fund management company sells you the units directly, possibly by referral, whereas in the case of the load fund an authorized sales agent sells you the units.

By buying a no-load fund directly from the sponsoring company, you will pay no sales charge or "load". Registered representatives of a broker-dealer or mutual fund trading company charge you a "load" or commission ostensibly for extra services rendered to you.

What is the Market? What is Trading?

There is an ongoing debate as to whether the net investment performance is better in a costlier load fund or a no-load fund. Either way, I don't see how a commission cost could affect the trading returns of professional money managers of the funds. The same managers make decisions for both types of fund and presumably they try just as hard to get the best results for each. They don't care whether you paid a load or bought the units directly on a no-load basis.

However, for new traders or for people who lack the skills or the time to find the appropriate funds, I actually prefer the costlier load funds. If you are going to entrust your wealth to professional money managers in the first place, then there is nothing wrong with paying a fee to a professional to find you the most suitable manager for your needs.

With load funds or no-load funds, there is likely to be no commission cost for redeeming the shares, but in both cases annual management fees run from 0.5% to 2.5% or more of the value of the invested money, depending on the cost to maintain the research and administration of the fund. This cost may seem small, but it can eat up your portfolio income.

On the other hand, if you choose to make your own trading decisions, like selecting what fund is best for you, then you ought to ignore mutual funds altogether and buy major market index funds (like DIAMONDS, SPDRS or QQQ) or closed-end funds on a securities exchange and pay the normal brokerage commissions. Or just buy a few of the best quality Dow 30 industrials instead.

5 So, Mr. Trader, you decided to take control of your own affairs

Trading is hard. I like to say that if trading was easy, where we just sat around hitting the "easy" button to make money, there would be no farmers, steelworkers and factory workers doing the real work. Trading successfully is a life skill that has to be developed over time. Some people pick it up quickly and others do not. However, I think the harder you work at it, the quicker success will come to you. And once you reach a point where you think you know it all, you realize there is more to learn.

May 1, 2007

Building a trading plan

To construct a trading plan, you, the independent trader, must understand that it's your wealth and your business is to protect that wealth at all costs and then grow it when business opportunities come along.

The first step is to pay more attention to risk than reward. It's nice to have big dollar wins, but it's more important to not have big dollar losses.

Remember that a 90% loss in a position requires a gain in that holding of 1,000% to recover. If you lose as much as you win, in percentage terms, you soon have few assets remaining. Try a few iterations of lose 90% followed by win 90% — eg, start with 100 > then lose 90% = 10 > then gain 90% = 19 > then lose 90% = 1.9 > then gain 90% = 3.61 > then lose 90% = 0.361 > then gain 90% = 0.686.

After three full cycles, your $100,000 asset has been turned into $686, without taking commissions into consideration. Your broker no longer wants to talk to you, but at least you have some funds to go to a fine restaurant.

A defensive mindset plus the guidelines I recommend can really help you take the necessary defensive posture so that kind of thing never happens to you.

Here is an analogy I use. Many traders think of themselves as a player — a scoring forward or whatever. But the key to success is to realize that you are, in sports parlance, the team owner.

What is the Market? What is Trading?

The owner has a set of goals and objectives. He or she hires the manager and coaches to fit the strategy and they employ and instruct the players to carry out tactics that hopefully achieve success for the owner.

With financial assets, you have a capital management business to run. You do it for a profit. The better your strategy and tactics, the greater your profit will be.

An owner — whether of a sports team or business or the capital market — has to understand a little about everything in that business. He or she has to know the economy, the customers, the competition and the company. If an owner knows only sales and customers and nothing about purchasing, manufacturing, quality control, shipping, finance, etc, the business is likely to soon fail. The financial services industry, however, doesn't want you to think like an owner. They want you to rely on their products and services; that's the business they are in.

But your business is to keep and grow your wealth. With an owner's mindset, you must start each day with a plan to do that. In trading, we call it the daily set up, which I do in part in my Daily Report at BillCara.com, by looking at various markets and the key factors that drive prices and then focusing on what's happening to the stocks in my watchlist.

The market is like a journey. You start from a place and then head off along a certain path. If you know where you are starting from and where you are going, you'll undoubtedly get there.

There is never a need as an owner of capital to act out of character. If you try, your journey will only get side-tracked. Let's be honest; that happens a lot with most people. As each of us is a unique person, the place to start your journey as a trader is with a realistic assessment of your personality. The best person for that task is yourself.

After you have decided whether your nature is basically: (a) conservative; (b) enterprising; or (c) speculative, your next decision is to choose what line of approach you will take to trading in the capital markets. The clear alternatives are: (a) fundamental; (b) technical; and (c) quantitative. A less clear one is (d) economics.

Fundamentalists are interested in paying one dollar for two dollars or more in good assets — assets that, in time, are certain to appreciate in value. People in this group are seldom willing to pay five or 10 dollars for one dollar of prospective (and possibly uncertain) earnings and/or dividends. Regrettably, in 1999 there were far too few true fundamentalists in the market.

Lessons from the Trader Wizard

That's why fundamentalists are always looking for good assets, what they refer to as "value", "quality" and/or "growth" assets. Sooner or later they find them. Their modus operandi has also been called the "margin of safety" approach.

Technicians, on the contrary, are interested in the business's stock price much more than its assets. In fact, even if the assets might be valued at a dollar, technicians will pay four or five dollars a share or more, if the price action in the market leads them to believe the stock will rise to 10 dollars. Some even become successful with this approach.

Quantitative traders are in between the fundamentalists and the technicians. A lot of "quants" have MBAs and little else going for them. These people like to work with computer spreadsheets and time-series data of all types — corporate, market and economic.

You'll see I cover this material when I talk about trends, because that's what a quant studies.

Recall that earlier I stated, "Regardless of whether you are conservative, aggressive or speculative, the first and simplest rule to trading is that if any trade causes you to worry, do not make it. Or if you have already done so and you are worried about it, then sell it".

Implicit in my remark is that the personalities and philosophies of people are wide-ranging and when they become traders these traits should become a basic part of their approach to trading. Just as there are all types of people, there are all types of traders and that is what makes the market.

There is no type of personality best suited to the market and no right or wrong strategic approach to trading. It's just who we are. The point is that we should trade consistently as who we are as people.

Now you know that there are many effective strategies for each kind of trader — the conservative, the enterpriser or the speculator — and they may be fundamental, quantitative or technical. Take your choice.

As for me, being in the business of trading for many years, I recognize a bit of all three personality traits in myself and I happen to like elements of all three strategic trading approaches. You probably will too as you mature as a trader.

At present, I am probably an "enterpriser-speculator" who favors a combined "quant-technical" approach, which sounds like a mouthful. In full retirement (which is not that far off), I'll be more conservative. In my seventies and eighties, I will probably lean toward exchange traded funds (ETFs) exclusively.

Trading is something people can do until they die. My Dad, in fact, was computer trading individual stocks in banking, auto and aircraft manufacturing, mining and steel when he was 85. You might even say he was a day trader.

In terms of the frequency of trading, I prefer trading a position every couple of months for 7-10% gains, if possible, but mostly in the blue-chip stocks of the global S&P 1200 and just a few others. My goal over time is to add to my core holdings by sticking to my values and my plan. As I get older, I recognize my values change a little. I trade less frequently, and more conservatively.

In writing a popular blog, I recognize that not all my readers are like me. My readers are as varied as the United Nations.

Three basic aspects of markets you will have to learn

- Compounding
- Calculating asset growth
- Risk-adjusted return

The wizardry of compounding

Earning income on income is one of the most important success factors in trading, especially for conservative or enterprising persons.

If you want to know how long it takes for your assets to double in value, use the Rule of 72: At various rates of return, divide 72 by the yield, ie, at 6%, it is 12 years; at 10%, 7.2 years; at 12%, 6 years.

By doubling your rate of return on capital, the assets will double in half the time. Once you understand the importance of rate of return, you will start to work on the tactics that can consistently double it for you, and you will be more wary of taking on risks of losses that will reduce your returns. As I said earlier, a 90% loss will require a 1,000% gain to make a full recovery.

Consistent savings and prompt reinvestment of all earnings can grow your assets at an astounding rate.

Here is a table view of the wizardry of compounding:

Lessons from the Trader Wizard

Rate of return (%)	Average annual return on capital (%) with re-investment				
	5 years	10 years	15 years	20 years	25 years
6	6.8	7.9	9.3	11.0	13.2
7	8.1	9.7	11.7	14.3	17.7
8	9.4	11.6	14.5	18.3	23.4
9	10.8	13.7	17.6	23.0	30.5
10	12.2	15.9	21.1	28.6	39.3
11	13.7	18.4	25.2	35.3	50.3
12	15.2	21.0	29.8	43.2	64.0

How to calculate asset growth

Use this table to project the growth of assets with an equal amount invested at the start of each year, compounding at different rates of return.

Years of holding	Growth factor: per year compounded				
	6%	7%	8%	9%	15%
1	1.00	1.00	1.00	1.00	1.00
2	2.06	2.07	2.08	2.09	2.15
3	3.18	3.21	3.25	3.28	3.47
4	4.37	4.44	4.51	4.57	4.99
5	5.64	5.75	5.87	5.98	6.74
6	6.98	7.15	7.34	7.52	8.75
7	8.39	8.65	8.92	9.20	11.1
8	9.90	10.3	10.6	11.0	13.7
9	11.5	11.9	12.5	13.0	16.8
10	13.2	13.8	14.5	15.2	20.3
15	23.2	25.1	27.2	29.4	47.6
20	36.8	41.0	45.8	51.2	102.4
25	54.9	63.2	73.1	84.7	212.8
30	79.0	94.5	113.3	136.3	434.8
35	111.4	138.2	172.3	215.7	881.2
40	154.8	199.6	259.0	337.9	1779.0

To see the growth of the asset base, multiply the annual compounded percentage return rate by the years of performance at that rate — eg,

What is the Market? What is Trading?

$1,000 each year for 10 years (ie, a $10,000 outlay) at 9% = $1,000 X 15.2 = $15,200. After 40 years after consistent reinvestment at 9% returns, the value would be $337,900, on a $40,000 outlay.

If the annual rate of return was 15% instead of 9% for 40 years, you would still have committed $40,000, but the total value would have compounded to $1,779,000.

If a trader could manage to commit $10,000 per year to a program that compounded the asset at 15% annually, in 20 years that $200,000 would grow to $1,024,000 and in 40 years it would be $17,790,000. Inflation-adjusted, tax-sheltered growth of this kind would be outstanding.

What this table also proves is the great fallacy of mutual funds, where traders can afford to give up 3% or more in annual marketing, administration and management costs with no significant damage to ultimate returns. Another downside with lower top-line performance, of course, is that the ultimate return is severely damaged over time.

Understanding risk-adjusted return

In order to make sound financial decisions, you need to understand the importance of risk-adjusted returns. That means knowing where the market's been and where it stands today.

The current US T-Bill rate (July 2007) is just under 5%, whereas at November 2003 it was 1% (http://bloomberg.com/markets/rates/index.html).

Suppose you are considering buying a stock which is deemed to have "average" risk relative to a typical share of stock. Say it offers 8% return. Is this a good investment? Would a satisfactory return be 10%? What return should you demand?

The answer is that if the long-term average risk premium of an S&P 500 stock is 9.2% and the current risk-free return (T-Bill yield) is 4.8%, then I would seek a 14% total return from equities that would be the average quality of an S&P 500 company. For every point the T-bill rate increases or decreases from there, I would seek a point higher or lower in return.

As you can imagine, the higher the T-Bill rate, my probabilities of earning the required risk-adjusted return decrease. As the Fed raises rates, at some point I have to withdraw my capital from the market, or decide to take on greater risk.

Market professionals use a measurement called the Sharpe Ratio to study the potential risk of an annualized return of a portfolio. The Ratio takes the excess return over and above the risk-free return and divides it by the average amount of the deviation of the return from the mean return. A Sharpe Ratio of 1.5 is usually considered good.

Five mistakes even professional traders make

Let's take a look at mistakes made by all traders — even smart ones:

- Wall Street fixation
- Not doing your own thinking
- Being stubborn and inflexible
- Neglecting inflation
- Being the greater fool

I've said that by understanding what the market truly is, knowing your place in it and then taking responsibility for your own decisions, you are on the road to success. But it's not all roses without thorns.

Wall Street fixation

Wall Street is constantly spinning you. And you have become fixated.

Let me give an example. When was the last time you saw an earnings estimate from Wall Street? Probably today, right? But when was the last time you saw anybody post the actual earnings numbers in a table beside actual share prices and major market index prices, so you can see how the corporation is really doing?

Instead, you are advised to listen to the sell-side earnings estimates. Does it take a rocket scientist to figure out that game? If a company wants to be on Wall Street's good side, they purposely shade their discussions on the conservative side so that the analyst's estimates are always a penny shy. That gives the sell-side some ammunition to recommend a "buy".

Corporations that want their stocks to temporarily fall in price a bit (maybe the insiders are accumulating), or analysts who want to help their broker-dealer employers accumulate positions in a stock, will be generous in their estimates so they can hammer the stock on the release of earnings that come up a bit short.

There has been a big improvement in the Wall Street research business in the years following the 2000-02 bear market, but the only way to totally stop the nonsense is to separate brokers from dealers and to make the analysts totally independent.

Remember: "when it's about money, people are funny".

What is the Market? What is Trading?

Another problem I frequently see is that somehow people seem to think that any advisor who works for an HB&B is imbued with the full power and knowledge of that firm's empire. I hear it all the time, eg, "Morgan Stanley thinks the airlines are going to take off!"

Well, no. With respect, in that situation your equity salesman, in the Boulder Colorado office might believe airlines are a screaming "buy", but having worked for that organization I can tell you with confidence that this individual probably thinks the same way when interest rates and oil prices are at record high levels. He may simply like the airlines.

The HB&B bond trader in Boston or the file clerk in their London corporate finance department or even that advisor's mom in Colorado is just as likely to have a worthwhile and contrary opinion. All of them may or may not even know what the firm's research department has opined and if they do, they don't always agree.

At the end of the day, you and your advisor have to be thinking on the same wavelength. You have to be dancing in the same rhythm.

Being over-influenced because you don't do your own thinking

You are in charge. Be responsible. You shouldn't be at all inclined to follow what others are recommending or what they are telling others they are doing in the markets. This is your journey.

I say that because the HB&B makes a lot more money trading *against you* than selling *to you*. The trading rooms of the banks are where most of the corporation's profits are made, not in their retail customer-service charges.

But that doesn't mean they aren't always selling products. The so-called banking experts you see or read in the media may seem to be giving you a professional opinion, but in fact they have a vested interest in selling you something — even when they infer they don't.

About the "game": I laugh when I hear people say they are playing the market. To the contrary, the market is a game that plays people, even the pros. The marketplace will try to throw you off your plan by making it seem so complex you end up guessing at most every decision.

Trading is straightforward, but you still have to think your way through it. If you are properly organized, it takes no more than five minutes a day to review the day's market statistics, look at the news and results for your corporate holdings and apply common sense. It may take another five minutes a day to do some specific research and look up information.

Lessons from the Trader Wizard

Any student can do that 10 minutes of daily homework. The point is that *every trader has to*! If you just guess at every decision, your chances are 50:50 at best. Sooner than later, you will be transferring assets either to a "thinking man" or a "con man".

Being stubborn and inflexible

The slogan "buy and hold" is misleading if you happen to think it is going to make you a winner. When holding means doing nothing, it is all too often a mistake.

It's human nature that traders are reluctant to admit mistakes or willingly switch from plans gone awry. They tend not to adapt to changing economic, industry or corporate conditions. They hold bonds and utility stocks as their prices plummet during periods of rising interest rates; they rationalize they are earning the originally anticipated interest or dividends. They often refuse to sell inherited stock despite corporate losses, dividend cutbacks and plunging stock prices.

Market conditions change. Buy and hold is no longer an option. Today it's a big mistake.

Think of trading like driving down the street or highway. At times, depending on the circumstances, you will exercise more or less caution. Experience pays. It helps you to slow down or speed up, as and when required. Trading is much the same.

Over the long run, it's true that quality stocks will be worth more than you paid, unless you paid a ridiculous price. They are usually worthy of the market risk. But if you hear your advisor or people you respect questioning whether the stock market is too high or too frothy, then it probably is.

During those times when amber lights are flashing, making trades for cash and fixed income is the safe move, even if your assets grow slowly for a while.

By the same token, it's usually the case that after prices have fallen 15%, 20%, 25% or more in the short term, traders still only wish to make safe trades. But that is precisely when they should be taking some *extra* long-term risk.

While I perpetually advocate a cautious approach to capital markets, I also believe it pays to use *extreme* caution no more than 15% or 20% of the time and that is almost always when the local barbershop is abuzz with stories of high profits in the markets.

What is the Market? What is Trading?

On the other hand, you don't need to be cautious when everybody around you is complaining of low, low stock prices. In fact, I have a belief that when the world is in a state of panic, you ought to throw caution to the wind.

Neglecting inflation

If you are a taxable trader (the unwilling or unwitting chattel of the nation), for every dollar you invest, you must get a return large enough to pay the tax on your income. You must also earn enough to make up for the loss of purchasing power in the period you held that trade.

To calculate the rate of return you need, simply divide the anticipated inflation rate by the difference between 100 and the rate at which you are taxed. If your income is taxed on average at say 40%, with inflation at say 5%, you will be getting poorer unless you grow your assets annually by 8.33% (ie, 5/(100 - 40) x 100%).

The biggest problem with inflation is that the public does not know how bad it is. Almost all inflation data is created by governments that are biased toward the understatement of inflation data. After a while of disbelieving the reported data, we tend to put out of our mind the long-term devastation that inflation wreaks.

Consequently, this situation has caused retirees to have underestimated their financial needs in their final years. In fact, as Michael Panzner points out in *Financial Armageddon*, the retirement system is one of the four biggest economic and financial threats to society today, and solutions are not being implemented.

Knowing that a solution will require massive money printing, I have in recent years, particularly in times when wealth creation has slowed, turned to over-weighting "hard money", ie, precious metals — probably to the extreme.

Greed and the greater fool

I don't look upon precious metals as anything more than a hedge against the falling value of paper money. Other people are different. They see it as glitter. Every day in the capital markets there are reports of drowning by greedy traders trying to swim upstream holding gold bricks in their hands.

Over-reaching people tend to ignore the importance of steady, above average percentage returns. I am always amazed when, after a properly timed trade, the trader who bought, say, IBM at 80 won't sell it a week later at 92.

What could possibly have happened within IBM that week that warrants such an extreme move, but prevents its stock from reverting to the mean?

After an extreme upside move, 98% of the time there will be a pull-back in stock price. So what's wrong with a 15% profit in a week or a month, or even a half year? You don't take that gain because you have been lured by other traders telling you the gain will soon be 20% or 25% and you begin to think there must be a greater fool than you who will buy it higher.

Then there is the sell-side pulling you in the opposite direction. When it comes to the sell-side, when all is said and done, all is said … These people don't do what they tell you they are doing. In fact they are doing just the opposite. That's why they call you the retail client and themselves the wholesaler.

Even the notion of "retail" trader is based on The Greater Fool Theory. In order to get access to your money in the future – which is their ability to earn commissions – the sell-side needs you to retail that stock to some other person.

I suppose it's possible that the Wall Street firms that employ the "TV talking heads" are neither trading against you nor selling you something. They could, as they say, be working for you on the buy-side, like a mutual fund.

But if that is the case, many of them must be simply incompetent because if you ever check thoroughly into their track record, including the losing funds they often close, you'll be truly astonished at how pathetic many are.

According to surveys (see the Morningstar ads for proof of this), 80% of all trading advisory services are wrong more often than they're right. And more than 80% of professional money managers under-perform the market index.

It's often so bad, I can't believe it. That is to say, I know it's bad and it's more than a simple case of incompetence. I mean, we're talking Harvard and Wharton School MBAs here, so who's kidding whom?

I've known it for years. Facts don't lie. How can that be? Well, even the Pope employs some wayward souls. Don't ever think the life's ambition of everybody employed as HB&B advisors or managers is just to make money for you.

What is the Market? What is Trading?

Their knowledge of trading statistics and details may be higher because they are immersed in it, but, in most cases, you — whoever you are — are just as smart and have just as much common sense as 99% of the best of them.

I can say this based on 25 years' experience in all aspects of the securities industry, having risen to the corner office on the penthouse floor of the stock exchange tower in a global money center.

Summary

In thinking over the biggest issues facing independent traders today, I believe that more than any other factor, they too often parrot back the musings of the sell-side without understanding that the sell-side just uses that patter to do its job. Consequently, traders end up selling long positions when they should be adding to them and vice versa.

In my case, I frankly don't give a damn what anybody else thinks or says or writes about the market. I'm concerned only with the actions of buyers and sellers, as well as my interpretation of the reasonableness of those actions. I have taken the time to thoroughly study capital markets from A to Z and I'm able to make up my own mind.

In time, so can you. Depending on whether you happen to be a conservative, enterprising or speculative person by nature, whether you live in the East or West, whether you are young or old, there is a road to success accessible to all people.

A strategy for the conservative trader; how to deal with inflation

The conservative trader stresses safety and income and is always fighting the effects of inflation. He aims, first and foremost, to preserve his capital and second, to earn a moderate, stable return on his money. At the end of the day, his success is measured in inflation-adjusted terms.

Traditionally the conservative trader puts a significant percentage of his money into fixed income. If he does buy a bond, he usually holds it until maturity, which may be 10 years or more. These bonds are not normally actively traded.

Such a strategy may be great for peace of mind, but just like keeping money in a bank account, it's often poor protection against inflation. And there is no longer a need to do this, because like stocks, you can trade bonds on the NYSE.

Lessons from the Trader Wizard

Let's suppose you are primarily a saver of funds in a bank savings account. My strong advice is to consider a securities market alternative. That's because, if you're not already in the fixed-income securities market, you'd be better off with an equivalent risk/reward return as high as you can get in today's US two-year government or corporate bond market (3Q07).

You should be invested in high-quality equities too, because the best ones pay consistent, high dividends and also appreciate in price over time.

Therein lies the nature of a realistic strategy for conservative traders. Find securities that are about as safe as your bank account and buy them.

If, on the other hand, you continue to deposit your money in your bank and stay out of the capital markets, then you must be prepared to accept portfolio attrition due to the effects of inflation.

In our society, we talk a lot about inflation, mostly because it's almost always with us. I'd like to believe in the accuracy of the government Consumer Price Index (CPI) measure of inflation, but I can't. The cost of the government's so-called basket of goods and services never seems to square up with mine. You probably agree.

The last great inflation cycle terminated in 1980, thankfully, but it took interest rates of over 20% to stop it. As money and credit tightened during that time, the stock market collapsed and there were many corporate and personal bankruptcies. I know people who committed suicide over the loss of their financial assets at that time.

Since then, the world has enjoyed a period of disinflation, which means we've still had inflation but at a much slower rate of annual increase.

As a trader, you will have to manage the influences of inflation on your holdings. But, in the parlance of the race-track bettor, there are, thankfully, "horses for courses".

For example, during the 1970s and 1980s, the purchasing power of the conservative trader's savings would have been cut in half every decade unless certain actions were taken. At the peak of the interest rate cycle in 1981, in order to maximize safety and income, the conservative trader in North America was best served buying 30-year US or Canadian government bonds and good quality Dow 30 blue-chip stocks.

Early in the third quarter of 2007 (3Q07), it's a different situation altogether. You have to deal with the circumstances of the day.

What is the Market? What is Trading?

As recently as 4Q02 and 1Q03, most people were still scared of the bear market that had started in 2000. The conservative trader probably felt secure with a 5% return on a top-rated, long-term bond. He knew that at maturity he could always get back his full capital position.

But such a trade soon proved to be a bad one. The "stable" 5% coupon bond that he bought at 100 in 2002, was quickly selling below 90 in 2003. So, that particular trader got locked in. You see: if, as and when the economy starts to expand (as it did in 2003), interest rates will move higher as well. That is bad for bonds.

The point here is that trading in any instrument including bonds is not always a great financial strategy unless it's appropriate to the time. The market is about prices and time.

It always pays to understand why you are making the decisions you are. As for bonds, unless you are at least somewhat knowledgeable about interest rate trends and cycles, you are just guessing. Very few people make good returns that way.

But for now, a good rule of thumb is that if interest rates are at cycle highs and likely to come down, it pays to buy 10- to 30-year long bonds. If interest rates are at cycle lows, or likely to rise, it pays to buy two-year bonds.

Often you don't have to be an expert in the bond market to tell the times when interest rates are reaching the high and low extremes. Just read the newspapers or listen to the TV reporter tell you "interest rates have just made a 25-year low" or "interest rates are at the highest level in eight years".

If the bond market is to your liking, the media will occasionally tell you when to buy them and when to switch or sell them. For conservative traders, my simple guidelines (later) will tell you what to buy.

When the time is appropriate, just do it. Don't think about it. Don't talk about it. It's nothing personal. Like I say, this is not rocket science.

A strategy for the enterprising trader; zeroing in on corporate management

An enterprising trader takes risks somewhere between a conservative trader and a speculator. He looks for total returns (which is income plus capital gains) averaging at least double the current or near-term anticipated rate of inflation and he will sacrifice some degree of safety in pursuing higher than average returns.

Lessons from the Trader Wizard

In a 5% inflation environment, that 10% return would be roughly 2% in dividends and 8% in appreciation. As inflation moves up to say 6%, his goals would move higher to say 2% in dividends plus 10% in appreciation.

This 10%-return goal is a minimum and 15% (ie, a tripling of the inflation rate) would be a maximum for the enterprising trader. Goals beyond that, over the long-run, would involve speculation and, therefore, be appropriate to a different type of trader.

The typical enterprising equities trader buys and sells some stocks after holding them for about 12 months; others he holds for, say, 10 years.

Later, I'll show you how to find high-quality, dividend-paying, blue-chip stocks that are appropriate to your needs, but for now I'd like you to go to the Value Line website (http://valueline.com/dow30/) and click on the reports of each of the Dow 30 stocks.

I believe that most of you would be shocked at how successful just trading in Dow 30 blue-chip stocks over the past 20 years would have been. That's all it would have taken to make you considerably richer than you are today.

As an example, look at General Electric. Between 1993 and 2003, GE (adjusted for stock splits that gave traders 600 shares for each original 100) grew their annual dividends from $0.22 to $0.73 (2002) per share for a total over 10 years of $4.28 per share. Every year, the returns on stockholders' equity have been between 20% and 25%, while per-share sales, earnings and cash flow have all grown year-over-year. The GE stock price, adjusted for splits, soared over those 10 years from about $7.50 to about $30.50. As General Electric has posted many consecutive years of excellent results, it would have been an outstanding holding in an enterprising trader's portfolio — a hold, that is, until the market started going goofy in 2000 with GE's PE ratio up to 50.

If you look at Wal-Mart, 3M, Microsoft, Johnson & Johnson, Procter & Gamble and a few other stock components of the blue-chip Dow 30 Industrials Index (my favorites), you'll see pretty much the same outstanding total return growth picture.

Now if you happen to be self-employed, would you not agree that if you ran your own company as well as many of these Dow 30 corporations are run, you'd be successful?

Think about this question because therein lies the nature of an enterprising strategy: Find companies that are managed better than you could do for yourself. Buy the shares and hold them for a few years. Otherwise, invest your money in your own business based on the higher returns you can get there, and stay out of capital markets as a trader.

That's good advice to the young MBA student too. Investing in somebody else's company (possibly one where you're employed) is a good deal only so long as you can get better total financial returns there due to excellent management performance. The same common sense applies to investing in your own company.

If you know, believe or hope that you can manage earnings and cash flow growth rates in your own company that beat any of the highest-quality Dow 30 corporations, then you're ready to go out on your own. If and when you can get those performance results, bankers will line up to lend you money and traders will want to buy your common shares.

But don't dream of what's required. All you have to do is look at the track record of the blue-chip Dow 30 stocks. That's the standard you have to beat. It's a tough one.

A strategy for the speculative trader; seeking hidden opportunity

Speculation does not necessarily mean gambling or guessing. In fact, speculation may be every bit as much a strategy for success as any conservative or enterprising trader strategy. It depends entirely on your trader personality and how you go about your business. It must be in your personality and philosophy to be a speculator, of course. Then you have to become skilled at it.

The trading speculator has a philosophy that if something extremely positive or negative can possibly happen in the market, it always does! Such events cause volatility and therefore opportunities.

Here is a bit of a case study: A few years ago, the CEO of Coca Cola died of cancer. In spite of the fact that Coke (KO on the NYSE) had global sales at the time of about $20 billion and net profits of $5 billion, plus a very competent executive management team that had long been alerted to their leader's ill health, news of his death dropped the stock price several dollars. This meant the market capitalization for KO declined by several billions in a matter of minutes. However, was the corporation any less an excellent long-term trade for conservative and enterprising traders? Clearly, in that case nothing had changed.

So, in true Chinese philosophy where "crisis equals opportunity", speculative traders stepped in and bought the stock. A couple of days later, they sold. In the interim, they earned over 5% capital appreciation.

Lessons from the Trader Wizard

Was this a gamble? Hardly! It was merely an honest to goodness speculative trade, carefully thought out in advance and executed in a timely manner.

If there is a severe or sudden market pullback, the speculative trader will stand ready to buy low. But he does have to have a good reason for each purchase and be able to explain it. Mostly, he seeks to achieve the largest percentage gains in the shortest time. That's what a speculator does.

Since nobody is perfect, the speculator is taking extreme risk because he always faces the probability of losses. He may also buy and sell frequently in order to stem those losses and in doing so will capture smaller gains than the enterprising trader. But since he knows the losses will come, he looks for higher average percentage gains from his winning selections.

In the example of Coca Cola, a 5% gain in a week is equal to an uncompounded 260% gain in a year! Compounding is not a tool used frequently by speculative traders because they never know when the next opportunity is the big one or a loser.

A speculative trader strategy can be successful, but it takes more time and active management of a portfolio than other strategies. Note that I did not say it takes more skill or luck, just time and focus. Even if the potential for gain is tantalizing, most people don't really have that time or focus, so they should refrain from active speculation.

Speculative traders cannot afford to be gullible, that's for sure.

Too many people are afflicted with something I call "credulity syndrome". That is to say, they pretty much believe everything they hear. But the truth is, it's your wealth and other people want it. If that's the case with you, you ought to learn an expression we use in the capital markets: "If their lips are moving, they're lying!"

Until you prove (to yourself and your family) that you're not a credulous person, ie, a naïve trader, it will pay to pass on "opportunities" for quick profits and let them go to the next person. Maybe those traders can afford to lose 90% or more of their capital, but I'm thinking you can't.

So, if the story sounds too good to be true, it is! Buyer beware.

In my *Special Situations* section, I will provide guidelines to finding some good longer-term speculations and how to manage them appropriately.

As you learn to do that well, you'll start looking for shorter-term speculations. They abound. As a successful stock promoter once told me:

"There is never a shortage of good deal opportunities. I have my pick of several a day".

When you get good at the process of speculating, so too will you quickly spot those opportunities to make money.

Summary

This has been a lot of background material to read before I actually get into the "meat" of trading, but I believe it is an important introduction. These are the concepts I believe you need to grasp before running into stocks and bonds.

Part **2**

Cara's Approach to Trading Bonds, Bond Funds and Cash

In any event, the economic problems the Administration does not want to address are widespread. Higher energy, food and mortgage costs will break the budget of many Americans this time around. So, we are in a kind of a transitioning phase where bonds will become more attractive than stocks for a while. After stocks start to fall, the Fed will drop the interest rates and bonds will start to rally. But the momentum of falling stock prices will linger, and that is the time it will pay to be out of stocks and into bonds.

June 3, 2007

Cara's Approach to Trading Bonds, Bond Funds and Cash

1   What is a bond?

I think by now you get it. The price of assets can be lifted by the creation of wealth or by speculative means. One or the other. The latter is defined (by me in this case) as a ton of debt creating an ounce of wealth and also higher asset prices. This gives new meaning to the expression "lead balloon".

There is another popular expression in equity markets, which is that "what goes up will come down". I'm here to say that most of the time that's really not true. It just happens to be true today — because higher prices today are the clear result of speculation, which in turn has been caused by excessive money printing by the world's central banks. First it was real estate that took the hit; next it will be stocks and bonds.

April 28, 2007

I say you can't become a successful trader of stocks until you understand a little about the bond market. That's because bond yields and interest rates work in combination and together they are principal drivers of stock prices.

When you buy a bond, you are loaning your money to a corporation or government. In return, you receive a certificate or contract that states that the issuer will pay you interest at a specified rate, usually twice a year, until the principal debt is repaid, sometime in the future — perhaps 10, 20 or 30 years hence.

When most people buy a bond or debenture, they do so for income or security. Somebody else's obligation or debt is the buyer's asset — just like a stock except the owner of a bond doesn't hold any equity in the business. The asset is limited entirely to the debt, which underscores the importance of the contract.

To many of you, a bond is a secure, mostly stagnant holding that provides a fixed annual income and can be redeemed at maturity for the same amount of dollars used to purchase it when issued. But, as well as plenty of low-risk opportunities to attain capital gains or to increase total returns from income plus appreciation, there are risks with all kinds of bonds.

Cara's Approach to Trading Bonds, Bond Funds and Cash

Thus it's important that bond traders understand the agreement.

Obviously the type and quality of the debt is a prime concern to the trader. A bond is secured debt, whereas a debenture is unsecured debt. A bond may also have other features, like convertibility to stock.

The bond agreement will contain a security clause, while in the case of a debenture, there is no such security. Hence, bonds are typically more secure than debentures, but not always. A bond issued by Consolidated Moose Pasture is not as secure as a debenture from General Electric, for example.

Clearly, the financial strength of the corporation is a significant factor in determining the quality of the debt.

A straight bond is almost always priced relative to the current cost of money, which is reflected by the interest rate. Capital gain opportunities result from changes in interest rates.

How interest is calculated and paid

Interest on bonds is calculated on a daily basis and added to the sales price (but does not include the day of delivery). For US Government issues other than Treasury bills, the base is the exact number of days in a 365-day year. With other bonds, it's a 360-day year or 12 30-day months.

To figure out the yield superiority of 360-day bonds (versus 365-day bonds), divide the interest rate by 360 to get the daily return, then multiply the result by 365. With a 12% interest rate, the daily rate works out to 0.333%, so the annualized rate for 365 days would be 12.16%.

How bonds are rated

General description	Moody's	S&P
Best quality	Aaa	AAA
High quality	Aa	AA
Upper medium	A	A
Medium	Baa	BBB
Speculative	Ba	BB
Low grade	B	B
Poor to default	Caa	CCC
Highly speculative to default	Ca	CC
Lowest grade	C	C

Ratings may also have a + or - sign to show relative standings in the class.

Prices for high-grade bonds — rated A or better — reflect money-market conditions and interest rates almost exclusively.

The lower the rating, the more the bond prices are more closely attuned to business conditions generally, and to any changes in the quality of the issuer.

Medium-grade Baa or BBB bonds are the lowest category that qualifies for commercial bank portfolios.

Any rating of Ba or BB or lower is speculative and traders should not purchase these bonds without analyzing current financial statements and considering the industry prospects. Of course, if you want to speculate, Ba or BB-rated bonds pay over 8% and B-rated junk bonds pay 10% or more (3Q07).

Differences in bonds

Quality

Since you buy bonds for safety, stick to high-quality issuers and forget the small amount of extra interest ($5 to $10 per year per bond) that can possibly be obtained with the debt of a company that has a dubious credit rating.

Most corporate and municipal (but not Federal Government) bonds are rated by statistical services in nine categories from gilt-edged to extremely speculative. These ratings represent carefully calculated estimates of the degree of protection for both principal and interest, based on past performance, current financial strength and future prospects.

The two top statistical services — Moody's and Standard & Poor's (S&P) — usually come up with about the same rating for any particular bond.

Collateral

This is the property that stands behind each bond. Secured bonds may be:

• First-mortgage bonds backed by the company's real estate, plants, heavy trucks and so on, or equipment trust certificates such as the ones secured by railroad locomotives, freight cars, etc.

• Bonds guaranteed, according to principal and interest, by another corporation or by the government or a government corporation or agency. Examples of the former are foreign bonds offered for sale abroad by foreign subsidiaries or affiliates of US corporations and guaranteed by the parent company.

• Unsecured bonds (debentures) are backed only by the general credit standing of the issuing company. The trader should translate this credit into the company's ability to pay annual interest and amortization plus the principal sum when due. The projection should consider recent historic ratios and trends, and should apply to the total debt.

In practice, for most bonds, the ability of the corporation to pay is much more important than theoretical security, because legal obstacles to traders collecting a bond's security in the event of insolvency are formidable and time-consuming and often require litigation, which is the last thing you need in your life.

If an industrial bond is unrated, a rule of thumb for determining investment-grade is that interest charges should be covered over a period of five years at the following rate:

Bonds of:	Before Federal Income Taxes	After Federal Income Taxes
Industrials	5x	3x
Transports	4x	3x
Electric, gas and water utility	3x	2x

Serial and sinking fund bonds

Serial bonds are issues that are redeemed at various dates over a period of years. This enables a buyer of a new bond to select the exact maturity he desires: say in 10 years when a son or daughter is due to start college. Usually, all of the debt comes due at once, but if there's a sinking fund feature, there's extra safety.

Bearer or registered bonds

Historically, most bonds were issued in bearer form with interest coupons attached. Interest was paid, usually twice a year, by presentation of the detachable coupons to the paying agent. This is the origin of the phrase "clipping coupons".

In today's world of forgeries and scams, I would not deal in bearer bonds and I would only buy un-rated bonds from a top-flight broker-dealer who is a known bond trader.

Lessons from the Trader Wizard

Exchange-traded bonds

Bonds, like stocks, even trade on the New York Stock Exchange (NYSE), which operates the largest centralized bond market of any US exchange or other self-regulatory organization. A list of current bonds traded on the NYSE is available at: http://nysedata.com/bondsymbols.

The NYSE offers traders a broad selection of over 2,000 corporate (including convertibles), agency and government bonds and even foreign bonds. Most bond volume at the NYSE is in straight domestic corporate debt, with some 15% in convertible bonds.

In my opinion, the NYSE website is outstanding in many respects. For trading bonds, you'll find all the information you need at: http://nyse.com.

NYSE-listed bonds trade through the exchange's Automated Bond System (ABS), a terminal-based system for trading corporate, agency and government bonds. The ABS system maintains and displays prices and matches price orders on a price and time priority basis.

ABS reports real-time quotes and trades to market data vendors. Closing bond prices are available in the financial sections of major newspapers, as well as on-line.

How to read bond quotations and figure yields

You can get the daily bond tables from the on-line *Wall Street Journal* at: http://online.wsj.com/public/resources/documents/fbndsdec.txt.

Let's have a look at the bonds of AT&T taken from a previous year. If you need a primer on how to read bond quotations, there is a plethora of information in the *Wall Street Journal, Barron's* or *Investor's Business Daily* and you'll find no shortage of places to look by searching on Google. It's pretty simple when you get the hang of it.

Wall Street Journal: November 13, 2003 example

NYSE: Corporate bonds				
BONDS	CUR YLD	VOLUME	CLOSE	NET CHG
AT&T 6 3/4s04	6.6	35	101.53	-.13
AT&T 7 1/2s04	7.4	10	101.84	...
AT&T 7s05	6.6	95	105.75	...
AT&T 7 1/2s06	6.8	26	110	-.13

Cara's Approach to Trading Bonds, Bond Funds and Cash

Foreign bonds				
BONDS	CUR YLD	VOLUME	CLOSE	NET CHG
SeaCnt 7 7/8s08	8.3	90	95.25	88
TelArg 11 7/8s04	11.5	4	103.75	.75

For the AT&T 6 and 3/4s of 2004, the current yield is 6.6. That day, 35 bonds traded and the closing price was 101.53, down 13 cents on the day.

It's not difficult to use your broker to put in an open order for specific bonds, and you can change your order by the day depending on your fills and how interest rates are moving.

About prices and yields of bonds

Bond values rise when interest rates decline. Conversely, bond values fall when interest rates go up. So, the interest rate is the most important factor in the price of bonds — not supply and demand, as with common stocks.

Yields on short-term issues tend to react more quickly to changes in business cycles and monetary conditions and move to greater extremes in both directions. For example:

•   In easy money markets, when interest rates are relatively stable, short-term issues typically yield less than long-term ones.

•   In tight money markets, short-term interest rates are usually appreciably higher than long-term ones. Such has been the case from mid-October 2006 into early 2007.

By contrast, prices of long-term bonds fluctuate more than those of short-term issues. The reason is that "time is money".

A change in interest rates calculated for a few weeks or months involves a lesser change in price than the same change projected for years ahead. For example:

•   A rise of 1% in interest rates will mean a drop of about $10 for a $1,000 short-term T-bill, but

•   It can force a decline of $100 or more for a bond with 20 years to maturity.

Shrewd traders take advantage of this differential.

Lessons from the Trader Wizard

Your trading objective will require an understanding of the different types of yield. Yield is a matter of definition, for example:

- **Nominal or coupon yield.** This is the interest rate stated on the bond: 6%, 10.5%, etc. It depends on the quality of the issuing corporation and prevailing cost of money at the time the bond is issued.

- **Actual yield on the purchase price.** This is the rate of return per year that the coupon interest rate provides on the net price (without accumulated interest) at which the bond is purchased. It is higher than the coupon yield if you buy the bond below par, lower if you buy the bond above par.

- **Current yield.** This is the rate of return on the current market price of the bond. This is higher than the yield on the purchase price if there has been a decline in the price, lower if there has been a rise in the market value of the security.

- **Yield to maturity (YTM).** This is the rate of return on a bond held to redemption. When bought at a discount from par, YTM includes the appreciation to par from the current market price, or depreciation to par when bought at a premium.

- **Discount yield.** This is the percentage from par or face value, adjusted to an annual basis, at which a discount bond sells. It is used for zero-coupon bonds and for short-term obligations maturing in less than one year, primarily Treasury bills. Roughly, this is the opposite of YTM. If a discount bond with one year to maturity sells at a 10% yield, its cost is 90 ($9,000). The discount yield is 10 divided by 90 expressed as a percentage, or 11.11%.

To approximate the YTM for a discount bond:

1. Subtract the current bond price from the face amount.
2. Divide the difference by the number of years to maturity.
3. Add the annual interest.
4. Add the current price to the face amount and divide by two.
5. Divide (3) by (4) to get the YTM.

Example: A $1,000, 5% coupon bond, due in 10 years, is selling at 70 ($700). The coupon yield is 5%, hence the current yield is 7.14% (5/70) and the YTM is approximately 9.41%.

Cara's Approach to Trading Bonds, Bond Funds and Cash

1. $1,000 - 700 = 300
2. 300/10 = 30
3. 30 + 50 = 80
4. (700 + $1,000)/2 = 850
5. 80/850 = 9.41%

What you should consider before trading bonds

Going into debt makes most sense to an issuer when interest rates are low, but cheap borrowing costs tends to lead to more borrowing by traders, corporations and governments, which at some point leads to inflationary pressures that push up interest rates.

In addition to broader issues of concern regarding all debt securities, here's what to specifically look for in bonds:

- **Inflation.** As fixed holdings, the dollars invested and income received are worth less every year. With 10% inflation, each $1,000, after 20 years, will buy only about $150 worth of the same goods and services.

- **Lack of appreciation,** unless the bonds are bought at a discount and held to maturity (or, when traded, sold at a higher price). If you buy a new bond for $1,000, you will get back exactly $1,000 at maturity. The only chance for a profit is if interest rates decline sharply so that the bond value rises in the interim and you decide to sell before maturity. Why not buy at a discount, say $970, which produces a profit of $30 per bond at maturity?

- **High taxes.** All interest (except that earned by tax exempts) is taxable at the highest personal income tax rate. With capital gains, the realized appreciation is taxed at a lower rate.

- **Difficulty of compounding** (earning interest on interest). Unless you buy shares in a bond fund, there can be no automatic reinvestment, as with stock-dividend investment plans. The interest payments will have to be held in a low-yield cash account until there is money enough to buy a new bond: Over a couple of years, the difference between a 1.5% cash account and a 8.5% bond fund yield will add up to $70 per year per $1,000.

Nowadays, with the extreme volatility in interest rates, bonds should be bought for trading, not holding, unless you are unwilling to swap the ultimate security for interim profits.

Lessons from the Trader Wizard

As a rule of thumb

(1)   Buy short-term, high-coupon yield bonds when there is a probability of higher interest rates.

(2)   Buy long-term, low-coupon yield bonds when there is good reason to anticipate a decline in interest rates in the next six to 12 months.

Since you are giving up some current income when you buy bonds at a premium, look for a higher-than-current yield.

If you invest a large sum, ask for the minimum standards for commercial paper and watch out for any fund that invests in sub-prime debt, ie, ratings under A.

Discount bonds are excellent trading instruments for tax-advantaged accounts like offshore corporations and trusts that pay little or no tax on income, and sub-chapter S corporations in the US (basically a family holding company) where profits are funneled through the holding company to the owner(s).

Discount bond investments, which lead to a capital gain at maturity, can earn tax-deferred or tax-free income for shareholders because, in the US for example, only 40% of long-term capital gains are taxable to an individual. Hence, the result is to convert part of the investment income into tax-free income.

It pays to know the history of certain bonds before you buy them. For instance, US Steel Corp had for many years faced financial crises, which caused chaotic conditions for the bond holders. Prices were all over the board. A 4 3/8s US Steel bond, issued at $1,000, sold at 55 when the interest rate was 8%. When the cost of money went below 7%, its value moved up to about 59. But later, when interest rates soared to over 18%, its price fell to 39. When they started to fall again, the price jumped to about 66.

I recall reading, in the 1970s, a series of books by the "Dean of Bond Street", Sidney Homer, entitled:

(1)   *History of Interest Rates*
(2)   *Great American Bond Market*
(3)   *Inside the Yield Book: Tools for Bond Market Strategy*
(4)   *Price of Money, 1946-1969: Study of U. S. & Foreign Interest Rates.*

In his books, Homer advised traders to recognize the value of reinvesting interest, which I note in my section on the power of compounding returns.

Cara's Approach to Trading Bonds, Bond Funds and Cash

Over a 20-year period, Homer pointed out that more than half the total return from a bond comes from interest on interest. That is a powerful concept.

So, if you are a bond trader, to build capital and boost your income over the years, always reinvest periodic interest income in more bonds. If the coupon is small, Homer would advise you to hold the money in a savings account until you can add savings and buy more bonds. Today, of course, you could put that money into a money market fund.

In *Inside the Yield Book* (1977), Homer explains that all bonds do not act the same when there is a change in interest rates, which is a basic concept that too few people really understand to this day 30 years later.

Other things being equal, the volatility of bonds is greater: (a) the longer the maturity; (b) the lower the coupon; and/or (c) the higher the starting yield.

If you have substantial holdings in bonds, it would be worthwhile to ask your advisor to discuss your portfolio with an experienced bond analyst.

The relative safety of fixed income securities

Many traders believe that US Government bonds are safer than UK or Canadian Government bonds, for instance, but I hardly think that is true. Wherever the highest interest rate is — that would be where I'd invest, assuming a liquid market exists and the returns are calculated on my net costs.

To my thinking, within a large group of industrialized countries, the bonds of one country are as sound as another. If there is any question, I'd turn to Moody's and Standard & Poor's, the independent agencies that give sovereign ratings to government bonds of all countries.

I'm not going to get into the tax-benefits to North Americans of trading in municipal government bonds, because that's a market I'm not familiar with.

Income instruments that are safe, but ...

Bonds are a relatively inexpensive way for corporations to obtain funds for capital improvements and expansion. The interest is a tax-deductible business expense, so the cost of a 10% bond for a company in the 40% tax bracket is 6% (.10 x 60%).

Lessons from the Trader Wizard

When you buy a bond, you are loaning money to the issuer. In return, you receive a certificate that states the corporation will pay interest at a specified rate, usually twice a year, until the debt is to be repaid, as agreed, at a specified date, five, 10 or up to 40 years in the future.

Corporate bonds are debts to a corporation that may or may not be paid in full, however.

Corporate bonds might be safe, but they are not as safe as the government bonds of any of the industrialized nations. For example, just a couple of months after Enron Corp was reputed by Wall Street to be one of the world's strongest corporations, it was bankrupt.

In the turbulent times of today's financial markets, corporate bonds are no longer the safe secure securities they used to be. They may provide steady income and almost always return your capital, but, in recent years, their values have fluctuated as much, or more than, those of common stocks. In less than nine months, for instance, the price of top-quality AT&T 8.75% bonds fell from 98 ($980) down to below 68 ($680).

What this means is that traders who buy bonds must: (i) keep watching total returns, ie, interest income plus appreciation; and (ii) be willing to trade, not hold until maturity.

Guidelines for trading the bond market

To be a profitable strategy, a corporate bond portfolio must be closely managed like any other asset. It's unwise to buy bonds and forget them until maturity.

1. Remember the Rule of 72

A $1,000 8% bond compounded semi-annually grows to $2,000 in nine years. It then grows to $7,106 in 25 years and $50,504 in 50 years.

2. "Buy and hold"

While compounding is crucially important, I say that "buy and hold" is a dumb strategy for bond traders. Years ago, bonds were stored in a safety deposit box, but today they are represented by an electronic entry in a brokerage account. So when you know you have purchased these trading instruments for yield, which is a function of price, and price is constantly changing, why hold them until maturity?

Cara's Approach to Trading Bonds, Bond Funds and Cash

3. General guidelines

(i)   Trade bonds like you would trade stocks.

(ii)   If you anticipate higher interest rates, buy short-term bonds. If you're right, reinvest the redemption proceeds in high-yielding long-terms.

(iii)   Be cautious about locking in high yields unless you are happy with income alone. Over a period of years, the prices of high-yield bonds will swing widely and their total returns *will always* run behind inflation.

(iv)   If you anticipate lower interest rates, buy low-coupon long-term bonds and sell when you have an adequate capital gain. The percentage gains would be higher if you used margin where the cost of borrowing is less than the rate of interest earned.

(v)   Beware of administrative fees. If you leave the bonds in safekeeping with a custodian, any charge will lower your net rate of return. A $60-a-year custodian charge, for example, is a large dent in the $600-a-year interest on 10 6%-coupon bonds.

Buying bonds on margin

Some broker-dealers limit margin accounts with bonds, which are often about 33% for long positions and 50% for short selling. But, in recent years, banks are more liberal and will lend up to 80% on investment grade corporate bonds and over 90% on US Government securities.

Whenever the yield on bonds is higher than the interest rate on a loan, the income from the bond pays the loan cost. This is called a carry trade.

Speculating in high-yield bonds

Be very cautious with high-yield securities. It should be obvious that the higher the yield, the higher the risk.

There are two types of high-yield bonds and both types sell at low prices (and thus high yields) because traders can get somewhat comparable returns with much less risk:

•   Bonds of well-established corporations that have run into temporary trouble, usually not entirely of their own making. Under normal conditions, such securities would be fairly safe.

- Bonds of highly-leveraged companies, ie, of questionable quality (usually unrated) and not suitable for institutional portfolios. These are classified as "junk" bonds.

When you see debt-inspired common share buy-backs, the added leverage (also called gearing) enables the company to produce an instant earnings increase. This is because the after-tax interest cost is always less than the earnings attributed to the common stock they buy back from the market. Whenever you see interest rates at long-term cycle lows, there are a lot of corporations up to that trick, which has been the case in 2006 and 2007.

To cover stock that is selling at five times earnings, the company must earn 40% before taxes. By swapping for a 10% bond, it can save three-quarters of that cost. Shrewd speculators take advantage of this situation and obtain high yields and — with a little luck — appreciation as well.

Marginally strong corporations often offer to swap high-yield bonds for lower-coupon CVs or preferred stock. But the replacements may be every bit as risky and they pay less.

Now and then, because of unusual circumstances, a junk bond could be the debt of a high-rated corporation. For example, Teledyne 10% subordinated debentures 2004, were selling in 4Q03 at 825 to yield 12.1%. They were rated BB because they were subordinated to other corporate debt. But cash flow could have paid them off quickly if Teledyne so decided.

Tactic for a high tax payer, *a 45.3% annualized rate of return*

If you are in a high-tax jurisdiction, where say you pay taxes at a 70% rate and are willing to borrow heavily, bonds bought at the right time can provide after-tax returns of over 45%. This is possible because of a combination of deductions for interest and low 3% to 8% margins on the loan. The benefits may even be worthwhile for those in a somewhat lower tax bracket.

Mr. Smith, in the 70% tax bracket, bought $1 million 7% coupon bonds, due in 13 months, at 94.4375 ($944,375). He put up $29,540 in cash and arranged a fixed-interest loan for the balance. (For tax purposes in his jurisdiction, everything had to be over one year.) His interest payments were $44,710. In the 70% tax bracket, this meant an after-tax expense of $13,414. His total commitment was $42,954.

When the bonds are paid off at par, the capital gain will be $45,625. Since his capital gains will be taxed at a 28% rate (40% at 70%), the after-tax net

Cara's Approach to Trading Bonds, Bond Funds and Cash

will be $19,437. On the investment base of $42,954, that's a net return of 45.3%.

The danger here, of course, is that the price of the bonds will drop during the remaining 13 months of this bond, so that Mr. Smith will have to come up with more cash on the margin loan. With such a short maturity, this is not likely, but if it should happen it could be expensive.

Every rise of 1% in the cost of money would mean an extra $10,000 in margin. So, before you try such a deal, be sure to check with your tax advisor and be confident that interest rates are likely to rise in the interim.

To swap or not to swap

Swapping bonds is an important tactic in serious bond trading. The question is: to swap or not to swap?

On the surface, it appears best to sell a bond yielding 6.5% to purchase a similar quality bond selling to yield 8%. In theory, this is a gain of 150 points a year to maturity. However, this would be an incorrect assumption. The conventional yield to maturity assumes a reinvestment rate of 6.5% for one and 8% for the other. Actually, the reinvestment rate will be identical for both issues. Thus, the yield gain from the switch is narrowed and, depending on the time to maturity, may be almost eliminated.

There's the same problem in relating present and future yields.

To calculate if its best to accept $1 income today or $1.25 in four-and-a-half years invested in a 6% bond, ie, .03% paid semi-annually, use this formula to find the answer:

$$1/(1 + R)T \text{ where}$$
R = interest rate per period, expressed as a decimal
T = number of semi-annual interest periods

Answer:
Take the $1 yield today, because your return from the bond will be:

$$\$1.25 \times (1/1+.03)9$$
$$= \$1.25 \times (1/1.3048)$$
$$= \$1.25 \times 0.766$$
$$= \$0.96$$

If you add bonds to your portfolio, review them every six months, use the interest productively and consider swaps whenever there is a change of at least 1% in the prevailing interest rate.

Lessons from the Trader Wizard

The yield curve

I cannot leave the section on bonds without addressing the yield curve.

Inexperienced traders have two misconceptions about the bond market:

(1)   they presume interest rates are the same as bond yields, which are, in fact, not the same; and

(2)   they think the bond market goes up and down with all yields moving together. Everybody, however, should know that yields of different bond maturities behave, to some extent, independently of each other. In fact, short-term rates and long-term rates occasionally even move in the opposite direction.

It is very important to understand the yield curve and to keep monitoring it.

The yield curve is a line chart that, at any given time, shows yields for all securities having equal risk, but different maturity dates. It is used to compare a government's short-term Treasury bills with its mid-term notes and long-term bonds. The line begins on the left with the yield of the shortest maturity and ends on the right with the yield of the longest maturity. The next day, as the different yields change to a different extent, the line between the various yields will shift.

What's important is the overall pattern of yield movement — and what it says about the future of the economy and the capital markets. The yield curve is an important tool for economists, but it should also be one you use as well. It's probably the most important concept inexperienced traders could learn and apply.

In a healthy economy, income securities with longer maturities usually have a higher yield. This is the normal yield curve, which is sometimes called a positive yield curve.

If short-term securities offer a higher yield, then the curve is referred to as an inverted yield curve or a negative yield curve. This doesn't happen often, but when it does, it's a clear sign that bond yields, as well as interest rates in the general economy, are expected to decline.

At times the yield curve will go fairly flat.

Ordinarily, short-term bonds carry lower yields to reflect the fact that a trader's capital is subject to less risk. The longer you tie up your cash, the theory goes, the more you should be rewarded for the risk you are taking.

Cara's Approach to Trading Bonds, Bond Funds and Cash

Who knows, in fact, what's going to happen over three decades that may affect the value of a 30-year bond?

A normal yield curve based on a stable and growing economy, therefore, slopes gently upward as maturities lengthen and yields rise. From time to time, however, the curve changes into a few recognizable patterns, each of which signals an important turning point in the economy. When those patterns appear, it's often wise to change your assumptions about economic growth.

When bond traders expect the economy to move at slower rates of growth with possible negative changes in inflation rates or available capital (ie, liquidity), the yield curve slopes downward.

To help you learn to predict economic activity by using the yield curve, I have isolated four of these shapes — normal, steep, inverted and flat — so that I can demonstrate what each shape says about economic growth and stock market performance. This data was derived from TD Securities.

Normal curve: eg, December 1984

When bond traders expect the economy to have normal rates of growth, without significant changes in inflation rates, the yield curve slopes gently upward.

In the absence of economic disruptions, traders who risk their money for longer periods expect to get a bigger reward (in the form of higher interest) than those who risk their capital for shorter time periods. So, as maturities lengthen, interest rates typically get progressively higher and the curve goes up.

December 1984, marked the middle of the longest period of post-war expansion. Global economic growth rates were in a steady quarterly range of 2% to 5%. The major equity market indexes were posting strong gains. The yield curve during this period was normal and this is the kind of curve most closely associated with the usual comfort zone of an economic and stock market expansion.

Steep curve: eg, April 1992

Typically, the yield on 30-year Treasury bonds is two to three percentage points above the yield on three-month Treasury bills, ie, 200 to 300 basis points higher. When the gap gets wider than that — and the slope of the yield curve increases sharply — long-term bond holders are sending a message that they believe the economy will grow very quickly in the future.

Lessons from the Trader Wizard

This shape is typical at the beginning of an economic expansion, just after the end of a period of recession. Economic stagnation will have depressed short-term interest rates at that point, but once the demand for capital (and fear of inflation) is re-established by rising economic activity, rates begin to lift.

Long-term traders fear being locked into low rates, so they demand greater compensation much more quickly than short-term lenders who face less risk. Short-term traders can trade out of T-bills in a matter of months, giving them the flexibility to buy higher-yielding securities should the opportunity arise.

In April 1992, the spread between short- and long-term rates was five percentage points, indicating that bond traders were anticipating an extremely strong economy in the future and had bid up long-term rates to create a steep yield curve. They were right. The GDP, which is a measure of a country's economy, was expanding in the US at 3% a year by 1993.

Short-term interest rates (which slumped to 20-year lows right after the 1991 recession) had, by October 1994, jumped two full percentage points (ie, 200 basis points), flattening the curve into a more normal shape.

Equity traders who had seen the steep yield curve in April 1992 and had bet on economic expansion and growing corporate profits were rewarded; the broad equity market gained 20% over the next two years.

Inverted curve, eg, August 1981

At first glance, an inverted yield curve seems a contradiction. Why would long-term traders settle for lower yields when short-term traders take so much less risk? The answer is that long-term traders will settle for lower yields now if they think rates — and the economy — are going even lower in the future. They're betting that this is their last chance to lock-in rates before the bottom falls out.

Look at the situation in August 1981. Earlier that year, the US Federal Reserve had begun to lower the Federal Funds Rate in an attempt to forestall a slowing economy. Recession fears had convinced bond traders that this was their last chance to lock in 10% yields for the next few years. The collective market instinct was right.

A GDP chart demonstrates just how bad things got in 1981. Interest rates fell dramatically for the next five years as the economy tanked. Thirty-year bond yields went from 14% to 7% while short-term rates, which started much higher at 15%, fell to below 6%. For equity traders, the 1981-82 bear phase was brutal. However, traders who bought a long-maturity bond

73

definitely had success. I recall participating in an investment roundtable at the Toronto Press Club for a major publisher, calling those 15% government bonds held in a tax-deferred plan to be the "Buy of the Generation".

Inverted yield curves are uncommon and it pays to never ignore them. They are almost always followed by economic slowdown or recession, as well as lower interest rates across the board.

Flat curve, eg, April 1989

To become inverted, the yield curve must pass through a period where long-term yields are the same as short-term rates. When that happens the shape will appear to be flat or, more commonly, a little raised in the middle.

Not all flat or humped curves turn into fully inverted curves, mind you. Otherwise all traders would get rich simply plunking their savings into 30-year bonds the day they saw long bond yields start falling toward short-term levels.

On the other hand, don't discount a flat or humped curve just because it doesn't guarantee a coming recession. The odds are still pretty good that economic slowdown and lower interest rates will follow a period of flattening yields. That's what happened in 1989 when 30-year bond yields were less than three-year yields for about five months. The curve then straightened out and began to look more normal at the beginning of 1990.

Was this a false alarm? No, because GDP charts show that the economy sagged in June and fell into recession in 1991. Equity market charts show that the stock market also took a dive in mid-1989 and plummeted in early 1991. Short- and medium-term rates were four percentage points lower by the end of 1992.

As I write this book (August 2007), the 30-year Treasury bonds are yielding 4.82% and the 30-day Treasury bills are yielding 4.89%, so there is an inverted yield curve. The yield curve went inverted early in 4Q06. Many economists have forecasted economic slowdown and/or recession in 2008.

Applying your knowledge of the yield curve

Say you inherited $10,000 and want to have it available in 10 years. You have several choices:

(1)   A 10-year Treasury bond to be held to maturity. This would be fine if you expected interest rates to stay high.

(2)   A six-month Treasury bill to be rolled over at maturity repeatedly over the 10 years. This would be wise if you might need the money and if interest rates are high and expected to rise.

(3)   A two-year Treasury note that, at maturity, would be turned into an eight-year bond. This would be fine if short-term rates are high and expected to drop and long-term rates are low and expected to rise.

(4)   A 15-year bond to be sold after 10 years. This would be worth considering if you expect interest rates to fall, but it has the most risk.

As with all technical indicators, the yield curve is not always correctly interpreted, but it's a useful tool in trying to predict future interest rates. It can aid traders in visualizing the profit potential of various holdings with different maturities.

But with a thorough understanding, it can do so much more. It can serve as the foundation of your entire trading approach.

Similarly, an understanding of the bond market, interest rates and cash management will clearly be a help to traders who are mostly interested in stocks.

2

Choosing between bonds and bond funds

It is important to me that you all understand that when I say the most important thing you can do as a person trying to make better financial decisions is to learn how to hunt in the forest, with learned skills and experience, totally ignoring the noise of others who have conflicting objectives. I'm not a "guru forecaster" or entertainer. I'm a teacher with a ministry. Enough said. I concluded yesterday, "Life is a matter of confidence... Don't ever lose it."

May 11, 2007

If you do not have the resources to buy a block of bonds directly on the NYSE, consider a bond mutual fund or an exchange-traded bond fund.

A bond mutual fund: (i) may provide competitive returns, (ii) provides reinvestment of income for compounding; and (iii) can be purchased for a minimum outlay of $1,000 or so, plus sales commission.

Traders ought to consider the comparatively high commission costs included with bond mutual funds versus buying an exchange-traded bond or bond ETF directly. The typical sales load or built-in sales charges run 0.5% per year; management fees are around 0.5% of assets plus 0.5% for operational expenses plus 2.5% of the fund's cash income. Thus, the annual percent yield of a bond fund will be about 1.5 points less than the return of an average bond.

Maybe this cost is worth it to you, maybe not. However, if you have any understanding of interest rates, I suggest the management expense of a bond mutual fund is a heavy cost. I believe you can trade better directly in individual bonds or bond ETFs.

Including mutual funds, the most popular types of bond funds are as follows:

Open-end bond funds

These funds invest either partly or entirely in government debt. They diversify their portfolios by maturities rather than by types of bonds. Designed for the small- and medium-sized trading account, the sales charges are low, and often there are no redemption fees.

Cara's Approach to Trading Bonds, Bond Funds and Cash

The discounts of current price to NAV vary according to the type of bonds held and the management fee charged. Since the fund shares have no maturity dates, a trader is always at risk that the spread will become greater rather than smaller. So don't worry if you buy these traditional mutual funds for long-term income, but be cautious if you are seeking capital gains.

Closed-end bond funds

These units are traded on an exchange, but where the company is operated like a regular mutual fund. The proceeds from the sale of the company's treasury shares are invested in fixed-income debt securities. Actual returns depend on the skill of the asset managers and the composition of the portfolio.

The buyer of these funds is typically trading for a combination of high yield and some capital growth.

In trying to beat the competition, some aggressive managers of closed-end bond funds look for income via excessive trading or "alternative" investment tactics. They may be buying super high-yielding debt such as collateralized debt obligations (CDOs) or lending securities to traders who are short of those securities and will pay a small borrowing fee in order to avoid having to cover short positions in an erratic market.

I believe the concept of a bond fund should always be "safety first", particularly if the fund is meant or income purposes, so always check the fund's policies and current portfolio before you buy. These so-called alternative strategies of a particular fund manager may be profitable, but they can be very risky too.

Price-wise, these shares typically rise and fall with interest rates. In a rising-rate environment, some of these fund shares have suffered annual capital losses of one-third or more. Capital growth is likely when rates are falling.

With the collapse of the credit market in July 2007, however, the prices of these shares have fallen in a falling rate environment. There have been serious solvency issues in many cases.

Retractable bond funds

In these funds, the bondholder may redeem part of the total principal each year at par plus accrued interest. Usually, the redemption of bonds is callable by the issuer, so this feature would appeal to retirees who are interested in fixed-income.

High-yield bond funds

In these funds, the fund managers specialize in riskier, low-grade corporate issues and syndicated CDOs that have extra-high rates of return, say 15% a year or more. Risk diversification in your own portfolio is probably a good thing unless there is a liquidity crunch as there has been in July-August of 2007.

Introduced many years ago by a hero of mine, Michael Milken, high-yield corporate bonds (or junk bonds, as they are called), are possibly too risky for most individuals who should be thinking "safety first".

High-yield bond funds have two special features that appeal to speculators, including: (a) greater upside leverage compared to average-yielding bond funds, because these riskier bonds trade at bigger discounts to NAV; and (b) the downside cushion in a rising interest rate environment.

The latter happens because shares of bond funds selling at deep discounts will decline less in a bear phase (ie, rising-rate environment), than the prices of individual bonds. If, however, interest rates fall rapidly (ie, a bull phase for bonds) these high-yield funds rally hard because there is double pressure from (i) the rise of the overall bond market; and (ii) the enthusiasm of traders who purposefully bid up heavily discounted prices until they get close to net-asset values.

Bond ETFs

There are six excellent bond ETFs to choose from. These six funds will satisfy the needs of 98% of bond traders. Note that the 0.15%-0.20% expense ratio is a fraction of the average 1.5% levied on mutual funds.

#1 iShares Lehman 1-3 Year Treasury Bond Fund (SHY)

Average Yield to Maturity(%): 4.8
Weighted Average Maturity (Years): 1.9
Effective Duration (Years): 1.8

#2 iShares Lehman 7-10 Year Treasury Bond Fund (IEF)

Average Yield to Maturity(%): 4.7
Weighted Average Maturity (Years): 8.6
Effective Duration (Years): 6.6

Cara's Approach to Trading Bonds, Bond Funds and Cash

#3 iShares Lehman 20+ Year Treasury Bond Fund (TLT)

Average Yield to Maturity(%): 4.9
Weighted Average Maturity (Years): 23.2
Effective Duration (Years): 13.2

Each iShares Lehman 1-3 Year US Treasury Bond Fund has a credit quality of Aaa/AAA, and includes all publicly-issued US Treasury securities that have a remaining maturity of between one and three (SHY) or seven and 10 (IEF) or greater than 20 years (TLT), are non-convertible, denominated in US dollars, rated investment grade, fixed rate and have more than $250 million par outstanding. Each index is market cap-weighted and rebalanced monthly to help maintain maturity targets. Options are available. The expense ratio is 0.15%.

#4 iBoxx $ Investment Grade Corporate Bond Fund (LQD)

Average Yield to Maturity(%): 5.6
Average Credit Quality: A2/BBB+
Weighted Average Maturity (Years): 10.2
Effective Duration (Years): 6.1

iBoxx $ Investment Grade Corporate Bond Fund (LQD) is an exchange-traded fund designed to track the performance of Goldman Sachs $InvesTop Index. The index is a basket of 100 bonds designed to provide balanced representation of the US dollar investment-grade corporate market through some of the most liquid corporate bonds available. All 100 bonds in the basket are equally par-weighted and the index is rebalanced monthly. Options are available. The expense ratio is 0.15%.

Top LQD Holdings (approx. 1% each)

Mohawk Inds Inc, 6.12%, 1/15/16
United Technologies, 4.38%, 5/1/10
Embarq Corp, 7.99%, 6/1/36
Hsbc Hldgs Plc, 6.5%, 5/2/36
General Elec Cap Cor, 5%, 1/8/16
Deere John Capital C, 7%, 3/15/12
Jpmorgan Chase Cap X, 6.95%, 8/17/66
Merrill Lynch & Co I, 6.05%, 5/16/16
TXU Energy Co Llc, 7%, 3/15/13
Oracle Corp / Ozark, 5%, 1/15/11

Lessons from the Trader Wizard

#5 iShares Lehman Aggregate Bond Fund (AGG)

Average Yield to Maturity(%): 5.4
Average Credit Quality: Aa/AA-
Weighted Average Maturity (Years): 7.2
Effective Duration (Years): 5.0

iShares Lehman Aggregate Bond Fund (AGG) is an exchange-traded fund designed to track the performance of the Lehman Brothers US Aggregate Index. The index includes over 6,500 issues with more than $250 million outstanding. It is designed to represent the total fixed-rate, non-convertible US investment-grade bond market, excluding municipals. The securities in the index are denominated in US dollars and must have at least one year remaining to maturity. The index is market cap-weighted and is rebalanced monthly. Options are available. The expense ratio is 0.20%.

Top AGG Holdings (%)

FNMA Tba 30Yr, 5.5%, 12/15/36	5.3%
US Treasury Note, 6%, 8/15/09	5.3%
FNMA Tba 30Yr, 6%, 12/15/36	4.9%
Fhlmc Gold Tba 30 Yr, 5.5%, 12/15/36	4.3%
US Treasury Bond, 7.62%, 2/15/25	3.8%
US Treasury Note, 3%, 11/15/07	3.7%
FHLMC, 2.75%, 3/15/08	3.5%
US Treasury Note, 5.12%, 6/30/08	3.2%
US Treasury Bond, 8.12%, 8/15/19	2.8%
FNMA Tba 30Yr, 6.5%, 12/15/36	2.7%
Top Ten Total	39.5%

#6 iShares Lehman TIPS Bond Fund (TIP)

Average Yield to Maturity(%): 6.5
Average Credit Quality: Aaa/AAA
Weighted Average Maturity (Years): 10.1
Effective Duration (Years): 5.9

iShares Lehman TIPS Bond Fund (TIP) is an exchange-traded fund designed to track the performance of the Lehman Brothers US Treasury Inflation Notes Index. The index includes all publicly issued, US Treasury Inflation-protected securities that have at least one year to maturity, are non-convertible, denominated in US dollars, rated investment grade, fixed rate and have more than $200 million par outstanding. The index is market capitalization weighted and the securities in the Index are updated on the last calendar day of each month. Options are available. The expense ratio is 0.20%.

Cara's Approach to Trading Bonds, Bond Funds and Cash

Discussion of ETFs, including closed-end funds, versus open-end funds

What differentiates an exchange-traded fund from an open-end fund is that the open-end fund involves units of a pooled holding based on NAV calculated daily, and the units are purchased as a product from a mutual fund company and probably redeemed (ie, sold back), to that company.

On the other hand, an exchange-traded fund is a security of a corporation or trust whose shares are bought and sold on a securities market.

People who buy financial products buy and redeem mutual funds and those who trade securities buy and sell the shares or units like any other exchange-listed security. Securities may trade equal to the NAV or above (ie, at a premium) or below (ie, at a discount) to NAV.

ETFs can be passive-tracking instruments or actively-managed pooled funds called closed-end funds that are officially termed investment companies.

In the case of the listed investment holding companies, the price of the shares frequently changes during the day, based on supply and demand for the shares — often with no relation to the NAV of the underlying holdings. In fact, a closed-end fund often trades at a discount to the asset value of its holdings, which could make it more attractive to you.

Depending on the quality of management and how substantial the purchase discount, I like closed-end funds and index-tracking funds, but not mutual funds.

Guidelines in choosing bond funds:

- If you are not going to stick with a bond ETF, stay away from any fund that has holdings of NR (Not-Rated) issues. (i) For safety, choose those with the most AA- and A-rated holdings. (ii) For income, look for those that buy lower-quality issues, but are not rated less than BB.

- Calculate the average discount or premium for a closed-end fund. When a closed-end bond fund is selling below its average annual discount from NAV, it may be a good buy. If it's priced above that average, be cautious but not negative. Usually, the discount/premium will reflect the fund's portfolio composition.

- With higher-yielding bond funds, be skeptical about diversification claims until you check them out. When corporations fail, there is little chance they will pay interest or redeem the principal.

Lessons from the Trader Wizard

- For an open-end fund, check the repurchase price. If the fund distributor buys only at the lower bid side of the price spread, you will lose a few dollars on redemption.

- Look for frequent distributions. A fund that pays a monthly distribution assures a steady cash flow and, if the income is reinvested, compounds at a higher rate. Buy just before the distribution-declaration date.

3

Money market funds:

Cash is an asset class too

Just remember the expression, "Things are never that good, and they are never that bad." As we move forward in time, there is a constant reversion to the mean.

March 17, 2007

Cash represents an unallocated asset, but an asset class in itself. Cash is also a tradable asset too in that there are at least 10 international currencies that are popular with individual traders today whether they are traded in the cash or futures markets or as ETFs.

Putting money to work to preserve capital and beat inflation

Since your first goal as a trader is capital preservation, and some of the assets are likely cash, you have to take steps to fight inflation. You can do that with a high-quality money market fund, which is a form of savings account with a variable rate of return floating with general interest rates.

In recent years, we hear economists tell us daily that inflation has been beaten. In terms of inference, nothing they say can be a bigger lie. Inflation is never "beaten". It's like my color-blindness, it's all just a matter of degree. All we have to do is look at the constant increase in our daily cost of living and we know that, at the best of times, inflation is a problem.

What I very much resent in the media today is the common use of the term "mini-bubble", such as "there is a mini-bubble in housing prices in California and Southern Florida" as if inflation is not a problem elsewhere. This is a type of intellectual dishonesty that has crept into our daily lives and it needs to be confronted at every opportunity.

In any event, cash is an asset you have to manage like bonds. A good way is via money market funds, which offer individual traders a good deal, such as: (a) excellent liquidity (telephone redemption); (b) high yields (currently two points above bank savings account rates); and (c) convenience (banking privileges).

Cara's Approach to Trading Bonds, Bond Funds and Cash

There are investment companies that invest only in liquid assets such as Treasury bills and notes, as well as lower credit quality instruments such as CDs, commercial paper, repurchase agreements, and so on. They pay daily interest and thus compound income. Their yields reflect the current cost of money. But, check the credit quality before you place your money there. Some money market funds have failed in the July–August 2007 credit market fiasco.

Money market funds have many attractive features:

- Your money is always at work because interest is compounded daily. With Treasury bills, you buy at a discount and get full value at maturity … no compounding.

- There are no costs and all of your money goes to work immediately. Alternatively, with Treasury bills, bought through a bank, the cost is about $15 and you lose three days of interest and four days' discount on the discount. If you deal direct and send your payment to the Fed, you lose a week's interest and, at maturity, get no interest for five more days.

- Safety. Your money is used to buy prime debt of well-rated corporations or the US Government or its agencies. If you choose a fund that invests only in US securities, your yield will be a fraction of 1% lower, but you count on the Government guarantee and you sleep well at night knowing you have avoided any problems in credit markets.

- Easy redemption: done by telephone when proper procedures are set up at the outset.

- Banking privileges plus extra income.

- Quick benefits when interest rates rise. You get the extra return immediately rather than having to wait until buying new bills or notes. And when interest rates fall you continue to get the high yields for another month or so.

- The privilege of shifting to other funds under the management of the same advisory firm. Thus, you can use money market funds as a parking place while you decide the next trades you wish to make.

Lessons from the Trader Wizard

Since nothing's perfect, here are some drawbacks with a money market fund:

- When interest rates reached the historically low level of 1% in 2003, you could have done better with investments in short-term bonds bought at par or at discount.

- All interest income is taxed at the highest rate. In the 50% tax bracket, that 45 return drops to a net of 2%. When you buy common stocks that provide total returns of 10%-2% dividend and 8% appreciation — your net will be far greater and the realized gains on the capital appreciation will be taxed at the low capital gains rate. But, of course, with money market funds you'll get your capital returned with interest while the stock values fluctuate.

- Money market funds are not insured. CDs in banks are covered by an agency of government, but only up to $100,000.

- In an effort to out-perform the competition, some fund managers buy securities of lower-grade corporations, foreign governments and syndicated debt (including sub-prime mortgage paper) — all of which are comparatively risky, and could lead to solvency issues.

- There can be temporary losses if managers guess wrong on interest rates.

How money market fund assets are valued

Money market funds price their shares at $1 each. The stated yield as reported daily, reflects the interest earned. The base is the NAV per share. This is determined by subtracting all liabilities from the market value of the fund's shares and dividing the result by the number of shares outstanding.

Money market fund guidelines for selection by relatively large accounts

Know the fund manager. Look for a well-known, established management firm. No major bank, insurance company or mutual fund group will endanger its reputation by holding dubious investments in these funds.

Don't chase high yields. If this decision is part of a long-term strategy, look for reasonable rates of return and remember that you are not trading, but investing in a proven money manager, which, by definition, means fairly long commitments. As a frame of reference, compare the yields to those of 90-day Treasury bills.

Buy late in the day, but not after 3 p.m. You want to start earning interest immediately.

Look for short maturities — 60 days at the most. If you have large cash funds, this practice assures flexibility and the opportunity to move with interest rates. With long maturities, there can be problems when the cost of money changes suddenly.

If you follow a money market fund's interest rate tables for a couple of months, you'll start to see some obvious signals:

- When the average rate of maturity moves within a narrow range, interest rates are likely to remain stable.

- When the maturity jumps, say, from 35 to 40 days, there will probably be a sharp decline in returns.

Check the seven-day data, but focus on the 30-day figures. These funds are so huge that it takes time to make shifts.

Traders who seek the most conservative money market funds buy primarily US Treasury bills; while the aggressive traders look for funds that hold short-term debt instruments from emerging nations as well as some US dollar CDs.

If you have a small amount of cash available because most of your funds are invested in stocks and bonds, you might want to keep it simple by holding Treasury bills. Traders who are thinking ahead go into a laddering of 90-day Treasury bills with one-third of these funds maturing into cash each month.

Whenever you have a lot of cash on hand, however, you should put some thought into cash management, such as:

When interest rates are rising:

- invest in short-term money market funds; and
- do not invest in longer-term money market funds — you'll lose tomorrow's higher yields.

Lessons from the Trader Wizard

When you think interest rates are about to peak:

- put 25% into CDs;
- put 25% into super-yielding money market funds; and
- keep 50% in normal money market funds and wait for the peak.

When interest rates peak: Move another 25% from money market funds into CDs.

When interest rates are falling:

- hold the highest yielders;
- add to CDs;
- if they can be sold at profit, sell CDs for three months after buying them;
- reinvest in CDs, if available, or in super-yielders;
- move back into a 75% money fund — 25% CD profile when interest rates begin to reverse and climb; and
- shift from the highest yielders back into money market funds.

There are effective cash management strategies I know are used by the treasury departments of broker-dealers. But I have to admit treasury management is not my specialty.

As for cash management strategies and tactics, I operate differently to most people. I believe every trader should be 100% invested, long or short, in highly liquid equity securities. In my case, rather than buying a money-market fund, I try to write naked put options in stocks that I believe are rising in price. That's extra risk, and success admittedly depends on my market-timing ability, but the options premium is a much better return than I would earn in a money-market fund. Very seldom do I have the owner of the put option force me to buy the stock.

As you can see, there are many different approaches to trading bonds, bond funds and cash.

Part **3**

Trading Stocks (Also Called Equities)

As most traders are interested in trading equities, I will devote the most time and space to this part of the book. Before I get into a trading plan for equities, I wish to cover four basic knowledge elements that all traders have to master before they can gain confidence to trade equities successfully.

The four legs of the stool are labeled:

(1) macro-economic;
(2) fundamental;
(3) quantitative; and
(4) technical.

I always start from the top down by looking at (1) the macro-economic and government regulatory environment that a corporation has to manage. I do this to assess the environment picture and operating conditions for business corporations. Then I turn to (2) the corporation and how it deals with its employees, suppliers and customers. The next step is (3) to compare those results against industry peers and past-performance metrics. Finally, I look at (4) the stock price to see where it's been, where it's likely to go (according to mathematical studies called Time Series Analysis) and how that theory compares with my sense of the underlying enterprise value and the share prices of a company's peer group, industry, sector and broad market.

Trading Stocks (Also Called Equities)

1

Macro-economics: Where public and private sectors meet

The first Friday of every month, the capital markets (ie, stocks and bonds) are put through their biggest spin cycle of the month. It's called US Jobs Report Friday. Like CPI, the number is almost meaningless because it is a wild estimate and will almost certainly be revised. What the Jobs data does, however, is to add grist to the sell-side mill. Just a lot more yada yada by smooth talking noggins, trying to convince Joe Public they are "experts" and you ought to be following their advice.

I learned the patter too. I mean, if you want to survive in the securities industry in any capacity from chief investment strategist to mail runner, there are a few things you must be prepared to utter when your lips start moving. The US Jobs Report data is at the top of the list. CPI is another. Why? Because all people have a vested interest in their jobs and in the cost of getting to the end of the month, hoping not to be a dollar short.

May 4, 2007

Trying to understand economics, the Fed and the market

I believe that if a trader has a very basic understanding of the subject, macro-economic data could be used to interpret and forecast trading conditions and make better-informed decisions. Business owners and executives do this continuously and traders have to realize that their business is to manage the wealth under their control. Clearly, that is a business like any other.

The Internet offers traders free access to potentially valuable economic data. Where we go wrong is to overlook the data and focus on the "Talking Heads" who interpret the data in the broadcast media. These are well-educated, intelligent analysts and reporters, but they are either biased or paid to say what they say. Traders need better information.

What happens today — as in the past — is that when a US Government agency, like the Bureau of Labor Statistics, for example, publishes data such as the Consumer Price Index number, the "Talking Heads" of the media and Wall Street read the number like it is a sports report coming to you hot off the wire.

Economic data is made to seem as important as pulling a face card from the casino's blackjack dealer. The audience is advised to buy or sell because this number (an estimate in itself) is up or down a tenth of a percentage point from consensus expectation.

Isn't that an absolutely ludicrous approach to wealth management?

The fact is that economic data is just that — data — which is only an indicator of underlying conditions. Besides, the CPI data is materially incorrect and misleading. The US Bureau of Labor Statistics calculator states that the cost of living has increased by 7.37872 times in 50 years (year-end 1957-2007). That means $1,000 on all items of consumer expenditure in 1957 would cost $7,378.72 today. A moron knows better.

Consider your typical consumer expenditure list today and, if you are as old as me, compare them — apples to apples — to what they would have cost in 1956. Here's a list of comparables:

- housing, property taxes, insurance;
- auto costs, maintenance, insurance and repair bills;
- mass transit;
- hotel rooms;
- food and beverages;
- newspapers and magazines;
- dental and hospital/medical care; and
- school tuition and books.

In my case, the house my parents bought 50 years ago for $14,000 is now selling at 23 times that cost. The Coca-cola I bought in the local service station vending machine now costs 15 times as much. The mass transit ticket has increased 20 times in price. I could go on, but why bother? Entire books have been published on the issue of the flawed CPI. (Source: http://data.bls.gov)

Economic datapoints, you should know, no more strictly control stock prices than the way a school playground is laid out for activities from basketball to hopscotch. The kids will use it as they wish.

Conditions may set the framework, but clearly, players decide on the game. So my point is that economic data, like other data you receive, is carefully spun to you by vested interests. If those people want markets to go up, the data is used to paint a positive picture. If they want it to go down, the same data is used to paint a negative picture.

Lessons from the Trader Wizard

In today's economy, the school board has granted an extended recess and the kids have settled into a routine of watching a few ringers throw hoops. Soon the flock will get tired and want to get back to classes.

Today (November 2007), the US Federal Reserve Bank under Professor Bernanke's leadership has set a Fed rate of 4.75%. But if the Fed were to set a rate of, say, 3.75% or 5.75%, which is one full point higher or lower, would there be any difference? After a series of moves, there would still be a stable stock market. Traders would also still be worrying about if, and when, the next Fed rate would be set at 4.00% or 6.00%.

Nonetheless, economic analysis is still a truly important adjunct to securities analysis for serious traders. My point is that it is the change in the data that is important and how that change impacts thinking, which impacts market prices. Today, for instance, (November 2007), traders are hoping the Fed will cut the Fed rate to 4.25% from 5.25% in just a couple months, but if that were to happen the reason would be problematic. Traders would initially think that the rate cut would be a positive factor, and would rally equity prices; then they would think about the underlying reasons for the rate cut and would start selling stocks unless there were a series of rate cuts. All through this period, the spin artists for the various sides would be pushing the public to move from one extreme to the other.

By focusing on a few key economic statistics, I believe any trader should be able to acquire a reasonably full understanding of the real-world conditions in which corporations and professional traders operate, which is essential to drawing a link to future operations and financial strength of a company and its future share price.

In this process, rather than thinking that any one data series is more important than others, your consideration should be given to the inter-relationships between underlying economic conditions and securities prices, and the fact that financial markets are dynamic and constantly evolving due, in part, to changes in these economic conditions.

One caveat to new students of the market is that US data is only part of the economic picture. Traders, like corporate business managers, must increasingly deal with a global economy. Push and pull forces on stock prices — economic factors like interest rates, commodity and currency prices and so on — operate today in the international arena. Every Fed action or public speech must be put into the context of trying to stabilize interest rates and the US dollar in a global context.

In any discussion of economics (as I shall attempt here), one has to start from the premise that "those with the money set the rules". So the banks

Trading Stocks (Also Called Equities)

— and the most important bank, the US Federal Reserve Bank — is a good place to start one's analysis.

It is a basic fact that commercial bank lending facilitates personal and business spending. Another fact is that excessive spending generates inflation. Since the Fed controls bank lending in the US, it thereby controls inflation or, at the very least, the pressures that would create or destroy inflation in the United States.

Moreover, stock market indexes may run up or down in tandem with the economic cycle, or they may run counter-cyclical to it. But both have a cycle, and stock prices are linked to the economic cycle, and the economic cycle is linked to conditions set by or permitted by the Fed. Fed policy determines the actions of commercial banks, which happens to be the most important source of lending and, therefore, spending.

Bank lending is a key ingredient in the economic cycle — it drives the cyclic expansion of demand. Since lending can't grow beyond the limits set by commercial bank reserves, the Fed, when it wants to give the economy a boost, will encourage banks to lend more by increasing reserves at those banks. To do so, the Fed simply buys securities on the open market or from the commercial banks directly. The sellers (who are independent of the commercial banks) deposit some of the proceeds of the sale into their banks. Hence the banking system reserves grow from both sources.

Increased commercial bank reserves directly increase the money supply — given, of course, that banks can find borrowers (and they always do). Banks create money through loans, simply by crediting the deposit/checking accounts of their borrowers when they make those loans.

All commodities have a market price and the interest rate you must pay to borrow happens to be the price of money. So money is a commodity. Its price fluctuates according to the laws of supply and demand, depending on its use. The use of money is what this discussion is all about.

If money is used, say, to build armaments for warfare, that's probably inflationary. During wartime, wealth is destroyed. Historically, periods of war (over hundreds of years, affecting all markets) have been the only serious periods of inflation for otherwise stable economies. During peace time, the economic cycle is typically disinflationary, which is the best time to invest in stocks and bonds, particularly those that are low interest rate beneficiaries, such as the banks and mortgage companies, REITs, and companies that hold lots of bonds and bank debt as liabilities, like regulated telephone companies, other utilities and insurance companies.

Lessons from the Trader Wizard

During periods of economic expansion, which can occur when the business cycle is disinflationary or inflationary, the demand for money increases and interest rates rise, because consumers and businesses often need to finance increased spending.

Spending is financed by savings, by sales of assets, or (as we said) most importantly, by borrowing from banks. Every few years the price of things, including money, gets too high to finance spending from bank borrowings or diminished savings levels, so personal and business spending cannot keep up with the supply of available goods and services. Therefore, inventories build, business investment slows and the economy goes into a recessive phase.

Recession and disinflation, you can see, are quite different. Recession is bad. Low inflation and periods of disinflation are good.

As a recessive economy starts to recover, savings start to re-build, financial assets accumulate and debts get paid down. Cash becomes plentiful again. Interest rates begin to fall as the supply of funds exceeds demand for funds at current rates. This was the economic picture leading up to 3Q98, for instance.

With available cash to lend because of higher reserves on hand, and with a low enough interest rate to attract borrowers, bank lending starts to increase, which leads to higher spending, which, in turn, leads to increased total demand and economic expansion. Internationally, the US economy took the lead in 1998 (it doesn't always) and by late 1999, there were signs that other major industrialized nations were beginning to follow.

Excessive bank lending then leads to inflation when the higher demand for goods and services reaches a level that exceeds supply, at which point the Fed — all other considerations aside — would step in to reverse the cycle.

That process began in the US in 1999, and the Fed raised its rates to commercial banks several times until a recession ensued.

If the Fed abandons their responsibility to keep inflation in check, the trade-weighted US dollar falls in price, and the cost of imported goods — to a nation that is a heavy net importer like the US — rise, causing inflation to spiral higher.

Because the US is a debtor nation, the Fed often has to perform a balancing act between interest rates and the foreign exchange rate and their combined impact on US jobs.

Trading Stocks (Also Called Equities)

If US interest rates rise too much, the dollar will get too strong, causing businesses to stop spending on capital programs locally and start importing more from foreign vendors. Jobs will be lost. But if rates fall too quickly, the dollar will get too weak, causing imports to become needlessly expensive and inflation to return.

By 2003, much more spending by both business and the consumer was needed to boost the US economy, so to ramp up jobs and avoid the potential for deflation, interest rates were forced down by the Fed to 1%. As we subsequently learned, that rate was well below a reasonable point and the price of the US dollar soon collapsed.

A long-term balance between the supply and demand for money is needed and the Fed has for many years, under Chairman Alan Greenspan, and now under Ben Bernanke, played a controversial role in moving too far in one direction or the other. For political reasons (as in pressure from the White House and Congress) the job is not an easy one. Sometimes, like brats in the schoolyard who don't want to return to class, preferring instead an extended recess, there are many traders around who never want the Fed to tighten the money supply and borrowing conditions.

Many different schools of economic thought exist today, from the Keynesian/monetarist/demand-siders to the Kudlow-Laffer/supply-siders. All believe that different factors in this equation (ie, the business and economic cyclic process), have varying degrees of importance (which really is a political discussion). But the basic equation for the cycle, as outlined above, remains the same.

The world is as rife today with economic statistics as with the stats listed in the sports pages of our daily newspapers. Some are more important than others: in my view, the consumer and business spending aggregates are important economic numbers and, hence, must be routinely monitored by traders who use the big picture, top-down analytical approach that I recommend.

Regarding consumer spending, the most important statistics to follow are auto sales, consumer credit and new permits/housing starts. For business spending, the most important data are capital expenditures and inventories.

The effects on the capital markets of changes in data related to retail sales, employment and personal income are, I feel, difficult to analyze. This data, however, is sometimes helpful when analyzing individual stock groups, such as specialty retailers, recreation and leisure stocks, and the like.

All this data is reported on by a free service called Econoday, which is available through the NASDAQ website.

The world is strewn with economists, statistics, economic analysis and reports. I don't see the value of most of it and I certainly don't believe much of what I hear and read. But at the end of the day, I need to frame my trading analysis and opinions in my sense of the economy.

Economic analysis protocols I've used for over 20 years and still recommend

There are seven economic analysis protocols I follow:

(1)   "Fed Watching" to determine easing or tightening and its effect on the stock, bond, commodity and currency markets.

(2)   Interest rates and their effect on the bond, stock and currency markets.

(3)   Currencies and their effect on stock groups, global mutual funds, gold and the North American equity markets.

(4)   Consumer spending indicators and the impact of rising or falling spending behavior on stock group beneficiaries.

(5)   Business spending indicators and the impact of rising or falling spending behavior on stock group beneficiaries.

(6)   Inflation indicators and point-of-cycle studies for stock groups, interest rates and commodities.

(7)   Financial assets (ie, stocks and bonds) versus hedged holdings (such as gold, cash, equities short-selling and real estate).

Each of these studies gives a unique perspective of an important element of the global and regional economy. As traders routinely analyze this type of information, actively putting the data relationships together, a clearer picture of the economy emerges, which can be applied to better trading decisions.

Remember, stock prices are better understood by well-informed traders than by economists or media people.

The question is always: "What is the state-of-the-economy today, and why are the Fed and its counterpart central bankers taking their current actions?" The answer you get from one economist is never the same as that from

Trading Stocks (Also Called Equities)

another. It's a common joke that 10 economists will give you 10 different answers.

I feel that because of relatively high productivity gains in the United States, as well as economic weakness abroad (mostly in Japan and in the "Old Europe" economies), Americans enjoyed both a long cyclic expansion of their economy from 1981 through to 2000 and the deferral of the inflation cycle that didn't begin until 2002.

The crisis of September 11, 2001 was the turning point. That was when the US Administration under President George Bush made the fateful, and probably necessary, decision to wage a costly war against a concept they labeled as "terrorism".

This is not a book on politics, but the fact is, US politics and global capital markets are intertwined. Traders, knowing that we are humans and prone to errors in judgement, started focusing on the errors in implementation of the war effort.

In 2003, after global interest rates and commodity prices started to rise, and the large European and Japanese economies started to get settled into their growth mode, inflation returned. Initially there were only a few indications of this inflation cycle. Rising oil prices and then housing prices and then metals prices were the first signs of higher commodity prices.

My personal view, which I recorded in 1999, is that the Fed under Greenspan did an exceptionally good job of recognizing the sea change in digital telecommunications technology and in supporting the expansion of American intellectual capital in that environment. Fed-enabled bank lending and business spending in the area of intangible, Internet-related technologies (including software) in the late 1990s powered the strength of the US economy.

Without an excess of money in the banking system at that point, the Internet phenomenon would have been shackled. However, because of the surge in growth of the Internet, which was a window of entrepreneurial opportunity, the Fed-created ocean of money in the US (for whatever reason it was created, such as to combat Y2K), was channeled into capital investment, rather than personal spending on lavish lifestyles, as was the case in the 1980s.

Because of this capital investment, America made a giant leap ahead of global competitors in Europe and Japan in technology. In California alone in 1999, there were reportedly 250,000 new Internet-related millionaires who, after the 2000-2002 bear market, decided to invest that money in houses, which, in turn, started the housing bubble that surfaced in 2005 as speculators across America decided to get in on the action.

Excess money in the system in 1998–1999 also led to excessive speculation in "concept" stories. Skilful promoters, surrounded by tight insider control groups, gained hold of the pipeline to speculators as well as the float of stock in the hands of the public. Regrettably, the Fed under Greenspan did the same mistake in 2002. They dropped the Fed's Fund Rate too low (to 1%) for too long during the Bear market that ended in 4Q2002. That helped start the commodity boom in 2003 that reached bubble status in 4Q07.

A trader's job is to examine the decisions of central bankers and to determine their likely impact on the business environment and health of the private sector. This task takes a big-picture perspective.

The job of a nation's central bank is not to manage the capital markets, but to keep the domestic currency and interest rates stable, so that the nation's private sector can remain globally competitive.

Regardless of the Fed policy, the currency of the US continuously devalues.

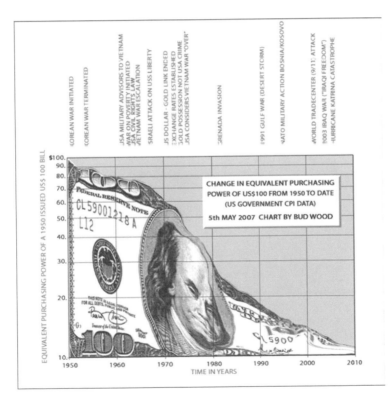

Trading Stocks (Also Called Equities)

2 Fundamental (corporate) data

When I am making decisions to support or not support a company, I look to the personal make-up of its Chairman and Chief Executive. I want to know how these people treat other people. I need to know if they believe in social equity or if they are the type of person who might work in darkened boardrooms to foist one over on us. I walk only on the ground I feel most comfortable. Over the years, if you do the same, you will find it pays off.

Qualitative assessments of a public company are just as important as the quantitative ones. Goodwill translates into higher share prices, lower cost of capital, happier employees and, ultimately, better decisions, higher profits and more rapid asset growth of a corporation.

Because of substantial bought-and-paid-for PR support of many of these companies, we, the owners and managers of capital, tend not to see beyond the veneer that is intended for us. We must look deeper because there are usually reasons why facts are hidden from us. I believe in transparency in capital markets, and in the notion that "sunlight is the best disinfectant". I hope you do as well.

July 1, 2007

Every day, traders are facing decisions on whether to buy, hold or sell a stock. That decision must be based on information, which I believe can be reached in less than 30 minutes of studying the corporation's quarterly and annual reports (both the statement of income and the balance sheet), and then putting your findings of value into the context of its current and recent stock prices.

Due to standards set by the SEC and the Financial Accounting Standards Board (FASB), which are the most powerful and influential capital market regulators in the world, a financial report must contain reams of detailed information.

You'll find loads of information for each Reporting Issuer (RI) on the source and volume of profits; data on off-balance-sheet financing, such as store/plant/equipment leases; allocations of hard-to-check sources of expenditures for interest; and research and development activities.

Trading Stocks (Also Called Equities)

This is really detailed information, but you'll be able to have it summarized for you by Value Line or Standard & Poor's — independent research services that I highly recommend. In particular, I advise all traders to print out all Value Line's quarterly reports of the Dow 30 analysis.

Neatly summarized in a binder of 120 pages a year plus some periodic hard-copy charts where you can write notes — not just about these 30 stocks, but about the stocks of other companies in their respective industries. I call it the peer group because business operations are not conducted in a vacuum.

http://valueline.com
http://stockinfo.standardpoor.com

So much of this corporate data is disseminated on the Internet — free and global, just seconds after it's publicly disclosed — that you can't say it was hidden from you. But you do have to know what to look for in the data in order to turn it into information.

How to read and analyze corporate financial data

Financial analysis is not easy for the uninitiated, but once you get the hang of it and use a screening service, you can use this knowledge to pick the best quality prospects from thousands of top-rated corporations. If you are speculative-minded, you can also find short-term stock bargains even in corporations of mediocre quality.

The key here is that the figures you'll read in a financial report have, at best, an indirect relationship with the corporation's stock price. But even some professional accountants and financial advisors fail to understand that.

In the 1990s, a "Big Four" audit partner of the private family holding company of one of the world's 25 richest men said to me: "I can't understand how, when the corporate numbers look so good, the stock price is falling." He was referring to a stock we were reviewing and I was taken aback at his deficient capital markets acumen.

Don't presume that all financial professionals understand the market!

I'm sure the same auditor, on looking at a worsening corporate position during 1999 and 2007 — the years of the market bubble, but declining corporate fundamentals in many cases —might have asked why most stock prices were going up.

The simple answer is that in the market, a rising tide floats all boats and vice versa.

Lessons from the Trader Wizard

So, you start with the knowledge that a stock is not a corporation. A stock is merely a price. A floating price.

Second, you know that, at any instant in time, the stock prices are accurate, more or less, because that's what real buyers and real sellers (in most cases) negotiate. On the other hand, as for the accuracy of corporate data, you have to keep your fingers crossed. Some corporations have deficient accounting systems and some corporate officers have even been proven to be cheaters.

In a recent case, the SEC alleged that a major health services company and its CEO were cheaters. And if they could have proved their case, which they didn't, that CEO was facing a sentence of up to 600 years in jail (which I suppose is 30 times "life"). (See http://sec.gov/litigation/complaints/comphealths.htm). In other cases, such as those against WorldCom, Enron and Computer Associates, very long prison sentences were handed down at the end of the day.

So you cannot always trust the corporate books or the executive officers, but you must always understand there is a difference between a corporation, which is represented by people and books of account, and assets and liabilities, and has a value, and a stock, which is just a floating price.

As an example, let's just say that IBM, the corporation, is slow to change its value, but IBM, the stock component of the Dow 30, changes its price significantly — sometimes 5% within minutes. With a $160-billion market capitalization, that's a change of $8 billion in minutes! This has happened. In fact it happens to the stock of all corporations.

At the height of the market bubble in 1999, during the week of 13 December, I watched Microsoft move up over $50 billion in a 10-minute period. As I wrote in my Dow 30 journal that week, "... in 10 minutes, MSFT grew by almost the total capitalization of McDonald's ($57b) or Philip Morris ($56b). At $85 billion, the personal fortune of Bill Gates now exceeds the gross national product of Portugal ($84b) and Ireland ($81b) in a single year, according to the Organisation for Economic Co-operation and Development."

In late August 2007, as I noted in my blog, the combined market cap of four Chinese companies had moved up and down by about $25 billion each day for three consecutive days. For three days, these corporations had not changed their value, however.

Back to IBM; to determine its current and prospective financial condition and its past and prospective earning power and growth, you'll have to examine the corporation's basic figures and ratios as reported in its quarterly financial summaries.

Trading Stocks (Also Called Equities)

With some practice, you'll figure out a reasonable going concern value (sometimes called enterprise value, fair value or equity value) and, when comparing that figure to its current stock price, you'll have an indication of its desirability as a potential purchase or sale.

IBM the corporation is 99.9% the same entity whether trading at 82.50 (as it was at the end of August 2003) or 92.50 (about 10 trading days later). I can assure you that the corporation never gained $20 billion in going concern value in that brief stretch, just like it didn't drop $8 billion in the following week.

But enough for now about stock prices, let's stick to the financial reports.

Publicly owned corporations issue financial reports on a quarterly and annual basis. What you need to review can be found in: (a) the balance sheet; (b) the profit and loss (or income) statement; (c) the change in financial position; or (d) the "flow of funds" data. In each of these you can find or derive:

1.   The key quantities: net tangible assets, changes in components of working capital, sales costs, profits, taxes, dividends, etc.

2.   The important rates or ratios: price/earnings, profit margins, net worth per share, growth rate, profit rate, etc.

3.   The relations between significant ratios: to compare the performance of the corporation with some standard, such as its own past performance, the industry average or some overall business-stock-market average.

The analysis we will discuss applies primarily to industrial corporations. With proper variations, they can be used for a better understanding of utilities, transport or finance and insurance companies.

How to read a corporate balance sheet

The balance sheet is the snapshot (not a moving picture) part of a corporate financial report. As at a specified date, the balance sheet shows the financial strength of a company.

A balance sheet is a summary of assets, liabilities and shareholders' equity. But, not all information worth reading in a balance sheet is in the body. Sometimes, balance sheet notes are as informative as the figures themselves or the trends you can spot between snapshots of the figures taken at different times.

Lessons from the Trader Wizard

You can get into finer detail, but the key points of a balance sheet are restricted to:

Current assets and liabilities

These show cash and liquid assets and currently payable debts. Generally, the ratio should be 2:1, which means that, after all accounts are paid in cash, 50% of the current assets (at least in terms of book value) are still available to the stockholders.

The average current ratio of a corporation varies with the type of industry. Utilities and retail stores have rapid cash inflows and high turnovers so they can operate effectively with low ratios. Again, watch the trend, which is usually more important than the absolute dollar amount.

Accounts receivable

When trade receivables rise at a rate faster than that of sales, it's a yellow caution flag. Also, if interest rates are high, financing customers can be mighty costly and can lead to a future cash squeeze or write-offs. Refer to the president's letter to learn if an increase in receivables represents, in his opinion, higher future sales.

Inventories

With inflation, inventories should increase at the same rate as sales. If there is a sudden rise, check the text of the report to find out why. Management may be smart in stocking up in anticipation of higher costs of raw materials, or it may have miscalculated customer demand. A 10% jump in inventories results in more income, but probably means a 30% decline in real net earnings. Maybe they have deliberately misstated inventory.

During my auditing career in the early 1970s, my firm, PWC, sent me to observe an inventory count at a scrap steel yard in Toronto Harbor. As audit senior of the parent steel manufacturer, I knew that these particular records were always a mess. One pile of a certain metal grade showed grotesquely high tonnage whereas others showed minus totals in the books. So, I took my Polaroid camera and did the natural thing — assigned three separate teams to do their inventory counts. I went not with management, but with the crane operator who had no axe to grind. I was astonished at the different calculations by management. I got a call that Saturday afternoon from the PWC partner asking me to put away my camera. Why? It was intimidating the client! To me, it was common sense and I couldn't understand why every auditor didn't follow this practice.

Trading Stocks (Also Called Equities)

That was an important lesson in life. If you want to play the corporate game, you are expected to go along with the accepted norms — the rule applies even to the supposedly independent auditors, I discovered. However, if you want to be a trader, there is an absolute and total need to be independently and objectively minded. You must see the facts for what they are.

In my case, I was fortunate to learn that lesson soon after leaving business school. The lessons I never learned in business school, but in the streets and the scrap yards.

Gross property

Since these figures are usually stated at the lower of cost or market, ever-higher values for real property reflect corporate expansion, replacements and acquisitions. But a lower figure could be beneficial too, if it is the result of the sale of unprofitable operations or unused plants. The important factor is not the size of the assets but the earnings they produce. Sound familiar?

Depreciation

Depreciation represents the accounting allocations for wear and tear of equipment and property. As a non-cash tax deduction, it provides after-tax money that will be used for replacement and expansion, so it should be an ever-rising figure. Watch for a sharp drop in any single year, as this could boost reported (but not real) profits.

Long-term debt

The lower the debt, the less the fixed payments will cut into profits. It's true that current debt will be repaid in ever-cheaper dollars, but when long-term loans keep rising, profits should be up even more to keep pace. Loans have to be repaid sometime.

Stockholders' equity or book value

This is the net worth behind each share of common stock, ie, what's left after deducting all liabilities from all assets. This is a key figure. It can be used to calculate two very important indices: profit rate (PR), which is the return on invested capital, and earned growth rate (EGR), which is the annual rate at which retained earnings are plowed back into the corporation. To find the PR, divide the per-share income by the per-share book value. To find the EGR, subtract the dividend from the earnings, and then divide by book value.

Companies with relatively low PRs and EGRs are considered speculative. Interestingly, natural resource companies, like base metal miners, that have low PEs tend to be indicators that the commodity price cycle is advanced, and the high metals prices cannot be sustained.

Dividends

Watch the trend more than the dollars. Check the percentage of dividends to earnings. Except with utilities, a dividend of more than 50% means too little money is left for future growth. And when a company reports a deficit and still pays a dividend, watch out. That's not any way to operate a business successfully — or a household for that matter. But today, corporations are borrowing funds from banks to pay dividends that exceed free cash flow. They are depleting the company's assets in a practice known as "return of capital", which has nothing to do with the concept called Return On Capital.

How to read the statement of income

The best source of useful corporate information in the annual report is the statement of income. That's because it reflects a period of a quarter year or a full year of operations, whereas a balance sheet is a snapshot of a moving picture.

We are all like a company. A snapshot of you or me tells somebody very little about us; it usually misses information like our interests, values, goals and objectives, job, family and so forth, and sometimes the picture is taken with a little window dressing.

But if we were a company, traders would need to know all that. So in addition to a balance sheet snapshot, we also need an operating statement.

What to look for in the operating statement

The statement of income — or operating statement, as it may be called — is there to explain how much money came in and went out, and, in broad terms, how the results affected shareholders.

Revenues, primarily from sales of products

With 3%-5% inflation in the economy, corporate revenue figures ought to rise annually by at least this much; but if they don't, have a deeper look. Now and then, it's a fact that lower revenues may be an indication the company is focused on generating profits rather than volume. But, for the most part, a company's flat to lower sales does indicate a problem. Traders need to see if it could be a pricing issue, which could possibly be an industry issue, or a unit-volume problem, which is more likely a management issue.

Trading Stocks (Also Called Equities)

Also note that inflation data that is understated by government authorities causes corporate revenue to look better than it actually is.

Operating income

This is what the company has left over after paying all production, sales and administrative expenses. Use this to determine:

(a)   The source of earnings: whether entirely from operations, the result of accounting changes or the inclusion of the proceeds of the sale of buildings/divisions, etc. Neither of these last two items actually reflects management's money-making skill.

(b)   The profit margin: the ratio of income to sales. To calculate this, divide gross profit by revenues. More important than the percentage is the trend.

Net income

This is the well-known "bottom line" expressed on a per-share basis. If earnings are flat or down, read the CEO's message to find out why and what steps were taken to improve the situation. This is a key factor in the trend of corporate profitability. Even if earnings are up, remember that they should be discounted because of the effects of inflation: ie, a stated 8% gain should be reduced to a real increase of about half as much.

Quick review of corporate results

If you have a lot of time on your hands, you can review the detailed corporate reports filed quarter-yearly with the securities commission and available to anybody who cares to investigate. For help from a trustworthy source, I'd turn to Standard & Poor's or Value Line.

You could also turn to a Wall Street analyst, but first ask yourself if the analyst is an independent one and also a competent one. I do believe that after the quality of research fiasco of the 2000–2002 bear market, and the changes made by the SEC and the broker-dealer community, that the major sell-side firms are doing a much better job today of separating their duties from the wishes of their corporate finance departments. Unfortunately, the bottom line is that there are always pressures to cause analyst bias, which cannot be regulated or legislated. So, the public must protect themselves at all times by getting multiple sources of independent reviews.

As an aside, isn't reading a review by a broker-dealer's analyst a little like expecting good behavior of the fox in the hen house? All sell-side firms are constantly on the search for business from listed corporations. That's why I often ignore their "opinions" and why I just look at how they lay out the corporate facts, which, by itself, makes my task easier.

Occasionally I discover a sell-side analyst who I find insightful, articulate and helpful, and I invest my time in following the work of that analyst. Some of these people truly are brilliant.

Traders have to go about their business totally objectively. We need facts, not stories and "personalities" with entertainment value. But, if there's one message you'll get from these pages, it's that you can't generally trust people on Wall Street unless they are truly objective in their work and you build up a confidence in following them.

That includes what I refer to as "financial entertainment television". I believe that Bloomberg Television and BNN (in Canada) are good value for your time; well worth watching, though with lots of room for improvement.

CNBC adds value by displaying market prices and introducing news headlines, which helps with market awareness, but otherwise the sell-side could do a more professional job by directly producing financial TV rather than just advertising on it.

I respect some CNBC commentators. One of them is "chief commentator" Bill Seidman. The others may be super "nice" people, but nice doesn't cut it when capital is at risk. Traders need facts and unbiased opinions, not cheerleading.

When reviewing corporate results, you ought to look quickly for:

- Trends in sales, earnings, dividends, receivables and debts.

- Information: (a) from the tables: corporate financial strength and operating success or failure; and (b) from the text: explanations of what happened during the year and what management expects in the future.

- Positives: new plants, products, personnel and programs.

- Negatives: plant closings, sales of subsidiaries, discontinuance of products and future needs for financing.

Value Line offers free research on the Dow 30 Industrials that summarizes this information in detail.

Regarding corporate reports, be sure to always read the auditor's opinion and the CEO's message. Somebody once told me to read a corporation's annual report "Chinese-style": from back to front. Start with the auditor's report, I was told. If the auditor makes cautious statements or if, in the CEO's "management discussion", there are hedging phrases such as "except for" or "subject to", be alert. That can signal future problems and/or write-offs, which you ought to then be looking for.

Next, review the financial summary (usually toward the end). This is a digest of financial data for the past five or 10 years and provides an overall view of corporate performance.

By reading the broad text of a report of a company whose shares you hold, you can get an idea of the kind of people who are managing your asset, learn why and what they did or did not do during that period, and gain some idea of future prospects of the corporation.

If you're holding, say, 10 stocks in your portfolio, over a quarter year (ie, 90 days) you'll be getting a corporate financial report about every nine days. If you just stick to a quick review, that's not a lot of work.

After you get the hang of it, you'll review a whole report in about 10 to 15 minutes. That is, you'll be able to cover all you need to in that short time. Remember, you're not buying the company, just a few shares or a bond.

When looking for possible danger signals, I look at:

Projections

In the stock market, past is prologue, meaning that past experience is an indicator of things to come. I'm always wary when analysts consistently forecast corporate earnings that are beaten, and set 12-month price targets that are too low. I also tend to ignore a CEO who fails on consecutive quarterly reporting to meet earlier guidance.

I tend not to be as optimistic as others whenever I see a company's enthusiasm for its new products, processes or personnel. As I see it, a company requires at least two to three years or more to turn new products into major sales and earnings, or to get mergers and acquisitions to run smoothly, or to find out whether a new CEO's reputation is justly deserved.

Google (GOOG) was a new issue in recent years that had been well-hyped prior to the IPO. I needed about six quarters of public reporting and guidance from management before I could adequately assess whether the company could live up to the hype. Eventually, in the case of Google, I thought so; hence, I added the company to my list of the Cara Global Best 100 Companies.

Lessons from the Trader Wizard

Disappointments

Management does not always perform 100% to budget, but in financial matters the ability to meet budget, and to speak frankly about missed performance, is a good basis for shareholder confidence. Traders who do not trust the CEO should never hold that company's stock.

If there were operating failures during a quarter, traders should expect to read logical explanations. If management offers a sales forecast in one quarter, it should be referred to in future quarters, successful or not.

Information

When corporate reports are issued to shareholders, traders need to see full disclosure and clear explanations. Important subjects should never be hidden or glossed over with clichés, but too often they are. Meaningless phrases like "a year of transition" or "we have identified the problem and are taking corrective steps", should lead to skepticism.

Footnotes to the financial summaries are where traders often find negative information. For competitive reasons, a CEO cannot reveal everything, but there should be no reason for the management to withhold information on problems such as a government investigation, a major lawsuit or a delay in filing a quarterly report, and to try to hide it in obscure footnotes.

Controversy

I have a simple philosophy in life: if there's smoke, you ought to be looking for the fire.

When securities regulators start making negative remarks about a company, listen to them and not to the company. Even though I often criticize these public employees for serving the vested interests of corporations and other parties whose objectives are not aligned with the public, their civil service mandate is to work for you.

At the end of the day, however, it's not going to be a regulator that keeps you out of bad trades. That's only done by doing your homework and using your own analysis to make decisions.

Once you've read several annual reports and feel comfortable delving into the details, you'll be able to take advantage of your knowledge to find trades that match up with your needs.

Trading Stocks (Also Called Equities)

Eliminating problems

This rule is so crucial to good trading: always think risk before reward. Decide to sell any of your holdings where you cannot say a loud "OK" to three criteria: (1) comfort; (2) quality; and (3) value. There are hundreds of other opportunities in the market that will prove more rewarding.

Whenever you have funds available for trading, ask your advisor for the firm's best current trading ideas. When you have narrowed this list to four companies, do a quick study of the corporate financial reports. This should be easy since the summarized information is readily available on the Web and you will now know what to look for. Services like Value Line, Standard & Poor's and Yahoo Finance can help you cut down your research time.

Finally, review your final choice(s) against all the stocks you presently hold. If and when you decide to change your portfolio, don't get too enthusiastic until your homework is finished. Their management has yet to meet your standards regarding comfort, quality, and value. It may take weeks or months for that to come. In the meantime, you have to assess the stock's price performance against (i) macro-economic conditions, (ii) peer group price performance and, (iii) lastly (when you are ready to buy), technical analysis.

If you adopt this simple protocol, you will soon discover your portfolio contains less risk.

3 Combining corporate and market data for quantitative analysis

The bottom line is that all traders need a systematic approach or trading discipline that includes some degree of flexibility. In other words, there is both art and science involved in trading for success.

June 7, 2007

The Forbes.com glossary defines quantitative analysis as "the use of advanced econometric and mathematical valuation models to identify the firms with the best possible prospectives".

InvestorWords.com defines it as "the process of determining the value of a security by examining its numerical, measurable characteristics such as revenues, earnings, margins and market share".

I'm looking for anybody who can explain that gobbledygook.

The quant "gurus"

NASDAQ.com claims to have an outstanding screener of "eight quant studies" from people like Peter Lynch, David Dremen and The Motley Fool. Are these people "quants" or basically just good traders with a disciplined approach to trading?

After you pull up the "guruanalysis" page (http://quotes.nasdaq.com), enter a stock symbol. Each of the studies will produce a buy, sell or hold opinion. Methodology, in each case, is explained, which helps your understanding of their trading approach.

http://quotes.nasdaq.com/asp/MasterDataEntry.asp?page=guruanalysis

This free research facility is a powerful one, as you can see by the left-hand-side drop-down window, you can instantly find much information on the stock you are interested in.

The more you use this facility, the more adept you will become at understanding the principles used by these leading traders. But you still

115

need to have a basic understanding of the fundamental and technical data underlying this quantitative research.

With experience, you'll see that there's an appropriate time for all approaches to decision making, ie, fundamental, quantitative and technical. Furthermore, with respect to gurus, there are times in the market that favor the value traders like David Dremen and times that favor others who are looking for growth or quality.

Unfortunately, the "guru" moniker applies to many market personalities simply because they or their companies have done a great job of marketing on television and at popular investment conferences!

At the end of the day, you and I need to understand all approaches to trading, including the quantitative. Like a juggler of balls, you don't ask which one has the highest priority. You simply use them all.

One quant tool that I once used as a worthwhile screener for growth, value or quality stocks came from Reuters (http://investor.reuters.com). With the recent turnover of the Reuters business there have been many changes, including to the website and tools, so the usual free screening tools might be unavailable.

Another quant tool comes from DividendDiscountModel.com (DDM). DDM calculates the present value of the future dividends that a company is expected to pay its shareholders, but it can also calculate the expected return implied by the current dividend yield and projected dividend growth. I use it to screen for income from top quality Dow 30 and S&P 500 stocks (http://dividenddiscountmodel.com).

The automated decision system "gurus"

More than 25 years ago, I wrote in a magazine article that one day computers would beat the chess grand masters. Whereas the notion was unthinkable at the time, I thought it was inevitable. Times change. Today, I'd put my money on the computer.

Because of the incredible power of computers, there are many software systems that have been developed specifically for the automated buying and selling of securities. These are referred to in the financial services industry as "black boxes", mostly because nobody knows what's inside; just that it's supposed to work. Many don't, many are overpriced and many are unavailable to the average person.

Lessons from the Trader Wizard

In fact, there are so many automated decision systems in the capital markets today, the majority of all trading is done by execution of computer-generated orders from these systems. Back in 1993 when I built my own and tried to sell it on Wall Street (through a well-connected sales professional), I found the task impossible as the market had already been flooded by well over 200 such systems.

Today there must be thousands, although I suspect that, like some of mine, most have been put on the shelf and others ought to be, for all the good they do.

However, the issue is, do I believe that results like 25%-50% annual gains are possible from these automated trade decision systems? My answer is a qualified "yes" and here's why.

In June 1993, the editor of Canada's *Financial Post*, a leading newspaper, studied my system for a day and was impressed with the results. For about 850 stocks (where full data was available) of the *Business Week* 1000, back-testing for four years, using a protocol that switched only from long to short and back for every stock in that group over that time (meaning we were fully invested 100% of the time), I proved +85% wins plus average gains that exceeded average losses. The average holding period, by design, was about one year.

Excellent results! No, they were much better than excellent.

What I do know from that experience is that a person who operates a so-called expert automated decision system must also be an expert trader. These systems are merely decision-support tools, not magic black boxes that will guarantee financial success.

FinancialPicks.com is a black box system I once looked at. From January 10, 2000 to October 30, 2003, this system claimed to have gained 1807%. A subsequent ad showed the 2000-2005 performance at +3795%. With a win percentage of 58%, by keeping the average gain above the average loss, promoters of this system claim to have multiplied the starting capital 18 times in less than four years, and 38 times in five.

But claims like these are not always believable even if the promoter is a credible one because there is always a big difference from paper trading and back-testing to the real thing. When an order hits the market, the reality is that it changes the market. The market is a pricing mechanism that factors in all bids and offers.

Trading Stocks (Also Called Equities)

Here's why I don't care to get involved with most of the promoters of black boxes you see on paid-TV infomercials and the like. Like the Financial Picks example, most are sold by Multi-level Marketing (MLM) people or TV hucksters, most of whom have little understanding of capital markets trading. They sell these systems to people who are seeking wealth the easy way, without trying to understand trading basics. That's a formula for disaster. Many promoters of these products, in fact, end up under investigation by securities regulators.

My belief is that if a black box system is capable of producing results like this one claims (3795% gains in five years) for market novices, and is still being sold by MLM people, then it is probably not worthy of your time or money. Otherwise, it would sell itself.

As proof, I point you to the track record of the best-managed mutual funds on Wall Street, 80% of which cannot even keep up to the major market indexes in terms of their performance.

4 Technical (market) data analysis

I find it interesting how traders of stock prices can dismiss the fundamental, technical and economic data today, in favor of a highly subjective bully pulpit report from the FOMC in order to gather enthusiasm to bid prices even higher.

At the end of the day, if we stick with long positions in the shares of quality companies, adding to these share positions when the prices cycle through the bottom of a bear phase, we will enjoy a solid portfolio growth. And when we speculate about the activities of central bankers, gnomes and politicians, what we are doing is assessing risk to our wealth preservation and growth plans.

June 3, 2007

Later in this book (and in my next one) we'll get deeper into the tools of technical analysis and, in particular, the aspect of it that most appeals to me, which is time series analysis. For now, however, I'd like to cover a few basic elements of a technical report.

Technical analysis studies

Rather than try to cover the material in detail, I will point you to sources of information that I find useful. For example, I highly recommend any books or seminars by John Murphy (http://murphymorris.com) or a friend of mine, Martin Pring (http://pring.com). These people cover the full spectrum of the technical analysis field and do a solid job.

For on-line charts, I like three Internet services:

*   http://stockcharts.com
*   http://bigcharts.com
*   http://investertech.com (which I offer, with modifications, as http://billcara2.com)

There is a lot of technical analysis software in the marketplace, some of it very costly; but most of it is a complete waste of time and money.

Trading Stocks (Also Called Equities)

Recently I have observed trading-software-based, get-rich-quick schemes being sold via slick television infomercials. I researched a couple of the software packages, including speaking to the developers and couldn't find credibility in the marketing claims whatsoever. You'd probably waste time and money if you go down this path.

There is no magic to investing and trading. There is certainly no rocket science. As a student of the market, you ought to just try to keep it simple. When you get into the field of technical analysis, try to learn the basic concepts and when you start to smell the rocket fuel, it's time to back off.

When dealing in price series data, the subject is timing

Technical analysis is based largely on one dynamic: market prices. A stock or a bond is just a price, and traders trade prices. People invest in assets only if they have a need to control them and cause them to serve our interests. Trading is different. None of us can control the price, and the price and the trader are mutually exclusive.

As securities prices change literally by the second, for various reasons, a trader must have an understanding and appreciation of the time factor before it is possible to become a successful trader.

For traders, there are always times when you have to make a buy or sell decision and times when you should decide to let things ride. Because market prices are either rising or falling; the outlook getting better or worse, you are constantly making decisions. You cannot escape the time factor.

However, the longer you study and participate in markets, the more you will be conscious of its rhythms, the more you will see that the capital market is a natural phenomenon where, over time, people are just acting like people, with their habits, their mood swings and all.

Thirty years ago, an academic named Burton Malkiel wrote a popular book in which he stated his belief that stock prices are completely random, that you don't know from day to day what's going to happen in the market. Some serious trading disciplines subsequently developed from this theory. All I can say is that the man never traded stocks, bonds or commodities.

To my knowledge, there isn't a single person who trades these instruments for a living that believes that prices are random. To sum up, *Random Walk Down Wall Street* is a book that real-world people avoid.

Here is a book I recommend: The Book of Ecclesiastes, Chapter 3, best sums up the notion of cycles: "There is a time ..."

Lessons from the Trader Wizard

To everything there is a season and a time for every purpose under
the heaven:
A time to be born and a time to die; a time to plant and a time to
pluck up that which is planted;
A time to kill and a time to heal; and a time to break down and a time
to build up;
A time to weep, and a time to laugh; a time to mourn, and a time to
dance;
A time to cast away stones, and a time to gather stones together; a
time to embrace, and a time to refrain from embracing;
A time to get and a time to lose; a time to keep and a time to cast
away;
A time to rend, and a time to sew; a time to keep silence, and a time
to speak;
A time to love, and a time to hate; a time of war and a time of peace
…

Ecclesiastes acknowledges that there is a time when things are low and a
time when they are high... From birth to death, from sowing seeds to
harvesting the crop, we all have a cycle. So does the market.

I accepted the notion that the market does have cycles once I came to an
understanding that the market is "just people acting like people".

It's even people like you and me who program the black box computers to
execute buy and sell programs in the market. The so-called "artificial
intelligence" of computers is actually human intelligence, directed by natural
laws. No magic involved there.

The market doesn't represent chaos or randomness any more than does
your life or mine. Life might be fast and seemingly chaotic at times but
mostly it's just a lot of routine, based on the same fundamental needs
shared by all human beings, filled with the same basic emotions of fear and
greed, happiness and unhappiness, and so on.

You have your good days and your bad days, your good moods and your bad
ones. You do some things right and some things wrong. The market is the
same.

If there wasn't a sense of order and discipline to our lives, we'd all be in the
nut-house. We do not even have to get into a discussion of lunar phases,
menstrual cycles, the four seasons and the like, to know that there is a
rhythm to life.

Trading Stocks (Also Called Equities)

As a study of markets, rather than Makiel's *Random Walk*, I strongly recommend the more practical Dow Theory from Charles Dow, of which three theorems stand out:

*   price discounts everything;
*   price movements are not totally random; and
*   the "what" is more important than the "why".

I'm going to cop out from getting into the broad subject of technical analysis in detail. It would be a little like trying to teach golf over the Internet rather than something you just have to experience for yourself.

StockCharts.com will give you the basic information you need (http://stockcharts.com/education/overview/techAnalysis1.html). When you start to get the hang of technical analysis, you can move on to looking at special situations that professional and semi-professional chartists make available free on their websites (http://stockcharts.com/def/servlet/Favorites.CServlet?obj=ID369857).

Students, keep in mind that technical analysis is just one of four approaches to making trading decisions (technical, fundamental, quantitative and macro-economic), and all these resources are needed in your school bag.

Understanding my basic approach to technical analysis

I use mostly time series analysis involving price data trend and cycle indicators, to supplement fundamental and quantitative studies, plus a healthy dose of intuition and common sense.

The use of indicators in technical analysis is hardly perfect. If you wrap yourself up in these technical indicators, you will start to think they represent a scientific approach to trading. But, the fact is indicators involve more art than science. Some of them work some of the time.

Because momentum oscillators like stochastics and the relative strength index use the same time series data and the same mathematical concepts in their formulations, they are biased toward similar results. Nonetheless, they are extrapolative or predictive indicators of forward prices and, because of their nuances, I use a few of them together as well as in concert with moving averages-based trend indicators.

At the end of the day, if you can be 60% or 70% right in your decisions and keep your average percentage loss below your average percentage gain, you'll be a highly effective and successful trader.

Lessons from the Trader Wizard

There are several very good free services on the Web for learning about technical indicators. I strongly recommend all students of the market read and master the principles at the StockCharts.com website.

Trend and cycle indicators

The most commonly used cycles oscillators are:

- momentum;
- rate of change;
- relative strength; and
- stochastic.

(i)   The momentum oscillator has three weaknesses:

- the indicator does not fluctuate between set limits, meaning that overbought and oversold levels have to be continuously re-set for each stock;
- price motion tends to be excessively volatile; and
- unusually high or low prices at the start of the indicator window (eg, seven trading days ago on a seven-day indicator) cause distortion.

(ii)   The rate-of-change indicator fluctuates as a percentage around the zero line, but still suffers from the last two weaknesses above.

(iii)   The stochastic indicator compares the closing price to the price range (high minus low) for the window period. This is actually an improvement on the above two indicators, which measure relative changes in only the closing price. But it too has a weakness. Stochastic movements can be erratic and many analysts use the internally smoothed slow stochastic indicator (%D), which they find more reliable. The slow stochastic does a three-period smoothing of the fast stochastic oscillator (%K), which reduces volatility and improves signal accuracy.

$$\%K = \frac{100 \times (\text{recent close - lowest low} \ (n))}{(\text{highest high} \ (n) \text{ - lowest low} \ (n))}$$

A problem with the formula is that traders can (and do) spike extreme highs and extreme lows in order to camouflage their intentions, knowing full well that many technically oriented traders follow these indicators closely. It's why I say that traders need to use more than one indicator in their work, and they need to weigh the evidence.

(iv)   The relative strength index (RSI) indicator addresses all three weaknesses: it is smoother (ie, not as susceptible to distortion) and oscillates on a scale between 0 and 100.

RSI, which is a popular momentum oscillator described by J. Welles Wilder Jr. in his book *New Concepts in Technical Trading Systems*, is my favorite indicator.

RSI compares upward movements in closing price to downward movements over a selected period. Welles Wilder originally used a 14-day period, but also used seven- and nine-day data to trade the short cycle and 21 or 25 days for the intermediate cycle.

Rather than use a single time period RSI, I use a combination of the most recent seven-month, seven-week, seven-day, and, occasionally, seven-hour price series data in combination. I refer to these as the Monthly, Weekly and Daily market-session timeframes.

I find the RSI to be smoother than simple momentum or rate of change oscillators and is not as susceptible to distortion from unusually high or low prices at the start of the window. It is also formulated to oscillate between 0 and 100, which enables pre-set "overbought" and "oversold" levels, that — when used to determine trading signals I call Buy/Sell Alerts — are typically 30 for oversold and 70 for overbought.

Depending on market circumstances — early or late in a Bull or Bear phase, for example, or during periods of extreme or minimal volatility, I may set the oversold or overbought levels at higher or lower than 30 or 70. Having said that, it is the discipline in using the RSI protocol as a decision-support tool that is more important than fiddling with the levels.

Trading signals using only RSI

Different trading signals are used for (a) range-bound, ie, side-tracking, or (b) trending, ie, flowing, markets. Buy or sell signals in trending markets are taken from oversold or overbought RSI levels, plus analysis of moving average converging and diverging (MACD) patterns.

(a) Range-bound markets

For the majority of stocks, set the overbought level at 70 and oversold at 30.

•   Go long when the RSI falls below the 30 level and rises back above it or on a bullish divergence where the first trough is below 30.

- Exit when the RSI rises above the 70 level and falls back below it or on a bearish divergence where the first peak is above 70.

Consider the effects of beta, ie, the measure of a stock's price volatility in relation to the rest of the market. For stocks with a high beta, such as the smaller technology companies and companies that are subject to extreme media hype, set the overbought level at 80 and oversold at 20.

For long-term oriented traders, and extreme trading situations like the possibility of a terminating primary bull or bear phase, use a combination of RSI-7 calculations for monthly, weekly and daily price series rather than relying strictly on a single data series.

If there is a possibility of a terminating bull phase, all three RSI-7 values must exceed 70, in which case I refer to that condition as the "distribution zone". My trading signal occurs in the distribution zone when the Daily RSI-7 falls back below it or on a bearish RSI-7-to-RSI-14 divergence where the first peak is above 70.

IDEALIZED MARKET PHASES

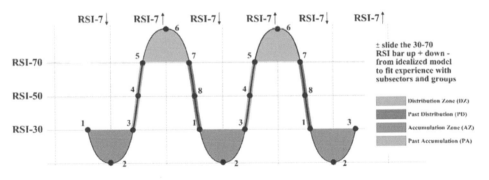

(b) Trending markets

In a trending market, unless confirmed by a trend indicator such as MACD, RSI divergences on their own are often not strong enough signals to trade.

- Apply only the signals that occur in the direction of the trend.

- In an up-trend, go long when Daily RSI-7 falls below 40 and rises back above it. Take partial profits on negative divergences between RSI-7 and RSI-14.

Trading Stocks (Also Called Equities)

- Exit using a trend indicator such as MACD.

- Go short in a down-trend when the monthly, weekly and daily RSI-7 rises above 60 and weekly and daily RSI-7 subsequently falls back below it.

Type of trader		Average position holding period
Intra-day	ID	< 1 session
Intra-week	IW	< 5 daily sessions
Intra-month	IM	< 18 daily sessions
Intra-year	IY	< 250 daily sessions (ie, < 50 weekly sessions)
Extra year	EY	> 250 daily sessions

Point of Cycle		Predominant tactic	
AZ	1 - 2	sell long puts + write puts + begin to accumulate stock positions	
	2 - 3	finish accumulating stock positions + (if extreme lows, buy calls)	
PA	3 - 4	buy some calls (conservative accounts)	expect to see MACD rising
	4 - 5	hold long position	(warning if not)
DZ	5 - 6	sell long calls + write calls + begin to distribute stock positions	
	6 - 7	finish distributing sticks + (if extreme downside tops, buy puts)	
PD	7 - 8	buys some puts (conservative accounts)	expect to see MCAD falling
	8 - 1	hold short positions	(warning if not)

Strategy depends on point of cycle

AZ = 1 - 3 = accumulation zone
PA = 3 - 5 = hold (past accumulation) = "too late to buy"
DZ = 5 - 7 = distribution zone
PD = 7 - 1 = avoid or stay short (past distribution) = "too late to sell"

Trading signals using the stochastic oscillator

Occasionally, the use of stochastics is helpful. Trading signals are the same for the stochastic oscillator as for RSI.

(a) Ranging markets

Signals are listed in order of their importance:

- Go long on %D bullish divergence where the first cycle trough is below the oversold level.

- Go long when either %K or %D falls below the oversold level and rises back above it.

- Go long when %K crosses above %D.

126

Short signals:

- Go short on %D bearish divergence where the first cycle peak is above the overbought level.

- Go short when %K or %D rises above the overbought level then falls back below it.

- Go short when %K crosses below %D.

(b) Trending markets

Because of the sensitivity of the stochastic oscillator, I use it in combination with RSI and MACD indicators. The MACD oscillator is a trend indicator, whereas RSI and stochastic oscillator are momentum indicators.

Apply signals only in the direction of the trend. Never go long when the stochastic oscillator is overbought, nor short when oversold.

The shape of a stochastic bottom gives some indication of the type of next rally. A narrow and shallow bottom indicates that the bears are weak and that the next rally should be strong. A wide, deep bottom pattern signals that the bears are strong enough to mute the next rally.

The same applies to stochastic tops. Narrow tops indicate that the bulls are weak and that the ensuing correction is likely to be severe. On the other hand, high, wide tops indicate that the bulls are strong enough to soften the correction.

Trading signals using MACD

The MACD indicator is primarily used to trade trends and, on its own without momentum indicators (RSI and stochastics) should not be relied upon in a range-bound market.

MACD (Moving Average Convergence Divergence) measures the distance between two moving average lines. The MACD was coined by Gerald Appel and is discussed in his book, *The Moving Average Convergence Divergence Trading Method*. World-leading technical analyst Ian Notley taught me how to use this technical indicator. Notley calls it the moving average departure analysis".

Signals are taken when the MACD crosses its signal line, also called zero line, which is calculated as a nine-day exponential moving average of MACD.

Trading Stocks (Also Called Equities)

First check whether the price is trending. If the MACD is flat or stays close to the zero line, the market is side-tracking and trend-based signals are typically unreliable.

Trending market

Because of the sensitivity of MACD, I use it in combination with a momentum indicator. MACD is a trend indicator whereas the RSI and stochastic oscillators are momentum indicators.

Signals are far stronger if there is either:

- a divergence on the MACD line; or
- a large swing above or below the zero line.

Unless there is a divergence, do not go long if the signal occurs above the zero line, nor go short if the signal occurs below zero.

- Go long when the MACD line crosses the signal line from below.
- Go short when the MACD line crosses the signal line from above.

5 How equity markets are sliced and diced

I set mental stops no worse than -8% from the cycle high, which, in the case of the Nikkei 225 is near the 16600 technical support level, or the FTSE at 6500 or the DJIA at 12750-12800. If violated, I would be out. These are the three most important equity market indicators in the world. If one breaks down, I have stated all along that because of inter-listings and the global influence of market drivers that the other major equity indexes were likely to also break down.

July 27, 2007

I like to say you wouldn't walk through a food market without looking at the signs above and along the aisles. There is a similar signage and structure to equity markets. Stock industries, groups and sub-groups have been categorized by what is called the Global Industry Classification Standard (GICS®), which is a service from Standard & Poor's and Morgan Stanley Capital International (MSCI), two leading providers of global indices.

Within GICS, there are 10 economic sectors aggregated from 24 industries, 62 groups and 132 sub-groups.

GICS was the first system that answered the global financial community's need for one complete, consistent set of global sector and industry definitions, which reflects today's economy and is flexible enough to change as the capital market changes. There are two other vendors that offer competing services, but I use GICS to navigate my way around.

Sectors

- GICS 10   Energy
- GICS 15   Basic materials
- GICS 20   Industrials and transports
- GICS 25   Consumer cyclical & discretionary spending
- GICS 30   Consumer non-cyclical & staple spending
- GICS 35   Consumer healthcare
- GICS 40   Financial
- GICS 45   Technology
- GICS 50   Telecommunications
- GICS 55   Utilities

Trading Stocks (Also Called Equities)

Energy

The energy sector (GICS 10) is comprised of companies engaged in the exploration, production, marketing, refining and/or transportation of oil and gas products, plus coal. This sector includes companies whose businesses are dominated by the following activities: the construction or provision of oil rigs, drilling equipment and other energy-related service and equipment, including seismic data collection.

Reuters (http://reuters.com) breaks down the energy industry into four groups. When you go to the link for the energy industry, you can click on the group link. For example, if you go to the integrated producers, you'll get a current group snapshot.

The energy industry may be comprised of oil and gas, coal and alternative fuels, but it's mostly about oil stocks, the prices of which are driven by crude oil commodity prices and global economic growth.

Within the energy sector, the biggest industry by far is the integrated oil and gas group with a market capitalization of $1.8 trillion, of which the key stock Exxon Mobil (XOM), a Dow 30 component, has a market cap of about $477 billion (http://Finance.Yahoo.com database as of August 1, 2007). Chevron-Texaco (CVX), about one-third the size of Exxon Mobil, used to be a Dow component.

For long-term oriented securities traders, the call is whether crude oil — presently about $77 a barrel (August 1, 2007), which is well above the 200-day moving average ($62.94) — is going to trend higher than expected to, say, a 2007 average of $75, or lower than expected, to say $60 within a 55-65 trading range.

In long-term forecasting of oil prices, a key factor to watch is the economic growth rates in North America, Europe and Japan, which have been lagging behind the emerging economies of China, India and Russia.

When oil prices are high and rising, long-term investors always take a look at Canada's western oil and gas industry, and the huge oil sands play. The oil sands, however, represent a high and rapidly rising-cost resource, which seems to lose luster every time world crude oil prices fall below about 55.

In addition, because the majority of crude oil is priced in USD, and OPEC countries are now demanding payment in Euros and Yen, there are currency issues to consider. European oil markets (IDE Brent) are playing an increasingly important role in the pricing of oil.

Petroleum futures have been around for some time. These contracts meet an essential need by establishing a mechanism to be used by commercial sellers and buyers to be sure of firm future prices, which they assure through hedging. But due to widespread fears of rising prices and temporary shortages, these contracts have also become a popular trading vehicle among speculators.

I suppose the rest of us, who put gasoline into our cars and fuel up our homes with oil, think we know a little about energy prices. But, in my view, the volatile energy futures market is not one for amateur speculators. It represents extreme risk. In 2006, a multi-billion-dollar energy hedge fund collapsed within the span of a few months because their traders misjudged energy prices. It's a tough game for the biggest of pro traders as well.

Nevertheless, energy cost and availability is a major driver of stock prices across the board, so the futures and commodities market is one that traders need to have a basic understanding of.

Basic materials

The basic materials sector (GICS 15) encompasses a wide range of commodity-related manufacturing or processing industries. Included in this sector are companies that manufacture chemicals; construction materials; glass; paper, forest products and related packaging products; and metals, minerals and mining companies, including producers of steel.

Reuters provides a basic materials industry report (http://reuters.com).

Trading Stocks (Also Called Equities)

The basic materials sector is mostly influenced by the economy and by oil commodity prices. Dow 30 components DuPont (DD) and Alcoa (AA) are leading large-cap stocks in this sector.

Typically, the chemicals, metals and mining, and paper and forest products stocks do well when factory utilization percentage numbers are high, the related commodity prices are high and rising (even though the commodity represents their cost of materials), and the economy is in full gear.

However, while high commodity prices (see Commodity Research Bureau's CRB Index) rise during periods of economic expansion, which tends to mean higher revenues and better pricing power for the manufacturer of basic materials, they also mean higher cost issues for commodity processors like DuPont and Alcoa and, ultimately, the consumer.

A significant factor in recent years has been the heightened demand from a rapidly emerging manufacturing-based Chinese economy, which has been growing at over 10% year-on-year.

Whenever stocks in the basic materials sector are reaching new long-term cycle highs, unfortunately the stock market, which is our primary focus of interest, is typically late in its long-term cycle.

Capital goods/industrials

The industrials sector (GICS 20) includes companies whose businesses mostly involve the manufacture and distribution of capital goods, such as aerospace and defense, construction, engineering and building products, electrical equipment and industrial machinery. The sector also covers companies that provide commercial services and supplies, including printing, employment, environmental and office services, and companies that provide transportation services, including airlines, couriers, marine, road and rail and transportation infrastructure.

Reuters provides a capital goods industry report (http://reuters.com).

For stock prices in the industrials sector to move higher, investors have to have confidence in a strong and healthy economy, which in the long-term picture typically requires a "living" yield curve (ie, spread between 30-year and three-month US Treasury debt instrument yields) of 200 to 300 basis points (bp) or more.

I definitely do not want to see a flat or inverted yield curve while holding a portfolio that is over-weighted in these stocks. The only mitigating factor is the inflation rate. If producers have what is called "pricing power", ie, the Producer Price Index (PPI) is relatively high, then these manufacturers are likely to be earning strong profits. Profits are what traders buy.

Over the years, this sector always does well in the US when Congress gets into a free-spending mode, including increases in the gargantuan defense budget.

Leading stocks in this sector are Dow 30 companies: General Electric (GE), Honeywell (HON), Boeing (BA), United Technologies (UTX), Caterpillar (CAT) and 3M (MMM). Also, as industrial goods must be shipped from manufacturer to distributor and ultimately to the user, the Dow rail and trucking companies of the US are stocks to watch. Federal Express (FDX) is another important company in this sector.

Trading Stocks (Also Called Equities)

Consumer, cyclical (discretionary spending)

The consumer discretionary sector (GICS 25) includes industries that tend to be the most sensitive to economic cycles. Its manufacturing segment includes automotive, household durable goods, textiles and apparel and leisure equipment. The services segment includes hotels, restaurants and other leisure facilities, media production and services and consumer retailing.

Reuters provides a cyclical consumer industry report (http://reuters.com).

Some economists will tell you that the American consumer drives the global stock market. That is a bit of a stretch and actually the consumer is becoming less of a factor every year. Today it is more likely to be the consumers in the emerging economy markets of China and India that actually drive global economic cycles and capital markets.

The more important point, however, is that the consumer discretionary spending sector involves some interesting stock groups and brand names and, in my view, some of the best opportunities to grow your personal wealth. This is also a sector that most people can relate to — it's about spending money.

The key stocks in this sector are Dow 30 components Disney (DIS), General Motors (GM), Home Depot (HD) and McDonalds (MCD).

Because of its huge move into distributing food and household consumables, Wal-Mart (WMT) can go in either this sector or in the consumer staples (non-discretionary spending) sector.

Lessons from the Trader Wizard

Consumer, non-cyclical (staple spending)

The consumer staples sector (GICS 30) comprises companies whose consumer businesses are less sensitive to economic cycles, such as manufacturers and distributors of food, beverages and tobacco and producers of non-durable household goods and personal products. It also includes food and drug retailing companies, hypermarkets and consumer super-centers.

Reuters provides a non-cyclical consumer industry report (http://reuters.com).

Along with stocks in the utilities and financials, the stocks in the consumer staples sector are always favorites early in a new bull market cycle when, typically, interest rates are falling or have quickly fallen to very low levels. However, later in an economic cycle as interest rates rise, stocks in these groups usually fall from favor. The key stocks in this sector are Dow 30 components Wal-Mart (WMT), Procter & Gamble (PG), Altria Group (MO) and Coca Cola (KO).

With a flat to negative yield curve, "defensive" stocks, plus consumer healthcare, out-perform some other stock sectors (eg, energy, basic materials and industrials), which suffer in a "stagflation" environment, ie, a stagnant economy (one that grows at 2% or less year-over-year).

The one big concern with this sector is that short-term rates — say yields on Treasury debt instruments of two-years or less — start to rise to a point where the high-dividend yielders of the defensive consumer staples and healthcare sectors no longer make sense to investors. And short rates rise when the Fed tightens.

Trading Stocks (Also Called Equities)

Healthcare

The healthcare sector (GICS 35) encompasses two main industry groups. The first includes companies who manufacture healthcare equipment and supplies or provide healthcare-related services, including distributors of healthcare products, providers of basic healthcare services, and owners and operators of healthcare facilities and organizations. The second regroups companies primarily involved in the research, development, production and marketing of pharmaceuticals and biotechnology products.

Reuters provides a healthcare industry report (http://reuters.com).

As people age, their consumption of healthcare products and services grows rapidly. In fact, today, the pharmaceutical industry is the world's largest. And so too is the industry's number of lobbyists in Washington.

Another fact is that as baby boomers turn 55 (as most have), they consume about 100% more drugs than when they turned 50.

One of the reasons the pharmaceutical and biotechnology industry is so huge today, in my view, is that society across the world (in Asia, Europe and the Americas) has become the most stressed out and the most drugged up since the beginning of time.

People today are taking so many pharmaceuticals, they've either forgotten the reason why or else they simply rationalize the use of drugs.

Still, this GICS Sector 35 does provide opportunities for various types of securities traders. The speculative trader will follow the biotech industry in

search of the discoverer of the next blockbuster drug. The enterprising trader will stick to the discounted cash flow models of the senior drug manufacturers. The conservative trader will like the business model of the drugstore retail chains and the drug wholesale distribution firms.

Two things always seem to come into play when the economy is starting to look shaky: (1) government starts to ratchet up the work of regulators; and (2) civil law suits seem to get popular. This is usually the "perfect storm" condition for attacking healthcare companies and some of the consumer staples companies like the tobacco companies.

Financial

The financial sector (GICS 40) contains companies involved in activities such as banking; mortgage finance; consumer finance; specialized finance; investment banking and brokerage; asset management and custody; corporate lending, insurance and financial investment; and real estate, including REITs.

Reuters provides a financial industry report (http://reuters.com).

There are a number of financial service ETFs that warrant some research. The most popular is the XLF (which is the Select Sector SPDR-Financial)

Occasionally, it makes sense for investors to buy the ETF and hedge (ie, short) the ETF's worst component issues.

As bank customers get overloaded with debt, there is a limit to the revenue growth of the banks. Moreover, as interest rates rise, so too do the bad debts of banks and the narrowing margins on their loans.

I like to compare results of the key money centre bank group, Citigroup and JP Morgan, which are components of the Dow 30 Industrials. In addition to comparing them to Bank of America (BAC) and Wells Fargo (WFC); and foreign banks HSBC (HBC), UBS (UBS) and Credit Suisse (CS) and Deutsche Bank (DB); I also check them against other DJIA components General Electric (GE) and American Express (AXP).

What's good for the large-cap banks is good for the mid-cap banks, so I also look at the US regional banks, which includes a list of US-traded foreign banks and the savings and loan banks.

This sector also includes the insurance industry group, including American International (AIG), which came under regulatory investigation and had criminal charges laid against its senior executives in 4Q04.

Trading Stocks (Also Called Equities)

Whenever economic factors converge to create a rising interest rate situation in the US, I believe it is inappropriate to over-weight or even market-weight the banking industry and sub-industry stocks that are directly interest-sensitive. However, there are many investment bankers that are minimally interest-rate sensitive (eg, GS and LEH) that I like.

Technology

The technology sector (GICS 45) covers the following areas: (1) technology software and services, including companies that primarily develop software in various fields (such as the Internet, applications, systems, database management and/or home entertainment) and companies that provide information technology consulting and services, as well as data processing and outsourced services; (2) technology hardware and equipment, including manufacturers and distributors of communications equipment, computers and peripherals, electronic equipment and instruments; and (3) semiconductor and semiconductor equipment manufacturers.

Reuters provides a technology industry report (http://reuters.com).

When you looked at the technology sector in the 1970s, it was all about IBM. Today, it's Microsoft (270B), Cisco (193B), Google (160B) and Intel (150B) as well as IBM (160B). These five companies comprise almost 25% of the total $4 trillion information technology sector.

There are multiple industry groups and sub-groups in the technology sector, and they are listed with market cap totals at Finance Yahoo (http://biz.yahoo.com/p/8mktu.html).

Technology is a huge sector, and there are always some good stocks to hold long. However, unless there is clear strength in the global economy — in terms of real wealth being created — and a softening of interest rates at the short end, I am not inclined to venture blindly into this sector.

Unless a company can report both: (1) better than excellent results and (2) higher guidance, for the quarter, the stock is likely to suffer a setback even if the performance results are not that bad. You see, in a bear phase, "not bad" just doesn't cut it for high-beta, high PE stocks.

On the other hand, after a big sell-off in a sector, what I look for is for stock prices not to fall following a poor-to-average performance report and guidance.

Telecommunication services

The telecommunication services sector (GICS 50) contains companies that provide communications services primarily through a fixed-line, cellular, wireless, high-bandwidth and/or fiber-optic cable network.

We now live in a digital world where wireless communications has become the leading segment of the telecommunications sector — far exceeding fixed-line communications. The computer sector and the telecommunications sector are now basically one technology sector, differentiated by the monikers B2B (business to business) or b2c (business to customer).

Trading Stocks (Also Called Equities)

The key stocks in the telecommunication services sector are Dow components AT&T (T) and Verizon (VZ). Both companies have undergone extreme re-organizations and restructuring in recent years. They are being positioned to compete with cable operators by replacing fixed-line services with wireless services.

These are mostly capital-intensive, interest-sensitive stocks (at least, the old fixed-line group is), which tend to rise and fall with the financial sector.

Reuters provides a telephone and communications services industry report (http://reuters.com).

Following the 2000-2003 bear market, which was particularly devastating to the telecommunications sector, there was a sector recovery that missed the bull rally in the other sectors. The new long-term bull phase of this sector did not start until late 2005.

The future (as well as the present) belongs to wireless. Yes, cell phones are ubiquitous, even in every nook and cranny of the developing world, where you'll even find seven-year olds with their own phones.

As that sub-industry group matures, the next one to benefit will be high-speed wireless voice and data communications that will usher in the era of Internet TV. That will truly make the world a smaller place.

As I see it, there are millions of entrepreneurs out there (in small-cap companies) who are packaging up mind-boggling solutions to customer needs and selling them.

Looking around the world, I like a number of superbly managed large-cap telecom services companies, mostly in the fast-growing mobile phone market of emerging economies such as China and Russia.

For longer-term growth, I like China Telecom (CHA) and China Mobile (CHL), Russia's Mobile TeleSystems (MBT) and Vimpel-Communications (VIP), plus Microcell International (MICC), which services several emerging economies. All are large-cap stocks and companies that have made my Global Best 100 list based on quality, growth and value factors.

Utility services

The utilities sector (GICS 55) encompasses those companies considered electric, gas or water utilities, or companies that operate as independent producers and/or distributors of power. This sector includes both nuclear and non-nuclear facilities.

Reuters provides a utility industry report (http://reuters.com).

Investors, who do like the safe and reliable income from dividends need only to determine the S&P ratings on all the stock components of the Dow Jones Utility Average, S&P SPDRS (Amex: XLU) or the HOLDRS (Amex: UTH). Then they have to find the highest-rated companies in these groups that pay the highest dividend yields. For investors who find it a bit too risky investing in individual stocks, many financial advisors recommend the SPDR Utilities or the HOLDRS (Amex: UTH), and I agree.

As with all securities, there is an element of cyclicality in the utilities sector. You should try to add to your positions when the market is down, which results in a higher-than-average dividend yield.

When assessing the quality of the companies in this sector, I recommend you don't listen to the sell-side, because when they have an axe to grind you most likely won't be told about important issues like Moody's or S&P's credit-rating changes.

Trading Stocks (Also Called Equities)

What you have to do with the individual utility sector stocks is sell them on S&P's or Moody's rating downgrades. Don't even bother to read the report.

Generally, where current bond yields are rising, and prices of bonds are sinking, the capital intensive, debt-burdened utility sector should be under-weighted. And when bonds start to move higher, it's usually a good time to look to this sector again.

Of course, bonds also do well when the economy is in recession or slow-down mode, which negatively affects the profits of the utilities. So the best time to buy them is when interest rates are softening, but the economy is gradually strengthening.

In light of today's global warming and pollution issues, I believe that nuclear power is the best alternative to hydrocarbon-based power. My overall choice for a nuclear power utility is Exelon Corp (EXC). The biggest supplier of uranium to power utilities is Cameco Corp (CCJ).

6 Countries

Years ago, I once had a private meeting with then Finance Minister of Canada, Michael Wilson, about my investments/analysis in securities in other countries. When it came to Germany, I mentioned a few names and he offered rhetorically, "Why not Deutsche Bank? When you invest in a country, why not through their large banks, which in effect is like holding a mutual fund since they cover the economy?"

Michael Wilson had been a senior officer and director of Dominion Securities, Canada's largest component of HB&B, a company I also once worked for, and still have a high regard for. Mr. Wilson is presently Canada's Ambassador to the US, and one of the smartest people I have met.

I never forgot that piece of advice about investing in a country's banking system. In terms of India, banks are the place you ought to be directing your capital until securities markets there develop further, as in Brazil. Eventually, I believe that will happen.

June 21, 2007

Global investing entails significant political and economic risk. But even the biggest global corporations disappoint their investors, so I believe that portfolio allocations ought to model approximately the S&P 1200 country composition, with one exception. As I see it, there needs to be a more significant weighting of stocks of companies that are headquartered in China, India and Russia, which, except for a few Hong Kong stocks, are not compiled in the S&P 1200 Index.

Students of the market ought to study the plethora of global stocks data at Standard & Poor's (http://www2.standardandpoors.com/spf/pdf/index/factsheet_global1200.pdf).

Trading Stocks (Also Called Equities)

Country composition of the S&P 1200 stocks:

	December 2005		August 2007	
Argentina	0.05%	3	0.05%	3
Australia	2.39%	50	2.87%	52
Austria	0.09%	2	0.12%	3
Belgium	0.56%	10	0.62%	10
Brazil	0.61%	17	0.83%	17
Canada	3.46%	60	3.63%	60
Chile	0.09%	10	0.13%	10
Denmark	0.19%	4	0.23%	4
Finland	0.53%	5	0.59%	6
France	4.69%	46	5.14%	48
Germany	3.24%	32	4.03%	33
Great Britain	11.56%	125	11.23%	121
Greece	0.13%	3	0.21%	5
Hong Kong	0.82%	18	1.00%	19
Ireland	0.35%	6	0.37%	6
Italy	1.74%	26	1.82%	22
Japan	9.45%	150	8.51%	150
Korea	0.85%	10	0.82%	10
Luxembourg	0.13%	1	-----	--
Mexico	0.39%	10	0.45%	10
Netherlands	1.61%	18	1.95%	19
Norway	0.28%	6	0.32%	6
Portugal	0.18%	6	0.22%	6
Singapore	0.26%	8	0.30%	8
Spain	1.88%	18	2.12%	18
Sweden	1.00%	20	1.14%	21
Switzerland	3.32%	22	3.32%	22
Taiwan	0.65%	14	0.75%	13
USA	49.50%	500	47.23%	500
Total	**100%**	**1200**	**100%**	**1200**

International market trading considerations: USA versus the world

When he was CEO of General Electric, Jack Welch once said: "Ideally, [GE] would build all our plants on barges." That may have been Jack musing on the management issues of operating in a world theatre, but I think the analogy is particularly well suited to talking about global securities trading.

Investors are, by and large, aware that conducting business in a global environment is inherently unpredictable. I suspect they know that numerous variables have a material effect on corporate operating results and share prices.

If international securities trading is something you have not thought much about, consider the issue in the following terms: Most of us have a pretty fair understanding of what goes on in our own homes, but not in the homes of our neighbors. Still, in the case of close-by neighbors, we might be able to venture a guess.

Now take that case to people in other countries, and we typically don't have a clue.

Publicly traded corporations are required by law, in all jurisdictions, to fully disclose their operations and their accumulated resources; but we are better equipped to understand that which is happening locally.

With regard to investing around the world and, in particular, buying stocks of globally active corporations, I believe the only successful approach is to take a defensive posture. As volatility is the norm for stock prices in the emerging world, I wait for extreme RSI lows at the bottom of trading cycles before buying and I typically sell into extreme rallies at the top.

American depository receipts (ADRs)

The ADR is a US-listed security that mirrors a foreign-listed security. There may be legal reasons that the actual stock cannot be listed for trading in the US market, but this factor should not concern you. If the underlying corporation is of high quality and its share price represents a good value to you, then don't hesitate to buy the ADR.

The big industry player in the ADR market has long been the Bank of New York. For a virtual smorgasbord of investor information and tools, I highly recommend the BNY ADR website (http://adrbny.com/siteguide.jsp). Also, perhaps the best source of information I have found on ADRs comes from JP Morgan (http://adr.com). It's a terrific free service, but, like any financial site, you have to agree to their terms of use.

JP Morgan has a particularly good daily review of foreign markets, which you can access prior to the market opening in North America. They also have the most extensive web-based research on US-listed foreign issues (mostly ADRs) that I have found.

Under the tab called "ADR Universe", you can analyze ADRs by region, by country and by industry sector. When you have located a target, you can immediately call up a plethora of financial and trading data.

Trading Stocks (Also Called Equities)

With a single click, you can even have this service provide you the list by cross-listed market, eg, if you wish to confine your search to NYSE-, NASDAQ- or AMEX-listed stocks. With another click, you will see a listing of the major institutional owners and mutual fund owners and their holdings. In fact, there is such a significant amount of information, I give this website a five-star rating.

Although many people look at the ADR market as a special situation, I see it a different way. These are just equity securities like any other. Moreover, I use the JP Morgan service as a research tool the same as I do others.

Believe me, you too will find this website to be invaluable when seeking out internationally listed securities that are commonly affected by changes in global interest rates, commodity prices and economic factors. The airline industry is an excellent example.

You know that I say the capital market is a marketing game. Wall Street and its counterparts across the globe like to keep their stories straight — for maximum impact. Stocks in industry groups tend to move up and down in tandem because analysts and money managers like to follow one another. Maybe it's safety in numbers, who knows? But it is clearly people acting in concert.

There is one other thing you need to know: an ADR might not trade in a 1-to-1 ratio with the underlying stock. It could be that the ADR represents 10 shares or 100 shares or half a share. You have to check. Otherwise, you'll be confused when seeing an entirely different price in the foreign market, even after adjusting for foreign exchange.

If you are looking to invest in a well-diversified fund where political risk of individual stocks or country funds is clearly a factor, why not consider the BLDRS Emerging Markets 50 ADR Index Fund (http://billcara2.com).

The ADRE ETF might get a little overpriced at times. However, there is going to be a point in the future when this particular ADR is appropriate for any investor who seeks a globally diversified portfolio.

The NYSE website has a list of all the non-US headquartered NYSE-traded stocks (http://nyse.com/international/nonuslisted).

Trading considerations of foreign stocks

Readers of my website are from 140 different countries, so it's impossible to write material that appeals to all. But for the purposes of building a

146

diversified global investment portfolio for active securities trading, I'm going to suggest the following percentage weightings, when fully invested:

45%   USA
8%   Americas, including Canada and Latin America
30%   Europe, including UK, Russia, Middle East and Africa
17%   Asia, including Japan, China and Australia

After the securities trading environments (including regulatory conditions) of economically emerging jurisdictions mature somewhat, these percentage weightings will change.

For example, by the year 2010, I could foresee a relative weighting of 40% in the US; 10% in the other Americas, with the increase being in Latin America (bringing it to 6% plus 4% in Canada); 30% still in Europe, but with a heavier group weighting coming from Russia and other Eastern European countries and less in the UK, Germany, France, Italy, Spain and Switzerland; and 20% in East Asia, with the increase coming in mainland China and India, Hong Kong, Taiwan, South Korea, Singapore, Australia and New Zealand, rather than Japan.

Trading considerations for Dow 30 stock watchers

I don't believe you should be trying to cut down a single tree in the forest without first surveying the environment. In trader terminology, you need a long-term perspective before you can start thinking trades. Fortunately, Value Line Publishing Inc. does a great job in presenting the big picture. Once you find yourself getting into the detail of too many small company stocks, I find it's best to return to a focus on the Dow 30 stocks for a look at the big picture.

Value Line presents a Long-Term Perspective Chart of the Dow Jones Industrial Average (1920-2006) at http://valueline.com/pdf/valueline_2006.pdf.

The following table is also available at Value Line: http://valueline.com/dow30/index.cfm. I use it every week to study the Dow 30 stocks. After that, I routinely look at fundamentals and charts of each of the Dow 30 components (via http://billcara2.com).

The Trader Wizard recommends the individual Dow 30 stocks to all traders, for the reasons — and with the perspective that — these companies are all engaged in global operations.

Trading Stocks (Also Called Equities)

Traders are aware that conducting business in a global environment is inherently unpredictable, and that numerous variables have a material effect on results or operations. So choosing among the biggest corporations lessens the risk.

As you will see in the fine print in all new issue sales prospectuses, these country risks include: economic and market conditions, including the liquidity of secondary markets and the volatility of market prices, rates and indices; the timing and volume of market activity; the availability of capital and inflation; political events, including legislative, regulatory and other developments (such as the formation of the European Monetary Union); competitive forces, including the ability to attract and retain highly skilled individuals and the ability to cost-effectively develop and support technology and information systems critical to doing business in the new economy; and trader sentiment.

Having provided that caveat, I submit that traders of Dow 30 stocks should not even be interested in examining the details of the international operations of these monolithic corporations. There is no amount of fundamental securities analysis one can do that has not already been done by the universal banks of the world, such as Merrill Lynch, UBS, Credit Suisse, Morgan Stanley and so forth. So give the raw data only a cursory view.

Since traders trade market prices and not assets anyway, there is an investment strategy that does work. It is the time series analysis of market prices and inter-related economic and market data. By that we mean the actions of traders are studied numerically where results are scrutinized for expected patterns of trading. For example, when interest rates rise, history proves that earnings and share prices decline for most companies in the financial services sector. We call these "interest-sensitive stocks". When commodity prices (for say oil, metals and wood) rise, history also proves that earnings and share prices increase for commodity producers.

It follows that groups of companies have share prices that rise and fall in tandem; for example, the pattern of Dow 30 stocks like ExxonMobil (XOM) are likely to move together.

So, traders need to start with a certain view of the market, which for Dow 30 stocks I break down into five groups:

(1)   Interest rate-sensitive: JPM, C, AXP, AIG and GE. (5)

(2)   Early economic-sensitive: WMT, MCD, PG, HD, MO, KO, DIS, JNJ, PFE and MRK. (10)

(3)   Economic-sensitive: T, VZ, GM, HPQ, IBM, MSFT, INTC and MMM. (8)

(4)   Late economic-sensitive: CAT, BA, UTX and HON. (4)

(5)   Commodity price-sensitive: XOM, DD and AA. (3)

I then group these stocks further into the ones I expect to act in tandem, and I may compare their charts to non-Dow 30 stock prices I expect to have similar patterns:

*   JPM, C, AXP and GE. Since AXP is heavily travel-sensitive, I also compare it to DIS. Since GE is also an industrial conglomerate, I compare it to BA, HON and UTX;
*   JNJ, PFE and MRK, plus other major drug stocks BMY, GSK, and NVS; HPQ, IBM and INTC, plus major computer industry manufacturer DELL;
*   WMT, PG and MCD;
*   CAT and BA;
*   AA and GM (since there is lots of aluminum in autos), plus AL and F;
*   UTX and GE;
*   XOM and DD, plus CVX, BP and GP (noting wood versus oil);
*   T and VZ;
*   KO plus PEP;
*   DIS and AXP plus CCL, FS and others in travel and entertainment.
*   HD plus LOW;
*   MO plus HAN (cigarettes) and BUD (beer); and
*   MMM plus AVY.

At a time when interest rates are at record low levels, I expect prices of JPM, C and AXP to be relatively high. Price-to-earnings ratios are also expected to be expanded beyond the long-term norm. When interest rates begin to move higher, the stocks to directly suffer will be the interest rate-sensitive ones and those with very high PEs. Commodity prices for oil and wood, which have been depressed for several years, show indications of moving to higher levels. Therefore, I expect that the commodity price-sensitive stocks to become more bullish in price patterns.

The world has enjoyed a strong economy for several years (as at 3Q2007), so all economically sensitive stocks should be, and are, bullish. Since stock prices are a leading economic indicator, traders should be looking for signs of price weakness in selected groups, before trying to guess at what the economy is likely to do.

There are four groups of economically sensitive stocks that traders should monitor:

*   Group 1 (WMT, PG and MCD), which are defensive stocks, but they should top out first from record high price levels, where low yields

and high PEs simply cannot be sustained for mature, relatively slow-growth companies.

- Group 2 (JNJ, PFE and MRK), which are also considered defensive stocks in the portfolios of global money managers and should top out next because of unsustainable prices relative to underlying corporate fundamentals.

- Group 3 (HD, GM and AA), which are the strength in the consumer durable sector, and should top out when personal spending slows and personal savings start to rise.

- Group 4 (CAT and BA), which are the beneficiaries of strong or over-heated economies when industrial capex reaches a peak, ie, when heavy goods like machines and planes are replaced.

Traders should list the most serious global factors that could materially affect the business operations of these blue-chip companies. Over the past 200 years, the facts show that prices of materials are flat to deflationary except in periods of war. That means, most of the time, financial asset companies like the banks and insurance companies are favored most of the time.

In wartime, prices become inflationary. Companies like GE, BA, HON and UTX are somewhat favored, because they make products that are used in wars and purchased by governments — and which can be sold at inflated prices, thereby increasing profits. These are referred to as the US military-industrial complex.

It has been said that no one knows where stock prices will go in the future, but prices represent data — and data, while it cannot be controlled, can be assessed and managed.

Time series analysis of the important data in the economy and stock market is a trader discipline that can be used to determine trends and cycles of stock prices. Widely held stocks, like Dow 30 stocks, will generally trade according to market factors that can be studied by time series analysis.

Unlike small and illiquid micro-cap and small-cap issues, which can be and are too often manipulated, large-cap blue-chip stocks represent a level playing field to serious traders.

New industries like the Internet pose the risk of major capital loss when markets turn bearish as they did in 2H1999 into 2000. At that point, the corporate metrics being used by Wall Street, and the market price data for

Internet companies, was too volatile for serious analysis, so risk-averse traders wisely avoided those stocks.

To sum up, with respect to the Dow 30 Industrials, I strongly believe that disciplined analysis of corporate fundamentals and stock price data of these few leading American companies can lead to decision-making protocols that produce superior trading results for all types and ages of traders.

At the very least, the Dow 30 Industrials is a good place to learn how to trade capital markets, and the free Value Line research reports that are published quarter-yearly (ie, every 13 weeks) on each company give students of the market a leg-up.

In falling markets, most stock prices decline, including blue-chip stock prices; but disciplined decision processes in a portfolio of "blue chip" Dow 30 stocks should keep the losses to a minimum, so that the trader's portfolio can grow strongly in bull markets. Capital appreciation over the long run should be the objective of all traders.

The Standard & Poor's 500 Index covers 500 stocks of large-cap US companies. Companies that are headquartered in other countries are included in other S&P indexes. The global S&P 1200 Index covers 1200 "blue chip" stocks of which the US S&P 500 comprises 41.7% in number and 47.23% (August 2007) by capitalization weighting.

Canadian securities

In building a truly international stock portfolio, when fully invested, I would have about 4% of my total holdings selected from the following list of high-quality Canadian securities.

The S&P/TSX 60 represents the Canadian component of the S&P Global 1200. This index, which offers exposure to 60 large, liquid Canadian companies, is the large-cap index for Canada. It is market cap-weighted, with weights adjusted for available share float, and balanced across 10 economic sectors.

The S&P/TSX 60 is the large-cap component of a series of S&P Canadian Indices, including the S&P/TSX Composite — the leading benchmark for Canada and the basis for the most highly traded futures contract in Canada.

You can electronically trade Canadian stocks (as you can US-, UK-, German- and Swiss-listed stocks) at Interactive Brokers (http://interactivebrokers.com).

Trading Stocks (Also Called Equities)

You can find them easily on the NYSE if they are dually listed stocks (http://nyse.com).

During the 1980s and 1990s, the strong dollar, government bonds and financial markets of the US were favored. Not so after 2002, when it became Canada's turn (and other natural resource-producing nations, like Brazil, Russia and Australia).

The S&P/TSX 60, which offers exposure to 60 large, liquid Canadian companies, is the large-cap index for Canada and represents the Canadian component (3.63% weighting by capitalization) of the S&P Global 1200. The S&P/TSX 60 is market-cap weighted and balanced across 10 GICS economic sectors. In building an international portfolio, I would invest from 4% to a maximum 5% of my holdings among the S&P/TSX 60 list.

With a rising Canadian dollar (versus US dollar) and an enormous natural resources base, Canada is very likely to outperform the US in the context of a growing global economy — in the higher inflation years — as it did in the 1970s.

In Canada, the ETF from Barclays Global Investors (which trades with the TSX ticker symbol XIU) allows an investor to buy the S&P/TSX60 Index Fund in Canadian Dollars.

If American securities traders wanted to hedge their dollars, they would buy the XIU on the TSX, rather than the AMEX ETF Canadian market tracker that trades in US dollars under the ticker symbol EWC (http://billcara2.com/tkchart).

With either XIU or EWC, your portfolio would be diversified across all economic sectors of Canada. Like any ETF, you can buy or sell EWC (the S&P/TSX60) in seconds and there are no switching fees, nor front- or back-end loads or trailer fees, and the built-in management costs are minimal.

Some of the best of the Canadian corporations are in base metals and oil and gas industries and, of course, there are the five big Canadian banks and a couple of large insurance companies in the financial sector.

Because they are dual-listed, you can find many leading Canadian stocks on the NYSE (http://nyse.com/about/listed).

A few of the best-known NYSE-traded Canadian stocks are CIBC, RBC, TD, BMO, Scotia Bank, Thomson Corp, Manulife, Research In Motion, Teck-Cominco, Cameco, Suncor and EnCana.

Lessons from the Trader Wizard

As Toronto has become a mining finance capital of the world, rivaling London, you will find most of the gold producers and exploration companies listed on the TSX. Many of these are also listed on the AMEX or the NYSE, such as Barrick (ABX) (http://billcara2.com/tkchart/tkchart.asp?stkname=abx).

You can also electronically trade Canadian stocks directly in Canada (as you can US-, UK-, German- and Swiss-listed stocks on their exchanges) via Interactive Brokers. (http://interactivebrokers.com/index.html).

If you typically take large positions, be aware that beyond the list of the 60 S&P/TSX stocks, and maybe 40 others, most Canadian stocks are thinly traded.

Trading Stocks (Also Called Equities)

Latin American stocks

In a well-diversified international stock portfolio, when fully invested, I would confidently hold up to 3% or 4% of my holdings in the S&P Latin American 40 list of large-cap securities. However, the considerable political, economic, currency and market risks of Mexico, Brazil, Chile, Argentina and their neighbors combine to prevent me from holding a bigger percentage.

As of September 2007, there are 100 Latin American companies listed on the NYSE, including 38 from Brazil, 17 from Mexico, 17 from Chile and 12 from Argentina.

The total of 451 NYSE-listed, non-US companies are valued at $9.6 trillion, but the Latin American stocks are valued at about $100 billion.

Of the S&P Latin American 40, which is a part of the S&P Global 1200 Index, there are 17 from Brazil, 10 from Mexico, 10 from Chile and three from Argentina (September 2007).

A list of the Latin American stocks that are traded on the NYSE can be found on the NYSE website (http://www.nyse.com/about/listed/4.html?ListedComp=NONUS).

Very popular NYSE-listed stocks from Brazil are: Tele Norte (TNE), Petrobras (PBR), InBev (ABV) and CVRD (RIO). Most of the Brazilian stocks had a great run during the 2003 to 2007 bull market.

From Mexico, there is: Telefonos de Mexico (MX:TELMEXL) in telecommunications, Alfa SA (MX:ALFAA) in the industrials, and Wal-Mart de Mexico (MX: WALMEXV) in the consumer staples sector. These particular stocks fared well in the 2002-2007 bull market.

Traders can diversify their portfolio across all economic sectors of Mexico or Brazil by holding the AMEX ETF market trackers that trade in USD under the ticker symbols EWW (Mexico), EWZ (Brazil) or the Latin America S&P 40 (ILF) or NYSE-listed, Mexican closed-end funds MXE and MXF.

Three high-quality S&P-rated Latin American funds, which have previously been five-star rated, are:

(1)   Genesis Condor Fund, Genesis, 21 Knightsbridge, London, England, SW1X 7LY. Tel: +44 20 7201 7200, Fax: +44 20 7201 7400.

(2)   Gartmore CSF Latin America, Gartmore, 8 Fenchurch Place, London, England, EC3M 4PB. Tel: +44 20 7782 2000, Fax: +44 20 7782 2075.

(3)   Threadneedle Latin Amer Growth 1, Threadneedle Investments, PO
       Box 1331, Swindon, England, SN38 7TA. Tel: +44 (0) 20 7309 7788.

UK and European stocks

In building an international portfolio, when fully invested, I would put 25%
to 30% of my holdings into Europe, which would comprise of, say, 17% into
the S&P/Europe 350 list of securities, 10% into the S&P/UK 150 list, and 1%
into the Eastern Europe emerging economies, such as Russia.

UK securities

In building an international stock portfolio, when fully invested, I would
have about 10% of my total holdings selected from among the UK components
of the S&P 1200 list of securities.

The S&P UK list contains 125 high-quality names, which represents 11.6% of
the S&P global list (30 June 2006). These are stocks of mostly very high-
quality companies whose stocks, at times, trade at about half to two-thirds
the PE multiple of the S&P 500.

If you wish, rather than trading foreign stocks (British, Canadian, German
and Swiss exchange-listed stocks) through the NYSE or NASDAQ, you can
directly and electronically trade them on their local (domestic market)
exchanges via Interactive Brokers (http://interactivebrokers.com/
index.htm).

Trading Stocks (Also Called Equities)

A list of British stocks that are traded on the NYSE can be found at the NYSE website (http://nyse.com/about/listed).

If you have a serious interest in British (UK) stocks, I recommend you go to the JP Morgan website for ADRs (http://adr.com), where you will find a lot of detailed information.

Some of the biggest British stocks trading in the US as ADRs are BP plc (BP), Vodafone plc (VOD) and HSBC plc (HBC), which are globally active, large-cap corporations.

The simplest and least costly way for most securities traders to gain a balanced investment exposure to the UK market is, in my view, through iShares MSCI Index Fund (AMEX: EWU).

Lessons from the Trader Wizard

"Old Europe" stocks (non-British)

The S&P/Europe 350 represents the non-British European component of the S&P Global 1200.

In building a truly international stock portfolio, when fully invested, I would have about 17% to 20% of my total holdings selected from among the list of European securities that includes mostly Germany, France, Switzerland, Italy and Spain.

You can electronically trade German- and Swiss-listed stocks (as you can US-, British-, and Canadian-listed stocks) at Interactive Brokers (http://interactivebrokers.com).

You can even find them easily if they are dually listed stocks on the NYSE (http://nyse.com/about/listed).

In the "Old Europe" group, there are some solid German and Swiss corporations. Active German ADRs trading on the NYSE are:

- SAP AG (SAP)
- Deutsche Telekom AG (DT)
- Infineon Technologies AG (IFX)
- Allianz AG (AZ)
- Bayer AG (BAY)
- BASF AG (BF)
- Siemens AG (SI)
- Fresenius Medical Care AG (FMS)
- Schering AG (SHR)
- E.ON AG (EON).

Active Swiss ADRs, mostly trading on the NYSE, are:

- Novartis AG (NVS)
- Syngenta AG (SYT)
- Logitech International SA (LOGI)
- Credit Suisse Group (CSR)
- ABB Ltd (ABB)
- Adecco SA (ADO)
- Swisscom AG (SCM)
- Ciba Specialty Chemicals (CSB).

Trading Stocks (Also Called Equities)

Traders can diversify their portfolio across all economic sectors of Europe by holding the AMEX ETF market trackers that trade in US dollars under the following ticker symbols:

* IEF (Europe S&P 350 index)
* EWO (Austria)
* EWK (Belgium)
* EWQ (France)
* EWG (Germany)
* EWI (Italy)
* EWN (Netherlands)
* EWP (Spain)
* EWD (Sweden)
* EWL (Switzerland).

East European stocks (including Russia)

The major capital markets story since 2000, in my opinion, has not been about China or India, but the transition of Russia to a successful trading nation.

For all the negativity in the West about matters of Russian corruption, murderous oligarchs, dysfunctional banks and inept civil servants, the bottom line is that in the past six or more years there has been: (1) remarkable success in all Russian capital markets; (2) a period of extraordinary change in the Russian tax code and budgetary and state financial system; and (3) several years of such enormous fiscal surpluses that the country is now a net creditor nation and holds sufficient foreign reserves to buy back 100% of its foreign-owned debt, with enough left over to fund close to a year's imports.

Compared to Russia, it is America that is the nation in deep financial trouble. I have been writing that for three years in my blog and nobody can refute it. Russia has strong economic growth (would you believe over 7% per annum?), strong wage growth and consumer consumption, and a strong ruble. In fact the ruble is so strong, there is a worry among Russians that it might be upwardly valued, which would serve to put the brakes on economic growth there.

Recessions in Russia have led to a very hard landing in the past, such as in 1998, which was a financial disaster of the highest order. Since that financial crisis, however, 100% of Russian bonds have been paid in full.

As a result, foreign direct investment (FDI) is pouring into many Russian sectors and industries, including oil and energy, telecommunications, automotive, retail, high tech and aviation technology. The corporate acquisitors include the biggest ones from America, Europe, India and China.

As to its democracy, the freely elected Russian legislative assembly (Duma) is a smashing success. President Bush's GOP could only dream of holding two-thirds of the seats in Congress, as does Vladimir Putin's Unity Party in the Duma. Moreover, President Bush himself would welcome the popularity Putin enjoys in Russia.

Of course, having ousted oligarchs like Khordorkovsky, Potanin and Berezovsky, and others who are alleged to have bought off Western lobbyists as well as faced the more serious charges of murder and tax evasion, Putin is subjected to a high level of negativity in the Western media.

Just like other emerging economies (such as China, India and Brazil), it is quite obvious that Russia is hardly perfect. Taking Yukos away from Menatep and having Khordorovsky face charges of tax evasion, did hurt the minority shareholders, and the 1998 collapse of the Russian bond market also did much harm. Recovering the country's reputation as a quality capital market will take some time. It will also take generations, apparently, to solve the impediments in today's civil service, banking and mortgage industries.

On other scores, like corporate governance, huge strides have been made in recent years, but improvement is still needed.

Russia has always enjoyed the geographic advantage of being the bridge between Western Europe and Asia-Pacific. For many years, the country has produced world-class math and science graduates. And for hundreds of years, Russia has managed to survive an oppressive and tragic history because of a strong family and work ethic.

Today, in a secular global market trend to higher commodity prices and rising demand, Russia abounds in oil, metals, forest and agricultural commodities. These commodities, including finished products, are being exported to the world — largely to China and Japan — and the result is enormous profitability for the Russian manufacturers and producers.

Russia is well known as one of the world's largest oil players. It holds about 5% of world oil reserves and produces about 10% of daily world oil production.

The following Russian sectors/stocks are worth watching:

- **Oils:** LUKoil, Tatneft, Purneftegaz and Bashkortostan refineries
- **Steels:** Severstal, NTMK and NLMK
- **Metals:** VSMPO and Norilsk

Trading Stocks (Also Called Equities)

- **Airlines:** Aeroflot
- **Telephones:** Rostelecom, Volga and Siberia
- **Utility stocks:** UES and Samaraenergo
- **Consumer stocks:** Pharmacy 36,6 and RBC
- **Aviation Technology stocks:** Ufa Machine (UFMO).

Foreign investors today can look to the Russian Trading System (RTS) Stock Exchange (http://rts.ru) as a phenomenally successful market and a market that still trades at a considerable discount to the PE multiple of the S&P 500.

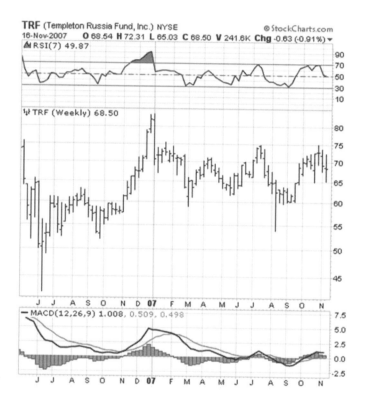

South Asia, including India, Malaysia and Singapore

Indian stocks

There is, I believe, a great case for a rapidly growing economy in India for years ahead, but perhaps less so for stocks. For several years I took a "wait-and-see" approach before adding Indian stocks to my global portfolio. Having said that, I now believe (1) that in maybe five years' time — say about 2012 — India will be the next great country of stock traders, and (2) about 2% of one's global portfolio should be positioned in the Indian banks to take advantage of the remarkable growth and stability of the Indian economy.

I hope to be early in picking winners. I selected ICICI Bank (IBN) and HDFC Bank (HDB) as two of the Cara Global Best 100 companies, based on financial strength and operating performance that excels. Today, however, I look at the broad market in India as something of a Wild West, with rampant speculation. In a bear market, therefore, I expect significant capital to be lost, and the capital markets set on their heels for the five-year window that I suggested.

India has never been without its celebrity supporters, and rightly so. In a *Fortune* magazine article on the "Economy and the World" (January 12, 2004), Peter Drucker is highly complimentary of India (and not so for China).

Here are some quotes from the eminent Mr. Drucker from this *Fortune* article:

> "The dominance of the US [over the world economy] is already over. What is emerging is a world economy of blocs represented by NAFTA, the European Union [and] ASEAN. There's no one center in this world economy. India is becoming a powerhouse very fast. The medical school in New Delhi is now perhaps the best in the world. And the technical graduates of the Institute of Technology in Bangalore are as good as any in the world. Also, India has 150 million people for whom English is their main language. So India is indeed becoming a knowledge center ..."

> "In contrast, the greatest weakness of China is its incredibly small proportion of educated people ... the likelihood of the absorption of rural workers into the cities without upheaval seems very dubious. You don't have that problem in India because they have already done an amazing job of absorbing excess rural population into the cities".

Whether or not you are comfortable with the judgments of this highly acclaimed 95-year-old management guru, I don't think you can argue against the continued outsourcing of jobs to India from America as well as an increasing number of Indian companies listing on US exchanges. The latter, in particular, is something I'd like to see happen more.

There are a number of India mutual funds, including a good one by Templeton (TIEIF) and the Morgan Stanley ETF (IIF) as well as the (Blackstone/Advantage Advisors) India Fund (IFN), but the funds, like the stocks, are volatile because that is the nature of the usually grossly over-hyped India market. A list of Indian stocks that are traded on the NYSE can be found at the NYSE website (http://nyse.com/about/listed).

Trading Stocks (Also Called Equities)

For a detailed look into individual stocks that trade on Indian exchanges, such as Bombay, as well as US-listed ADRs from India, I recommend you have a look at JP Morgan's ADR website (http://adr.com).

Traders can diversify their portfolio across economic sectors of South Asia via the AMEX ETF market trackers for Malaysia and Singapore that trade in US dollars under the following ticker symbols and the popular NYSE-listed, closed-end funds for India:

* EWM (Malaysia);
* EWS (Singapore); and
* IFN and IIF (India).

Chinese securities (including Hong Kong)

The Chinese economy is growing at the fastest pace of any large country in the world today because it has become a manufacturing powerhouse. Recently, there has been considerable debate as to whether China or India will lead the emerging markets. My money is on China, because of its society's more organized structure. However, India is close behind.

Management guru Peter Drucker thinks China's state-owned factories are a major economic and social disaster-in-the-making for today's investors.

Lessons from the Trader Wizard

He likes India's prospects better, and points to their highly educated population. But to my thinking, education and high IQ are not the only keys to financial success.

The former USSR republics have better-educated populations than most countries (including India) and yet Russia has struggled to develop thriving small-cap companies because their people have been slow to learn the old-fashioned entrepreneurial way of making money. China has done so, but India and Russia are still in the early development stages.

We all have reasons for our bias. In my case, the reason is probably that I've been to China twice and given speeches there, and I haven't been to India. Although there are substantial risks as Drucker and others point out, I have experienced the dynamics in person and I am a believer in the long-term economic and investor prospects for China.

Not a day goes by without the Chinese economy being mentioned in the media. In 2002, China exported eight times as many goods as India, and its gross domestic product grew twice as fast as India's 4.3% increase at that point. Maybe that's the reason China got 12 times more foreign investment than India for several years. In my view, this situation will continue at least through the IOC Summer Olympic Games in 2008.

While the Chinese economy is growing at the fastest pace of any in the world today, in terms of building an international portfolio, I would still only have about 3% of my holdings selected from Chinese stocks. I would like more, but the market risks are excessive.

Regardless of how fast the economy grows — and how alluring some of the stories promoted by Wall Street — you have to stick to sound investment principles.

Active Chinese ADRs trading on NYSE are:

- China UNICOM Limited (CHU)
- China Mobile (Hong Kong) Ltd (CHL)
- APT Satellite Holdings Ltd (ATS)
- CNOOC Limited (CEO)
- Asia Satellite Telecom Holdings (SAT)
- Petrochina Co Ltd (PTR)
- China Petroleum & Chemical Corp (SNP)
- Shanghai Petrochemical Company Ltd (SHI)
- China Southern Airlines Corporation Ltd (ZNH).

A list of Chinese stocks that are traded on the NYSE can be found at the NYSE website (http://nyse.com/about/listed).

Trading Stocks (Also Called Equities)

Standard & Poor's provide a list of the Hong Kong Exchange large-cap issues (www2.standardandpoors.com).

Traders can diversify their portfolio across the economic sectors of China by holding the AMEX ETF market tracker for Hong Kong, which trades in US dollars under the ticker symbol EWK and the NYSE-listed closed-end fund for China (FXI).

There are also many excellent Chinese mutual funds. Here are three S&P-rated funds for Greater China (the first two are five-star):

(1)   Manulife GF China Value Fund, Manulife Global Funds, 13/F Suite 5, 9 Queens Road, Central, Hong Kong. Tel: +852 2501 9100, Fax: +852 2810 9510.

(2)   Value Partners IF China B & H Fund, Value Partners Ltd, 608-609 Bank of America Tower, 12 Harcourt Road, Central, Hong Kong. Tel: +852 2880 9263, Fax: +852 2564 8487.

(3)   Fructilux Actions Chine Fund, Natexis Private Banking Lux SA , 51 avenue J.F. Kennedy, Luxembourg, Luxembourg. Tel: +352 46 31 16 1, Fax: +352 463816 505.

Lessons from the Trader Wizard

Japanese securities

International foreign-exchange and interest rate movements have a significant impact on the stocks you are trading. In trading Japanese stocks, perhaps even more than in the US, you must be cognizant of the global, regional and Japanese domestic economic environment.

Japanese stocks move in well-defined themes, which can change quickly. So, Japanese traders, especially individuals, love technical analysis and charts. Even if you are a pure fundamentalist, you must still be aware of key price points and trends. For consistent success you need to be acquainted with technical support and resistance, trend-lines and Japanese candlestick chart patterns.

Led by significant developments in technology, deregulation and restructuring, Japan is in a long-term economic recovery, following the inflationary disaster of the 1970s and 1980s. Its government now appears to be totally committed to improving the conditions essential for a sustained recovery.

The remarkable Japanese stock market's boom and bust history has had global economic and political repercussions. How about the Nikkei-225 rise from 86 in 1950 to almost 39000 in 40 years, with a 600% bubble growth in the last seven years? How crazy was that!

At its peak in December 1989, Japan accounted for 45% of the global market cap, larger than the total US market capitalization, which defied all common sense. Right at the top – months before the bubble burst – there were all the world-leading sell-side financial services firms touting the Japan market.

In *all* the booms, bubbles, bursts, and busts in stock-market history, the cycle peak is characterized by widespread maniacal greed. Fourteen years later in 2Q03, the cycle bottom was reached. The US media likes to refer to 1987 as the "year of the crash", but far more significant was the Japanese crash that began in 1990. The Nikkei 225 index shrank to just 20% of its peak size, dropping first from 38916 to 14980 in August 1992 and then, in step with the US market collapse that started in 2Q2000, down to 7699 in April 2003.

That was a good example of the cycles concept called "reversion to the mean". But from 2Q03, the country appears to be well on the road to recovery, supported by Chinese demand for Japanese export products attractively priced due to a lower Yen, stronger Yuan.

When fully invested, I like the Japanese market enough to put up to 10% of a globally diversified portfolio into these stocks, although for growth I would tend to look elsewhere.

Trading Stocks (Also Called Equities)

A list of Japanese stocks that are traded on the NYSE can be found on the NYSE website (http://nyse.com/about/listed/7.html?country=Japan).

Characteristics of Japanese stock trading

Although the securities trading environment is stable now, there are subtle intricacies of Japanese economic analysis and stock-picking that seem strange to Americans and Europeans. Japan stocks move in well-defined themes, and these can change quickly. Scarcity value magnifies demand and price movement.

Perhaps even more than in the US, you must be cognizant of the Japanese economic environment in a global and regional context — particularly with respect to China, but also Taiwan and South Korea. You must also understand the role that international interest rates and foreign-exchange movements can have on the stocks you are trading.

Currency movement (the yen versus the dollar) is a major factor in trading Japanese equities. If you buy these stocks or ETFs, paying US dollars, you can hedge your currency position by also buying Japanese yen in the currency market, but I suggest you'd have to be a big securities trader to do that.

Overseas Japanese listings and ADRs

If you don't have the time or inclination to study individual Japanese stocks, but just want exposure to the Japanese stock market in general, try the closed-end Japanese funds, the Japan Equity Fund (JEQ) (http://billcara2.com/tkchart/tkchart.asp?stkname=JEQ) or the Japan OTC fund (JOF) (http://billcara2.com/tkchart/tkchart.asp?stkname=jof).

In the US, many major Japanese companies have full listings of shares or ADRs, which are certificates issued by a US depositary bank representing foreign shares held by the bank, usually by a branch or correspondent in the country of issue.

Here is a list of liquid Japanese stocks I follow, which are listed on the NYSE:

- Advantest Corporation (ATE)
- Canon, Inc. (CAJ)
- Hitachi, Ltd. (HIT)
- Honda Motor Co., Ltd. (HMC)
- Konami Corporation (KNM)
- Kubota Corporation (KUB)
- Kyocera Corporation (KYO)
- Matsushita Electric Industrial Co., Ltd. (MC)

- Mitsubishi Tokyo Financial Group, Inc. (MTF)
- Nidec Corporation (NJ)
- Nippon Telegraph and Telephone Corp. (NTT)
- Nissin Co., Ltd. (NIS)
- Nomura Holding, Inc. (NMR)
- NTT DoCoMo, Inc. (DCM)
- Orix Corporation (IX)
- Pioneer Corporation (PIO)
- Sony Corporation (SNE)
- TDK Corporation (TDK)
- Toyota Motor Corporation (TM).

The 10 most active from the list above are HMC, SNE, MTF, CAJ, NTT, ATE, TM, and DCM. Other active ones are HIT and KYO.

Of the NASDAQ listings, there are two I like: FUJI and NSANY. Many other Japanese companies have an illiquid OTC ADR, which means that these are much better to trade in Tokyo, unless you do not mind the wide bid-offer spread and are just going to buy and hold.

Traders can diversify their portfolio across the economic sectors of Japan by holding the AMEX ETF market tracker for Japan that trades in US dollars under the ticker symbol EWJ. This is one of the most popular ETFs on the market.

When trading individual US-denominated Japanese stocks, always bear in mind the short-term effect of foreign exchange fluctuations. In recent years, the US dollar-Japanese yen pair has encountered some extreme trading moves.

There are also many excellent Japanese mutual funds. Three high-quality S&P-rated Japanese funds (which were five-star rated the last I looked) are:

(1)   Sirius Japan Opportunities Fund, R.S.I. Conseils SA Luxembourg, 11 Rue Aldringen, Luxembourg, L-2960. Tel: +352 46 54 52, Fax: +352 46 81 92 543.

(2)   Nippon Growth Fund Ltd, Banque Baring Brothers (Suisse) SA (no address available).

(3)   Vitruvius Japanese Equity Eur Belgrave Capital Management Ltd, 5 Lower Belgrave Street, London, England, SW1W ONR. Tel: +44 207 824 1200, Fax: +44 207 824 1202.

Other important Asia-Pacific markets, including Korea, Taiwan and Australia

Traders can diversify their portfolio across other important economic sectors of the Asia-Pacific region (not covered above) by holding the AMEX ETF market trackers for South Korea, Taiwan and Australia that trade in US dollars, namely:

- EWA (Australia)
- EWY (South Korea)
- EWT (Taiwan).

These are excellent markets for trading. I could write a book, or at least a chapter on each, but will have to settle for the simple opinion that I like these markets almost as much as Japan, China or India.

7   Knowing the playing field

This is the dance I talk about. The motion is back and forth. Bullish, bearish, bullish, bearish. Once you catch on to the phenomenon, it's like breathing. Occasionally, you get punched in the stomach by some market interventionist, which makes you scream, but after a while you start to play the game like Rocky. I'm already up to Rocky forty-something.

If you happen to be managing $10 billion, or more, it is not a fun game. But if you happen to be one of the Little People who has a clue, the whole business of personal wealth management can be as intellectually satisfying as pretty much anything.

June 3, 2007

A rising tide floats all boats (and vice versa)

I look at the capital markets as a series of waves that I try to interpret using a form of time series analysis, like the father of the Dow Theory, Charles Dow, once did.

I have also described this wave phenomena in trading action like a person (or a group) inhaling and exhaling. Whether it's like breathing or surfing waves, the market definitely exhibits a pattern of natural movement that, while irregular, is consistently ebbing and flowing.

I'll get into the "natural law" aspect some other time, but for now, let's stick to the water analogy.

In the stock market, because prices are set by "people acting like people" there is a time when most people are thinking and acting alike. That's called "the big wave" or the long-term picture. The intermediate-term picture is of course shared by fewer people and the short-term picture by even fewer people. The amplitude of these waves becomes smaller as fewer people participate.

The big wave is carried in and out by the tidal flow. On a flood tide, water is rising and it is falling during the ebb tide. Whether you're a boater on a wave — long, intermediate or short — you know that you are rising or falling;

Trading Stocks (Also Called Equities)

but regardless of the size of the wave, when the tide is flowing out (ebbing), you know your boat is sinking lower and when that tide reverses and starts to flood in, then you know your boat is rising. A rising tide floats all boats, and vice versa.

I'm not going to debate science, because I know that liars can figure just like figures can lie. I do know that when that tide is flooding, my boat is going to rise. Just like I know that when buyers outnumber sellers, when optimism exceeds pessimism, when the major trend is up, and so forth, that most stocks are going to rally. This is common sense. It's logical.

If we have been raised with a modicum of common sense, then why is market timing so difficult a practice to accept? Don't we all basically want to buy low and sell high so we can pocket the difference?

Can't we all see that the best time to hold a stock is during the flood tide and not hold it (or be short) during the ebb tide?

Well, I'll explain why it's so hard to tell. Actually, I'll give you an example. There is a popular financial TV commentator and economist who represents the interests of Wall Street, Washington and capitalists in general. Regarding a certain group of "Great American Stocks", ie, the Dow 30, there never seems to be one he didn't tell you to buy. This year, next or the years after that, he is always telling you to buy them.

Why? Because Wall Street, Washington and the capitalists benefit when they are selling you something. If you don't buy, they suffer.

Think about it. They see your role in society (and mine) as being the workers who toil for wages that are then spent on consumption, which goes back to them in the form of goods and services we buy and taxes we pay. We are chattels of the system that they have created and control. To keep you in line, they set up the rules of the capital markets to favor them and, by definition, hurt you.

By telling you only what they want you to know, which is their modus operandi, they abuse you. They abuse you when they put you into the mutual funds they manage or into high-risk products they tell you are low risk.

When they are actively wholesaling the big brands like General Electric, IBM and Exxon, they are selling the shares to you — always at the top of the cycle — only to buy them back from you at the cycle bottom, when they get you down and discouraged. It's their game and they continuously play you.

The spin on Wall Street is the same spin in Washington. It's the same vested interests being served.

170

Lessons from the Trader Wizard

I mention GE, IBM and XOM — even their headquarters are within a 15-minute drive, a few miles north of New York City. Close enough to quickly get into the Big Apple or Washington when necessary, but closeted in a small enough community that they can conveniently meet at the local clubs and restaurants and their kids can go to the same schools.

Now, don't get me wrong. I'm not into conspiracy theory. This is just how social and financial networks develop. In fact, once I recognized what the game is, in reality, I learned how to use this knowledge to my advantage.

Once I got it into my head that there is always a time to sell (Book of Ecclesiates, Chapter 3), which, as I've been telling you, is when the tide is ebbing, life became a lot easier. I could then, (from their own words) see many of these people for what they really are: insidious liars who put greed and gluttony ahead of any sense of morality.

If you think this is a little harsh, a little over the top, please read my Dow 30 Journal 1999 again. I said precisely the same thing for the nine months at the peak of the cycle — these white collar con artists were shoving stock down your throats without you realizing it. That was the point at which I decided to turn my life 180 degrees from the culture of the day to counter-culture.

I have always been seen by associates and friends as "different" because while I was in the money game, money was never my primary driver. Then the bear market of 2000-2002, and the related disappointments, investigations, charges and convictions — all of which I had been fore-warning — sealed the deal for me. I decided then how I would live out the rest of my life.

A study of market interrelationships

The market is not traded in a vacuum. By taking a top-down approach to studying market prices, you'll get to an end point with enough analysis and understanding of time series data where you will see that certain nested relationships exist in the ubiquitous mass of data.

Some of these relationships are on account of the industries, groups and sub-groups being affected by the same factors. Those factors can be characterized by: (a) interest rates (ie, prices of paper assets); (b) the economy (ie, the impact of consumer spending or business spending); and (c) commodity prices (ie, prices of real assets).

There are cycles in all the price data of all these different factors. At times, interest rates are low and, at times, they are high. By that we mean that

Trading Stocks (Also Called Equities)

there is a very long-term mean average price and sometimes interest rates are above, and sometimes below that mean average.

Same thing for commodity prices. Typically, when commodity prices are high, interest rates are high and when that happens, paper assets are priced low.

Goods and services are produced at high cost or low cost depending on the interest rate and commodity price cycles. When paper assets are priced low, the interest rates are high and the cost of production to the financial services industry and the utilities that have to pay these high rates is high. Therefore, their profit is lower than average.

That's when commodity prices are high — at the peak of the inflation cycle — and when the producers of natural resources (like the energy group or the metals group) have high prices, they also have high profits. But they sell to consumers who have to pay those high costs, and higher-than-average costs leads to lower-than-average profits. For instance, when the cost of fuel oil is high, the airlines suffer. When interest rates are high, the high-debt airline group suffers there too.

As in most things in life, what is good for one group is bad for another.

The trick then is to study the major factors in the capital markets and the inter-relationships that exist in the stock market as a result.

Sometimes I do this to make a decision; sometimes I do it to confirm my assessment of markets generally. I am always looking at the weight of the evidence, because often these relationships in the short term are inconsistent. But if you look long enough and hard enough, you'll spot the relationships and be able to act accordingly.

For instance, let's look at the oil price. It's part of the Commodity Research Bureau Index. So higher oil prices are typically followed by higher agricultural commodity prices and metals commodity prices. With a higher oil price, I'd like to see a higher gold price. But gold is priced in US dollars, so a higher gold price would mean a lower US dollar, which means a higher other currency like the Swiss franc or the Canadian dollar, as they are more asset backed.

If the US dollar is down and falling, I'd expect to see interest rates up and rising. Obviously, I'm looking at the trends, not the day-to-day prices.

Oil prices also affect the integrated producers and, in turn, affect the prices of the oil refiner and the oil marketer. When the marketer has higher prices, it usually means that the customers, like airlines, have lower prices.

Lessons from the Trader Wizard

Oil prices also affect the oil field services companies and the drillers, because higher oil prices leads to more production and exploration activity. If the driller group is up, so too should the sub-group offshore drillers.

Accordingly, the natural gas producers and pipelines should be up, but their customers, the utilities, should be down. And when I see utility prices down, I expect to see higher interest rates.

Are you starting to see how these things work? If so, you can easily extend this analysis into the general economy. Soon, you've covered all markets and all industries in all major countries.

Early in my securities industry career, I would study the price smoothing lines on the Notley machine for 24 hours straight (and occasionally longer), overlaying the different groups and sub-groups on top of one another. Not once would I look at a high-low-close-volume bar chart or any other kind of chart. Historical prices were not that meaningful. My interest was always focused on future trends and cycles.

In time — usually a couple of months starting from scratch — I would start to just breathe like the market. In and out. In and out. I could tell you when the pharmaceuticals were reversing up or the gold prices turning down. I could spot the time to sell the US and buy Germany.

The total focus on the Market Cycle Model became for me a natural living experience where I became one with the market. Seriously!

Then I'd go off to do a corporate finance deal for several weeks or get distracted on some other issue, and upon my return I'd have to get back in tune with the market once again.

There is definitely a rhythm to market prices, as there is attached to most natural phenomena in our life, like heart waves and brain waves, ECGs and EEGs, sheet music, the four seasons, lunar cycles or the ocean tides.

I could go on, but suffice it to say that the capital markets have rhythm — actually, they have many rhythms — and it's up to us, as students of the market, to find them and exploit them. Those who doubt me, and who believe in chaos theory and the Random Walk can listen to so-called experts and advisors from Wall Street and be misled.

It's true, the sell-side has a job to do: the same job, all the time. The sell-side also has an internal set of objectives and priorities that are quite different from yours and mine on the buy-side. Theirs is to maximize personal income, whereas we are trying to minimize risk and increase the total return of our portfolio.

Trading Stocks (Also Called Equities)

Fastest moving industries and groups

There is always an underlying cause for the stock prices of certain industries to be rising or falling faster than others. The major determinants to industry stock prices are: (1) interest rates; (2) the economy; and (3) commodity prices. This is what you should be mostly thinking about when looking at an overview of an industry.

Interest rates are going to affect the financials more than the materials and industrial products industries, for example. So look at the whole sector as a snapshot and think about the impact of rising or falling interest rates on:

- banks;
- insurance, conglomerate;
- insurance, full line;
- insurance, life;
- insurance, property/casualty;
- real estate;
- specialty finance;
- diversified finance;
- securities brokers; and
- savings and loans.

Within each industry there are groups and sub-groups. Within the selected retail group, for instance, there are sub-groups, as follows:

Men/general apparel
GAP (NYSE: GPS)
Abercrombie & Fitch (NYSE: ANF)
Urban Outfitters (NASDAQ: URBN)
Men's Warehouse (NASDAQ: MW)

Women's apparel
Ann Taylor (NYSE: ANN)
The Limited (NYSE: LTD)
Bebe Stores (NASDAQ: BEBE)
Cache Inc. (NASDAQ: CACH)
Dress Barn (NASDAQ: DBRN)
Intimate Brands (NYSE: IBI)
Paul Harris (NASDAQ: PAUH)
Talbot's (NYSE: TLB)
Coldwater Creek (NASDAQ: CWTR)
Guess? (NYSE: GES)

Teen/Tween Apparel
The Buckle (NYSE: BKE)
Pacific Sunwear (NASDAQ: PSUN)
Tween Brands (NYSE: TWB)
Hot Topic (NASDAQ: HOTT)

Department stores
Kohl's (NYSE: KSS)
Dillard's (NYSE: DDS)
J.C. Penney (NYSE: JCP)
Sears (NASDAQ: SHLD)

High-end department stores
Nordstrom (NYSE: JWN)
Saks (NYSE: SKS)

Discount stores
Wal-Mart (NYSE: WMT)
Target (NYSE: TGT)
Kmart (NYSE: KM)
Family Dollar (NYSE: FDO)
Ross Stores (NASDAQ: ROST)
T.J. Maxx/Marshall's (NYSE: TJX)
Fred's Inc. (NASDAQ: FRED)

Warehouse clubs
B.J.'s Wholesale (NYSE: BJ)
Costco (NASDAQ: COST)
Sam's Club (NYSE: WMT)

Home improvement stores
Home Depot (NYSE: HD)
Lowe's (NYSE: LOW)

Home Furnishings
Ethan Allen (NYSE: ETH)
Pier 1 Imports (NYSE: PIR)
Williams-Sonoma (NYSE: WSM)
Bed Bath & Beyond (NASDAQ: BBBY)

Drug stores
CVS (NYSE: CVS)
Walgreen Corp. (NYSE: WAG)
Rite Aid (NYSE: RAD)

Trading Stocks (Also Called Equities)

Grocery stores
Kroger (NYSE: KR)
Safeway (NYSE: SWY)
Whole Foods Markets (NASDAQ: WFMI)

Electronics retailers
Best Buy (NYSE: BBY)
Circuit City (NYSE: CC)
Radio Shack (NYSE: RSH)

Shoe retailers
Footstar (NYSE: FTS)
Payless Shoe Source (NYSE: PSS)

Books/music
Amazon.com (NASDAQ: AMZN)
Barnes & Noble (NYSE: BKS)
Musicland (NYSE: MLG)

Specialty/other
eBay (NASDAQ: EBAY)
Starbucks (NASDAQ: SBUX)
Tiffany & Co. (NYSE: TIF)
West Marine (NASDAQ: WMAR)

If people have jobs, they'll have money to spend. If they go shopping for women's clothes, maybe they go to Ann Taylor or maybe to The Limited or Jones of New York. When they pop into a department store, maybe it's Sears, JC Penny, Kohl's or Dillard's (if they're all still around). You get the point. Shoppers' dollars go into cash registers and eventually fall to the corporate bottom line, affecting stock prices. It's pretty hard for one store in a sub-group to be having an awful time of it while a competitor is enjoying good fortune.

If you have decided, for example, that the consumer discretionary stocks are moving fast, or are about to, get confirmation from the chart patterns of other groups in the same industry. Then start thinking about which might be the fastest-moving groups. It's pretty hard for people to be buying automobiles if they aren't shopping at the department stores. But when they start to spend, they will, sooner or later, start to buy cars, and when they do, they are also likely to be buying big-ticket appliances like refrigerators and stoves, etc, so get the confirmation from the auto manufacturers and the appliance manufacturers (eg, Maytag) and the entertainment appliance retailers (eg, Best Buy NYSE:BBY).

Lessons from the Trader Wizard

So, to find the fastest-moving groups, first find the fastest-moving industries and then look into the different groups with common themes, as in interest rates, commodity prices or major economic factors. When you zero in on a group, look at the sub-group components. Then look at fundamental, quantitative and technical factors of those stocks that Value Line or Standard & Poor's rate the highest.

Eventually, you will find a good trading candidate.

Trading Stocks (Also Called Equities)

8

Exchange-traded equity funds,

including closed-end funds

Look at the technical indicators on the charts and ask yourself if that looks like it is free of intervention. NOT! It's true. As the rich and powerful see that trend lines are close to being violated, and that unsophisticated traders will step into the trap, they deliberately move the price into the trap, close it, and then reverse the trend. They call it "eliminating the weak hands". But we are onto their tricks now, right?

Rates will not collapse until equity prices collapse. Meanwhile, the stage is set for rising commodity prices, and a weaker dollar that will be blamed on (who else!) China. End of story.

June 17, 2007

What differentiates the closed-end fund from an open-end fund is that the open-end fund trades in units of a pooled holding based on Net Asset Value (NAV) calculated daily, whereas the closed-end fund is a corporation whose shares are bought and sold on a securities market without a direct link to NAV.

Closed-end funds are officially termed investment companies.

In the case of the listed investment holding companies, the price of the shares changes during the day based on supply and demand for the shares, and not the asset value of the underlying holdings.

In fact, a closed-end fund typically trades at a discount to the asset value of its holdings, which could make it more attractive to you.

Depending on the quality of management and how substantial the purchase discount, I like closed-end funds. I like them in the form of country funds, gold funds and other types of specialized funds for the diversification factor, which I prefer to mutual funds.

Mostly I just like being able to buy them on an exchange like the NYSE, for a cheap discount-broker commission of less than one cent per share. And, while I prefer the use of limit orders, I like being able to click and buy in one second or less through a market order, when dealing in thinly traded issues,

Trading Stocks (Also Called Equities)

so that the broker can't use the time float or the knowledge of my market order to his advantage.

If you want to find the best-rated closed-end funds, look to Morningstar to do the research for you (http://screen.morningstar.com/CELists).

Buying major sector and country ETFs

Buying major market index tracker funds and major sector and country ETFs is referred to as "passive-but-aggressive" trading.

Because of their passivity, tracker funds might look on the surface like something I'd never recommend. On the contrary, I believe there could be a strategic role for them in your portfolio. You'll see them in my model portfolios for beginner traders and experienced traders alike.

ETFs are funds designed to track a major market index and whose units are traded on an exchange much like shares of listed companies. There are now hundreds of ETFs globally, with hundreds of billions of US dollars in assets.

For tracking the broad US stock market, the three main ETFs you should consider are listed on the American Stock Exchange (AMEX):

*   SPDRS, which track the S&P 500 index;
*   QQQ, which track the NASDAQ 100 index; and
*   DIAMONDS, which track the Dow Jones Industrial Average.

Product	Symbol
Diamonds	DIA
NASDAQ-100 Index Tracking	QQQQ
SPDRS	SPY
iShares MSCI-Japan	EWJ
iShares MSCI-Hong Kong	EWH

The QQQQ and SPY ETFs have gained in popularity because they lend themselves to arbitraging, hedging and trading opportunities.

ETFs are useful to three main groups of traders:

(1)   First is the short-term, after-markets trader, who could get a head start, for instance, on some market-sensitive news that breaks after NYSE/NASDAQ trading hours. As the ETFs are designed to be fungible, the arbitrage trader could pick up units in a Far-East-market cross-listed ETF such as the NASDAQ's QQQ, and trade it later on the AMEX exchange.

(2) The second group will be those market professionals who already hold a basket of US stocks, and who could use ETFs to hedge their stock positions.

(3) The third will be those traders — whether institutions or individuals — who buy the ETFs as strategic short- to medium-term holdings, possibly as part of pension schemes or retirement savings.

But all that still begs the question: for strategic reasons, are they any good for you?

With a passive fund, you'll get index returns at best with no chance of out-performance. If you happen to buy at the bottom of a market cycle, then you will do well holding them; but if you happen to buy at the cycle top, you will not. So, timing your entry is essential.

Some traders consider passive assets as the core. It contains the bulk of their holdings, say 50% to 70%, in a broadly diversified form, in leading companies on an indexed basis. This means allocating the other 30% to 50% of equity funds to actively managed stocks.

For the individual trader who is short of expertise, time and/or money for trading in securities, ETFs could play a significant role in your strategy. For such traders I recommend 70% to 80% of equity exposure in ETFs.

If you are in a younger age bracket, say your twenties or thirties, I'd recommend QQQQ, simply because they are more volatile, which in effect forces the trader to keep a closer watch on the market. In addition to the QQQQ, I'd recommend a holding in maybe four stocks that are constantly in the news: Goldman Sachs (GS), Google (GOOG), Research In Motion (RIMM), and Apple (AAPL). These companies can be particularly useful case studies for the younger students of the market.

If you are in the forties and fifties mid-range, I'd recommend Dow 30 Diamonds (DIA) in combination with quality DJIA stock components whose names come up in your typical work day, like Intel and Microsoft. I'd track these stocks against the Diamonds (DIA).

With an eye on retirement and during your retired years, I'd switch to the more conservative SPDRS ETF that tracks the S&P 500, and combine that holding with some of the financially stronger, more defensive components of the Dow 30, like McDonalds, Proctor & Gamble and Johnson & Johnson.

I'm hoping that, like the institutions, more individual traders will be convinced to take the "core-satellite" approach to their portfolio.

Trading Stocks (Also Called Equities)

Buying big-cap stocks and ETFs

When looking to buy a large-cap stock, you want to study the market from the top down. Securities prices are all you really need to examine. Let's face it, you're not going to uncover some hidden gems in the footnotes to the corporate financial statements or see something different in the important operating ratios.

Large-cap stocks have been analyzed every possible way by well-paid analysts and people shrewder than you or I, so forget it. Actually, have a quick read of the Value Line report to get a gut feel and then forget it.

The only way you are going to beat the major market indexes (those QQQQ, DIA and SPY ETFs) is to learn how to time the buy and sell trades. The only way you can do that is to learn how to use the tools of time series analysis.

Have hope, because the huge majority of professional traders and retail traders have never cottoned on to the tricks of market timing that I'll show you. It's not that they don't know them (or some of them at least), it's that they're too busy making all the mistakes I talk about here. They're parrots; they do what somebody tells them to do. At least, the majority of them simply don't think for themselves. I mean that as much as I mean anything I've got to say to you.

When you learn to think for yourself, you'll see how quickly you get good trading results from effective market timing. Sometimes being shown how makes all the difference in the world. After being introduced to the RBC Trend & Cycle system of Ian Notley in January 1981, and for the next three years of hard study, I was able to drop most of my undisciplined trading habits.

The transformation was remarkable. I recall being in the securities industry for less than two years when I met with Toronto's top-rated technical analyst, who had left his job to become vice-chairman of a mutual fund group he and his partners were starting. As I was then a money manager with the country's leading broker-dealer and starting to get some media publicity (remember, I was a late starter), I figured he wanted me to help manage some funds for the new company. But, instead, he asked me to take over his personal account as he no longer had the time to watch over his portfolio.

It seems he was interested in my independent thinking and totally objective approach to securities analysis. I had a system to buy and sell and nothing could dissuade me from changing my protocols.

Lessons from the Trader Wizard

He knew, of course, that Wall Street is a game that plays people and he understood that I wouldn't let it play me. He paid me the greatest respect; he called me "The Mechanic".

I'm an emotional guy — I'm Italian — but when it comes to the job of trading, I trade without emotion. That's how I became the Trader Wizard. But I still prefer the moniker: "The Mechanic".

Now you might think this is not germane to big-cap stocks and Wall Street, but it very much is. You see, the big corporate "brands" have bought and paid Wall Street to parrot their version of capitalism. When everyone about you is saying "Buy! Buy!" you have to remove the rose-colored glasses and see the market clearly. You have to think and act independently.

In the hope that you get the message, here is an excerpt from my Dow 30 Journal Week 44-99: November 6 (10704.48):

> "We all know GE is one of the best-managed companies on the globe, but does it deserve a price/earnings multiple, on Trailing Twelve Months (TTM) earnings, of 43.6, or a price/cash flow (TTM) of 26.7? We're talking about a very mature company with almost 300,000 employees and a market cap of over $440B. GE's operating margins are below 14% and its profit margins are under 10%. This is not some early life-cycle high tech wonder. Isn't this (GE situation) all about an asset bubble?
>
> In preparing for this article, we used the historical quotes program of bigcharts.com to go back to the last such bubble, the infamous Black Monday when that bubble burst, October 19, 1987.
>
> We were there on the firing line that day, and it was, as the media like to euphemistically say, not a pretty sight. Truly, to people who were responsible for Other People's Money (OPM), it was sickening. The best-constructed and managed portfolios were destroyed in a few hours.
>
> There were many so-called "players" who committed suicide.
>
> On October 5, 1987, GE had closed at 62 5/8. On the 19th, GE hit a low of 38¾ and closed at 41 7/8. Similarly, PG closed on October 5, 1987 at 103½, and after hitting an intra-day low price of 60, closed on October 19 at 61 3/8. At the time, PG's PE ratio dropped from about 22.7 to 13.5. GE's dropped from about 19.6 to 13.1.
>
> Once again, PG's PE ratio today is 40.6 and GE's is 43.6. Think about it."

Trading Stocks (Also Called Equities)

"Figures don't lie, but liars figure."

Wall Street did not want you to see reality (of over-bought valuations) in 1999-2000. You ended up holding the bag. Admit it! Sometimes you can be fooled by the changing stories of the small- and mid-cap companies and their promoters; however, with big-cap stocks, at least, there is absolutely no excuse.

Buying small-cap and mid-cap stocks and ETFs

When looking to buy a small-cap stock or a mid-cap stock, you should be looking for a track record. The story might be good, but you're really looking for some trading metrics you can analyze, like profit margins and growth rates of cash flow and (if available) earnings.

If you're looking for an efficient stock screen, I'll offer a plug for my friend John Cheng who runs a pretty fair data service called Investertech.com. Like me, you may have difficulty in navigating or understanding John's descriptions of his indicators, why he lays out pages like he does and even why he fails to correct obvious spelling mistakes and data errors. But the bottom line is that he offers a vastly under-rated product at a reasonable price.

John is a former Wall Street trader who built a database service with technical and fundamental tracking tools. He uses the same approach as I do in that he looks at data in industry sectors, groups and sub-groups. He then runs technical and fundamental screens to come up with high quality, high-growth companies whose stock is reversing trend. He puts these tools into a user's hands without comment about the corporations or the stock prices. The interpretation is strictly up to you.

I recently decided to do a deal with John Cheng so that Investertech can now be seen as http://billcara2.com. Eventually, I will get around to creating user screens and group studies that will follow the protocols I use when trading.

9   Selecting equity mutual funds

As you know, I happen not to be interested in forecasting price points, which I know from experience is a mug's game. Our job as traders is to figure out trend direction and to stay on the right side of it.

April 4, 2007

Is your long-term average annual net return below 8% for a balanced fund, 10% for a large-cap equity fund, 14% for a small-cap fund, or 20% for a micro-cap fund? If so, you need help in selecting them.

In terms of guidelines for selecting equity mutual funds (and, to a lesser extent, closed-end investment companies), the long-term performance record is the key.

The only way any trader can judge the future is on the basis of past performance. Mutual fund managers are rated on a quartile system among their peers ie, their last quarter, or last year, or their last three-five-10 years' performance ranked in the first quartile or the third quartile, for example.

It's too much to expect that first quartile performance is always attained, but I wouldn't invest in a fund if it cannot reach the top half (ie, first two quartiles) every time.

When you look at a fund's record, you have to keep in mind the objective of the fund: income, growth, balance, speculation or whatever it may be. There is a different risk profile for each type of fund, which is why the fund tables separate the different types for you.

What you want to know, for a certain type of fund, is how and if the fund's goals have been attained, preferably over more than five years. But a five-year track record is still worth studying.

Unless you are willing to settle for safety and income alone, you need a balanced fund or a growth fund.

The balanced fund should have attained average annual total returns (realized gains, reinvested income and unrealized appreciation) at least 3% greater than the yield of a triple-A-rated corporate bond, which has been averaging 5% returns in recent years. So a relatively low-risk balanced fund ought to

185

be returning at least 8% net or else your portfolio is under-performing. A growth-oriented fund should return about 50% more than that because you're taking more risk. There should also be a performance premium for the growth funds that invest in smaller and riskier stocks.

Recall that, over several years, the average risk premium of the typical S&P 500 stock is 9.2% and for small company equities it has been 14% (with a 4.8% Treasury bill yield). Because the risks are that much greater for micro-cap stock funds, I'd expect at least 2.5 times the average return of a balanced fund.

Pay attention to the fund's long-term average return in good markets and bad. Several major funds have never been first in performance in any one year, but they may do better than the market in good years and not as poorly in bear markets.

Also look for the fund's record in both up and down markets. In up years, the fund should beat the market. In down years, the losses, if any, should not be greater than that of a stock-market average such as the DJIA.

I happen to know through my career experience, a person who manages a group of mutual funds badly. Once or twice in the past 20 years he's been one of the country's top-performing money managers. But in almost every other year he's ranked at or near the bottom. Not just for one of his funds, but three of four of the country's 10 worst performing ones. Not only is he consistently in the bottom quartile, he is likely to be in the lowest decile.

Sometimes our perspective is conditioned by our circumstances. Perhaps his clients remain loyal in hopes of striking it big again.

Like "cool" is "hot" to some people, or "hold" means "sell", I guess it's all in how you look at something. The word perspective says a lot. Traders need to be aware.

The importance of what to buy

I seek to buy quality. To search for it, you have to decide whether you are looking for growth or value or both. In my case, I always look for growth, but at a reasonable price. That's not the Growth at a Reasonable Price (GARP) mantra, by the way, but, as I see it, the quality of the peer performance metrics of a corporation, as well as the long-term proximity of the market price range to the company's enterprise value.

We'll discuss these concepts now. Bear in mind that quality is partly a subjective assessment and partly a comparison of corporate performance to a peer group.

10   <u>About growth</u>

In technical jargon, equity markets are ether range-bound (ie, they are side-tracking) or they are trending (ie, the major market indexes are moving up to a newer trading range), or they are moving down. The primary job of a trader is to stay on the right side of the trend and to make decisions that exploit it. The next most important job of a trader is to determine, within a long-term trend, the market phase or cycle of the current price motion, and to make decisions that exploit it. There could be either a bullish or bearish phase within a bull or bear market trend. Traders are always focused on risk before reward, which is why my communications here seem overly negative on the sell-side. I respect their job — always looking on the bright side in order to sell something — but I also know my job is on the buy-side, which is to make the right decisions that, over the long-run, will protect and grow the portfolio.

Because of the substantial bought-and-paid for PR support of many of these companies, we, the owners and managers of capital, tend not to see beyond the veneer that is intended for us. We must look deeper because there are usually reasons why facts are hidden from us. I believe in transparency in capital markets, and in the notion that "sunlight is the best disinfectant". I hope you do as well.

July 1, 2007

Search for "growth-oriented" common stocks

The search for "growth-oriented" common stocks should be guided by the same standards used by professional money managers.

Here is a case of consistent corporate growth:

In the first year, on a per-share basis, the book value is $10.00, earnings $1.50, dividends 50¢, leaving $1.00 for reinvestment. This boosts the book value to $11.00 per share. At the same 15% rate of return, earnings in year two will be $1.65, dividends 55¢, so there will be $1.10 for reinvestment. And so on. At the end of five years, on a per-share basis, the book value is $14.60, earnings $2.19, dividends 79¢, with $1.40 added to book value. Thus the underlying worth of the company is up 46%, and in normal markets this will be reflected in a higher valuation for the stock.

That's solid growth.

Trading Stocks (Also Called Equities)

Year	Book value per share	Earnings per share	Dividends per share	Reinvested per share
1	$10.00	$1.50	$0.50	$1.00
2	$11.00	$1.65	$0.55	$1.10
3	$12.10	$1.81	$0.60	$1.20
4	$13.30	$2.00	$0.70	$1.30
5	$14.80	$2.19	$0.79	$1.40

The point here is that growth doesn't have to be on a rocket trajectory, it just needs to be consistent.

In a search for growth, professional portfolio managers are guided by standards. Here are some standards developed by Wright Investors' Service. Unless you have other reasons, these should be the absolute minimums for listing a company on your approved list:

- Earned growth rate (unadjusted, per share): +4%
- Stability index: 60%
- Equity growth (annual rate per share): +4%
- Dividend growth (per share): +4%
- Sales (revenues): +4%

Now let's see how these standards for growth corporations can be used to make rewarding selections in our search for growth stocks.

There are several definitions of growth but basically, with common stocks, growth is in the eye of the beholder. What type of trader are you?

1.   The conservative trader wants growth, but not at the expense of safety or income.

2.   The enterprising trader seeks appreciation, but also looks for some return for the use of his money.

3.   The speculative trader sees growth as a rise in the price of the stock and is little concerned with what happens to the company itself.

Unfortunately, in Wall Street, seeking growth is too often based on management reputation — or hopes — and rising stock prices, not on the underlying reasons.

Lessons from the Trader Wizard

Too many analysts judge growth by broad subjective standards. They assume that because a company is in a growth industry, it automatically becomes a growth company.

Or they relate higher sales with higher earnings without digging into the reason for these increases.

Here's an example: The Internet is a growth industry, at least it is for the foreseeable future. There are a number of companies that are engaged, directly or indirectly, in one or more aspects of communications between businesses and/or people. But which are the growth stocks?

Even some of the leading corporations in a growth industry should not be considered growth stocks. For instance, shares of established companies like Amazon (AMZN), Yahoo (YHOO) and eBay (EBAY) may already be selling at prices that overly discount the future potential of the industry and/or the company.

In the opinion of many professional traders, there is no longer a question about the business model of these corporations, but at what price/earnings multiple should these stocks no longer be viewed as valid growth stocks?

There's also the danger of selecting the wrong company. One or two exciting quarters do not translate to a growth stock. If the company is new and small, how do you know there can be real future progress for five or 10 more years?

Even an industry or a company that has been growing rapidly for the last five or 10 years may show little or no growth in the next decade. The need for its products or services may have leveled off, competition may have moved in, new techniques or equipment may be more efficient or capital needs may be so great that profits will be limited.

If it's a more mature organization, how can you be sure that the corporation has not reached a plateau for several years? On the other hand, a new company in a new growth industry may show future promise far greater than in the past. The tough, testing days may be over, and now management can turn its attention to making money.

Growth in a stock is different than growth in a company. There's growth in a stock only if traders think so, because it takes more buyers than sellers to drive a stock price higher. Even then, be sure the underlying facts justify such confidence.

Trading Stocks (Also Called Equities)

It sounds easy to pick growth stocks, but a true growth equity is relatively rare because the corporation must combine growth with profitability and the common shares must also be available at a reasonable market price.

Regardless of what you may hear or read, true growth is to be found in the increase of the underlying worth of the corporation as measured by stockholders' equity (often called book value), which represents the assets behind each share of common stock.

If you don't know what to look for, you probably won't find it. So now I'll tell you what to look for and I'll give you an example.

In my opinion, a growth corporation should earn 15% a year on its equity and grow its equity by 10% a year, year after year, as a minimum. You will be surprised at how many of the Dow 30 Industrial stocks meet that criteria. To find them, spend a few minutes looking through the data, which can be found for free from Valueline (http://valueline.com/dow30/index.cfm).

You might want to expand your horizons to include the S&P 100 constituent stocks too.

Multex "Growth" Screens, they say, help you identify companies that are enjoying consistently strong sales and/or earnings growth while avoiding companies that have fueled growth by short-lived or extraordinary means. The Accelerating EPS Growth screen helps you find companies where the EPS is growing at a healthy pace, and where that growth has been accelerating over the past 12 months.

Differentiating the valuation of growth from price

Trading for growth is wise, as long as the price you pay is reasonable. The problems develop because of Wall Street's tendency to swing from unsupported optimism to equally false pessimism. Corporate growth is not reflected by these changes in stock price.

Remember an earlier example of IBM trading in 3Q03. At the end of August, it was 82.50 and two weeks later, 92.50. In mid-September you couldn't call IBM a growth stock because the price was up over 12% in two weeks. A week after that it was back down again $8.

There are times when certain stocks become popular as growth stocks — as they did in the late 1960s and again in the late 1990s — when institutions kept buying with little or no regard to value. Metrics like earnings and cash flow were replaced by "stories" of website "hits" and so on.

Lessons from the Trader Wizard

This was mass mania, not trading. The higher the price of the stock, the greater was the buying — at least for a while. Although corporate earnings of quality stocks continued to grow steadily, the prices of some of these shares soared to outlandish heights — 50, 75, 100 and 200 times profits or more. Many of these companies were just growing hot air, not cash flow or profits.

Their questionable rationale was: These are already famous brands that will continue to grow and grow, so "buy, hold and get wealthy".

How stupid can one get?

One didn't have to even look into the new "dot bombs" to see that the world had gone nuts. Adjusted to today's number of shares, GE, one of the world's largest corporations, with earnings of $0.51 per share, was trading normally in the $6 range in 1993, and about $8 with $0.58 earnings in 1994, and about $10 with $0.65 earnings in 1995, so how come the same stock was priced at up to $60+ in 2000 when earnings were just $1.29?

Isn't 50 times earnings much more than double what GE should have been selling at during the best of times?

You might have heard of the phrase, "Growth is in the eye of the beholder". That's fair, but when you're looking through rose-colored glasses supplied by Wall Street, you ought to take those glasses off. They're dangerous to your financial health!

In the long run, corporate growth will determine the value of a stock, whereas for the short term, there may be very little direct relationship between price and value. In fact, the shorter the term, the less relationship there is. Therein lies the basis for needing to understand market timing.

Even with a true growth company like GE, a trader must be patient if they're looking to buy the stock. If you paid over $40 in mid-1999 for GE, you did not see that price again well into 2004 and it was still at those levels in 2007.

You simply can't chase stocks. You have to find the good ones, like GE, and buy at the low end of their price cycle, which may come along once every year or two or possibly once every five or six years. Listening to Wall Street tell you to buy all the time because you can't time the market, will just lead you astray.

I happen to respect GE as much as anybody. They do things right. But the Book of Ecclesiastes, Chapter 3, tells us about the rhythms of life and how

Trading Stocks (Also Called Equities)

we must act. "There is a time ..." Well, with GE, the time to sell was early in 2000 and the time to buy was early 2003.

I'd like to relate a personal story. I have a long-term friend (of almost 20 years) who used to work for General Electric Corporate in a strategic planning unit. He used to read my Dow 30 Journal and pass it along to one of his past associates at GE headquarters. They were troubled that I was discussing shorting GE in the upper 50s during 2000.

Later (1Q02) in the high-30s, after a 15-point drop, they wanted to know how far I thought GE stock would drop and I replied to the low 20s. I gave them my reasons, which are the same ones I have given you: GE's normalized earnings and cash flow multiples indicated a low 20s price at that point. Prices always revert to the mean, because in time, people use their common sense.

The response of my friend's associate at GE was "Gosh I hope not. Our pensions couldn't take it." But what does mentioning pensions have to do with anything other than hope? Hope springs eternal, but has little to do with stock price.

In December 2002, I was having a lengthy long-distance chat with my friend when I said that the current 24-25 was about what I had predicted and he replied: "No, in fact, you forecasted 22 and I told my associates that you were right on the mark when the stock touched that level in October." It did so again ($21.30) in February 2003.

I've never tried to pin-point an intermediate-term or long-term high or low price. There are too many cross-currents in the markets to do it effectively. There are no high-technology systems you can buy that back-test successfully either.

There is only one approach and that is a combination of what I write in the Bill Cara Blog. You will never read that I profess to calling tops and bottoms of price cycles. I know it can't be done consistently by anyone.

Opportunities to make profits abound, however, because Wall Street causes plenty of trouble when a company — no matter how solid or profitable — fails to live up to analysts' consensus predictions. Remember: we're talking about Wall Street analysts.

When IBM reported quarterly earnings were up "only" 13.2% a while back, the stock was knocked down eight points in a day. There was no logic to the selling — yet that's the way too many money managers act, and the way Wall Street wants them to.

Lessons from the Trader Wizard

Even serious professional traders fail to let facts get in the way of their hope, opinions and forecasts on occasion.

This IBM case is one example of many that shows that unless you are speculating, it doesn't pay to follow Wall Street's lead. If you were a speculator, you could have stepped into IBM a day or so after the 8-point sell-off and profited nicely on a short-term trade. Years later IBM is still a solid growth stock. And in the years ahead, it will be selling at a much higher price than today simply because real traders recognize the importance of long-term growth and profitability.

But that's the way Wall Street works. It's a game that plays people. Wall Street earns its commissions and bonuses based on the volume of trading and the profits made by their own proprietary traders. There is a vested interest by the broker-dealers to whip up your emotions, to make simple things appear like rocket science so you have to follow their lead, so you trade more than you want to or should, and at prices you should not.

How to relate future earnings and current market prices

Relating future earnings and current prices of stocks involves a combination of formulae and hope. The details vary by institution or advisory service, but the basic principles are similar. All of them require a certain amount of accuracy in the assumptions.

The most conservative approach is to project earnings for a short period, over say three to five years. With this measurement, stocks that are selling at very high multiples of current profits often appear more reasonably priced in terms of projected future earnings.

The problem is, in today's environment, I don't know how even the best-quality management can accurately estimate corporate earnings more than 18-months out.

Theoretically, the most exact formulation of a future earnings figure is the exact number of years (even fractions thereof) of estimated true earnings included in the current price of a stock. This period is called the "pay-out time".

The PE multiple is the number of years of current profits represented in the price of the stock. That is, if a stock sells at 60 times its latest 12 months' earnings, it will take 60 years for earnings to add up to the price you have to pay for the stock today. But, you don't have 60 years! The hope is, of course, that extraordinary corporate earnings growth will reduce that time span.

Similarly, the price-to-future-earnings multiple is the number of years of future earnings that add up to the stock's current price. The lower this multiple, the shorter the pay-out time, and (other factors being equal) the better the investment value of the growth stock being considered.

In a rapid-growth company like Google, traders are focused on price-to-future-earnings multiples, not just for the next 12 months, but for two and three years out.

Applying this technique assumes that earnings will continue to grow for years into the future at the same constant rate, which is often true of established corporations with histories of consistent growth, but it is a rash assumption for most small companies, even those that are growing at very high rates today.

The bigger a company gets, the tougher it is to maintain the same rate of growth. Traders refer to this concept as the "Law of Big Numbers".

For example, it is a lot easier to add $1 million to $10 million in annual earnings than $100 million to $1 billion in earnings, even though the gain is 10% in both cases.

At some point, even the best-run small companies will slow their growth rates. A reasonable frame of projection reference is considered to be five years.

Many firms now prepare five-year advance budgets. With a true growth company, this is a period long enough to balance out temporary dips and yet short enough to be somewhat in the ballpark. But even five years is an impossibly long time to accurately estimate anything as complex as corporate results.

If you see a long-range budget published in management's notes in an annual corporate report, save the notes for your research file. It makes for fun reading in subsequent years.

Another approach is to relate the present stock price to its projected future cash flow. This ratio is comparable to the PE multiple, but adds an extra assumption, which is that the financial structure of the company will remain much the same. Large loans or issues of fixed-income securities, however, can make a sizable difference in the accuracy of projections.

Lessons from the Trader Wizard

A growth stock price evaluator

The biggest risk in buying and holding growth stocks lies in overestimating their probable future rate of growth in earnings. Too many traders project recent earnings growth automatically, but they don't have access to complete data and end up making frequent revisions. Later, when such forecasts go wrong, the price of the high-flying stock can collapse. So, in projecting future earnings and cash-flow growth rates, I recommend being conservative.

In today's environment, a sustained 10% compound annual growth rate (CAGR) of earnings is barely acceptable; 15% is very good; and only a few leading corporations can maintain a 20% growth rate for many years.

These 20% earnings growth companies are candidates for the Cara 100, which is my list of the 100 best companies, either globally or in a regional market, like: (1) US; (2) Canada and Latin America; (3) Western and Eastern Europe, Middle East and Africa; and (4) South Asia and Asia-Pacific.

American business is too competitive; expansion into new products and new markets is too expensive; and unforeseen events are too frequent to permit even the best new companies like Google to maintain super-growth rates — say 30% or more — for longer than a couple of years. Yahoo! and eBay have discovered the Law of Big Numbers. All companies do.

For successful trading, you have to be realistic. It is every bit as important not to lose money as it is to make profits. A Growth Stock Price Evaluator table can be used to project earnings or cash flow when looking to establish the reasonableness of a forecast. It is most useful when studying fast-growing companies, ie, companies with above-average growth rates.

Here is how to weigh prices of growth stocks in terms of their future gains in earnings or cash flow. Example: The stock of a small high-technology corporation is selling at 30 times net current, per-share earnings, which sets a time span of 30 years. You estimate that, over the next five years, earnings will grow at an average annual compound rate of 20%. The table on the following page shows that, if this projection is correct, the stock will be selling at 12.1 times its anticipated five-years-hence profits.

Trading Stocks (Also Called Equities)

Forecasted earnings (or cash flow) compound annual growth rate:

10%   15%   20%   25%   30%   40%   50%

Here is how many times five-year's projected per-share earnings or cash flow the stock now sells at:

When PE=	10%	15%	20%	25%	30%	40%	50%
12	7.5	6.0	4.8	3.9	3.2	2.2	1.6
14	8.7	7.0	5.6	4.6	3.8	2.6	1.8
16	9.9	8.0	6.5	5.2	4.3	3.0	2.1
18	11.2	9.0	7.3	5.9	4.9	3.3	2.4
20	12.4	10.0	8.1	6.6	5.4	3.7	2.6
22	13.7	10.9	8.9	7.2	5.9	4.1	2.9
24	14.9	11.9	9.7	7.9	6.5	4.5	3.2
26	16.1	12.9	10.5	8.5	7.0	4.8	3.4
28	17.4	13.9	11.3	9.2	7.5	5.2	3.7
30	18.6	14.9	12.1	9.8	8.1	5.6	3.9
32	19.9	15.9	12.9	10.5	8.6	5.9	4.2
34	21.1	16.9	13.7	11.1	9.2	6.3	4.5
36	22.4	17.9	14.5	11.8	9.7	6.7	4.7
38	23.6	18.9	15.3	12.5	10.2	7.1	5.0
40	24.8	19.9	16.1	13.1	10.8	7.4	5.3
42	26.1	20.9	16.9	13.8	11.3	7.8	5.5
44	27.3	21.9	17.7	14.4	11.9	8.2	5.8
46	28.6	22.9	18.5	15.1	12.4	8.6	6.1
48	29.8	23.9	19.4	15.7	12.9	8.9	6.3
50	31.1	24.9	20.2	16.4	13.5	9.3	6.6

This evaluation technique can be reversed. For example, say today the stock is selling at a 30 PE, but you are not so sure about its future profits. From experience, you are willing to pay no more than 12 times future five-year earnings for any growth stock. Checking the table, you find that the average annual earnings growth rate must be 20% compounded annually to meet your objectives. This stock just meets your criteria.

Finding growth stocks objectively

In theory, the ideal growth stock is a reasonable price for a proven growth company, in a proven growth industry, with proven competent management and promising prospects for continued growth in the next decade. Its executives will be alert to new developments, and if they're not creating new products and markets, they will be moving their current ones into growth areas.

You see, a true winner must meet a much broader spectrum of requirements beyond the obvious growth of earnings, equity and dividends. The most reliable index is stable, superior corporate growth during both prosperous and difficult economic periods. Then you have to focus on that corporation's stock price.

In searching for growth stocks, try to weigh the corporation's past performance with its future realistic prospects. The best choice is a company that combines a strong past record with an equally strong future. Look for future prospects of a superior rate of net return on common shareholders' equity, an outstanding balance sheet and a wide institutional ownership and following.

Those are the subjective tests of real growth and are a solid base for your trading decisions. In practice, you will probably have to settle for something less, because:

- Conservative traders will be willing to pay a higher price for established growth leaders.

- Enterprising traders may settle for fast-growing companies in not-so-fast-growing industries, especially if they can be acquired at reasonable prices.

- Speculative traders will tend to compromise on the required past performance. They will make their decisions primarily on future hopes, even if they come high. For speculators, one really "hot" stock can offset a great many losers or mediocre performers.

Traders who are consistently successful in finding fast-growing companies rely on formulas. They look for firms that have outstanding management, enjoy robust markets for their products or services, provide good expectations for continued profitable growth and have proven records of performance. The way you do that is to look at the numbers. Figures don't lie. For a quick screen for "growth" stocks, I go to Reuters (http://multexinvestor.com).

Trading Stocks (Also Called Equities)

Johnson Survey of America's Fastest Growing Companies specializes in young firms and so uses four-year data. Their entry criteria are less stringent than those of many professional money managers (see Wright Investors' Service) but, because they know that the growth of these firms can often be more exciting than profitable, they set strict standards and don't hesitate to downgrade or remove companies.

The Johnson Survey selections are based on:

*   growth in net income per share;
*   uninterrupted gain in annual profits for the last three years; and
*   evidence of continued growth at the time of listing.

From a master list, they then choose those corporations with the largest and most consistent year-to-year gains in earnings and whose stocks are selling at the lowest PE ratios. Periodically, they eliminate companies when: (1) the average annual growth rate of profits per share, through the last fiscal year, drops below 10; and (2) annual earnings fail to rise by at least 5% over those of the prior year.

In selecting stocks for managed accounts, Wright Investors' Service by the Winthrop Corporation (http://wisi.com) is an excellent service.

WISI relies heavily on two fundamental measurements of corporate growth and profitability: earned growth rate (EGR) and profit rate (PR) because these measures best reveal the ability of management to grow the money entrusted to them by stockholders.

Earned growth rate

The EGR is the annual rate at which net earnings increase the company's equity capital per common share after payment of the dividend, if any. It is a reliable measure of capital growth because it shows the growth of the capital invested in the business. That's what successful trading is all about!

EGR = (E - D)/BV
EGR = earned growth rate
E = earnings
D = dividend
BV = book value

The book value is the net value of total corporate assets, ie, what is left over when all liabilities, including bonds and preferred stock, are subtracted from the total assets (plant, equipment, cash, inventories, accounts receivable, etc). It is sometimes called stockholders' equity and can be found in every annual report. Many corporations show the book value, over a period of years, in their summary tables.

A good growth company will increase equity capital at a rate of at least 6% to 8% per year.

Example: Johnson & Johnson (JNJ), a member of the Dow 30 Industrial Average, qualifies as an outstanding growth company over many years with an annual earned growth rate of 16.5 to 20.5. To determine the EGR for JNJ for 1992, take the per-share earnings of $0.62 and subtract the $0.22 dividend to get $0.40. Then divide by the book value at the beginning of the year: $1.97. Thus, the EGR for 1992 was 20.3%. It stayed at 20.3 in 1993, but fell to 18.1 in 1994, down to 17 and 16.8 in 1997 and 1998.

For 2002, the EGR was up to 18.7%, which you get by taking the per-share earnings of $2.23 and subtracting the $0.80 dividend to get $1.43. Then divide by the book value at the beginning of the year ($7.65). By 2005, JNJ's EGR dropped to 17.4, and for 2006 the EGR was about 16.7.

Value Line's EGR estimates for JNJ for 2007 and 2009-2011 are 15.8 and 13.5 respectively. What this is telling me is that JNJ is becoming less of a high-growth company, which will result in a lower-than-past-average PE multiple.

Profit rate

The PR is equally important in assessing true growth. It also measures management's ability to make money with your money; it shows the rate of return produced on shareholders' equity capital at corporate book value. PR is calculated by dividing the earnings per common share by the per-share book value of the common stock at the beginning of the year.

PR (profit rate) = P/BV
P = profit per common share for last year reported
BV = book value

Again, using JNJ as an example:

1992: $0.62 / $1.97 = 31.5%
2002: $2.23 / $7.65 = 29.2%
2005: $3.50 / $12.73 = 27.5%

JNJ's EGR and PR are on the decline, but still well above the average. You might want to keep tabs on all the Dow 30 blue-chip stocks and compare them to the average for the Dow 30. So, whether you like the EGR or the PR calculation, the analysis will clearly differentiate the companies you follow

Trading Stocks (Also Called Equities)

in the market from those that can and those that cannot make money on money. I stick to the former.

Added guidelines

There are other factors that can be just as important in discovering and evaluating growth stocks. Some of them are:

Improving profit margins

This is an excellent supplementary test for a growing company, particularly for one whose stock is just breaking into the growth category as defined by Wall Street. Improving profit margins almost always mean larger earnings per share soon.

The profit margin (PM) shows a company's operating income, before taxes, as a percentage of revenues. It is listed in many annual reports and most statistical analysis. It can be easily calculated: divide the net operating income (total revenues less operating expenses) by the net sales.

In 1969, Boeing Company's PM was a meager 0.1 and its stock was trading below 10. By 1975, the PM was up to 2.1 with little change in the stock price but by 1977 the PM was at 5.5 and, the next year, the stock soared to over 50.

The use of the PM measure has drawbacks. Internal corporate changes can result in a higher PM, but not greater or faster growth. A consumer goods manufacturer, for example, could boost its PM by shifting from direct sales to wholesale distribution.

Plowed-back earnings

The fastest-growing companies will almost always be the smallest dividend payers. By re-investing a substantial part of profits (preferably 70% or more), a company can speed expansion and improve productive efficiency.

A growth company plowing back at a rate of 12% of its invested capital each year will double its real worth in about six years.

Take another look at JNJ. Its payout rate for dividends, as a percentage of profits, has been 34% to 39% for over 30 years. That's one reason why it was able to boost its working capital from $325 million in 1970 to $1.2 billion in 1980, to $8.3 billion in 2000, and to $18.8 billion in 2005, while over the same period, it was growing its net income from $84 million in 1970 to $400 million in 1980, to $4.8 billion in 2000 and to $10.5 billion in 2005. Now that's growth!

Lessons from the Trader Wizard

Strong research and development

The aim of research is knowledge; the aim of development is new or improved products and processes. A company that uses re-invested earnings largely for new plants and equipment will generally improve its efficiency and the quality of its products, but it will not grow as quickly in the long run as a company that spends wisely for researching new and better products.
A prime test for aggressive growth management is whether a company is spending a higher-than-average percentage of its revenues for research, new product development and new process development.

With good management, dollars spent for R&D constitute the most creative, dynamic force for growth available for any corporation. It is not unusual for thousands of dollars used for R&D to ultimately make millions of dollars in additional sales and profits.

Another advantage is that, dollar-for-dollar, research spending is better than other forms of investment because it is fully tax deductible as a current business expense. Most plant and equipment spending must be capitalized and then written off over a long period of years. But, up to about one-half of corporate outlays for R&D is footed by the government via tax savings in the year the money is spent.

Acquisition-minded management

Back in the mid-1960s, the words "growth" and "acquisition" were almost interchangeable. Some of the hottest stocks were those of conglomerates that appeared to be acquiring a new company every month. Share prices of Gulf & Western, Litton, City Investing, National General and other such merger-minded conglomerates soared. But, when the inevitable collapse came, only a handful of the "glamour" companies survived, and the stocks of most of those took a severe beating.

Recently, the same phenomenon happened, with the inevitable result. Tyco International (NYSE:TYC) is an example of an acquisitor run amok. From a $10 price level in mid-1996, TYC ran to over $60 in 2000, but six months later had fallen to $10 again.

Today, TYC's two senior officers are in prison on criminal fraud convictions facing as much as 30 years in jail. The news that came from the trial was incredible. For example, CEO Dennis Kozlowski sent a case of the world's most costly champagne to an analyst who had pumped the stock in his reports. What a tangled web is Wall Street.

In late 2001, during the height of these hi-jinks, my neighbor (who had worked for Tyco for several years before branching out on his own), told me

201

he was holding TYC stock in his retirement plan. He and his wife had just had a new baby and were moving to a new home soon. He wanted to know what I thought of TYC because he said if he sold it he could afford to put in a new swimming pool. (Isn't it strange that a lot of decisions are made this way?) I opined that the stock in the high 50s at that point was in a final promotional push by Wall Street and could possibly hit 60. I urged him to put in an order to sell the whole position at 59.85. Within the next month, TYC twice hit 60. He could have had that swimming pool fully paid for if he had sold. A month later, the stock was in the mid-20s and four months after that it was under 10. A couple of years later, judging from human nature, my friend is probably still holding onto the stock.

The point is that when the corporate acquisitions are coming so fast that the auditors and financial analysts can't keep up, it's time for you to look elsewhere for growth opportunity. I get very nervous when I see people like Tyco's former CEO Kozlowski making the rounds of major financial entertainment television programs in order to pump his stock, which is then used as inflated currency to buy out other companies.

Calculating growth rates

Annual rate of per-share earnings increase	Justified PE ratios			
	5 years	7 years	10 years	15 years
2%	15	15	13	12
4%	17	17	16	16
5%	18	18	18	18
6%	19	19	20	21
8%	21	22	24	28
10%	23	25	28	35
12%	25	28	33	48

There should be only a small premium when a low growth rate remains static over the years. A 5% annual gain in EPS justifies the same PE no matter how many years it has been attained.

But when a company can maintain a high compound annual growth rate (CAGR), say 10% or more for earnings, the value of the stock is enhanced substantially.

Why you ought to be cautious trading in acquisition-minded "growth" companies

Taking control of other companies is a way for a corporation to grow quickly. Some of the fastest-growing corporations are always on the lookout for takeover possibilities. In boom years, the trick is to keep their per-share earnings rising, no matter by what device. Many of these "acquisitors" have created the appearance of growth where, in many cases, none existed.

If the buyer issued $1 billion in stock for assets carried on the corporate books at $400 million, the purchase was listed on the acquisitor's books at $400 million. Later, if these assets were sold for $500 million, the headlines in the annual report would show a $100 million profit, even though there was a real loss of $500 million. If the acquisition had been made at true value for $400 million cash, there would have been no question about the dollars gained or lost.

Under generally accepted accounting principles (GAAP) and SEC rules, one would presume these mythical profits to have been eliminated in recent years, but now that we've seen the Enrons and the Worldcoms, there are situations today that should be viewed with suspicion. With shifts in depreciation policy, revaluation of assets, etc, these "profits" via mergers and acquisitions can be more paper than real. And if Wall Street is underwriting their stock issues, do you think they're going to tell you what's really going on?

Caveat: Be cautious about empire-builders. Corporate management that seeks growth at any price, and in almost any area, must be closely watched. In recent years, Tyco was a good example of acquisitor management gone astray.

It's a tough task to run one major corporation, let alone several, especially when they are in different areas. Look at the record. Almost daily there are announcements of divestments of divisions or subsidiaries that once were touted as "ideal fits for future progress". A good example is Chrysler, which was purchased by Mercedes for about $35 billion, subsequently took billions in losses, and then sold recently for under $10 billion.

Going into that deal, Mercedes was a close Number 2 to BMW as a luxury car brand. What did they hope to do with a lower-priced, mass market brand? That was a costly mistake.

General rule: if you own the stock of a company involved in a new merger or acquisition, hold it if you respect the proven moneymaking skills of the senior executives. But don't buy more stock for at least one year and then only when you are convinced that, by steadily rising profitability and growth, the combination is working. Management styles, marketing policies and personnel practices vary widely and in most cases, are difficult to fit together.

Trading Stocks (Also Called Equities)

Corporations can make growth as well as buy it. Internal growth — or organic growth as the analysts like to say — is often more feasible, often faster and more durable, and it avoids confrontation with government.

Seeking growth from well-established companies

Corporations do not have to be youthful to have growth potential. There are opportunities with mature companies where there is: (1) new management; (2) R&D-based product developments; (3) mergers/acquisitions; or (4) a turnaround situation.

There is nothing wrong with holding the shares of seasoned companies like GE and IBM — other than, maybe, the Law of Large Numbers, which makes growth somewhat more limited. But, like many people and Swiss watches, the best run middle age and older companies work fine.

Reminds me of the story of the young bull who said to the old one, "Let's rush down to the herd and get ourselves a cow". The old one replied, "No, let's take our time and get them all."

Here are six corporate attributes to focus on:

(1) Strong position in an evolutionary market

GE executives refer to this concept as "the unfair advantage". They won't buy a company if they don't see that key. So find an industry that is bound to grow and check its top six companies. The leaders may be the best bets, but don't overlook secondary companies if you see a clear-cut advantage. They may provide greater percentage returns for your portfolio.

(2) Ability to set prices at profitable levels

"Pricing power" is especially important in service industries where greater volume can bring proportionately higher profits, as overheads remain relatively stable. The same approach applies to companies making or distributing branded merchandise. Marketing today is often about "brand".

(3) Control of a market

IBM (IBM), Google (GOOG) and Research In Motion (RIMM) are in dominant positions in the information technology industry, not because of price, but because of an ability to engineer effective solutions that include new products and high-quality customer service at a reasonable price.

Lessons from the Trader Wizard

(4) Growing customer demand

This means a total market that is growing faster than the global, regional or national economies. In the early years of new items, almost any company can prosper because the demand is greater than the supply. Later, when production has caught up, only the strongest and best-managed firms survive and expand their positions.

(5) Adequate funds for R&D

With few exceptions, future growth of any corporation is dependent on finding new and better products, more efficient methods of doing business, and so on. Look for a company that is building for that sort of future. Intel (INTC) and Cisco (CSCO) are good examples.

(6) Strong technology base

Technology is a valuable, but not essential, asset. High-tech is often a synonym for productivity, but it is productivity that usually drives earnings growth. Growth companies usually start with expertise in specific areas and then move out into other products and/or markets.

I like to watch the growth of corporate earnings and dividends of mid-tier S&P 400 stocks. Large, successful corporations continue to make more money and pay out higher dividends than small-cap companies. There are, of course, frequent years of downturn, but they do not last long and soon the growth rate returns to normal.

Part of a growing corporation's gains are due to inflation but the quality companies continue to move ahead, usually.

You should not buy shares of any company that has not grown at a faster average rate than the economy or at a rate faster than that of inflation. That standard should apply to sales, earnings, dividends and return on shareholders' equity. These are metrics I use to determine candidates for the Cara 100.

Core holdings in your portfolio are long-term commitments, not only of your capital, but of your time, so concentrate on the long-term averages, because there are times when growth can be erratic. At these times, pessimism or optimism is more meaningful in terms of providing you buying or selling opportunities.

Over the short term, psychology is the greatest moving force behind share prices. On a short-term basis, I trade against the emotions of other traders in the market because there is always a delay between perception and reality.

Trading Stocks (Also Called Equities)

Wall Street often moves on emotion and fails to react to facts. But in the capital markets, over the years, corporate earnings and cash flow determines the enterprise (going concern) values which, in turn, pushes and pulls the stock price. Remember this when selecting growth stocks. Once you have spotted real growth, you may have to be patient for this value to be recognized and accepted by other traders.

Conversely, the stock market, in buoyant periods, may stick with an "established" growth stock long after its growth has slowed and all that's left is a corporation with a reputation and hopes. As an example, Polaroid and Kodak remained institutional favorites until long after their per-share profits went flat or dropped. The same thing happened for most of the telcos and airlines.

Many traders just hate to sell, even when the facts are staring them in the face. Rather than play the latest-result-versus-Wall-Street-consensus earnings game, I feel that it is best to sell a stock when it reports two consecutive quarters with profits below those of the previous year. That's what I call a broken company, temporary or otherwise, and I want to be out of all positions in the stock.

One, or even two, mediocre growth years, however, should not be enough to remove a quality company from a watch list. Wal-Mart is an example. There are many more in the Cara 100.

Keep an eye on corporate progress as interpreted by a few Wall Street analysts. Once a company performs well enough to deserve widespread trader attention, it is a certainty that its management will work to retain that recognition. Those CEOs who cannot sustain trader interest are fired, much the same as field managers of major league sports teams.

Always investigate the reason for a slowdown in the important metrics of a previously successful corporation. It could be due to accounting changes, a shift in sales mix, or new product or regional market start-up costs. With quality companies, these dips can sometimes result in greater future profitability.

At the end of the day, do not fall in love with any stock. If the corporate future is dim, sell. You can always buy back if and when the outlook becomes promising.

Lessons from the Trader Wizard

Finding growth potential in unseasoned companies

Typically, you will find tomorrow's winners in today's unseasoned companies rather than in say a mature but failing company that is undergoing a corporate make-over. The latter we refer to as "putting lipstick on pigs".

While there may not be much of a track record to study among the thousands of unseasoned companies, there are clues to look for.

Although the market capitalization (price times number of outstanding shares) is said to be under $1 billion, and a company in the upper range is not "small", these typically (but not always) grow faster than large-cap companies, and so too does the share price of the good ones.

I tend to look at the Russell 2000 small-cap stocks at long-term cycle bottoms. Take, for example, the first up leg of the bull market that started between 4Q02 and 1Q03. The small-cap index (Russell 2000) in eight months (early March to 7 November 2003) was up +58.3% versus +33.5% for the S&P 500 large-cap stocks. (See http://bigcharts.marketwatch.com/quickchart/quickchart.asp?symb=rut.)

A subset of the small-cap market is the micro-cap company, ie, those companies that have a market capitalization below $100 million and have been in existence fewer than 10 years and listed on the stock market fewer than five. This is the domain of the speculative trader.

Search criteria

Basically, much of the same criteria apply to searching for attractive small caps (and micro-caps) as to large caps, so if you are an enterprising or speculative trader and wish to expand your analysis to include unseasoned companies, you should:

- First read the auditor's report at the front of the annual report. Determine just how dependent the company is on its ability to raise new capital to sustain its operations. Many dot-com companies had good management and business plans in 2001, but they couldn't find traders to tide them through as venture capital money had all but completely dried up. Remember, with small companies, if "it" can happen, it usually does.

- Next, read the annual report backwards. The footnotes may tell you whether there are significant problems, unfavorable long-term commitments, etc.

Trading Stocks (Also Called Equities)

- Analyze management's record in terms of growth of revenue and earnings and, especially, return on stockholders' equity. Discard any company that has not averaged a 15% profit rate over the past three and, preferably, five years.

- Find a current ratio of current assets to current liabilities of two-to-one or higher. This indicates the company can withstand tight credit markets (like those of 3Q07) and will also likely be able to obtain money to expand.

- Look for a low debt ratio with long-term debt under 35% of total capital. This means the company has staying power and could be around long-term.

- Unseasoned companies tend to have volatile stock prices. Compare the PE ratio to that of larger companies in the same industry: If the multiple is lower or if it's above 30, be wary. Obviously, start-up companies are special situations.

- Look for stocks of companies that sell at half their growth rates, with strong management, little debt and an internal rate of return on capital invested that is high enough to generate the internal growth you are seeking.

All these criteria also apply to large, established corporations. You want a proven record of able management as shown by fairly consistent results over a period of time. It's possible, but just harder to find in an unseasoned company.

Guidelines for evaluating unseasoned growth companies

Given a T-bill risk-free return of say +4.8% (September 2007) and an average seasoned company equity return of +9.2%, I would be looking for a minimum total return (including dividends) of +14% per year for Cara 100 companies. For unseasoned growth companies, however, I need at least an additional 3% return to satisfy my risk concerns.

Annual growth in earnings per share	Rating
Less than 4%	Unacceptable (I need to see earnings)
4-10%	Below average
10-14%	Average
14-20%	Good
20-25%	Very good
Over 25%	Excellent

Lessons from the Trader Wizard

Annual return on equity	Rating
Less than 6%	Below average
6-12%	Average
12-16%	Above average
16-20%	Very good
Over 20%	Excellent

In total I am seeking minimal returns from unseasoned companies of +17%. And since I wouldn't be expecting dividends, the price growth of +17% would be needed. That's not an insignificant target.

I think this table is helpful to explain the concept. Each company is going to apply the concept differently. A young company may have a big burn rate, but also be flush with cash from a recent public financing. The bar for earnings growth and return on equity metrics would not be as high.

For an example of an unseasoned company that I selected for the Cara Global Best 100, have a look at NetEase.com (NDQ: NTES), which develops computer games in China.

With the help of an associate, Karl Leutenegger, and a large team of volunteers from the BillCara.com blog, a Cara Microcap 100 list has been created. Monthly reports will be available in the first quarter of 2008.

Trading Stocks (Also Called Equities)

11   About value

Traders know there is a difference between price and value. Right now, for instance, traders around the world are watching central bankers print money at excessive rates (several multiples of the global economic growth rate), which devalues fiat money and increases the value of hard money (ie, gold and silver, which are storehouses of value).

Not to put too fine a point on it, but does anybody really believe that the value of these precious metals dropped -3.24% and -2.24% respectively in a single day, Friday? Why Friday? So you can sit and twist all weekend. The Treasury Secretary and Fed Chairman would like you to return to capital markets on Monday with an attitude adjustment, whereby you are transformed from Gold Bull to USD Bull. Some people actually put their trust and faith in the Treasury Secretary and Fed Chairman. I don't know why, but they do.

June 9, 2007

During the 1998–2001 market bubble, dot-com corporations represented the antithesis of value. Most of these intriguing recent start-ups had only their "story" to propel them to high stock prices. Most had no cash, no current assets and their so-called business model was not based on any business reality.

This was one boat full of dream merchants that value-conscious traders gladly passed by. Not since the 1960s has there been a situation in the capital markets that so proved the reality that price and value have quite different meanings.

However, and this is my point, there is intrinsic value in every company, even recent start-ups. It's up to us to find it and compare it to the share price.

Balance sheet checklist for value-conscious traders

The balance sheet shows the financial position of a company as of a given date, usually the end of either the calendar or fiscal year. Value traders have to familiarize themselves with the concepts.

Trading Stocks (Also Called Equities)

Here is a typical balance sheet to study:

	31 Dec Current year $ Millions	31 Dec Prior year $ Millions
ASSETS		
Current assets		
Cash	9.0	6.2
US Government securities	-	2.0
Accounts and notes receivable	12.4	11.4
Inventories	27.0	24.6
Total current assets	48.4	44.2
Other assets		
Receivables due after one year	4.7	3.9
Surrender value of insurance	0.2	0.2
Other	0.6	0.5
Total other assets	5.5	4.6
Fixed assets		
Buildings, mach. & equip. – cost	104.3	92.7
Less accumulated depreciation	27.6	25.0
	77.6	68.4
Land	0.9	0.7
Total fixed assets	77.6	68.4
Total assets	**131.5**	**117.2**
LIABILITIES & STOCKHOLDERS' EQUITY		
Current liabilities		
Accounts payable	6.1	5.0
Accrued liabilities	3.6	3.3
Current long-term debt	1.0	0.8
Fed. income and other taxes	9.6	8.4
Dividends payable	1.3	1.1
Total current liabilities	21.6	18.6
Reserves	3.6	2.5
Long-term debt	26.0	20.0
Stockholders' equity		
5% Cumulative preferred shares		
($100 par: auth. & outst. 60Mil.)	6.0	6.0
Common shares ($10 par: auth		
2.0 Mil outstanding 1,830,000)	18.3	18.3
Capital surplus	9.6	9.6
Retained earnings	46.4	42.2
Total stockholders' equity	80.3	76.1
Total liabilities and equity	**131.5**	**117.2**

Lessons from the Trader Wizard

The balance sheet is where you get a fully detailed breakdown of the company's capital or assets and liabilities (in each case, both current and long-term), as well as its net worth, more commonly known as stockholders' equity or book value.

Let's examine the balance sheet in the following example. The data and explanations are digested from an old NYSE-published booklet called *Understanding Financial Statements*. For convenience, the dollars and our calculations have omitted the $ millions.

Notes:

1. **Total assets.** This figure ($131.5 at the end of the current fiscal year) represents all the assets a company uses in its business, whether these assets are owned or leased. They are reported at original cost less depreciation or amortization (except for inventories, which are the lower of cost or current market worth).

2. **Net working capital.** This equals total current assets ($48.4) less total current liabilities ($21.6), for a net of $26.8 million. Current assets are of varying liquidity: cash and highly liquid government securities (in the prior year), fairly liquid accounts receivable, and less liquid inventories. Other assets of $5.5 million include longer-term receivables (possibly holdings in subsidiaries) and the surrender value of insurance.

3. **Fixed assets.** This figure shows the value of buildings, machinery, equipment ($104.3) and land ($.9). Except for land, fixed assets have a limited useful life. Each year, a provision (accumulated annually) is made for depreciation ($27.6) due to wear and tear, so that the value of the assets will not be overstated.

    The increase in fixed assets ($104.3 in the current year versus $92.7 in the prior year) is probably due to expansion and/or improved facilities and equipment. A large boost in fixed assets should, hopefully, be followed, in the next year, by a corresponding increase in products and sales, and a reduction in costs due to more efficient operations. If there is only a small change in fixed assets for several years, the company may be heading for trouble. It may not be keeping itself competitive.

    The higher valuation for land ($.9 versus $.7) represents the acquisition of additional property. Natural resource companies (oil and gas producers and mining corporations) that use up some of their assets each year show depletion allowances. Despite some theories to the contrary, these are not important factors in corporate profitability.

The best companies are those that make enough money to consistently plow back substantial sums in improved facilities and equipment.

Note that this balance sheet contains no items for intangible assets: goodwill, trademarks, patents and copyrights. They have no direct relation to corporate profits or growth. Under accounting rules, their value is normally amortized on an annual basis. Such items are omitted in computing the net tangible assets attributable to the common stock.

4. **Current liabilities: $21.6 million.** These are monies owed or debt obligations due within one year. They include:

   a. Money owed to suppliers for raw materials, parts, other supplies and items needed to conduct the business. Ordinarily, when sales are expanding, there will be an increase in this category.

   b. Accrued liabilities such as unpaid wages, salaries and commissions.

   c. Current maturity of long-term debt due in the next year. Many loans have provisions for repayment of a fixed amount annually.

   d. Taxes due. Sometimes, Federal income taxes owed is shown separately.

   e. Dividends payable, as declared by the directors, but not paid by year-end.

Note at the end of the current year, the company had $3 more current liabilities than in the preceding year ($21.6 versus $18.6). That's a considerable sum when sales were up only $5.8. In this case, fortunately, much of the difference was represented by higher inventories.

Watch the liabilities in the annual report of any company in which you plan to invest. A fast-growing corporation must plan carefully for its future financial needs. When current liabilities grow faster than current assets, there can be difficulty, unless the firm has adequate borrowing power. Here, current assets grew $4.2, so the extra $3 in liabilities is not out of line.

5. **Long-term debt: $26.0.** This shows the money due a lender (such as an insurance company) or lenders (such as individual bondholders) after one year. During the current year, the company paid off $1 in its debt, but had to borrow an additional $7.

6. **Stockholders' equity: $80.3.** This shows the re-invested earnings ($46.4) and the amount of money invested by stockholders. This is also called book value. It is an accounting term showing what the common shareholders actually own: $80.3 in the last year, which is a small $4.2 million increase from the prior year.

7. **On a per-share basis** (calculated by dividing the total by the number of common shares outstanding), it shows the assets behind each share of common stock. That's a low 5.5% increase, well below the 10% to 15% that is characteristic of true growth corporations. The $6 figure is based on 60,000 shares of 5% cumulative preferred stock with a par value of $100/share.

   In event of a liquidation of the company, the holder of each share of this stock would receive $100. In many cases, such stock can be redeemed, at the company's option, at a fixed price. $18.3 is based on 1,830,000 shares of common stock. The par value is listed at $10. Since the stock was sold at a price above par, the company received an additional $9.6 million, which is shown as capital surplus.

   Par value, or the stated value of "no par common stock", is an arbitrary amount having no relation to current market value (ie, price) of the common stock or to what common shareholders would receive in liquidation. (Market value is the amount traders are willing to pay momentarily to buy a share of common stock.)

8. **Retained earnings or earned surplus: $46.4.** This represents the operating earnings retained by the corporation to date (ie, not paid out in dividends). It is not a tangible sum or an amount on deposit in a bank. That's why most companies dropped the term surplus and refer to earnings retained and invested in the business.

Income statement checklist for value-conscious traders

The statement of income is where you find out how much money the company took in last year, how much had to be spent for expenses and taxes, and the size of the resulting profits (if any) that were available for distribution to shareholders or for re-investment in the business.

Trading Stocks (Also Called Equities)

Here is an example (SOURCE: NYSE) and a checklist of review points:

STATEMENT OF INCOME (and Earned Surplus)

	Year ended 31 Dec	
	Current year $ Millions	Prior year $ Millions
Sales	115.8	110.0
Less:		
Cost and expenses:		
Cost of goods sold	76.4	73.2
Selling, general & admin. expenses	14.2	13.0
Depreciation	2.6	3.5
	93.2	89.7
Operating profit	22.6	20.3
Interest charges	1.3	1.0
Earnings before income taxes	21.3	19.3
Provision for taxes on Income	11.4	9.8
Net Income (per common share)	9.9	9.5
Earned surplus, begin. of year	42.2	37.6
	52.1	47.1
Less dividends paid on:		
Preferred stock ($5 per share)	(.3)	(.3)
Common stock (per share)	(5.4)	(4.6)
Earned surplus, end of year	46.4	42.2

These figures are interesting, but when expressed as amount per share of common stock, they are important for comparisons to: (a) corporate results of prior years; and (b) those of other companies in the same or similar businesses.

Remember, neither business nor the capital markets operate in a vacuum.

Let's examine the income statement in this example.

1. **Sales or revenues.** The $5.8 increase ($115.8 versus $110) is fair but not exceptional. If the industry boosted sales by 10%, this 5.3% gain would not be satisfactory. When reviewing a sales figure, be sure to see if the unit sales figure has grown or if the larger dollar volume is merely derived from price rises. In the case of pricing power, remember, it might not be as good next year or the year after that.

2. **Cost of goods sold.** This $76.4 shows the outlays for raw materials, wages, salaries, supplies, power, etc. Since sales were up $5.8, the increase in costs ($3.2) shows that expenses were kept under control and that the profit margin remained stable. The lower the cost of goods sold, the larger the profit margin.

3. **Selling, general and administrative expenses.** This item varies with the type of business. In a steel company, most of the money probably would be spent for selling and administration. In a cosmetics company, the majority of such costs would be for advertising and promotion. Again, the company appears to be able to keep these expenses in line (up only $1.2). Note: this category may include R&D costs that, in many reports, are shown as a separate item.

4. **Depreciation and depletion.** These expenses differ from the other expenses because they are not an actual cash outlay. Every piece of machinery and equipment or other fixed assets has a limited life. Tax rules set maximum depreciation allowances to be used and require it to cost-based. Depletion is similar to depreciation, but represents the reduction in value, as used, of natural resources such as coal, timber, copper, oil and gas.

    The higher the amounts provided for depreciation and/or depletion, the lower the net reported income. Conversely, large deductions make for a high cash flow (the total of net income plus deductions for depreciation).

    Some analysts consider cash flow and not earnings as a better forecaster of future dividends. But consideration should also be given to working capital, projected capital expenditures, new products and markets, etc.

5. **Operating profit:** $22.6. As a percentage of sales, this indicates the pre-tax profit margin, 19.5%, an improvement over the 18.5% in the prior year. Normally, manufacturing companies have pre-tax profit margins (after depreciation and depletion) of about 8%.

6. **Interest charges:** $1.3. This is the cost of borrowed funds. It is a deductible, before-tax expense. Bondholders like to see at least three dollars of available earnings for each dollar's interest the company must pay. There's no trouble here, because there are 17 dollars (before provision for Federal income taxes) for each interest dollar.

7. **Earnings before income taxes.** This is the operating profit: $22.6 minus interest of $1.3 equals $21.3.

8. **Provision for taxes.** This $11.4 is just half of the operating profit. With a few exceptions at the state level, the rate of corporate income taxes has not varied much in the past several years.

9. **Net income for the year.** This is maybe the most important figure to the trader. The $9.9 was about 4.2% higher than the net of the previous year. It represents an 8.5% return on each dollar of sales: 9.9/115.8. This was slightly down from 8.6% in the prior year.

    The best companies are those that maintain or increase their profits each year: in total, in percentage of sales and in relation to stockholders' equity. The average net income to sales depends on the type of business.

    Food retailers hope to report a profit of two cents per sales dollar; manufacturing companies average about six cents per revenue dollar; and cosmetics and drug companies can go up to thirty cents of every sales dollar.

    The important figure is the return on equity, which is the return on the shareholders' investment: $9.9 divided by $80.3 (the stockholder's equity) equals 12.3%. This 12.3% was a touch better than the average profit rate reported by the Dow 30 corporations at that point some 20 years ago. In recent years, it is well below average.

10. **Dividends on preferred stock:** $300,000. This is a standard guide for the investment grade of a preferred stock. In this case, the company covered its preferred dividend fully 33 times. On cumulative preferred stocks, dividends that have not been paid in the past, in addition to the current year, must be paid before any dividends can be paid on the common stock.

11. **Net income available for common stock:** $9.9. This shows the capital that can be used to pay dividends to owners of the common stock. When divided by the weighted average of shares outstanding, it reports per-share earnings, the most widely used criterion for judging corporate progress.

    If a company has no senior securities (such as preferred stock), all of the net income is available for common dividends. Fast-growing companies tend to reinvest +80% of their net income, thus leaving little for dividends.

    Corporations with steady revenue, such as utilities, usually pay out 60% or so of their profits. (In order to keep attracting new capital, some companies have boosted the percentage of payout to 80% or more.) This policy does not leave much for investing in the future, so be wary of such companies, even though the yields may be attractive.

For income-oriented traders, look for companies that distribute a bit more than half their annual income. For growth-oriented traders, buy shares of low dividend payers.

12. **Retained earnings**. At the end of the year, the company added $9.9 (net income) to the $42.2 shown at the beginning of the year. This made a total of $52.1 before payment of $5.7 in dividends on preferred and common stock. The balance, $46.4, showed that the company was worth $4.2 more than at the end of the prior year. Reinvested earnings became part of other assets (inventories, receivables, etc.) or were used for new plants and equipment. That 10% increase in earned surplus was about double reported by the average large corporation during that period.

Keys to determining a stock's fair value

Like anything, if you don't know what you're looking for, you probably won't find it. Value traders are looking for corporations whose value, based on certain parameters they establish, is not recognized in the stock price.

Value traders look for the existence of these factors:

1. A current cash dividend of 4% or more.

2. Cash dividends must have been paid for at least five, and preferably 10, years without a decrease in dollar payout.

3. Total debt less than 35% of total capitalization.

4. Minimum of net working capital for liquidity equal to two times current liabilities.

5. Current dividend protection ratio should be 1.4 or more, which is $1.40 earnings for each $1.00 dividends.

6. Current PE ratio of 10 or less. Interest rates today (4Q03) are at historic lows. As interest rates increase (ie, the cost of capital increases), value traders will lower the required PE ratio to, say, 8 or even 6.

7. Next year's profits should be expected to be higher.

Trading Stocks (Also Called Equities)

8. **Gain-to-loss ratio or minimum of 2:1:** ie, based on past market action and future prospects, the probable gain should be twice as great as the possible loss, which is a potential gain of 10 points versus a five-point decline.

For another test of whether a stock is undervalued, try calculating the average 10-year growth rate of earnings, and then assign a price-earnings multiple that is increased by .8 for each 1% of profit rise. With zero growth, the PE is 8; with 1% average rise, it is 8.8; with 2%, 9.6; and so on, to a 20 multiple for a growth rate of 15% or more.

Next, multiply the average dollar earnings for this period (ie, 10 years) by the assigned PE to find the price at which the stock should be sold. To find the buy price, subtract one-third of the final figure.

Example:

> ABC has boosted its profits by 10% annually for 10 years. The assigned PE ratio is 15.8; the average earnings per share have been $3. Thus, 3 X 15.8 = 47.4. Subtract 33% to get a buy price of 31.6.

The best way to learn how to find value is to work through case studies.

Using balance sheet and statement of income figures in the last case study, let's look for value:

	Current year	Prior year
1. Operating profit margin	19.5%	18.5%
2. Current ratio	2.24	2.38
3. Liquidity ratio	41.7%	44.1%
4. Capitalization ratios:		
Long-term debt	24.4%	20.8%
Preferred stock	5.7	6.3
Common stock and surplus	69.9	72.9
5. Sales to fixed assets	1.1	1.2
6. Sales to inventories	4.3	4.5
7. Net income to net worth	12.3%	12.5%

1. **Operating profit margin** (PM). This is the ratio of profit (before interest and taxes) to sales. The operating PM (also referred to as top-line margin) ($22.6) divided by sales ($115.8) equals 19.5%. This compares with 18.5% for the previous year. (Some analysts prefer to

compute this margin without including depreciation and depletion as part of the cost because these have nothing to do with the efficiency of the operation.)

When a company increases sales substantially, the PM should be widened, because costs of rent, interest, real property taxes, etc, are fixed and do not rise in step with volume.

The PM is useful for comparison, but can be misunderstood when the corporation changes the types of products sold or its method of distribution. When a finance company acquires a retail chain, sales and profits may increase substantially even though the PM on combined revenues is considerably below that of the finance company's former PM.

2.	**Current ratio.** This is the ratio of current assets to current liabilities: $48.4 divided by $21.6 equals $2.24. For most industrial corporations, this should be about two to one. It varies with the type of business. Utilities and retail stores, for example, have rapid cash inflows and high turnovers, so they can operate effectively with lower ratios. In your analysis, check the past record and watch for any major shift in this ratio. When the ratio is high (5:1), it may mean that a company is not making the best use of its liquid assets. It may have too much money invested in securities, which provide high yields for a while, but they do not expand the business.

3.	**Liquidity ratio.** This is the ratio of cash and its equivalent to total current liabilities ($9 divided by $21.6 equals 41.7%). The liquidity ratio is important as a supplement to the current ratio because, despite a high current ratio, the immediate ability of a corporation to meet its current obligations or pay larger dividends may be impaired. This 41.7% liquidity ratio (down from 44.1% the year before) probably indicates a period of expansion, rising prices, heavier capital expenditures and larger accounts payable. If the situation persists, the company might have to raise additional capital.

4.	**Capitalization ratios.** These show the percentages of each type of holding as part of the total position in the corporation. Though often used to describe only the outstanding securities, capitalization is the sum of the face value of bonds and other debts plus the par value of all preferred and common stock issues, plus the balance sheet totals for capital surplus and retained earnings.

Bond, preferred stock and common stock ratios are useful indicators of the relative risk and leverage involved for the owners of the three types of securities. For most industrial corporations, the debt ratio should be no more than 66% of equity or 40% of total capital. In this instance, the long-term debt plus preferred stock is 43.1% of the equity represented by the common stock and surplus, and 30.1% of total capital. Higher ratios are appropriate for utilities and transports.

5. **Sales to fixed assets.** This ratio is computed by dividing the annual sales ($115.8) by the year-end value of plant, equipment and land before depreciation and amortization ($104.3 plus $.9 equals $105.2). The ratio is, therefore, 1.1 to 1. This is down from 1.2 to 1 the year before.

    This ratio helps to show whether funds used to enlarge productive facilities are being wisely spent. A sizable expansion in facilities should lead to larger sales volume. If it does not, there's something wrong. In this case, there were delays in getting production going at the new plant.

6. **Sales to inventories.** This ratio is calculated by dividing annual sales by year-end inventories: $115.8 divided by $27 equals a 4.3:1 ratio. The year before, the ratio was 4.5 to 1. This shows inventory turnover, which is the number of times the equivalent of the year-end inventory has been bought and sold during the year. It is more important in analyzing retail corporations than manufacturers. A high ratio denotes a good quality of merchandise and correct pricing policies. A declining ratio may be a warning signal. Note: A more accurate comparison would result from the use of an average of inventories at the beginning and end of each year.

7. **Net income to net worth.** This is one of the most significant of all financial ratios and is derived by dividing the net income ($9.9) by the total of the preferred stock, common stock and surplus accounts ($80.3). The result in this case is 12.3%. This shows the percentage of return, in profits, that corporate management is earning on the stockholders' investment. The same basic information is shown on a slightly different basis, as the profit rate (PR). This 12.3% is a decrease from the 12.5% of the prior year. It's a fair return, meaning it is not as good as that achieved by a top-quality company, but better than average. The higher the ratio, the more profitable the company.

    Any company that can consistently improve its net income to net worth is a true growth company. But be sure that this gain is due to operating skill, not to accounting tricks or extraordinary items.

Lessons from the Trader Wizard

Using quantitative analysis
to find "value" stocks

Detailed financial analysis involves careful evaluation of financial strength plus operating income, cost and earnings figures. That study is called traditional fundamental analysis. But it is also important to study ratios and trends, both within a corporation and in comparison with those of other companies in the same industry. The latter study is called quantitative analysis.

Usually, analysts prefer to use five- or 10-year averages. These can reveal significant changes and, on occasion, spot special values in either concealed or inconspicuous assets.

Example: When there is a wide difference between the book value of assets as carried on the balance sheet and their current market value (determined by the stock market), there may be important resources such as holdings of valuable real estate or oil and gas.

When trying to find value, here are the key ratios to consider:

Operating ratio. This is the ratio of operating costs to sales. It is the complement of PM (100% minus the PM percentage). Thus, if a company's PM (top-line profit margin) is 10%, its operating ratio is 90%. It's handy to compare similar companies but not significant otherwise.

Profit margins vary according to the type of business. They are low for companies with heavy plant investments (Alcoa~13%) and for retailers with fast turnover (Wal-Mart~6%), and high for marketing firms such as those providing information and computer software (Microsoft~47%) and for those manufacturing consumer products (Johnson & Johnson~32%).

Interest coverage. When a company has a large amount of senior obligations (bonds and preferred stocks), it is important to know that profits will be adequate to cover the payment of annual interest. This figure is the number of times the annual total interest is covered by the earnings. The usual acceptable minimum ratio for an industrial corporation is three to four times interest needs. For Alcoa (2002) it is 5.0x, but Boeing (2002) is only 2.5x.

Keep in mind that when a company (except utilities or transportation firms) has a relatively high debt, it means that traders shy away from buying its common stock. To provide the plants, equipment, etc, which the company needs, management must issue bonds or preferred shares (straight or convertible) to attract traders.

Trading Stocks (Also Called Equities)

There are some tax advantages in such a course, but when the debt becomes too high, there can be trouble during recessive times. All, or almost all, of the gross profits will have to be used to pay interest and there will be nothing, or little, left over for the common stockholders. Boeing, for example, has seen little improvement in its stock price for eight years, and in the past three years its long-term debt has increased a greater amount than its net profits.

On the other hand, speculators like high-debt situations when business is good. This means that when profits soar, all of the excess, after interest is paid, will accrue to the common stock.

Typically, railroads and airlines, which have tremendous assets (almost all financed by debt obligations), are popular in boom times. Because of the financial leverage involved, an extra 10% gain in traffic can boost profits far more percentage-wise.

When high-debt corporations like utilities have relatively small year-to-year changes in earnings, these fluctuations spread across a large amount of senior securities are no concern to the long-term oriented trader.

Pay-out ratio. This is the ratio of the cash dividends to per-share profits after taxes. It reflects management's policy. Fast-growing corporations pay small dividends, less than 30% of each earned dollar; stable, profitable companies pay out about 50%; and utilities, which have almost assured earnings, pay 70% on average.

A high dividend is attractive, but for growth, look for companies that pay small dividends or none at all. They use retained earnings to improve the financial strength and operating future of the company; and retained earnings are tax-free.

Example: For about 10 years until 2001, Intel Corp (INTC) paid an average of 4% dividend to net profit. The reinvestments paid off, as the price of Intel stock rose from about 2 to 75 (pre-split). In recent years, where the growth of dividends has slowed following a period of relative silence from management, the share price languished, so the Intel Board approved a substantial increase in dividend pay-out in the past year and the share price has begun to attract a different type of buyer.

Price-to-book value ratio. This is the market price of the stock divided by its book value per share. Since book value (BV) trends are relatively more stable than earnings trends, conservative analysts use this ratio as a price comparison. They keep in mind the historical over- or under-valuation of the stock which, in turn, depends primarily on the company's profitable growth (or lack of it).

Because of inflation, understatement of assets on balance sheets — and in boom times, the enthusiasm of traders — often pushes this ratio rather high.

On average, only the stocks of the most profitable companies sell at much more than twice book value. Stocks of high-growth, profitable companies, such as Microsoft with a price to BV of about 22%, do sell at higher ratios (usually), because traders believe these great corporations can continue to rack up ever-higher profits (as they have done in the past).

But when there's a bear market, this type of stock usually falls farther than those selling at more logical price to equity ratios.

Price/earnings (PE) ratio. This is calculated by dividing the price of the stock by the reported earnings per share for the past 12 months. Thus, the stock of Microsoft, with per-share profits of $0.90 in 2001 and selling at an average of 26, had a PE ratio of 35. This information is printed in stock tables in many financial publications.

For the Dow 30, I use http://valueline.com/dow30.

There are two caveats when using PE ratios in your analysis:

(1)   They are best made with stocks of quality corporations that have long, fairly consistent records of profitable growth. They will not work out well with shares of companies that are cyclical, erratic or untested.

(2)   Wall Street is often slow to recognize value and always takes time to come to intelligent decisions. Analysts tend to think that if a PE ratio is below the average for a company's industry group, there must be something wrong with the company. There is no assurance that real value will be quickly recognized in the capital markets.

Investment tax credit. For years, tax credits led to a large and growing share of corporate earnings, particularly in the auto and aircraft manufacturing sectors. In some high-tax jurisdictions, corporations are allowed to take up to a 15% investment tax credit for long-life capital assets purchased. This is designed to encourage business to replace old machinery and equipment. On a $100 million new capex investment, there's a $15 million tax credit. That's why it's important to note how much profit is due to tax benefits, including tax recoveries, rather than profitable operations.

If you want income, it makes little difference where the cash for the dividend comes from. But to the growth-minded trader, such gains from tax credits are not a true measure of corporate growth.

Trading Stocks (Also Called Equities)

Investment tax credits are difficult for inexperienced traders to figure out. They are explained in the notes to the annual reports, but not always for easy analysis by the average trader. If you are puzzled about the failure of a stock to rise appreciably after higher earnings have been reported, try to see if those extra earnings came from tax credits (not so meaningful) or continuing operations (very meaningful).

Cash flow. This yardstick is important in determining value. Reported after-tax net earnings do not reflect actual cash income available to the company. Cash flow is a calculation of earnings after taxes plus charges against income that do not directly involve cash outlays (sums allocated to depreciation, depletion, amortization and other special items).

If a company were to show a net profit of $30 million plus depreciation of $100 million, the cash flow would be $130 million. There are different types of cash flow, such as distributable cash flow and discretionary or free cash flow. To calculate the distributable cash flow per share, deduct provisions for preferred dividends (since these are required to be paid); then divide the balance by the number of shares of common stock. Free cash flow then is the distributable cash flow minus the common share dividends.

In an effort to keep earnings high in inflationary times, accountants exercise "judgments" that tend to overvalue some assets and understate depreciation expenses. As a result, some companies are paying dividends with money they do not have or must borrow and, in effect, are distributing assets, ie, returning capital (some call it cannibalizing the corporate structure) to keep the stock price up.

According to some analysts, the accounting for cash flow has become, due to shareholder pressures on the company to perform, a complicated area that reflects management's interpretation of GAAP.

Examples:

- When Company A owns over 20% of Company B, Company A can book B's earnings, even though there is no transfer of funds.

- A manufacturer continues to show depreciation of $100 million a year on a facility, yet, because of inflation, the real replacement cost is $150 million.

- A book and magazine publisher reports, as revenues, millions of dollars of receivables that have not been collected which, subject to returns, may never be.

Lessons from the Trader Wizard

Distributable cash flow: This is the amount of money a company has earned in the current year to pay dividends and/or invest in real growth. If this is negative, there are problems. If it's positive, fine, unless the company pays out more than this figure in dividends and, thus, is liquidating itself. Buyers of Canadian business trusts liked the 15%-20% annual returns but, in fact, were receiving a return of capital from many of them.

A company like Exxon Mobil (XOM), due to high capital expenditures and hence depreciation and amortization of assets, has very high distributable cash flow versus net earnings. That is why it can pay out a high percentage of earnings as dividends. In 2006, for example, Exxon Mobil is expected to have per-share cash flow and earnings of $8.50 and $6.40 respectively, with a $1.28 dividend, so while the dividend pay-out ratio (to net profit) was 20%, dividends as a percentage of cash flow was 15%. In 2002, however, cash flow and earnings per share were $2.88 and $1.66 respectively, with a $0.92 dividend, so while the dividend pay-out ratio was a very high (for ExxonMobil) 58%, the dividend as a percentage of cash flow was 32%. Now in 2007, it appears that Exxon will generate $9.20 and $6.75 in per-share cash flow and earnings respectively. The annual dividend (paid quarterly) ought to be $1.37, which will be back down to a payout of 20 percent of net profits and just 14.9 percent of cash flow. Exxon is a Cara 100 Global Best Company.

Discretionary cash flow: The amount of distributable cash flow is the capital remaining from current earnings after allocations for dividends to common shareholders.

Companies ultimately have to have the capital in some form (cash savings or borrowing) to grow with. Some companies that require heavy capital expenditures plus pay high dividends often have negative cash flows because their earnings are insufficient to meet the various pay-outs. When these companies borrow funds in order to pay those high dividends, they are depleting their assets; therefore the stocks of those companies would never become core holdings in my portfolio.

On the other hand, highly profitable companies, such as Exxon Mobil, have high cash flows by any measurement, so, over the long-run, XOM is going to stay in the Cara 100.

Yes, there are times when I write calls and sell XOM, but over the years, my goal is to add to my positions by writing puts and buying the shares. When I can do that at an increasingly lower cost base per share and those shares are constantly paying out higher dividends ($0.92 in 2002; $0.98 in 2003; $1.06 in 2004; $1.14 in 2005 and $1.28 in 2006), then my cash-on-cash return is greater than any real estate asset I can buy.

Trading Stocks (Also Called Equities)

One caveat regarding cash flow: Investment value is a total concept that should be based on realistic, conservative accounting and not on judgments that may be legal and, to some extent, accepted, but which artificially boost corporate profits, such as we saw in recent years with Canadian business trusts.

For a quick screen for value stocks I go to Reuters (http://reuters.com).

Seeking "value" in stocks of potential turnaround companies

Most speculative buyers of "value" are really momentum traders (and I have been accused of being that), but let's not quibble.

Value investing is an approach used by fundamentalists who look for situations where they are able to buy stocks of quality corporations at undervalued prices. If the term "Deep Value" is used, this typically involves a long-term turnaround situation after a fundamental corporate disappointment.

While I look for companies that trade in a range that approximates fair value, give or take 10% or 20% due to short-term market inefficiency, there are deep-value traders who look for potential turnaround companies. The premise there is that the company is labeled as "broken" and, to be fixed, must have new capital, a capital structure re-organization or new management, which takes time to do.

The deep-value approach is the beancounter's way of finding turnaround stocks. That's basically investing in the assets of companies, not trading of its stock. The expected hold period may be five or 10 years. To a trader like me, that would be a mistake.

Investing in turnaround value, which is a legitimate business typically done by private equity is based on financial facts — facts that are important to statisticians and accountants, but also to value-oriented investors. They examine going-concern value in terms of cash, current assets and proven profit-generating assets that may be under-used. This is not the rosy, intangible promises of big future earnings.

If you want to find value on your own, you'll have to learn how to analyze financial reports — at least as deeply as I go into in this book. It's an approach that relies heavily on economic forecasts and an analysis of a corporation's present balance-sheet strength and past operating performance, plus indications of the future if certain changes are made to the company.

If you decide to select stocks strictly on the basis of price-to-book-value and the corporation's potential ability to make money, you are probably

228

going to pick winners eventually. However, you have to be more patient than most people I know. It takes time for such stocks to rise to a point where you can take the sizable profits you thought were available for the taking.

The big factor here is time. In time, everything changes — sometimes for the good, sometimes for the worse. That's the problem I have with true-value investing with turnarounds.

I don't expect to be in and out of a stock in a day, but 13 weeks would be nice. I just haven't found corporate turnarounds working that way.

Also, during periods of high levels of economic growth, where price-earnings multiples expand beyond the norm, it is not easy to find value. Strict value-oriented traders might miss the cycle altogether.

But if you have done your homework and there is no major change in the way the corporation is operated or in the products it makes and the markets it serves, you will almost certainly make money in the long run. I think value traders succeed ultimately because they tend to apply more forethought, patience and common sense than the average trader.

But that's not to say that I'm a deep value-oriented individual or even a value-oriented trader. I don't particularly enjoy digging deep into corporate financial reports to the degree I did at a younger age. When you're in your 20s and 30s, you can afford to be patient.

Trading Stocks (Also Called Equities)

12 Growth + approximate fair value = quality [the Cara 100 concept]

Unlike medical terminology, market terminology is rather imprecise, and different people will use the same words to mean different things. The argument I am offering here is that the market is as complicated as we choose to make it, and in listening to every guru who has an opinion, and a different methodology of every type imaginable, we are making it tough on ourselves.

I have a very simple mechanical system. I contain my subjects of prime interest (my portfolio watchlist) to a limited number of high quality companies. Then, with the knowledge companies go through periods of thick and thin like we all do, I simply accumulate positions when the Monthly-Weekly-Daily Relative Strength Index (RSI) technical indicator is below 30, and distribute when it is over 70 for each stock.

August 5, 2007

Quality is my Holy Grail. It's what I put behind my selection of the Cara Global Best 100 Companies.

Finding "quality" companies: stable long-term profitability

With publicly traded companies, quality is like a charismatic personality. If you have it, what else is needed? In the market, traders have to separate the high-quality companies from the rest. Quality is primarily the record of a corporation's financial strength, its record of profitability and growth and its prospects for continuing a comparable record in the future. I judge these factors within the GICS sector, sub-sector and industry group classifications, where my goal is to find the peer group leaders.

For easy reference, most traders can refer to Standard & Poor's Stock Guide. This rates corporations on the basis of an appraisal of past performance of earnings and dividends and relative current standing:

A+ (highest)
A (high)
A- (above average)

231

Trading Stocks (Also Called Equities)

B+ (average)
B (below average)
B- (lower)
C (lowest)

Unless there is a special reason to do so, never invest in the common shares of any corporation rated by S&P below B+, particularly in times of difficult credit market conditions such as we have in 3Q2007.

In searching for quality in a small-cap stock, professional money managers are guided by standards such as these developed by Wright Investors' Service several years ago:

Investment acceptance:

• Market value of publicly held shares:	$100 million
• Trading volume (annual):	$25 million
• Turnover (annual):	less than 50%
• Ownership by institutions:	15
• Shareholders:	5,000

Financial strength:

• Total capital and surplus:	$50 million
• Equity capital as percent of total capital (include preferred stock and long-term debt):	50%
• Long-term debt (as % of total capital):	maximum 40%
• Fixed charges (ratio of pre-tax income to interest and preferred dividends):	3.5:1
• Working capital (ratio of current assets to current liabilities):	2:1
• Convertible securities:	max 30% of stock with 15% dilution

Profitability and stability:

• Profit rate (return on equity capital):	11%
• Stability index:	60%
• Dividends:	min payout 10% max 75% of earnings
• Dividends as % of return on equity:	5%
• Operating income (% of total capital):	15%

All of this data is calculated for at least five years.

Lessons from the Trader Wizard

For the first three categories, (investment acceptance, financial strength and profitability and stability) the Wright ratings are:

A = Outstanding
B = Excellent
C = Good (acceptable)

Some recent Wright Quality Ratings of Dow 30 components:

GE   AAA11
MMM ABA7
DELL AAA14
DIS   ABD3

I recommend that every trader visit Wright Investors' Service (http://wisi.com) and register (free) for the demonstration. If you like it, subscribe.

The Internet is also full of what is called "free stuff". Some of it is terrific.

For a helpful screening center for quality stocks, I go to Reuters (http://multexinvestor.com).

How to determine prudent price-earnings ratios for quality companies

On the following page is a quality stock price evaluator table based on PE.

Analysts use such a table for assessing fast-growing companies that have above-average growth rates. You have the same task and you need to know what represents a prudent PE ratio.

For example, a small-cap tech company is selling at 40 times earnings and you estimate that it will grow its earnings at a compound annual growth rate (CAGR) of 20%. This table shows that if your estimate is accurate, the stock will be trading at 16.1 times its anticipated five-years-hence earnings. This probably sounds reasonable to you.

But measures like the following evaluator table don't tell you the prudent level of PE multiple for a particular stock. In our example, the future PE will be just 16.1, but how does that compare to another company that may have a higher or lower quality rating?

How does it compare to one that may boost dividends, say, at a +20% annual rate?

Trading Stocks (Also Called Equities)

Relative to concepts like earnings predictability, stock price stability and price growth persistence that are evaluated by Value Line for each of 1,700 companies — why do you think that 16.1 times a five-years-hence earnings price is reasonable?

If you are going to trade on the basis of PE, you have a lot to consider.

Here is the number of times a company's 5-year out-projected earnings currently sells for:

PE	Expected compound annual growth rate of earnings (%)						
	10	15	20	25	30	40	50
12	7.5	6.0	4.8	3.9	3.2	2.2	1.6
14	8.7	7.0	5.6	4.6	3.8	2.6	1.8
16	9.9	8.0	6.5	5.2	4.3	3.0	2.1
18	11.2	9.0	7.3	5.9	4.9	3.3	2.4
20	12.4	10.0	8.1	6.6	5.4	3.7	2.6
22	13.7	10.9	8.9	7.2	5.9	4.1	2.9
24	14.9	11.9	9.7	7.9	6.5	4.5	3.2
26	16.1	12.9	10.5	8.5	7.0	4.8	3.4
28	17.4	13.9	11.3	9.2	7.5	5.2	3.7
30	18.6	14.9	12.1	9.8	8.1	5.6	3.9
32	19.9	15.9	12.9	10.5	8.6	5.9	4.2
34	21.1	16.9	13.7	11.1	9.2	6.3	4.5
36	22.4	17.9	14.5	11.8	9.7	6.7	4.7
38	23.6	18.9	15.3	12.5	10.2	7.1	5.0
40	24.8	19.9	16.1	13.1	10.8	7.4	5.3
42	26.1	20.9	16.9	13.8	11.3	7.8	5.5
44	27.3	21.9	17.7	14.4	11.9	8.2	5.8
46	28.6	22.9	18.5	15.1	12.4	8.6	6.1
48	29.8	23.9	19.4	15.7	12.9	8.9	6.3
50	31.1	24.9	20.2	16.4	13.5	9.3	6.6

Analysts usually translate a current PE ratio into an adjusted figure corrected for estimated future growth of per-share earnings or cash flow. I never could find a helpful formula, and then I discovered a table produced by Standard & Poor's that saves the trouble of lengthy calculations.

Lessons from the Trader Wizard

Prudent price-earnings multiples (using S&P ratings)

If you project earnings per share (after taxes) to grow in next five years at an average compounded annual rate of:	With these quality ratings				
	B	B+	A-	A	A+
	(These are approximate prudent multiples that represent the maximum current price to pay.)				
5%	12.0	12.9	13.7	15.0	16.7
6%	12.5	13.4	14.3	15.8	17.4
7%	13.0	14.0	14.9	1B.5	18.2
8%	13.6	14.5	15.6	17.1	18.9
9%	14.1	15.1	16.2	17.8	19.7
10%	14.6	15.7	16.8	18.5	20.4
15%	17.4	18.7	20.1	22.0	24.5
20%	20.2	21.8	23.4	25.7	28.6
25%	23.0	24.7	26.6	29.3	32.7
30%	25.2	27.3	29.4	32.5	36.2
35%	28.5	31.0	33.5	37.1	41.5
40%	31.9	34.8	37.7	41.7	46.7

S&P designations. If not rated, use B. For unseasoned companies, use a conservative rating based on the comparison with similar companies, preferably in the same industry.

Trading Stocks (Also Called Equities)

13 The importance of when to buy

Where we are is that some traders are saying, "We can't time markets," and that is a pile of rubbish. Would you rather just turn your capital over to the sell-side, and let them have their way with you?

I suggest that people who talk silliness either do not yet understand capital markets or they don't have a grip on themselves. For that reason, and thinking ahead fearing I would hear such talk, I decided to step up to the plate and, once again, try to use the market as a laboratory where I can teach and some people can learn.

June 9, 2007

The sell-side will say you cannot effectively time the market. However, if you are fortunate to acquire one skill in this life, it is knowing when to buy and sell securities. Of course, if you always buy at the right time, whether it is securities or physical assets, the selling becomes easy. Perhaps, although unlikely, you will never have to sell.

Tools and techniques of overall market buy/sell timing

You'll have to learn that being in the right place at the right time in the market is usually not due to luck. Once you have decided only to buy shares in companies you have decided represent high quality, successful trading is due to understanding and applying the concepts of market timing.

Timing is crucial for meeting your goals with any type of trading. With conservative holdings, it is not as important as with speculative ones, but is still an aid that can help you achieve extra profits and avoid unnecessary losses.

When you buy the stock of a high-quality company at a reasonable price, you will eventually make money. Good timing reduces the patience period.

The trouble with stock market timing is the market itself. There are short-term factors and there are long-term factors.

The shorter the timeframe, the more that timing becomes an important issue. Many long-term changes in stock prices result from "rational" or "fundamental" economic, monetary, financial and corporate factors and

Trading Stocks (Also Called Equities)

forces. However, short-term changes are due to psychological factors, such as fear, hope, confidence and uncertainty — almost anything but the facts.

You can make money (temporarily) when you buy the best securities at the wrong time. In a bear market, if you hold them through their inevitable decline, you will end up a winner when they bounce back again.

You can often make money by buying a poor security at the right time. But the best of all trading worlds is when you buy the right security at the right time.

Types of timing

Broadly speaking, there are two kinds of timing: fundamental and market.

Fundamental timing

How do you determine whether or not it is a good time to invest in common stocks? Action is taken against a background of the fundamental factors that influence stock prices: the economic, monetary and political influences; the earnings, dividends, financial strength, ratios, yields, interest rates and, of course, future prospects for the economy, the industry and the company.

With fundamental timing, the trader acts with the confidence that the stock market, over a period of time, will adjust to price levels reflecting these rational factors. Successful fundamental timing requires a continuous business and economic forecast.

Such an approach pays little heed to the many psychological and short-run market forces that affect week-to-week, month-to-month and, often, year-to-year fluctuations in stock-market prices. With fundamental timing, the trader works in general areas: low (or buy) ranges and high (or sell) ranges.

A widely used guide is the PE ratio. The typical fundamentalist believes that, over a decade or so, the market tends to sell within a broad range of a multiple of profits: for the DJIA, from a high of 16 to 18 to a low of 10 to 11.

This means that when the Dow stocks sell at more than 16 times earnings, the market is becoming overvalued and some stocks should be sold. Similarly, when the PE ratio of the broad Dow index falls below 10 or 11, it's time to consider buying some of these stocks.

This type of timing takes patience and is used only by very long-term traders.

238

Lessons from the Trader Wizard

Market timing

Market timing is judging whether and when to buy and sell specific stocks based strictly on market prices. This recognizes that, most of the time, the prices of common stocks move together and that there are four kinds of market-price movements:

(1) **Major bull and bear market swings:** These are sometimes, but not often, less than two years' duration; usually, they last longer, but include many short reversing fluctuations. Analysts may be able to spot the long-term trends, but are more lucky than wise in predicting interim actions. Typically, bear markets move prices down faster than bull markets move them up.

Remember the psychology: fear is a more powerful emotion than greed. Disillusion and deflation panic traders more than illusion and inflation exhilarate them.

(2) **Intermediate market movements within a major bull or bear market:** These usually run for about four to eight months. These are ever-present, ever-changing and are most rewarding with groups of stocks. After 70% of the stocks in a group start to rise in price, ie, their three-week (15-day) moving averages are rising faster than their 10-week (50-day) MAs, this is an intermediate cycle rally. In a confirmed bear market, it could last up to about four months (a good time to cover shorts), and in a bull market it could last eight months or more (a time to buy).

(3) **Seasonal market movements of a month or so.** These can be superimposed on intermediate swings. They tend to follow established patterns and often concern only a few stock groups significantly, but generally apply to all securities.

(4) **Very short-term fluctuations of days, possibly weeks.** These are important mostly to day traders, but have importance also in executing longer-term trades.

The conservative trader wants to catch the turn of major (multi-year) bull or bear markets; the enterprising (less conservative) ones watch for immediate movements (four to eight months); the speculative trader relishes the seasonal swings; and the day traders are alert to the day-to-day fluctuations.

All serious traders should understand the broad trend and cycle movements of the stock market in order to sharpen their timing.

Trading Stocks (Also Called Equities)

Overall, while I do admit that market timing is always difficult, it clearly is not impossible. Technicians rely on chart patterns and indicators, and fundamentalists look for signs of value bargains or overpricing. Economists and quantitative analysts also have their tools. They all recognize that there are patterns that can be used successfully by traders. For example, they know that, on the average, the price of a stock will swing 20% to 25% every year. This spread represents the profit that traders look for.

There are hundreds of trading timing tools, called "indicators" by market timers, that attempt to spot and pinpoint all four of the different market movements (long-term, intermediate-term, seasonal and very short-term). Some work some of the time.

Use relativity ratios to analyze such price movements. These measure the change in the price of a stock (or group of stocks) against an index.

(A) The "beta". Beta is based on the S&P 500 Stock Index, which is the professional money manager's proxy for the overall equity market. A stock with a beta of 1.25 has 25% more volatility (and thus risk) than the market. This means that it is likely to fall or rise 25% more than the general level of stock prices.

In terms of trading, the conservative trader would choose low-beta stocks, which are those stocks that have a beta below 1.00. In a down market, they decline less than average and in a rising market, their gain would be relatively smaller. The aggressive trader would concentrate on high-beta stocks.

It is important to keep abreast of developments in this area because stock/group betas can change markedly over the years. In 1973, drug stocks had a beta of .79, so were considered defensive. By 1979, the industry beta had risen to 1.24, ie, 24% greater volatility than the overall market. Recently their beta has fallen to just under 1.00.

(B) Stock/bond yields. This ratio can be useful in determining when to move from bonds to stocks or back. It was not overly valuable in years when there were super-high yields for most fixed-income securities, but is a good one today. As a frame of reference, the premise is sound, which is that there is always competition for capital between stocks and bonds.

The total return of common stocks (ie, dividends plus capital appreciation) is weighed against the interest of bonds. This relationship, while crucial to your understanding of capital markets, has changed over the years, especially since interest rates began to rise in the 1960s and 70s and then fall in the 80s and 90s.

Lessons from the Trader Wizard

Back in the early 1960s, the difference was small — less than 1%. Most people preferred equity to debt. In the bull market years of the early 1970s, when stock prices were high and thus dividend yields low, the bond advantage widened so that many traders moved into bonds, especially with the stock-market downturn in 1974. Then, a timing signal was flashed in 1979 when the spread widened to over 4%, which was a clear signal that, to seek income, it was wise to shift some savings to bonds.

By and large, yield spreads are of more concern to professionals than to amateurs, but if you can come to understand them, you will better see what's happening in the capital markets' big picture. Your trading timing will be sure to improve.

(C) Value timing. This involves the use of PE ratios for market timing: to buy when the multiple of a specific stock is below the long-term average ratio, and to sell when it rises well above it.

This works better in theory than in practice.

Value timing tells you when a stock is under- or over-valued, but it cannot indicate when a favorable price movement will occur. Wall Street is slow to change its prejudices.

The price movements you want — and can believe in — may take months, even years, and are signaled by market action that reflects psychology more than logic.

Within any one year, the price of a volatile stock may fluctuate as much as 100%, but there may be little or no change in its fundamental value. Thus, by buying an under-valued stock at the wrong time, you can tie up your money and miss potential profits that you might have made by buying a fairly valued stock or even an over-valued stock, at the right time.

During 1999, the prices of most equities zoomed up and up. They soared far beyond traditional values and the fundamentalists expressed dismay. But prices kept moving up under the pressure of institutional buying.

According to fundamental standards, even an aggressive trader should have sold GE at between 40 and 50 in 1999, when the PE ratio soared above 25. But GE roared to a high of 60 with a multiple of over 30-times earnings in 2000. In retrospect, the fundamentalists were right, as usual, but their timing was wrong. By 2001, GE had fallen way down, to 22 — along with almost all the Dow 30 Industrials.

The value approach, particularly when combined with technical analysis, can be extremely rewarding and relatively safe. The big losses take place

Trading Stocks (Also Called Equities)

when you fail to heed the signals on market action and the facts of corporate growth and profits.

Guidelines for "when" to buy a stock

All decision rules for buying boil down to this: it's not *what* to buy, but *when* to buy that counts most. Note that I didn't say "counts always". But, if and when it's the right time to buy a stock, the turkeys are going to fly like eagles and the dogs run like ponies.

Used appropriately, market timing is an effective tool for seeking trading profit: it can help you buy and it can help you sell. Knowing when to buy is next in importance to knowing when to sell. Of course, you have to learn both.

Generally, I say buy stocks of corporations when you see that they have:

(1)   under-valued assets, ie, when the business value of the assets is greater than the stock market value;

(2)   bright business prospects, ie, when corporate revenues and earnings have compound annual rates of growth that lead or are close to leading their industry group; and

(3)   popular management (thanks to the marketing power of the media).

So much for the general approach.

But "buying" means buying a stock, not the company. There is a difference.

Guidelines for buying a stock

Patience. For conservative long-term traders, you should buy only if and when you can anticipate total returns to be at least 40% in the next 24 months. That will likely assure that you achieve average annual total returns of at least 15% on your money. If you are a short-term trader, your time horizon is less — usually three months or less. I say if you can get a 7% trading profit within two months, 10% profit in three months, or 14% profit in four months, take it. This tactic works very well for the large-cap blue-chip Dow 30 stocks or the S&P100 constituent stocks.

Market momentum. Once the big picture looks favorable, then zoom in on the target. You start by looking to buy a rising market, then a rising industry sector, then a rising group, then a rising stock. When selling short, ie, where the buying comes later, you would do the reverse in that you would look for a falling market, then a falling industry sector, then a falling group, then a falling stock.

Buying the trend reversal. It's my experience that unless you are willing to hold a position for a while, the best time to buy a stock is when its price is rising shortly after reversing a declining price trend. I look at the long-term (monthly data), intermediate-term (weekly data) and short-term (daily data). The buy signal comes when the intermediate-term moving average has reversed a falling trend and has intersected the long-term MA, which is flat or rising. This indicator must be confirmed by the action of the short-term MA intersecting the intermediate-term MA and rising.

Buying on the break-out. There is one concept that some traders use in timing purchases, especially in a bull market. They buy high and sell higher. I don't like this particular tactic, because I believe in cycles trading rather than pattern trading, but if the break-out applies to a downtrend line, then it's no different than buying on the trend reversal, which is a good tactic, in my view.

Trading mostly in a 20–40 range since October 2000 to August 2007, except for two brief dips into the teens, DELL went above 30 in May 2003. Market timers who bought on the break-out saw their stock go quickly to 37 by the 4Q and to over 40 by year-end 2004. Then it headed south to 20 by mid-2006, at which point it should have been bought again. I prefer to buy the dips, although in the case of DELL, those who bought the break-out also did very well.

Buying the dips. In a seasoned stock that trades for weeks or months in a clearly defined range, you can buy the dips. When you come across a stock you like, say DELL, that is trading in a consistent price range, you could buy it when its price dips, eg, when it dropped to a short-term $19.14 on July 21, 2006, I recommended you buy. See my blog entry entitled "DELL enters My Accumulation Zone" (http://www.billcara.com/archives/2006/07/dell_enters_my.html). Within a year, DELL hit a high of $29.61 and is still above $28 (August 2007).

If you are adding to core positions in a rising phase of a bull market, you ought to be buying the dips. But since the media is almost always telling you the market is bullish, you may take your eye off the ball in a bear phase of a bull market or a bear market. That is when the important trend reversals occur, which is when you ought to be buying most of your new positions.

Volume. With the use of the stock options market, the significance of volume alone may not be as significant as in the past. For example, to disguise his interest in accumulating a block of stock, a major buyer might, in fact, sell stock and simultaneously buy enough call options to allow him to meet his objectives.

Still, traders who follow volume statistics believe that significant changes in volume precede significant changes in price. The logic here is that unless a substantial number of people are interested in the stock, its price will move within a narrow range. Only when there is additional activity will the stock price change significantly, which is to say, they go up when corporate prospects are bright and down when gloomy. When corporate sales increase, corporate insiders tend to have the confidence to put up their money to back their opinion. Vice versa on the downside.

In my experience, volume is a better indicator for timing the purchase of small company stocks. I used to work with a speculative trader who religiously followed the large block trades of micro-cap "penny" stocks. Whenever he would observe a significant block trade after a sustained downtrend in prices, he would buy the stock. He didn't care about the company in the least. The name could have been Consolidated Moose Pasture for all he cared. But, inevitably his purchases turned into huge gains. In fact, that trader entered a national securities trading contest using that tactic and came third out of several thousand contestants.

Absence of hype. There is a saying in the market that "stocks aren't bought, they are sold". What this means is that there are tens of thousands of listed stocks, but only a few in your portfolio and, typically, you bought them only when somebody sold them to you. So I look for the absence of hype when buying a stock, because I know that independently minded contrarian traders are more successful than those who get caught up in the hype.

Timing errors

The usual timing-related errors made by traders are:

Not selling in the Distribution Zone. That is, soon after the price trend and cycle of the stock has reversed from up to down. If a stock is held at a loss and switching could strengthen your portfolio, the tendency is to take no action. As a result, you soon get locked in with your worst performing stocks.

Not selling losers. It is a shame to refuse to sell stocks when they soar to unusually high levels far beyond any normal range and logical maximum value. This happens when even bad stocks become popular. By definition, this is the time to be selling — because the danger of a price drop is far greater than the probability of a further meaningful gain. You should sell them all, even companies such as GE. Best bet: Depending on how risk averse you are, set actual or mental stop orders at 8% to 12% below current market prices in a strong market. By doing so in 2001 with GE, you would have obtained a sale well above 50, on its way to 22.

Not buying in the accumulation zone. That is when the price of the stock is at a low point of cycle (POC), even though the prospects for profitable growth by the company and the industry are good. It is looking the gift horse in the mouth to refuse to buy at the point at which stocks are unpopular and bargains can be found. It is a sad fact that when stock prices are really low, as they were in 2001–2002, most people are unwilling to buy and that when stock prices are really high, as they were in 1999–2000, most people forget the logical prospects and buy avidly.

I'll describe, with an illustration, POC theory elsewhere in the book.

Summary

The basic rules for the successful timing of trades are to buy stocks when they are technically over-sold and unpopular and to sell when they become fully priced and are very popular.

If all this means "buy low and sell high", then do it, and if you are ridiculed for your clichéd or simple approach to trading, so be it.

To all those losers who say you can't time the market, I say "phooey".

George Soros didn't make himself a billionaire shorting the British pound without being a market timer. Warren Buffett didn't earn an annual 26% portfolio performance without expert timing either. There is nothing wrong with market timing as practiced by those two traders.

Mastering the market requires much more of traders than just reacting to it. You'll have to learn when to buy and when to sell, and that means having a plan in place where you have the skills to be proactive. As I say, I prefer the tactic of buying stocks mostly on the trend reversals and occasionally on short-term weakness, ie, on the dips.

At the end of the day, timing is a tool you have to have in your toolbox, but it is double-edged sword. Unless one is nimble, bad timing also cuts profits and often leads to losses.

Guidelines for "when" to sell a stock

Overall, it's emotionally easier to buy than to sell a stock, so knowing "when" to buy is not quite half the challenge. A little harder is knowing "when" to sell.

Trading Stocks (Also Called Equities)

Selling stocks is a more difficult challenge than buying because taking a loss is always hard to do and it's not easy to sell a stock when it's high-priced, popular and profitable. Moreover, there is a double-edged sword to bad timing: you can turn paper losses to real losses.

Yes, selling is an emotional experience for many people. But if you can't overcome your emotions and master the techniques of trading, which includes pulling the trigger to sell, then you can't become a good trader.

You can love your stocks, but how can you make real profits and avoid real losses if you don't ever sell them? For successful trading, the timing of sell decisions is crucial and doing so demands strict adherence to guidelines.

If you don't follow a guideline for selling, you fall prey to human nature. It is only human to want to boast about one's profit-making skill in the world of high finance, but that is basically just stroking your ego. Others don't want to miss the top of the price cycle, which is fear and greed at work. So you need to learn how to sell.

Let's begin with the facts. Stocks are merely prices. They're not your children. Moreover, they are prices set by people and forces other than yourself. You have virtually no say in the matter. You could, I suppose, operate on the "greater fool theory" that, regardless of how high the price of a stock is, a "greater fool" will come along and buy it from you. But what happens when the price cycle tops out and there are no more carefree buyers? You can quickly lose your profit and then end up with losses.

Here are some selling considerations:

(1) **Take profits when better gains are likely in another stock**. Stocks trade in rhythmic cycles. In addition to the regular cycles of most stocks, there are also counter-cyclical price patterns in the market. As stock prices tend to be based on profits to a degree, the counter-cyclicality in the markets occurs because products bought by one company are sold by another.

What's good for one company might be bad for another. For example, the airlines need cheap fuel costs, but their suppliers would like to see high fuel prices.

As fuel prices increase, the oil companies make greater profits. But then the costs to the airlines are higher and their profits fall. This knowledge leads to traders buying one group and simultaneously selling another.

Lessons from the Trader Wizard

(2) **Sell when the original reasons for the purchase no longer hold.**
There are three basic reasons you bought any stock:

- Your study showed that this was a sound company with good prospects for profitable growth.

- You believed that something good was going to happen: at the time you believed the stock may be split, the company was getting a big new contract, a new, profitable product, an acquisition, etc.

- Reports or charts showed that smart money was moving into the stock.

(3) **When the overall market trend clearly reverses.** On the long-term chart trend line on the DJIA (or any other standard stock-market indicator), there were obvious selling points in 1973, 1981, 1987 and 2000.

Items (2) and (3) are usually reasons for a quick rise in the price of the equity. There should be quick action. If there is not, sell. You were wrong.

For the first item (1), you only sell if you fear a bear market, because it's true that all boats rise and fall with the tide.

In my opinion, over the past 30 years there were four major stock market tops that strongly indicated selling was in order. Arguably there were others but, without question, all traders should have sold their stocks four times in 30 years and used the cash to buy them back (and a lot more) within one to two years later.

Technicians would say that whenever the 10-week moving average turns down and intersects a flat 40-week MA, that is a very good time to sell.

(4) **When an industry becomes unpopular.** In early 2000, it became clear that traders were questioning the viability of the corporate business models in the dot-com industry. There was clearly a price bubble in the market as stocks that were selling in the hundreds of dollars were not going to see any corporate earnings for many years, if ever. So reality finally overcame emotion and the bubble was burst.

But the damage wasn't localized. The dot-coms had hired people and leased office space and purchased expensive computing facilities for them. The employees bought homes as well as furniture and appliances

247

for these new homes, and they bought cars and spent money on gas for their cars to get to and from the workplace. They traveled extensively on business and took vacations. This huge money supply was circulating in the general economy, so earnings were up in many industry sectors.

When the dot-com bubble burst, the economic crash was felt world-wide. That happened long before the global crisis known as 9/11 in 2001.

The dot-com stocks' price crash, which began in March 2000, showed clearly that the market does not operate in a vacuum. A single industry might very well become particularly unpopular, but traders have to watch for the fall-out in other industries.

Dot-com stocks that were once so popular may never come back. At least half of them are now bankrupt. But other industries (like financial services, information technology, etc) that did in fact profit from the 1995-2000 boom in dot-coms, recovered.

The wise trader sold all stocks in the first half of 2000, including the best quality, and simply waited for bargains among these to re-appear.

The long-term trader has had to be patient in recent years because the aftermath of a stock bubble is usually a lengthy bear phase, which is exactly what happened from 1Q2000 through into 4Q2002.

After the Dow 30 Industrials 10-week moving average turned up and intersected the 40-week MA, patient traders can be confident the market has hit bottom as it did early in 4Q2002. Successful long-term-oriented traders once again started to buy the highest-rated quality stocks in the industries that were becoming popular again.

(5) **After a big score or a big change in your life.** If you just hit the lottery, got married, changed jobs, moved to a new home or just sold assets at a substantial profit, it's always a good idea to pull out of the market. You have to get your emotions under control.

During this period, when your mind is on other things, you may be too quick to listen to sales people urging you on to buy another stock. Rather, you should be thinking about selling your holdings. Let the market go for a few weeks. Give it a rest. Then, after you have cleared your head, you can make sure that the next stock you buy has a potential gain of 40%. You can focus on good buying tactics. Otherwise sit on the sidelines.

Lessons from the Trader Wizard

(6) **After three straight losses, sell everything.** If you have been following my guidelines and you still strike out three times in a row, there is a problem. I recommend you get out of the market while you study the reasons for your lack of success.

(7) **After eight months of a broad market rally in a bull market and a four-month rally in a bear market.** At some point, the up-moving stocks are likely to pause under the pressure of sales by profit-taking traders who take control of the market for a while. This is a good time to reassess your holdings.

Regardless of when you invested, judge the time span from the week the up-trend started, not the date you bought the stock. Look at the price chart and make believe you bought at the bottom of the cycle. Then mark your trading calendar eight months forward. This is a rule of thumb most traders don't want to accept, but it's backed by common sense and proven results. Use it flexibly.

In a bull market, if a quality stock has appreciated in price by 50% or 100% within eight months, it's time to consider selling. You'll probably have an opportunity to buy back your position inside two months at favorable prices.

(8) **On a breakdown of a consolidation pattern.** Quality stocks seldom spike upwards to a peak and then crash. They almost always form a consolidation area where the price moves up and down within a relatively narrow range. Hold as long as the stock stays within this channel pattern. But the minute there's a breakthrough on the downside, be prepared to sell and then, if the penetration is confirmed in the next day or so, sell.

(9) **If and when the dividend income falls short of your needs.** People who need maximum income on their money should not hesitate to sell and take their capital gains, if the return on their current trading is considerably lower than could be obtained elsewhere.

(10) **When the company plans to issue convertible debentures or convertible preferred stock.** This puts potentially more shares on the market and thus will dilute the corporate earnings. Also, CVs are usually issued when the market is most favorable and the securities can command the highest prices. Of 141 NYSE companies that issued CVs in the buoyant market of the late 1960s, the common stock of 70% of these companies fell 25% or more within the next nine months.

(11) **When your stock runs up on news that the company is to be taken over by another.** There are several good reasons to sell promptly.

249

Trading Stocks (Also Called Equities)

First, proposals do not always end in marriage, and second, there is no guarantee that a merger will be successful. Most important, the stock market sours quickly on acquisitions. In the 1960s, of 56 stocks that moved up on news of a proposed merger, 71% of them fell 25% or more within the next nine months. Sell quickly, because most of the declines occur in the first three months.

Of course, if you have reason to believe the takeover will be completed and then result in a much stronger organization, you will make your judgment on a different, sounder basis.

(12) **When your stock moves up too fast.** If you are fortunate to pick a stock that moves up 40% to 50% in a couple of months, definitely set a stop order. NYSE records show that of 55 stocks that achieved a 50% gain in a short period, 39 fell 25% or more within the next six months.

(13) **If there's a chance you could lose 20% or more in the next eight months**. Don't try to get the absolute top price when selling. When there's a significant 4-10% price decline with heavy volume, don't wait for an explanation. Nobody's going to explain it to you. Make your own move. The stock could whipsaw after you've sold, and you might miss a further 2% or 3% gain, but better a small profit than none.

(14) **Always sell too soon.** When a stock becomes overpriced, the risks of a severe decline are far greater than the rewards of further gains. Take your profits and go to another stock that will provide similar profits in the future.

Very few securities reach prices that reflect PE ratios well beyond their typical upper range. When they do, it's usually wiser to let others test the unfamiliar ground. Or set stop prices to protect your profits.

I believe very much in a concept called "reversion to the mean". The further a stock gets outside its normal trading pattern, the more I believe it will swing back. This oscillation can be charted around a zero line, which is simply the long-term trend or norm. At the upper peak of this oscillation, I'm a seller, and at the apparent low point in the cycle, I'm a buyer.

Since I can't tell whether the peak has been reached, I will almost always sell too early. Similarly, on the downside, I usually wait too long before buying.

Lessons from the Trader Wizard

The key to success is not to hit the top and the bottom, but to try to consistently meet a goal of 40% portfolio gain per year. I never do, of course, unless the market is particularly favorable to the type of trading I favor, but 20% to 25% per year is not too bad. If you check the hundreds — even thousands — of professionally managed mutual funds, you sure won't find many at the 20% performance level over 10+ years.

But by learning to sell too soon, you'll become successful with your trading program. A net gain of 24% compounded annually will double your assets in just three years (if you recall the rule of 72). I believe that is a reasonable goal for residents of a zero-tax country. I agree it's really tough for those in a high tax bracket.

(15)   **When insiders are selling.** When there are twice as many (or more) sellers than buyers, something unfavorable might be coming up. Many traders use this indicator to get out before bad news might hit the wires. I list it here because I could be wrong, but if I'm part of the typical management of a solid growth corporation, I too would be a seller, simply because I wouldn't want all my eggs in one basket.

If I'm an expert in, say, the field of discount brokerage, I'd be selling some of my management option shares and using the proceeds to invest possibly in Ameritrade (AMTD), if that was a stock that I believed had a possible 40% upside in 12 months. So, I can't fault others doing it.

(16)   **When you start to doubt yourself.** If you have difficulty asking yourself, "If I were making a brand new trade, would I buy this particular stock at this price and at this time, above all others?" If the answer is an unqualified "yes", then hold. But, if you have doubts, set up target selling prices on both the up- and down-side. And, if the answer is a clear-cut "no", then sell at once.

(17)   **Use stop orders and allow the market action to make the sale.** Stop orders placed with a broker can protect your profits or minimize your losses. There is, of course, a risk that your broker uses this knowledge to trade against you, but the market is what it is. If you are so concerned, then find a new broker.

There are two handy ways to implement stop orders:

(1)   **Enter a good-until-canceled stop order.** This will vary with the price range and the volatility of the stock, but as a rule, 6% below the purchase price or, if higher, to 8-10% below the recent cycle high price. With a stock at 50, set the stop at 47.00. Use

251

Trading Stocks (Also Called Equities)

pennies above the usual rounding (eg, 47.10), because in a fast-falling market your round-number stop may not be executed. If the stock goes up to 55, move the stop up.

(2)   **Use a mental stop order**. This requires discipline and constant surveillance of the stock market. It is valuable only for the disciplined trader. Every day you should set a price below which you do not want to own the stock. Each night, you should check the closing price and then decide your next day's action. That's called a trading plan. If the price trend is down and the volume is up for several days, you should act promptly.

The difficulty with a mental stop order approach is that it is too easy to delay or change your mind. Most people wait for a rally. By the time they do act, they have lost a couple more points than anticipated.

If you have a strong personal discipline as well as the time to observe intra-day trading prices, then "mental" stops are best.

Summary

Because I recognize that it's emotionally difficult to sell a stock, especially if it's at a loss or if it has failed to reach my target price, I prefer the tactic of selling stocks mostly on the basis of mechanical systems. I also establish general percentage gain targets, and sell when I determine that better percentage gains are available in other stocks, which I determine on the basis of trend and cycle reversal studies.

To help me in my trading, I use a form of time series trend and cycles analysis that can be described as a "trading oscillator" and theoretical market phases model.

14 Cara 500 market phases model and oscillator

I take capital markets seriously. I have simple systems or protocols to follow that help make that 65% of trades I do winning ones and not losers. I use time series analysis of market data. I don't read and then be influenced by the offerings of other publishers. Let's leave it at that.

August 16, 2007

A secret strategic weapon:
The Cara Trading Oscillator and the
Cara Market Phases Model

This is a daily, dynamically updated program that will help to pinpoint each of 500 stocks and ETFs on a three-wave time series model (long, intermediate and short-term). This will become an on-going premium service with attached PDF reports.

The Cara 500 represents the 100 top-quality tickers in each of five markets, as follows:

(1)   USA;
(2)   Canada and the Americas;
(3)   UK and Europe, including Eastern Europe;
(4)   Asia-Pacific and Southern Africa; and
(5)   Global ETFs.

I combine these 500 global stocks into (6) a Cara Global Best 100, which I write about in my free blog (http://billcara.com).

I have also compiled Cara 100 lists specifically for:

(7)   the Emerging Economies (Brazil, Russia, India and China);
(8)   fast-growing microcap stocks with market caps of under $1 billion;
(9)   high-quality high-risk speculative stocks with market caps typically, but not always, under $100 million; and
(10)   high-dividend-and-interest income securities.

Trading Stocks (Also Called Equities)

For the purposes of explanation, this book will show the Cara Global 100 only. In the coming year, I will publish separate books on (a) the specific methodologies used to select all Cara 100 stocks, in every category, and (b) the detailed formulation and description of my Market Phases Model and Trading Oscillator.

Part 4

Specialties to Trade

Yes, trading gives us hope in the same way that the struggling people in other lands managed to take control, doing it one stop at a time to build a mountain. Working together we can do it. In a virtual world, you and I and our brothers and sisters do not have to lock arms and raise our rifles to get ahead. We must, however, connect intellectually. We must share the same dreams, and we must plan, organize, implement and control our actions the same way that others have planned, organized, implemented and controlled us in order to get theirs. So the question is, are you going to adapt to the changes that are being forced upon us, or are you and I going to work together to bring about the change that benefits us? I think I know what you want. It's now up to us to put it together.

June 26, 2007

Specialties to Trade

1   About trading options

What we can do before Financial Armageddon inevitably strikes is to watch prices. We can continue to buy them when they are low and sell them when they are high based on relative historical performance and trading patterns. We can stick to trading the shares of quality corporations and buying risk-adjusted high-performace fixed income securities if that is our need.

We do not have to listen to the random noise that permeates the market place today, having our chain jerked from day-to-day. If we use preventative measures like put and call option strategies and stop orders, we ought to let a trending market (ie, extreme moves up or down as the case may be) take care of our decisions. That takes a little knowledge and much discipline. Other than writing about these things, I cannot do more.

June 8, 2007

Options on stocks are time-based contracts, each with an expiry date.

In buying or selling an option, you are buying or selling time. As you learn throughout this book, there is no concept more important in capital markets than time.

Rather than try to educate you directly, I'll point you to the best source of information, which is the Options Institute Online Learning Center of the Chicago Board Options Exchange (http://cboe.com/LearnCenter).

Another excellent source of options education plus tools is at Yahoo Finance (http://biz.yahoo.com/opt).

As a time-based trading instrument, options on stock are rights to buy or sell a specified number of shares (ie, 100 per contract) of a specified stock at a specified price (the striking price) before a specified date (the expiration date). Beginners may have to read that sentence a few times.

By definition, options are diminishing assets and they pay no dividends. And, the closer the expiration date, the less time there is for their value to rise or fall, which limits the trading or speculation interest in them.

Specialties to Trade

While it's not altogether simple, I view the act of buying an option alone without it being part of a larger plan as speculative trading, and selling an option as conservative trading.

Options are tools that enable trading strategies. I'm not in the club that likes to call an options trader a gambler, because it's simply not true. If you believe that, then you must also believe that soldiers and hunters have no right to guns. It's how you use the instrument that matters.

The most popular and widely used option is a "call", which is the right to buy the underlying stock on certain specified terms. A "put" is opposite to the call as it is the right to sell the stock, also with the terms attached.

For sophisticated traders, there are seemingly complex combinations such as spreads, strips, straps and straddles. All this, however, you can learn with several hours study.

The cost of an option is called the premium. It varies with the duration of the contract as well as the type of stock, the general activity of the stock market, and the corporation's status and prospects. By looking at the options data for a stock, you can see that premiums run as high perhaps as 15% of the value of the underlying stock.

For an example, let's turn the clock back to 5 November 200X, where for about $270, the trader could control 100 shares of Dow 30 ABC (the name's not important) selling at 74.53 ($7,453) for about 45 days. Once the price of ABC stock moves close to the exercise price of the option at 75, both stock and option will usually move together, often in small fractions of a point. Thus, the $270 investment can be just as profitable in absolute dollars as the $7,453 investment (not counting any dividends ABC might declare in the next 45 days).

What I find most interesting about the options market is that a single trade involves both prudent trading and speculation together. When options are used to protect positions or to acquire stock as part of a trading strategy, the other side of the trades in these puts and calls are speculations. So, one side of the trade is trading in the traditional sense and the other is probably speculating.

That means that traders who participate in the options market also have to know how to trade with skill. After all, if you wanted to drive your auto off the highway onto the racetrack, first you ought to know a few more things about driving.

Because of the time factor, simply buying call options can be risky to the speculative trader unless you know how to trade both the stocks and the options on the stocks. When the price of the stock declines, the value of the call option can drop faster and further percentage-wise than that of the stock and will probably expire worthless.

You have to be careful when speculating with calls. And, as the broad market tends to move up say 80 or 85% of the time (over say 20 to 40 years), you have to be careful buying puts as well.

However, selling (writing) calls on stocks you own can be a conservative strategy.

With experience, and the support of a knowledgeable broker and a good market, I believe a call-writing trader should obtain total returns at an annualized rate of 18-20%, which would be 13-15% from option premiums and 3-5% from dividends (as long as the stock is owned and used as collateral rather than cash, but, even with cash for margin you are going to earn interest on your credit balance).

Mystique

For some reason, there has always been a mystique about options. I suppose it's because options trading represents a zero-sum game where, at the bottom line, there is one winner and one loser and no other value created except for the employment of intermediaries.

Let me tell you about the day I thought I was going to be summarily fired from my position as a money manager with Canada's leading broker-dealer. It was all about options trading. Actually, when it comes right down to it, the issue was more to do with the mystique about options.

For background, you should know I happen to like options trading and learned to do it early in my securities industry career.

But, in my case, things almost didn't turn out so well on a matter related to options. As a money manager working for Canada's 800-pound broker-dealer gorilla, I had become an options expert in my own right. I had even been published in national journals. One day, during the absence of our departmental president, one of the other money managers came to me inquiring about options. After a brief educational session, he seemed excited and wanted to try using them on his own accounts.

This colleague was an elderly and particularly cautious man who was an heir of a world-famous family. He showed me the family's extensive investment portfolio and I immediately saw a ton of Canada's largest gold-mining company stock.

Specialties to Trade

The brother of our firm's chairman and CEO was a director and soon-to-be chairman of that gold mining company, and I just happened to be personally managing that particular family's portfolio as well, so I knew I'd be on uncertain ground when I advised my colleague to start trading "the crown jewels" in stock options.

I recommended a simple covered call-writing strategy. Remember, this was the biggest investment bank in the country, full of very conservative people who did not understand exchange-traded options — which, at the time, was a fairly new concept.

But, I also knew and understood the gold market fairly well too (as a trader, analyst, retail and institutional salesman, and underwriter of gold stocks) and I happened to know this particular corporation inside and out.

But, in terms of the market, I knew that when gold bullion prices go south, the stock prices of the major producers are soon to follow, so you have to trade these stocks — and more so the options — nimbly. "Nimble" is a favorite word of mine.

Gold had bottomed in mid-1982 at just under $300 and in the following year had spiked to the 400-500 range, whereupon I had correctly forecast that it would decline again for at least a year. So I believed the major gold stocks presented a great opportunity then to write (ie, sell) covered calls against a long stock position where, like my colleague, you don't want to (or because of family or business reasons can't) sell the stock.

If and when you're looking strictly for income, writing covered calls is an effective trading strategy. I can't say the same for writing calls naked (or even buying calls unless, of course, you have done your homework and trading like that is part of your speculative strategy).

If you sell the call when you also hold the underlying stock, you are "covered". If you have to borrow the stock to cover you, you are "naked".

The seller of a call option is looking to earn the option premium today, hoping the contract expires worthless later. The buyer, who takes the other side of the contract, is speculating on a rally in gold prices, whereupon they either sell the call option or exercise it at expiration. Being a zero-sum game, somebody wins and somebody loses.

When dealing in gold commodities and gold stocks, there is always the buzz of a potential rally in prices. Because of this interest, call options on gold stocks usually trade at excessive premiums. It can be a call writer's sweet dream, but could also be a nightmare.

Lessons from the Trader Wizard

So following my advice, my colleague wrote something like 2,000 calls, representing 200,000 shares, or about $4 million of his family portfolio. He took into income the premium of over $10,000 and was extremely happy to have received this "found" money.

On Monday, our boss returned from vacation and, after reading the trading blotter and spotting the big options trade, literally exploded. I heard it of course, because I occupied the adjoining office to his. I didn't think much of the commotion until he burst through my door waiving paperwork. "What have you done! (So-and-so) told me you put him up to this. He doesn't have a clue about options trading! Explain!"

After gathering myself, I did explain. I must have been effective explaining options to a boss who didn't understand them because I wasn't fired, as I had feared. I did agree to watch my colleague's position carefully and this episode did turn out successfully, as I had expected. The buyers of those calls were the losers and we were the winners. Were we speculating or trading? I definitely think the latter.

In my opinion, for 20-25 years after exchange trading of options was organized in 1974, no part of the securities markets has changed more. In the beginning, the number of options was limited, the volume was small and price changes were closely related to those of the related stocks. But in time, that became less so.

Today, there are options on everything from stocks to indexes, commodities and futures as well as esoteric things I don't even want to get into. Annual volume of equity options is into many billions of contracts representing probably trillions of shares of stock in the aggregate.

People say options are a cross between trading in stocks and trading in limited-life warrants or commodities, because they permit holders to control, for a specified time with a small amount of capital, a relatively large asset.

It is a mature and sophisticated market today, but options prices occasionally move inexplicably with little relation to the price movement in the underlying securities. So you have to be careful. Still, I believe that every trader should use options as part of an overall trading strategy. With careful management, options can boost income or bring short-term gains. Buying and selling techniques can also be structured for tax benefits.

Trying to figure out options premiums

When a stock trades at its exercise price, the options premium percentage, as a percentage of the underlying stock price, will vary simply depending on the volatility of the stock price. This is the table I use to explain the options premium percentage differences of low, average and high-volatility stocks:

Months to expiration	Premium as % of price of underlying stock		
	Low volatility	Average	High
1	1.8-2.6	3.5-4.4	5.2-6.1
2	2.6-3.9	5.2-6.6	7.8-9:2
3	3.3-5.0	6.7-8.3	10.0-11.7
4	3.9-5.9	7.9-9.8	11.8-13.8
5	4.5-6.8	9.0-11.2	13.5-15.8
6	5.0-7.5	10.0-12.5	15.0-17.5
7	5.5-8.2	10.9-13.7	16.4-19.2
8	5.9-8.9	11.8-14.8	17.7-20.6
9	6.4-9.5	12.7-15.9	19.0-22.2
10	6.8-10.1	13.5-16.9	20.2-23.6
11	7.2-10.7	14.3-17.9	21.4-25.0
12	7.5-11.2	15.0-18.8	22.5-26.2

- **Dividends and rights**: As long as you own the stock, you continue to receive the dividends. That's why calls for stocks with high yields sell at lower premiums than those of companies with small dividend payouts.

  A stock dividend or stock split automatically increases the number of shares covered by the option in an exact proportion. If a right is involved, its value will be set by the first sale of rights on the day the stock sells "ex rights".

- **Commissions**: These depend on your broker-dealer.

I could get into detail here about Smart routing and Directed routing, but if you happen to have a serious interest in trading options, there is a plethora of such information at options specialist brokers like Interactive Brokers and OptionXpress (both of which are Cara 100 companies, by the way).

Strategies for writing call options

Writing (ie, selling) calls is a trading strategy for conservative traders. It is not a speculation. If you think it is because of the risks involved, then by your definition all trading must be speculating.

In writing calls, you start off with an immediate and certain profit rather than an uncertain, potentially greater gain.

Lessons from the Trader Wizard

You have three choices. You can trade them (1) on-the-money; (2) in-the-money; or (3) out-of-the-money.

On-the-money calls

These are written at an exercise price that is at, or close to, the current price of the stock.

Example: On 5 November, Mr. Smith buys 100 shares of ABC at 74.50 and sells a May call at a striking price of 75, for 5.50 ($550). The buyer acquires the right to buy this stock at 75 any time before the expiration date near the end of May.

Mr. Smith will not sustain a dollar loss until the price of ABC goes below 69, which is $74.50 less the premium income of $5.50. He will probably not have the stock called away from him until its price moves above 80.50.

Let's see how the trade might work out for both sides.

By May, say ABC has moved up from 74.50 to 82 (ie, +10.1%) so the call option is now well in-the-money. The buyer can exercise his option, pay $7,500 and acquire the shares, which are now worth $8,200, from Mr. Smith. After deducting about $600 costs (ie, the $550 premium paid to Mr. Smith plus two commissions), he will have a net profit of $100, which increases his capital over six and a half months by +18.2% (ie, 100/550) on this trade. This call buyer was able to take advantage of the leverage of options.

But if the price of ABC moves up to only 77.50, the call buyer will take a loss of $350, while Mr. Smith will keep about $615, which is the $550 premium plus two quarterly dividends of about $37.50 each, minus a $10 commission paid on the call sale.

On a trade of $7,450 plus $10 commission, Mr. Smith then made +8.3% (ie, 615/7460) for a Six and a half month hold, which is about +15.3% annualized return.

Typically, the call would have been exercised earlier, resulting in a much higher return.

If the price of ABC soars to the mid-80s or higher (really how high can this mature and stable blue-chip ABC go?), then Mr. Smith would lose out on the gains he could have made by not selling the call against his position. But isn't he going to be satisfied with a return of +16% to +24% per year?

If the price of ABC falls, the call option expires worthless. But Mr. Smith has applied that $625 gain against his cost of ABC, which lowers his cost base to

68.25. In fact, he can write a new call against his position after the first one expired. Over a period of years, Mr. Smith can do quite well with call premium income and dividend income in this relatively stable core stock position.

With all calls, there's flexibility and, often, several alternative strategies.

In-the-money calls

This is a more aggressive technique that requires close attention, but one that can result in fine profits and tax benefits for those in high income-tax brackets. The calls are written below the current stock price.

Example: You buy ABC at 209 and sell two in-the-money calls, at a striking price of 200, for 25 ($2,500 each). If ABC goes to 250, you buy back the calls at 50 ($5,000 each), take an ordinary loss of $5,000, then sell the shares for a $4,100 gain. In a 50% tax bracket, the loss saves $2,500 in taxes, and the after-tax gain is $3,280.

If ABC declines, there are no ordinary losses for tax purposes. But you can still make money if the stock ends its option period between 209 and 185. Between 209 and 201, everything is a capital gain. At 201, if the call is exercised, there's an initial $5,000 capital gain. You must deliver the shares for an $800 loss and can buy another 100 shares at market for another $100 loss. But the net is a satisfactory $4,100 — all taxable at the low long-term rate.

At 200 or lower, the calls are worthless, so you pocket $2,500, after taxes, as ordinary income. From this, deduct the $900 loss on the stock for a net gain of $1,600.

Deep-in-the-money calls

These are calls that are sold at striking prices below the current quotation of the stock. Writing them is best when the trader is dealing in large blocks of stock, because of the almost-certain commissions that have to be paid when the underlying stock is called. The best selection is a dividend-paying, low-volatility stock of a well-known company that yields about 4.75%.

The call seller always accepts a limited, but certain, profit, rather than a potentially bigger gain.

There are two approaches:

(1)   **Using the leverage of options**: when the exercise price of the call is below that of the current value of the stock, both securities tend to

264

move in unison. Since the options involve a smaller dollar position, there's a higher percentage of return and, in a down market, more protection against loss.

For example, ABC is selling at 97.63. The call price at 70 two months out is 28, so the equivalent price is 98. If ABC goes to 105, the call should keep pace and be worth 35.

If you bought 100 shares of the stock, the total cost would be about $9,800. Your ultimate profit would be about $550, close to a 5.5% return. If you bought 10 options, the dollar profit would be a 22.4% return on the smaller $2,900 position. If the stock does not move, you can let it go or buy back the calls at a small loss. If ABC declines, your maximum loss is $2,900, probably much less than that of the stock.

(2) **Creating cost**: basing your return on the total income received from the premium and dividends.

For example, In January, you buy 1,000 shares of ABC at 39.50. You sell April 35 options for 6.88 each, thereby reducing the price per share to 32.63. There's a 45¢ per share dividend due before the exercise date.

If the call is exercised, the total return will be $7.33 on a $32.63 position, which is a 22.5% gross profit in four months. Even after commissions, the annual rate of return is excellent, and the stock will have to drop below 33 before there's a paper loss.

Out-of-the-money calls

These are written at exercise prices well above the current quotation for the stock. They are best suited for traders who want to combine modest income and capital gains and still retain ownership of the stock.

Example: In March, Mr. Smith buys 300 shares of ABC at 50.50, then writes three October calls, at the striking price of 60 at 1 ($100) to get $300 immediate income.

If the stock stays below 60 for the next seven months, he keeps the premiums, dividends and stock, and writes new calls.

If ABC goes above 60 before the end of October, Mr. Smith can protect his position by buying back the calls just before the exercise deadline. He will have to put up cash to do this but, like he did with ABC, he will keep the stock with its 9½ points of unrealized gains. By repeating this process, he will strengthen his portfolio and add to his income.

This approach has risks:

- in a rising market, such good deals are hard to find because the price of the stock must have declined sharply and quickly in order to have the 60 option still listed;

- the stock may move up just as rapidly and be called before the expiration date;

- the price of the stock may continue to drop. Mr. Smith takes in cash but has paper losses.

Still, with quality stocks the risks of substantial declines are small if calls can be written again and again, as explained earlier.

Guidelines for writing options

- Be disciplined. Have a minimum of $25,000 in securities and be ready to write options every month, or more often if the situation looks unusually promising. Don't have all your money in the same types of securities and try to space the dates on which the options can be exercised.

- Set a target rate of return. If you want a 15% annual return, you will have to wait for premiums of over 10% for six-month contracts or 6% for three-month expiration dates. The dividends and turnover will bring such income.

  Unless you are very confident in correctly assessing the stock-price trend, it's wise to start thinking about getting out if, and when, you double your money or can buy back the option at a net cost half of that of your position cost. For instance, if you bought a call at 1, get ready to sell at 2.10 (the extra amount to pay for commissions). If you sold a call at 4, buy it back when its value drops below 2. You can possibly make more if you hang on, but in today's volatile market, that's probably too risky.

- Focus only on stocks you'd like to own based on their merits.

- Until you get experienced at this, try to write long-term calls (six to 12 months). The longer the option period, the greater the percentage of premium. With most stocks, profits require at least four or, in erratic markets, six months.

Lessons from the Trader Wizard

- Try to keep capital fully employed. Well before an option's expiration date, be ready to sell another one. You are dealing in percentages, so keep those premiums rolling in. Except in a roaring bull market, the odds are that you will retain the stock. It's best to have a list of 10 stocks: five in your portfolio, five others for replacements. Generally, the premiums move with the price of the stock.

- Own the stock on which you sell a call. When you become an expert, you can buy the stock immediately after you write the option. Before then, don't try to outsmart the professionals. It's best to buy the stock and then wait for a profitable option. Once you have decided that the stock is fairly priced or, better yet, undervalued, wait for a temporary dip to buy. Then be patient and don't write a call until you know the total percentage return you want.

About writing naked calls

If you keep a substantial margin account and have experience in trading options, you are permitted to write "naked" calls (that is, selling calls without owning the stock). This can be risky if the stock is volatile and could move up a lot. With options, you could cover your position by buying another call even though it's at a higher price than where you sold the option. You will lose some or all the premium, but keep the stock and its paper profit.

When you write an option, you are betting that the stock will not fluctuate greatly, that is:

- it will not go up by more than the amount of the premium (if the exercise price is below the present market price); or

- it will not go up beyond the exercise price plus the amount of the premium (if the exercise price is above the present market price).

About writing put options

This is my favorite. Writing (ie, selling) puts is an effective trading strategy (not a speculation) used by proactive traders. It's a way of trying to make something happen; and if it doesn't, you get paid anyway.

In writing puts, you receive an immediate gain but, until the expiration date, you must be ready to buy the stock if it starts selling at or below the exercise price. Maybe that's your objective. If so, put writing is a good trading strategy, because it provides income and also the opportunity to buy stocks at below current prices.

Specialties to Trade

Most traders write puts against cash (unless they have a lot of marginable high dividend-paying stocks). These are naked options, so you must meet substantial margin requirements and probably have readily available assets of $25,000 or more.

Example: ABC stock is at 53 and you like it, but will only buy at a lower price. You think it will probably stay level or go higher. You hope that it falls to your mental price level. So, you write an in-the-money put at 50 and receive 2.25 ($225). If you guess right, and the value of the stock remains the same or rises, you earn the $225 income from the premium and nothing else happens, as the put you sold expires worthless.

As long as ABC stock stays above 50, the put will not be exercised. But once it falls below 50, you must be ready to buy the stock (or buy a comparable put). If the stock falls to 49, you will have the 100 shares of stock put to you at 50. But, while you have to pay $5,000, your cost is reduced by the $225 premium income, so your net cost was 47.75.

This is an excellent strategy for patient traders who have the cash resources available to bottom pick markets. The problems start when you write puts right at the onset of a bear market as one of my partners did in the spring of 2000. In our example, ABC probably fell through the 47-50 level on its way to 25-30. If you indiscriminately wrote a lot of puts in 2000, you unfortunately bought a lot of stock losses.

Guidelines on writing naked puts

Writing naked puts is approximately the same risk as writing covered calls. But selling the puts has the following extra advantages:

- lower commissions, because unless you are writing out-of-the-money calls, you must include the cost of selling the stock when called;

- less margin money than needed to write the same amount of covered calls; and

- when cash is used as margin, you may get a higher yield on your money from the broker-dealer than you receive from dividends on stock. If the broker pays LIBOR less half a point, then you probably were earning 4% or more through 2007. You're not earning the dividend tax credit, but if a lot of your stocks are in the 0-2% yield range, then you might as well be in cash anyway.

Lessons from the Trader Wizard

A conservative trader should only write naked puts if:

- the underlying stocks are fundamentally strong;

- there are sufficient funds in the account to complete purchases of put stock; and

- you aren't afraid to buy back puts if you change your mind or the market does it for you.

Strategies for buying call options

In some months, 90% of all calls (or puts) expire worthless, although many positions have been rolled over, which is also costly, so I guess you can say buying options naked is extremely risky. This sounds intimidating, but in reality most losing options are rolled over before the expiry date.

Still, there are significant risks to buying call option contracts (as opposed to writing), so it's best to buy them in a broadly rising market, and to buy them in the stocks of a rising industry group or peer group. Obviously if you're buying puts you'd want to do that in a weakening market, within an out-of-favor industry group.

There are two broad approaches to buying calls:

- Buying long-term, out-of-the-money call options at a low premium (usually one or less). By diversifying with three or four promising, but very risky situations, you might be lucky to win big enough with one of them to more than offset a loss on another.

- Buying short- or intermediate-term, in-the-money or close-to-the-money options of popular, volatile stocks. Example: a call with two months to expiry, a stock within 5% of striking price and a low-time premium. If the stock rallies strongly and pushes the premium to double your cost, then sell. If you have three or more options, sell when you have a 50% gross profit. One expert says: "Never pay a premium of more than three for a call on a stock selling under 50, nor more than five for one trading over 60."

The striking price of the option and the market price of the stock should change by about half as many points as the change in the stock price: for example, if a 30 option is worth five when the stock is at 30, then it should fall 2.50 to 2.50 when the stock falls five to 25, and when the stock moves up six to 36, it should grow by three to be worth eight.

269

Specialties to Trade

Here are some guidelines for determining how much to pay for newly listed calls where the time premium is high:

- Watch the spread prices. When trading a particular month's option, always look at the premiums on the adjacent month options to see if they are in line.

- Watch for unusual situations. Normally the prices of options move with the prices of the underlying stocks. But there are periods when premiums move up and down on their own. Often call premiums drop more than the related stocks.

Example: In November, when ABC stock was at 23.38, the 25 May calls were quoted at 2.38. By late December, the stock was up a touch to 24, but the option, which, theoretically, should have dropped about 5% with the time factor, fell 16% to 2.

If this unusual spread increases, it might be worthwhile to buy back the call and look for more rewarding premiums in the August calls.

Strategies for buying put options

Put options can be bought either for profit or for protection, but time is of the essence. Like any option, a put is a wasting asset, since its value will diminish with the approach of the expiration date.

As I have stated, a put is the opposite of a call. It gives the option owner the right to sell a specified number of shares (usually 100) of a specified stock, at a specified price before a specified date. Puts have the same expiration months, dates and pricing structure as calls.

But a put is a distinct entity. Its intrinsic value increases with a decrease in the value of the related stock. You buy a put when you are bearish and anticipate the market or stock will decline. During 2000-2002, puts became very popular.

Properly handled, they can extend the range of trading and tax strategies, open new profit opportunities, provide bear market protection and, in fast-moving markets, yield excellent rewards.

As with calls, the attraction of puts is leverage. For a few hundred dollars you can control stock worth thousands. Generally the premiums will be smaller than those of calls because of lesser demand. In a bear market, there are more optimists than pessimists. The best candidates for stocks involving puts are any of the following conditions:

Lessons from the Trader Wizard

- **Stocks paying small or no dividends.** You are hoping for the value to decrease. Dividends tend to set a floor for stocks as, even in bear markets, yields are important.

- **Stocks with high price/earnings ratios.** These are more susceptible to downswings than stocks with lower multiples. A stock with a PE of 30 is likely to have a lot more leeway for a drop than one with a PE of 15.

- **Volatile stocks.** These are issues with a history of sharp, wide swings. Stable stocks typically move slowly, even in active markets.

How a beginner can trade options effectively

The options market opens new opportunities for traders of all types. Instead of risking their money in worthless low-priced stocks, speculative traders can, with the same outlay, get better action in options of top-quality companies like Google (GOOG). There are also effective trading strategies for conservative and enterprising traders.

Trading is for cash, so there are no margin calls. The positions are relatively small, the potential is large, and there are always opportunities to hedge. Always think in percentage terms. Because they are traded in high volume daily, there's instant information and gains or losses can be taken any time during the life of an option's contract.

In short, it's a market to get to know, particularly if you are adept with numbers.

Once you get the swing of trading options, you should find a skillful broker-advisor, do your homework and then start making trading decisions. For newbies, I recommend OptionsXpress. The cost is double the deep discount brokers but you also get the help of a broker-advisor whenever you need it. More experienced traders often switch to the Interactive Brokers platform, which offers much lower commission costs.

You can start by dabbling with one or two puts and calls. But to really get involved, I'd say you should work with at least $10,000 in capital, spend enough time to frequently check your positions and have a real-time, reliable source of information.

Concentrate on volatile, low-dividend-paying stocks. If you have time to watch developments closely, you can let your profits run, but for most traders, the best rule is to set target prices that will produce gains of 10-25% (net of commissions) depending on the volatility of the stock and the overall prospects of the capital markets.

271

Specialties to Trade

The sale of multiple call options against a single stock position can assure extra protection in a decline, added income if the stock levels out and bigger returns when there's a modest advance. This tactic works best following a strong market advance, or when there's likely to be a temporary lull or fallback. But don't try multiple writing with volatile stocks. Their rapid price swings can quickly narrow the profit zone.

It's important to have a frame of reference for the value of the option, so follow the market trend and always watch the time factor.

Checkpoints for trading options

The action of the underlying stock will be the determining factor in options profits and losses, but gains are easier to come by when you understand and appreciate the following points:

*   **Time before expiration.** The longer the period before the exercise date, the greater the chance for appreciation. Unless you are sharp, observant and lucky, it seldom pays to trade in calls with less than two months to run. In that situation, profits can be made only with volatile stocks in an erratic market and that's no spot for the amateur.

*   **Volatility.** The best ones are options on stocks that swing over 25% in a year. This criterion rules out slow-moving utilities and basic materials and favors technology.

*   **Price of the stock.** The greatest percentage gains can be made with stocks priced $20-$50; the lowest percentage gains with options on stocks costing over $100.

*   **Striking price of the option.** This selection depends on your experience and trading goals. Buying deep-in-the-money calls offers the best leverage, because their premiums are relatively small.

*   **Yield of the stock.** In most cases, the higher the dividend rate of the stock, the lower will be the premium of the option. For easier profits, stick with low- or no-dividend payers.

Trading guidelines

*   **Stick with high-quality stocks until you are experienced.** When trading options, the risks are enough without adding the danger of poor trades.

*   **Pick options with small premiums where the stocks appear to have prospects of moving quickly in price.**

Lessons from the Trader Wizard

- **Buy call options where the underlying stock is trading below, but close to, its striking price.** The premium will be smaller and will rise when the stock moves above the exercise price.

- **Buy a call option or write a put option when the market is going against your prospective position, but when you anticipate a turnaround soon.** This seemingly risky tactic will give you the benefit of both the temporary and long-term price changes.

- **Use limit orders; don't enter market orders unless you are in a fast-moving market.** Give your broker a specific price or, at least, a price range at which to buy. In fluctuating markets, an active option can move more than a half point and can cut deeply into your potential profits.

- **Calculate your *net* return, after commissions.** Commissions can add up.

- **Don't average down.** Gamblers on a losing streak double up. If they bought a call option at four and it drops to two, they double up to get an average cost of three. Now the option price need only move up one point to get out even. If it zooms, they make more money. But like most theories, this sounds better than it is. The markets are not random, like gaming tables. A trend in motion is more likely to continue (in this case, down) than to reverse over the short life of an option.

- **Keep a good bookkeeping system.** Options can become frequently traded, so good records make it easier for your accountant to prepare any necessary filings and to provide corroboration if you are audited.

- **Be persistent.** Once you have decided that you will write options as part of your trading plan, keep on doing so regularly, regardless of what the stock market does.

- **Watch your timing.** It's best to write a call when the stock has risen to a price that you think is too high. If you bought the stock at 50 and it has moved quickly to 65, look for a sudden reversal. If that seems likely, write an out-of-the-money call at an exercise price of 60. If you can get a four-point ($400) premium; you gain downside protection to 61. If the stock is called at 60, you still do well: a 10-point profit in the stock plus four points on the call for a total $1,900 return plus dividends.

- **Timing is also a major factor in the value of the option premium.** The closer the expiration date, the lower the premium. In July, premiums on January calls will be at least half a point less than premiums on comparable February options. The reason for this is that the demand dwindles because traders looking for gains are beginning to move out of the market. This leaves fewer buyers, primarily short-term speculators, to make the market.

- **Look to protect your capital**: When the price of your stock has dipped below your net-after-premium price: (a) sell the stock and simultaneously buy a call with the same striking price and expiration date as the one originally sold (this maintains most of your capital for reinvestment); (b) buy a call to close out your position and write a new call for a more distant expiration date. (See the example of Mr. Smith earlier.)

- **Use margin wisely**. Leverage can boost profits. Under the regulations in most countries, stocks can be purchased on 50% margin. Since long-term call premiums run up to 12%, buying the stocks on margin makes sense. If the stock price is unchanged or declines by expiration time, the option buyer loses his entire position. If the price rises 12%, the cash buyer comes out about even. But if he uses margin, he has a 24% gain (not including commissions and interest costs).

- **Watch the record dates of high-dividend stocks**. I tend to stick to trading optionable stocks that have low or no dividends to avoid the surprise of having an even more nimble trader exercise an option that appears above parity in order to capture a large dividend.

- **Define your trading goals:**

    - If you want maximum safety for your portfolio, write calls on stable stocks that pay sizable dividends. For example, in the Dow 30, that would be Altria (MO), AT&T (T) and Verizon (VZ). The lower premiums will be offset by higher yields.

    - If you want greater total returns, write out-of-the money calls on stocks that pay modest dividends and which are moving up in value.

    - If you want to be aggressive, focus on volatile stocks where dividends are low and the market action volatile. The premiums will be high, but the odds are that in bull markets the calls will be exercised and you lose your stock. Or, in a bear market, the stock price will decline for a paper loss.

Lessons from the Trader Wizard

Mistakes with options

Every options trader makes mistakes. We are all human.

The biggest mistakes include:

- **Being too bullish**. Stocks rise and fall. No matter what your long-term forecast for the stock, it usually has little effect during the short life of most options. This applies especially to buying options. So, I believe it is unwise to put all your money in options on one side of the market.

- **Underestimating loss potential**. When selling covered calls, your profit is limited, but your potential loss is almost unlimited if the stock plunges. Use a stop-loss order to sell the stock when it has declined to a predetermined price. At that point, the short call can be continued naked or bought back.

- **Failing to include all costs in calculating profits**. Since the profit from writing call options is always limited, be sure to consider commission costs.

Summary of option strategies

In order of risk-to-reward level, according to one's outlook for the underlying stock:

(1)   If you are *very* optimistic:

- sell put with strike price above market;
- sell put with strike price at market;
- sell put with strike price below market;
- buy call with strike price above market;
- buy call with strike price at market;
- buy call with strike price below market;
- buy stock on margin.

(2)   If you are *moderately* optimistic:

- buy stock, sell put;
- buy stock, sell call with strike price above market;
- buy stock, sell call with strike price at market;
- buy stock, sell call and put, both at market;
- buy stock, sell call and put, both with strike prices away from market.

Specialties to Trade

(3)   If you are neutral:

- buy stock, sell one call with strike price above market, one at market;
- buy stock, sell two or more calls with strike price above market;
- sell put and call both with strike prices at market (straddle);
- sell call with strike price at market, sell put with strike price below (combination);
- buy stock and one put with strike price at market (call).

(4)   If you are *moderately* pessimistic:

- buy stock and two puts;
- sell call with strike price at market or lower, buy call at higher strike price (bear spread);
- sell naked call with strike price above market;
- sell stock short, buy two calls;
- sell stock short, buy one call at market (synthetic put);
- sell naked call with strike price at market;
- buy one call and two puts, all with strike price at market.

(5)   If you are *very* pessimistic:

- buy put with strike price at market;
- sell naked call with strike price below market;
- sell stock short, buy call with strike price above market (partial put);
- buy put with strike price below market;
- sell stock short.

2 Trading the commodities, futures and currencies contract markets

Traders always deal with information they have today. What comes down the road or may come down the road is more nebulous, so we have to deal with it as it takes shape at a later time.

August 22, 2007

This section provides a brief overview of markets such as commodities, metals and foreign currencies, and "collectibles". I am interested in them mostly for the information I can glean that will help me in my other trading programs.

Basically, these markets are dominated by professionals. But the trading techniques are easily grasped and can be utilized by anyone who takes time to learn the ground rules, understand what's happening and do his or her homework.

I learned during my college days back in the 1960s not to go head-to-head against professionals who can play the odds in real-time. I saw one of my closest friends, also recently out of his teens at that point, win an automobile in a card game. He later told me he knew how to count the cards while in play and he automatically re-computed the odds. He didn't lose often. In business school one day, he recited from memory the closing market prices of stocks in published order on that morning's financial page, column after column.

I too have a good memory, but I decided right then and there that it would be best for me to devote my time to understanding systems and procedures — ie, how things work — rather than memorizing everything, in order that I might compete with traders with encyclopedic knowledge.

I have been told I too have an encyclopedic memory, and my ego used to fancy that, but I'm now glad that I learned how to study logic and apply a systems approach to problem solving. That's because computers are machines that have infinite memory and processing capability. And, when you click that buy sell key on your keyboard, the market doesn't know or care who you are — man, superman, or machine. In the capital markets, you can't fool anybody.

Specialties to Trade

The most important fact you need to understand about markets for commodities, financial and index futures and currencies is that they are (like options) zero-sum, time-based contract markets. *Time is of the essence.* You are always trading against time, but when you are involved in the contract markets, there is always an end point when time runs out.

Most traders find these markets quite risky and believe trading them should involve only money that you can afford to lose. I tend to agree, but while there can be a higher level of risk when you go from options trading into commodities, futures and currencies markets, I also know that they offer opportunities to build capital quickly and, under certain conditions, can be used conservatively to hedge and sell short.

Most important to me is that these markets can give the student of the market a tremendous amount of additional information to study when making even the simplest decisions to buy or sell a stock.

Assuming you want to trade in these futures markets, success with speculation requires the same research and projections as are required for profitable trading elsewhere.

As I say, however, I consider this end of the spectrum of time-based contracts to be highly speculative trading better suited to professional traders.

But where there are high-risk and high-reward possibilities, there will be participants who use systems of one kind or another to get a leg up. Professional commodities and futures traders use time series analysis in their decision-making process, but they also consider fundamentals such as shifts in government support policies, changes in interest rates, the outlook for crops, damage due to drought or storms, unusual demands for particular metals and so on. This is detailed work.

Because of the size and resources of the capital pools involved, and the stresses on the players to perform to high expectations, there have been spectacular gains and losses in futures trading in recent years.

There was George Soros, who hit the Bank of England for a loss of $10 billion on a position costing him $1 billion. But there was also the disastrous Long-Term Capital Management hedge fund that collapsed. And the failure of the Barings Bank on account of a single trading officer who got offside in his positions. More recently, the biggest futures trading debacle was the multi-billion dollar disintegration of capital under management of Amaranth Advisors.

If you're going to invest here, as in all capital markets trading, you must be able to spot situations where the potential rewards of tomorrow are greater than today's perceived risks. Then with the odds in your favor, and the use of leverage, you can achieve excellent profits — usually quickly.

Hopefully.

With the usual conservative trading in equity markets, patience is essential. The longer you wait, the more probable — and ample — your gains. But with speculative trading in futures contracts, profits should come fast, because in most cases your capital is not providing income and is probably diminishing due to costs of interest and commissions, as well as the constantly reducing time premiums you paid to enter your positions.

But, anybody can learn the systematic approach I take to capital markets. It's like learning to ride a bike ... as you get a little more practiced, you learn to lean into the wind on windy days. The market gives you the same opportunities to right yourself. Why? Because it's all about natural law, logic and common sense.

About Moving Averages (MA)

As discussed earlier, the simplest systems approach to risk management that I learned in my career is called the moving average (MA). Because of getting hooked on the MA, I learned a little more and soon became a trend-and-cycles disciple, using increasingly more sophisticated tools.

Based on many years' experience, I believe that any price series, once established in a trend (in either direction), has a strong tendency to persist before (sometime down the road) it reverses trend. This isn't that different to riding a bike down a path — you assume it's a straight one until you spot the corner.

There are different ways to study trends, but with commodities trading one of the most commonly used technical indicators is a moving average. When I was first exposed to commodity traders while working at Dean Witter 25 years ago, I thought of MA's as a simple tool for simple minds.

Later I came to understand that it does help you stay on the right side of a trend. And in commodities trading (or for that matter any capital markets trading), just knowing where you stand is half the battle.

MA is a progressive average in which the recent closing price of a commodity is added to earlier numbers and then divided by the time span. Each day, the price of the last sale is added to the accumulated total and the earliest figure dropped. Thus, with a 10-day MA, you total the closing prices for the past 10 days and divide it by 10 to get the base data.

Actually, you don't do this, a computer does. On Day 11, you drop the Day 1 price and add that of Day 11 to calculate the moving average, and so on.

Everybody has their own system. The more volatile and speculative the market, the shorter the MA needs to be. Futures traders like to use fibonacci series 3-, 5- and 8-session MAs in their time series analysis work. Day traders use minute and hourly data. Long-term oriented conservative equity traders tend to use 200-day MAs. I'd say the majority of traders use the 50-day (10-week) MA somewhere in their market studies.

The value of the MA, experience shows, is that as the result of more buying than selling, no commodity can stage an up-trend without its price moving above the MA. Vice versa on the downside. Trends and cycles rise when there is more buying than selling. It's the simplest concept really.

When the closing price of a commodity crosses the MA by an amount exceeding their predetermined amount of the maximum penetration in the same direction in any one day — no matter how long ago this occurred — traders act: buying when the breakthrough is up, selling when it's down.

Unlike the stock market, where stocks tend to move in a group, each commodity tends to develop its own pattern. There are small groups like the precious metals group, for example, where platinum and silver often follow gold, but not always.

To sum up, to be successful in the long-run in the commodities and collectibles markets, you are going to have to compete against professionals. Like a card game, these markets are zero-sum. There is a winner and a loser. So, if in fact you are going to venture in, it is important to keep abreast of multiple developments in markets and to act only in a few instances where the opportunities for gains are substantially greater than the possibility of losses.

Advice for the commodity trading novice

The markets for commodities, financial and index futures and currencies are where the biggest profits are made. Regardless, most speculators in these markets are losers, which concerns me. If you are a novice trader newly acquainted with these expert markets, it will pay to apply the following advice.

(1)   **Read books about commodity trading.** Then decide if you have the nerves and the funds to start speculating in these markets.

(2)   **If you can't afford to lose, you can't afford to win.** If you are not in a position to accept losses, either psychologically or financially, you

have no business speculating in any type of market, particularly futures or options. Remember, unlike stocks, commodity trading is a zero-sum game. You either win or you lose.

(3)   **Choose an experienced broker.** Deal only with a reputable company that: (a) has extensive commodities trading services; and (b) includes an experienced broker-advisor who you can trust and who knows the markets that interest you.

(4)   **Get current information.** All the statistics you will need are available in government reports, business publications and newsletters, so inside information is not a serious problem in commodities markets. Study the data and then review your conclusions with your commodity-trading advisor.

(5)   **Focus on a few commodities; preferably those in the news.** Staples such as corn, wheat and hogs always have strong markets. But I believe the easier speculative profits can be made in the active groups, such as gold, metals and petroleum. Maybe my thinking is due to my never having been a farmer (therefore with no relevant experience or expertise) and the fact that my introduction to futures and commodities trading came by way of a trader of pork bellies, who I gather ended up serving more expert traders his lunch.

(6)   **Adopt the Zulu Principle.** To succeed, you will have to become something of an expert in both the fundamental and technical aspects of at least one commodity or futures contract.

The Zulu Principle is a term that arose in the 1960s and it describes superficial expertise acquired from library books and magazine articles in a single obscure subject, like Zulus. As an aside, for a brief time, leading up to the free elections in South Africa, I became the chief financial advisor to the Zulu nation, by appointment of Prince Buthelezi (long-term Home Minister of Republic of South Africa) and his associate at the time, Sipo Mzemela. It's true, but that's another story.

(7)   **Prepare a trading plan.** Without a road map, you can't find your destination. Before you turn over cash to your broker, test your trading hypotheses on paper until you feel confident. Set up a game plan like this:

•   **Never meet a margin call.** When your original margin is impaired by 25%, your broker will call for more money. Do not send in more money (except in the most unusual of circumstances). Liquidate your position (before your broker does) and accept your loss. This is a form of stop-loss safeguard. When a declining trend has been established, more losses can be expected.

- **Unless you are sure, don't.** Don't get carried away by the unreal world of computer numbers, arrows and squiggly lines. You are trading real money. If there is any serious doubt in your mind about the trend of the price of a commodity or futures price, do not buy or maintain a position. It's much better to miss a few profit opportunities through caution than throw money away recklessly.

(8) **Be alert to "situations".** Information is the key to profitable speculation. As you become more knowledgeable, you will pick up pointers, such as:

- If there's heavy spring-summer rain in Maine, buy long on potatoes. They need ideal weather.

- If there's a rash of tornadoes over large portions of the US Great Plains, buy wheat contracts. Chances are the wheat crop will be damaged, thus changing the supply and demand ratio.

- There are, of course, many other factors to analyze before reaching any final decision. As with everything involving the profit potential of money, knowledge plus luck are both important.

(9) **Look for a ratio of net profit to net loss of 2:1.** Since most traders have more losing trades than winning trades, choose commodities where potential gains, based on trend studies, can be more than double the possible losses. When making such projections, include commission costs as they can be a major factor when dealing in small units and small price shifts.

Trade with the major trend, and against the minor trend. With copper, for example, if you project a worldwide shortage (due to the needs of emerging BRIC economy markets or whatever) and the market is in an up trend, buy futures when the market suffers temporary weak spells. As long as prices keep moving up, you want to accumulate a meaningful position.

The corollary to this is to never average down. Adding to your loss position increases the number of contracts that are returning a loss. By buying more, you put yourself in a stance where you can lose on more contracts if the price continues to drop. Generally, if the trend is down, either sell short or stay out of the market. And never (well, hardly ever) buy a commodity after it has passed its seasonal high or sell a commodity after it has passed its seasonal low.

(10) **Avoid thin markets.** You can win big when a thinly traded commodity takes off, but the swings can be too fast for you. Prices might soar or plummet and the amateur trader can get caught with no chance of closing positions.

Watch the spreads between different delivery dates. In the strong summer market, the premium for January soybeans is 8¢ per bushel above the November contract. Buy November and sell January. If the bull market persists, the premium should disappear and you will have a limited profit. Carrying charges on soybeans run about 6¢ per month, so it is not likely that the spread will widen to more than 13¢ per bushel. Thus, with that 8¢ spread, the real risk is not more than 5¢ per bushel.

(11) **Deal in percentages.** Don't take a position unless your profit goal is at least 10 times your commissions. I used to visit a casino with a player who had the idea that every day he would skillfully play 21 until he extracted $2,500 from the casino dealer. I've seen amateur commodity speculators take the same approach. They think they can dip into the market and automatically remove money. To do this, they must be right 60% of the time, or have bigger percentage wins than percentage losses, in order to cover the loss trades and hefty commissions.

(12) **Margin requirements are irrelevant to profit and loss objectives.** Margin is not a cost, a purchase price, a measure of value or a measure of available capital. It's a security deposit and nothing more.

(13) **Remain a student of the market.** Devote time to learning how markets inter-relate and why prices move as they do. You should know, for example, why economic recovery in Europe means higher soybean prices in Chicago and why higher soybean prices can pick up the price of silver in New York.

Some of the comments from above, from several well-known sources, are repetitive ... on purpose. If you are not doing well as a trader, it will pay to strictly follow these guidelines. If you still are losing consistently, you ought to seek and heed expert counsel because commodities and futures trading is a tough business.

Specialties to Trade

Trading in commodities and futures funds

Fund management

There are professionally managed commodities or currencies funds that you can buy into. If you do, you should be trying to accomplish through a skillful manager what you presumably can't do for yourself.

In studying the fund's history you should be looking for:

Track record of limited losses — This fund should have been working well for the long run, with a management track record based on say 8 years' experience rather than 8 times one year's experience. There are many funds that experience one good year followed by several very bad ones.

Stopping losses is more important than making gains in the commodities business. To keep losses low, look for proof that a fund's positions have been closed out at definite points over the years when major trends and cycles reversed.

Continuous profits — Don't go with a manager who talks of an ability to hit tops and bottoms. Purchases can never be made only at the bottom, nor sales at the top, of market cycles. There is no need to, however, as the market is a continuum of price motion. You need to find a manager who can demonstrate ability to make profits continuously, through thick and thin.

Whenever there's a sustained move, a well-run fund should capture, as profit, a large slice of the middle of the move. As long as the move continues without a valid crossing of the MA in the opposite direction, positions should be maintained.

Caveat with commodity trading funds

Watch the tax angle. For the individual, the important factor is the period of holding. Because most gains and losses in commodity funds are short term, they are taxed at ordinary rates and/or with limited deductibility.

Commodity funds are limited partnerships, so your share of realized gains and losses will be passed along directly to you, the timing of which could be painful in a high personal tax situation.

One fund I read about finished the year with $1.8 million in profits (all taxable) and $1.2 million in unrealized losses, which are not tax deductible. A net gain of $600,000, but a tax bill of about $900,000. Ouch!

Trading in financial futures

With financial futures, you are playing the interest-rate game, so they are a little different than commodities. Some of us, even some economists and bankers, know a thing or two about interest rates. But can we make money in financial futures?

Financial futures include the following contract instruments, among others:

- E-Mini 30-year US T-Bond (CBOT);

- US Treasury Notes (2-, 5- and 10-year notes) (CBOT);

- Fed Funds 30 Days;

- 10-year Interest Swap (CBOT);

- Municipal Bonds (CBOT);

- Canadian Bankers Acceptance 3 Month;

- German Bonds (DB, LIFFE);

- UK Gilts Long (GT, LIFFE);

- LIBOR — 1 Month;

- Short Sterling (SS, LIFFE).

Futures contract specifications

In the past few years, the unprecedented swings in interest rates have exposed businesses and financial institutions to severe risks. To protect themselves from these hard-to-predict fluctuations, professional money managers have developed the financial futures market. These futures contracts are now traded on about a dozen exchanges and are a major force in the financial world.

Its growth has been explosive.

Basically, financial futures are a form of the same type of time-based commodities contracts that are widely used with wheat, corn, copper and other foods and metals. They are standardized packages of debt securities whose prices move with interest rates: up when the cost of money falls; down when it rises.

Specialties to Trade

In familiar terms, here's the situation: A bank buys a 20-year, 8% bond at issue, for $1,000. If the market interest rate was to rise to 12%, the value of the bond drops to about 66 ($660). Similarly, if the cost of money should decline to 7%, that bond would sell at around 112 ($1,120). At maturity, the bond would be worth 100 ($1,000) again.

But in the meantime, the banker has problems. If he needs extra funds in a hurry, he must sell at a loss.

Like any businessman, the banker would prefer to have stable, predictable assets. That's where the financial futures market and hedging comes in. It enables the money manager to take positions in the futures market to protect positions in the cash market. When the cost of money changes, the loss in the cash market is offset by a profit in the futures market. And vice versa.

In each position, someone has to take the opposite side of the contract. This may be a speculator seeking a quick profit by buying or selling short, according to his view of the cost of money in the days or months ahead.

In the futures market, the profits can be big and fast, but the losses can be bigger and faster. As a conscientious commodity trader once warned, "You can make enough money in a morning to send your kids to college. But in the afternoon you can lose enough to have to sell your house."

All futures, as you know by this point in the book, are a zero-sum game: for every winner there's a loser. In the stock market, at least, you will usually be moving with the majority. If the market goes up, nearly everyone wins. If it goes down, nearly everyone loses — but only for a while, because stock prices eventually trade based on corporate value and the value of most of the quality corporations are constantly rising.

Using a case study, here are two examples of how financial futures were used in the past for hedging:

Long hedge. It was late winter and Mr. PM, a portfolio manager, expected an inflow of $1 million in the spring from client retirement fund savings. He planned to invest this money in five-year, 8% high-yielding notes priced to yield 9.01%. But he feared a drop in the rate of return before he actually received this cash.

To lock in his position, he bought 10 futures contracts at $100,000 each for 95 16/32nds ($95,500). He put up $10,000 in margin: $1,000 per contract.

Lessons from the Trader Wizard

Soon, interest rates dropped, as he expected, so the price of the notes rose to 99 16/32nds ($99,500). He chalked up a $40,000 profit ($4,000 per contract).

When the $1 million in cash came in, the price of the notes was up to 100. Now he had to pay $1 million, but his actual cost was $960,000 since he had a $40,000 gain in the futures market. Thus, the yield on the 8% notes was the targeted 9.01%.

Short hedge. In mid-fall Mr. BD, a bond dealer, contracted to sell bonds held in his inventory to a buyer. The interest rates would later rise so that his holding would be worth less than their current 99 8/32nds for a yield of 8.18%. As a hedge, he sold 10 futures contracts at 98 24/32nds ($980,750). Three weeks later, interest rates were up as expected, so the dealer bought back the contracts at 93 24/32nds ($930,750) for a $50,000 profit – enough to offset the loss in the value of the sold bonds.

Mr. PM, the portfolio manager, could also profit. In the first example, if he bought in anticipation of a drop in the cost of money, he would make the $40,000 profit. In the second example, if he looked for a rise in interest rates, he sold short and covered his position for a $50,000 gain.

In both cases, if interest rates moved opposite to his guess, Mr. PM would have lost money. But he would not have waited until the expiration of the contracts. Knowing that 75% of all trades result in a loss, he would have taken a quick, small loss, probably by means of a stop order.

Lack of safeguards

At the risk of being repetitive, I want to re-emphasize some of the dangers of trading financial futures (and, of course, all time-based contract markets). For the amateur, these markets lack many of the safeguards of stocks and bonds, which I believe can be summed up as follows:

(1) **No ban on inside information.** With stocks, executives and brokers who use inside information to anticipate or cause stock movements are subject to severe penalties and even jail. Futures traders have no such restraints that I am aware of.

(2) **No screening of customers.** With the tiny margins, anyone can get into the game and, with minimal governmental regulation, can be persuaded by commission-hungry brokers to get in over his/her head.

(3) **Stock orders must be processed when received.** Futures traders can place orders for their own accounts and the public at the same

time. This can create a conflict of interest and, possibly, force amateurs to pay too much or receive too little.

(4) **Pooled funds sponsored by brokerage companies can influence the market.** For small traders, the big advantage is a negative one: that they can lose no more than the money actually put into the funds.

(5) **Limited public disclosure.** Traders who own 5% or more of a company's stock must publicly disclose their holdings, because they are deemed to be investors. Large commodity traders do have to inform the Commodity Futures Trading Commission and the exchanges, but that information is of little use to small speculators.

If you wish to trade commodities and futures, the New York Mercantile Exchange (NYMEX) and Chicago Mercantile Exchange (CME) offer computer-simulation demos that use actual trading data and prices for a theoretical $250,000 paper account. Each day, these systems show what your decisions would have gained or lost.

Individual brokers also offer similar computer simulation programs (such as http://lind-waldock.com).

Competing with professionals in hedging

Few amateurs understand all of the risks of speculating in financial futures. The following important variables utilized by professionals were cited in *Forbes*:

(1) **Basis.** This is the difference in price or yield between the closest delivery month of a Treasury bill or Treasury bond futures contract and the present cash market price of that same instrument.

Let's say that you want to hedge a position in Treasury bonds. What could happen is that the cash market drops 1½ points, while the futures market falls only one point. That's a half point against you. With a hedge where you bought $100,000 in bonds and sold a $100,000 futures contract, you would have lost $15,000 on the bonds you owned and earned back $10,000 on the short sale of the futures contract.

(2) **Cheapest to deliver.** All sellers have the right to deliver those securities that are "cheapest to deliver" from a pool of securities. For bonds, the maturity must be at least 15 years. Usually, the highest-interest-rate, longest-maturity Treasury bond is the cheapest to deliver.

(3)   **Cost of financing a cash position.** When the annual cost of carrying a 5% Treasury note (assuming almost full-value loan) is 4%, there's a positive carry of 1%. But at a 6% cost, there would be a negative carry of 1%. That can make a big difference in the ultimate profit.

The professional understands these extra risks and trades accordingly. Too often, however, the amateur does not know, or understand, such important variables.

Strict guidelines to go by

If you have money you can afford to lose, time enough to keep abreast of developments, strong nerves and a trustworthy, knowledgeable broker-advisor, trading in financial futures may be rewarding and exciting. But don't rush out to get started.

Beginners are urged to follow these guidelines:

(1)   **Make dry runs in computer simulations for several months.** Pick different types of futures contracts each week and keep practising until you get a feel for the market and risk and can chalk up more winners than losers.

(2)   **Set a strategy and stick to it.** Don't try to mix contracts until you feel comfortable and are making money.

(3)   **Set stop and limits orders, not market orders.** A market order is executed immediately at the best possible price. A stop order, to buy or sell at a given price, becomes a market order when that price is touched. A limit order is the maximum price at which to buy and the minimum at which to sell.

(4)   **Buy long when you look for a drop in interest rates.** With lower yields, the prices of the contracts will rise.

(5)   **Sell short when you expect a higher cost of money.** This will force down the value of the contracts and you can cover your position at a profit.

(6)   **Buy a lucky charm.** Mine is a silver-plated horseshoe. Even pro traders guess wrong. No matter how intense your research, there will always be unexpected changes resulting from political or economic activity or changes in the weather somewhere in the world. You will be surprised at how much markets can move on the basis of seemingly innocuous information. So if you get caught, just put it down to circumstance.

Specialties to Trade

Trading in the "soft" commodities markets

With commodities, you are playing the farmer's game, so they are a little different than financial futures. Some people know a lot more about these products that most of us.

Commodities include the following contract instruments:

> Cattle/Hogs/Meat Commodity Futures
> Feeder Cattle (CME)
> Lean Hogs (CME)
> Live Cattle (CME)
> Pork Bellies (CME)
> Grains/Cereals/Oilseed Commodity Futures
> Barley (Alberta)
> Canola (WCE)
> Corn (CBOT)
> Corn Mini (XC, CBOT)
> Cotton (NCE)
> Feed Wheat (WCE)
> Flaxseed (WCE)
> Hard Red Spring Wheat (MGE)
> Oats (CBOT)
> Rice (CBOT)
> Soybean Meal (CBOT)
> Soybean Oil (CBOT)
> Soybeans (CBOT)
> Soybeans Mini (XS, CBOT)
> Wheat (CBOT)
> Wheat (Kansas)
> Wheat Mini (XW, CBOT)

Miscellaneous commodities futures include:

> BFP Milk (DA, CME)
> Butter (DB, CME)
> Cocoa (CSCE)
> Coffee (CSCE)
> Lumber (CME)
> Orange Juice (CEC)
> Sugar #11 (CEC SU)
> Sugar #14 (CEC SE)

Commodity trading is one of the few remaining areas where an individual with small capital can strike it rich. However, according to one study, 75% of commodities speculators lose money. Moreover, their aggregate losses were six times as great as their gains.

Even the best commodities speculators lose more often than they win, but by keeping losses small and allowing profits to run, they can do well.

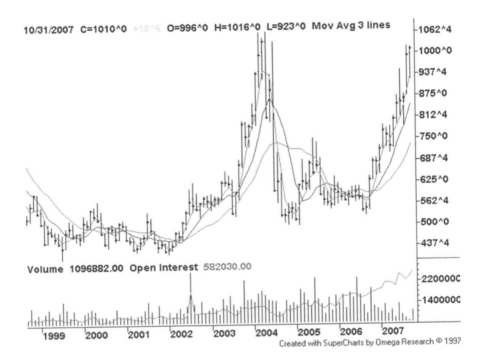

Profits, like losses, can be quick and large. In a few months in the 2H06, one speculator made a $12,500 profit on a $1,350 position, when the price of soybeans soared from $5.50 to $8.00 per bushel. That $1,350 was all that was needed to buy a 5,000-bushel contract for future delivery.

Roughly, commissions average about $35 per round trip to use a full-service broker-advisor, but self-directed trading can be much cheaper, as per the Interactive Brokers rate sheet; which can be found at http://interactivebrokers.com.

Specialties to Trade

The cash requirements for all commodities trading are low: 5-10%, varying according to the commodity and to the broker's requirements. But when there is extreme speculation, those margins can be raised quickly. There are no interest payments on the balance.

The lures of fast action, minimal capital and high potential profits are enticing, but before you start trading corn, wheat, soybeans, silver or any other commodity, heed these warnings from professionals:

(1)   **Be ready to risk at least $10,000: $5,000 at once, the rest to back up margin calls.**

(2)   **The odds are against making a profit on any one trade.** You have to make a hit big enough to offset the losses. Only a handful of amateurs last more than three years. The rest are broke.

(3)   **Emotional stability is essential.** You have to be able to control your sense of fear and greed, and train yourself to accept losses without too great a strain. Until a few years ago, some brokerage companies refused to accept female customers! What does that tell you other than that those particular brokers expected the clients to lose and they feared 'a woman scorned'.

Commodity trading is different from trading in stocks. When you buy a common stock, at least you are told you own part of the corporation and a share in its profits (even if it may not be true). But, if you whimsically pick a profitable company whose stock price tumbles soon after your purchase, the price of your stock will eventually move up. With commodities, there is no equity. You buy only time and hope. Once the futures contract has expired, there's no tomorrow. If your trade turned out badly, you must take the full loss.

The economic reason for a futures market is hedging (that is, removing or reducing the risk of a commitment by taking an offsetting one).

This example, taken from my notes in the past year, serves to illustrate the reasons for a trade. A farmer who borrows money to plant a 10,000-bushel soybean crop was asked by his banker in August 2006 to sell two futures contracts (5,000 bushels each) for November delivery. This contract calls for a fixed price, say $5.30 per bushel. If the November price was $5.00, the farmer would lose 30¢ per bushel in the cash market, but could make up the loss by buying back his futures contracts for less than he paid. The opposite happens if the November price rises. Either way, the farmer is assured of a return of $5.30 per bushel, so that he can repay his bank loan and probably turn a profit too.

Lessons from the Trader Wizard

On the other hand, a food processor that sells products throughout the year wants a pre-determined cost for his soybean purchases. He buys futures in the appropriate forward month. If the price rises, he pays more in the cash market, but profits when he sells the futures contract.

In both cases there must be someone to take the opposite side of the transaction. That's the role of the speculator. He assumes the risk because he thinks he can buy or sell the contract at a profit before the delivery date.

Here's what might have happened in 2003.

Note: In the summer of 2003, November soybeans moved from about $5.10 a bushel in late-July to $8.00 in 12 weeks. For some speculators, that was very profitable because the $2.90 move was worth $14,500 per contract on a margin of about $1,350! See: http://tfc-charts.w2d.com/chart/SB. The same thing happened in the summer of 2006, but the contracts ran from about $5.30 to $8.50–8.75 a year later.

The hedger, who needs soybeans for processing in November, buys (goes long on) one 5,000-bushel soybean contract:

June 4: Buy one November soybean contract at $5.30 for $26,500

Dec. 6: Sell one November soybean contract at $5.00 for $25,000

Loss: $1,500 — Commission $45

Total loss: $1,545

The farmer, who owns soybeans, will sell short:

June 4: Sell one November soybean contract at $5.30 for $26,500

Dec. 6: Buy one November soybean contract at $5.00 for $25,000

Profit: $1,500 — commission $45

Total profit: $1,455

Because industry buyers and sellers of futures contracts seldom match, the speculator moves in to take the opposite side of a contract. He holds the long contract as long as prices are rising (up to delivery date) and cuts his losses by selling fast when the market declines. Vice versa for the short sale.

Specialties to Trade

In almost every case, the speculator takes action long before the contract becomes due. That's the profit opportunity of trading in commodities.

Commodities options

These are contracts to purchase the commodity at a specified price on a specified date. As with stock options, the buyer pays a premium to the party granting the option. There's no margin, so the most the buyer can lose is the premium. The seller accepts a modest gain, rather than a possibly higher profit and takes the risk that the value of the contract will not drop too far.

If you trade commodities options in London, say on the London Metals Exchange, there is the issue of currency conversion and profit retrieval for anyone who doesn't hold a sterling account. The broker must convert dollars into pounds, and back again into dollars if there's a profit to be repatriated. That's expensive, so you'll want to hold a pound sterling denominated account if that's where you intend to trade.

Commodities mutual funds

Commodities funds, I feel, are a Wall Street pitch to let the little man gain profits previously possible only for the wealthy. For as little as $5,000, you can buy participations in a diversified portfolio managed by professionals.

The advertisement proclaims "Smart money goes where the profits are. In the past x years, a $100,000 portfolio in a conservatively managed commodities trading account has risen to over $500,000. Every active trader should have a portion of his assets in commodities. The rewards are high and, by tested techniques, losses are limited and profits can run."

Maybe so, but let's see how these funds operate. These funds are an outgrowth of "managed accounts" for wealthy individuals. They are similar to mutual funds in that brokerage firms sell limited partnership interests to the public, generally in five $1,000 units. The proceeds are pooled to buy or sell futures contracts in some large number (say 18) of the most active, most potentially profitable contracts.

Management typically uses a market-proven system that is supposed to automatically trigger sales and signal buying points. They are speculations and, usually, the fund is structured so that it will be closed out when 50% of the original capital is wiped out.

Participations can be bought and sold, with short notice, at the end of each monthly or quarterly reporting period. There are no dividends; only capital gains or losses. If you need cash funds in a hurry, you will have to sell at a loss if the market is down at the time. These are short term and taxable to the individual, at regular Federal income tax rates.

Look at the requirements in the fund's prospectus. While exact terms might vary, the proposals typically (last time I checked) call for:

(1)   Limitation of sales to individuals who have a net worth (excluding home, furnishings and automobiles) of: (a) $50,000; or (b) $20,000 and an annual income of $20,000.

(2)   No sales load. All of your dollars are used to trade in commodities.

(3)   Because of pooling, commissions are 20-25% below the regular rates charged to most individual customers.

(4)   Payments to the registered representative of 15-25% of total commission on a proportionate basis, eg, for a $5 million fund, the broker who sells five units ($5,000) will get 1/10th of 1%, which sounds small but, over a year, could be substantial. I read of an extreme example wherein one fund reported adjusted brokerage fees of $203,385 on fund assets of $7.2 million in three months!

In addition (and this is typical), the management group receives 20% of net profits plus 1% of net assets, calculated monthly, if the net profits exceed 3.2% of fund assets plus interest on the holding of cash reserves in Treasury bills.

The single biggest advantage of commodities funds is that the best ones have staying power. They have sufficient resources to keep going despite interim losses ... usually. But even some good ones go broke too, like Amaranth.

Never forget that these funds are speculations. There is no real wealth being created. The managers are trading against each other in a series of paper transactions. It is a zero-sum game.

Let me tell you a personal story. One of my associates was a proud and very successful commodities fund manager, who also had a popular radio show on the topic. One day over lunch, watching the ticker in the steakhouse frequented by market professionals, he noticed that commodity prices had gone against him, strongly. The more he fretted as seconds turned into minutes, the worse his positions seemed to get in the market. At first, he was anxious to return to his office. Then he grew disconsolate and sat back. Finally, he just gave up and said: "I've lost all my clients' money. I'm finished. I guess I have to leave town." All this over lunch!

Specialties to Trade

The individual buyers of these commodity trading funds must also be held to account. In fact, over the years, I discovered a lot about the nature of a person by the funds they buy.

Trading in financial futures

There is no shortage of tradable instruments created by Wall Street.

Trading in market-index and indicator futures

With market-index futures, you are playing the professional money manager's game. This is not a market for novices.

Major market-index and indicators futures involves trading in the following contract instruments:

Amex 10 Most Active
Amex 10 Most Active Volume
ASE Index
CRB Index
CRB Index Futures (RB, NYFE)
DAX Index Futures (AX, DTB)
Dow Jones — Composite
Dow Jones — Industrial Average
Dow Jones — Utilities
Dow Jones I.A. Futures
E-Mini Russell 2000 Index (CME)
E-Mini S&P Midcap 400 (CME)
Goldman Sachs Index (GI, CME)
London FTSE 100 (LZ, LIFFE)
Mini Sized Dow Jones (CBOT)
NASDAQ 100 E-Mini (NQ, CME)
NASDAQ 100 Futures (ND, CME)
NASDAQ Composite Index
Nikkei Index (NK, CME)
NYSE Composite Index
NYSE Index
Russell 2000 Index
Russell 2000 Index (CME)
S&P E-Mini (CME)
S&P 500
S&P 500
S&P Midcap 400 (CME)
Toronto S&P 60
Value Line Index (KCBT)

Trading in metals futures

After reading A.C. Copetas' book, *Metal Men*, about trader Marc Rich, you might want to stay away from these markets. Then again, maybe you see the potential for profit and want to learn as much as possible.

Of course, Marc Rich is (or was) also an oil speculator, which also might be a market that interests you.

With metals futures, you are playing the professional money manager's game. Most of us know a little about the metal markets, but the metal futures market is something else again. This is not a market for novices.

If you're an aspiring Marc Rich, the website http://ino.com offers good charts (including futures and spot prices) of the different metals contracts traded, such as:

- Aluminum (AL, COMEX)
- Copper High Grade (HG, COMEX)
- Gold (100 oz GC, COMEX)
- Gold NY Mini (YG, CBOT)
- Palladium (PA, NYMEX)
- Platinum (PL, NYMEX)
- Silver NY Mini (YI, CBOT)
- Silver, 5000 oz (SI, COMEX)

Trading in gold futures

To millions of people, gold is the finest form of tangible wealth. As my friend the gold miner Rob McEwen likes to say: "Gold is money."

Actually, gold is better than money. It is a symbol of security that protects the individual against inflation, confiscation of income through taxes, and worldwide threats of war and revolution. People enjoy the thrill and comfort of owning the precious metal as bullion or coins and boast of the profits from its ever-rising potential value.

While it could be a good speculative trade, unless you are into writing puts or calls, gold bullion is usually, unfortunately, a poor trade for income-seeking conservative traders. The gold futures market could even be dangerous. Extreme volatility usually ends up whipsawing most unsophisticated traders out of their positions.

If gold is bad, silver is worse and platinum and palladium possibly worse yet.

Specialties to Trade

Within five years from January 1975 — when Americans could first buy gold — it rose from US$197.50 to over US$870 per ounce. (Gold is internationally priced in US dollars.)

That was a huge gain, far above that of the stock market average or of fixed-income holdings during that period. But there was no income and many quality stocks did better, with far fewer risks and fluctuations. For the 20 years following the 1981 top, gold dropped to about $225, so long-term traders were badly hurt.

If you bought at the low and sold at the high, you might have stayed a step ahead of inflation during the 1970s. During that time, however, rather than buying bullion, which is the gold metal, you would have done better by owning shares of dividend-paying gold-mining stocks.

In early 1975, gold was selling at $197.50 per ounce. This was the peak for almost three years. Gold did not reach $243 until October 1978. After a year of seesawing, it then skyrocketed to over $800 per ounce. But, as had happened before, the price fell sharply. At best, the trader tripled his money — if the long position was sold at the cycle peak.

With gold-mining stocks during that period, he could have counted on steady income from dividends of over 10% a year from many of these mining companies. With compounding, that meant average annual rates of return of 12-20%, plus capital gains of 25-50%, depending on the stocks selected.

But those days of high dividends are gone. Management is retaining funds to pay for exploration and development of rapidly depleting resources. It is a fact that new gold discoveries are occurring much less quickly than mine production and sales.

Over the past 30 to 35 years, the best profits with gold bullion trading came from speculating, ie, buying extreme dips and selling after rallies, selling short and buying back at the next low, and so on. Gold tends to trade for long periods in trading ranges. If a trend takes the price outside those long-term trading ranges, you must be careful to not be positioned against the cycle moves.

The active trader made a lot of money: selling short in January 1975 at $197, covering his position in August 1976 at $104, holding until January 1977 to sell at $174; buying in 1978 to benefit from the surge from about $200 to $800; selling short and covering at around $500. Over the six years, if both smart and lucky, the trader might have made 30 trades and increased their capital 25 times.

Lessons from the Trader Wizard

If you wish to speculate in gold, there are many choices: from futures contracts to the physicals (bullion bars and coins and certificates) to the shares of companies and funds as well as options on the shares and funds, as follows:

(1)   **Gold futures contracts.** These give the speculator the biggest bang for their buck. Similar to contracts for commodities, they can be handled by most brokers and are actively traded on the New York Commodity Exchange and the International Monetary Market in Chicago.

See gold futures charts: http:// tfc-charts.w2d.com/chart/GD/W.

You can buy and sell 100-ounce contracts with different future delivery dates on margins of 5-15%. Thus, with gold at $400 an ounce, each contract is worth $40,000, which you can leverage with about $4,000. Make sure you have ample collateral; gold prices can move quickly and when they go down, you must come up with more cash or securities or the broker sells out your position at the end of the day.

Most brokers ask for a minimum balance of $10,000.

It's wise to set target prices. You can let your profits run, but to protect your holdings, give the broker a stop loss price: either at the price at which additional margin will be needed or at the average price of the last 30 trading days. Thus, if you bought a contract when gold was $370 an ounce and used a 10% margin, the sell price would be $350 if you were conservative. As the price of the metal moves up, boost the stop-loss accordingly.

Even stops may not protect you. Commodity traders try to knock off those stops late in the afternoon — eg, when the price of gold drops below $355, the professionals, knowing that amateurs have set stops at $350, will go short. This will drop the price again so that the trader may be able to buy back his contracts at about $340. He makes a quick profit and you're out of luck ... and money.

In bull markets, trading in gold futures can be very profitable. A five-point move is common. With a little patience, you can even pick up a 10-point intra-day move.

(2)   **Gold options.** These give you the right to buy gold bullion at a set price before a set date. The option may be on bullion at spot or forward prices. They are speculations that involve leverage. If you are a successful market timer, you can do well.

Specialties to Trade

(3)   **Contracts for Difference (CFD).** This is a contract between a buyer and seller, stipulating that the seller will pay to the buyer the difference between the current value of an asset and its value at contract time. If the difference is negative, then the buyer pays instead to the seller. Such a contract is an equity, debt, commodity or currency derivative that allows traders to speculate on movements, without the need for ownership of the underlying asset.

Contracts for difference allow traders to take long or short positions, and unlike futures contracts, have no fixed expiry date or contract size. Trades are conducted on a leveraged basis with margins typically ranging from 1 to 30% of the notional value.

CFDs are currently available in listed and/or over-the-counter markets in Canada, UK, Germany, Switzerland, Italy, South Africa, Australia, New Zealand, Singapore, Hong Kong, China and Russia, among other countries, but subject to restrictions by the US SEC on financial instruments that trade over-the-counter. In Canada, only accredited investors are permitted to trade CFDs.

In Canada, the trading of Gold CFDs at 1% margin is very attractive to some traders, including fund managers, who use the CFD to hedge positions.

(4)   **Companies listed on major stock exchanges.** Most of these are large and relatively stable US, Canadian, South African and Australian corporations holding a variety of mineral assets, but mostly gold. They provide detailed reports to stockholders, which are widely followed by broker-dealer analysts, and their shares can be bought and sold easily.

(5)   **Holding companies and Exchange-Traded Funds (ETFs).** These are securities of companies that hold equity interests in more than one gold-related company.

(6)   **Gold bullion ETF securities.** There are several countries, including the US, Canada, UK and Australia, that offer gold bullion ETFs. Some traders are concerned that the custodian banks are trading against the client, and so will not purchase such an instrument.

(7)   **Gold certificates.** The certificates represent ownership of a specific portion of physical bullion stores held by the custodial bank, such as the Scotia Bank. The sales price includes fees for insurance and storage, plus commissions, which (depending on quantity) range from 1-3%. The certificates are not negotiable or assignable, so they must be sold back to the dealer.

(8) **Gold coins.** These are non-numismatic coins, meaning they have been minted only for the collectibles market. The major forms are Canadian maple leafs, US medallions, Krugerrands, Mexican pesos, Austrian coronas, China pandas. Gold coins are minted in different sizes according to the gold content: 1 oz, ½ oz, ¼ oz and 1/10 oz.

You can check the daily value of coin holdings in the press or from radio/TV reports. Because of manufacturing and distribution costs, gold coins often sell at a 5-8% premium over spot gold prices. Local sales taxes in some jurisdictions can add another 8%. Before you buy, do your homework and calculate how much you can lose.

Some traders like to trade in gold coins and gems, because they can do so in secrecy, like with bearer bonds. However, with the Know Your Client (KYC) legislation and industry regulations being implemented around the world since the events of 9-11-2001, unless you plan to buy these on the street and keep them in a safety deposit box, your broker or financial institution will have to keep records that are accessible to the authorities.

(9) **Installment buying.** These are billed as "sure-fire" systems. They require periodic trading with the goal of building substantial holdings. You buy bullion on the installment plan and it is stored abroad, usually in a jurisdiction where there are no taxes on the asset or any related trading.

Usually, there are two types of installment contracts:

- Unit price averaging, which is where the trader agrees to buy a fixed amount of gold regularly, paying less when the price is low and more when high.

- Cost averaging, which is buying an amount at a fixed sum at periodic intervals and buying more when the price is low, less when high.

Guidelines for buying gold

Assuming you have a large appetite for the yellow metal:

(1) Unless you use a registered fund, never give discretionary powers to anyone over your own account without a formal trading agreement.

(2) Never commit more than half your money at risk. If you have $50,000, use only $25,000. Put the balance in money market funds for quick retrieval.

(3)   Limit the possible trading loss to 25% of the total account.

(4)   Paper trade your own account for at least one month before you commit any dollars. Make decisions, calculate margins, set stop-loss prices, etc.

(5)   Read all the broker-dealer and commodity trading firm bulletins and reports.

(6)   Use charts to check daily and weekly price movements and trends.

The Trader Wizard's experience in the gold market

I once traded a lot of gold stocks and became quite expert as a trader in the gold market. At the time, I could tell from the deutschemark–Swiss franc currency spread in what direction the gold market would be likely to move. I would get confirming signals from watching the spread prices on high-quality versus lower-quality gold coin collectibles. Sometimes, I would spend 48 hours straight without sleep on the Notley machine, which is a classy technical analysis service for institutional money managers.

I once organized a visit by the top three executives of North America's biggest gold producer at the time to meet over breakfast in the home cities of the gold mutual funds, including Toronto, San Antonio and Dallas. I got to know some of the gold producers inside and out.

I also attended 20 or more "gold shows" in places like San Francisco, New Orleans and Toronto. Most of the gold analysts and senior gold corporation executives and gold company underwriters were my friends. I got to know most of the gold advisory service market letter writers personally.

I've been underground in gold mines all over the country, including four mines at the Arctic Circle (coming home once with pneumonia and another time partially deaf). In one mine, north of Great Slave Lake, I had to climb down a rope ladder about 125 feet in a four-foot wide tunnel blasted straight into the earth. That was a life experience! A few minutes after reaching the bottom, we inadvertently walked into a part of the mine that, about 100 feet away, was being blasted by dynamite.

That day in the far north was a memorable one. The time I almost died, however, happened while visiting a mine that was in a deep valley on the Quebec–Vermont border, surrounded by mountains, where our floatplane had to land in a farmer's field.

I was traveling in the personal plane of the prospector who had discovered the $5-billion gold deposit at Hemlo in Northern Ontario. Thankfully, it was a new and very expensive plane because that day there was a small-craft wind warning, with notable wind shear at the top of these mountains.

As we approached the valley where the mine is located, the pilot told us to strap our seat belts tight. It was worse than I had imagined. The plane spun, my head hit the side wall so hard that I could only see stars and darkness. The pilot's console was flashing red; there was a siren blaring. We had flipped right over and were in a dive. But the valley was only about 750 feet deep. Obviously, thanks to a skilled pilot and a well-built airplane, we made it.

Because they are instructive, the two stories I most like to tell about gold are the following.

I once helped organize a trip to British Columbia, from north to south, for about 25 professional mining analysts. We flew in every type of airplane and helicopter possible. Three or four prominent gold letter writers accompanied us on that trip.

As we walked one property, it had become obvious to the professional mining analysts (most of them geologists) that there was nothing of value to see there. One of the market letter writers stopped to pick up a small rock — in an open field nonetheless. Pure rock.

Then the "guru" got excited and shouted to everybody that he had found a gold nugget. So the knowledgeable analysts began to play a game by telling him he had probably stumbled onto something valuable. And we all laughed. The lesson that was not lost on us that day is that this chap was serious. And he would be telling his popular market letter subscribers of his "gold discovery".

Another true story — one that had the gold fund managers laughing heartily at the New Orleans show — was told to me by a young broker I hired one year. Before joining my firm he had been part of a stock promotion group from Toronto that flogged to Americans what we call Northern Ontario "moose pasture".

After selling so much worthless penny stock to a New York City broker, the the promoter received a call from the broker who decided he had to see the property. He wouldn't take no for an answer, so arrangements were made to fly him to Toronto, then to the northern Ontario city of Timmins, then rent a car and drive a couple more hours.

My young associate hosted him. It was raining and entirely miserable that day. Nevertheless, they got to the property where the guide took his guest (who was dressed in a light trench coat and loafers) up and down the fields following the prospector's claim stakes on the property. After an hour of trudging up and down the same wet fields in Northern Ontario, the exasperated New York broker exclaimed: "But where's the mine?"

After I told them that story, the gold fund managers would see me on the convention floor and shout across the room, "But where's the mine!"

Of course, there was no mine. Just what we Canadians call moose pasture.

Oh, there are so many stories I could tell. Maybe just one more.

Once, while working for the Dean Witter organization in Canada, I used to field about 50 calls a week from US Dean Witter brokers asking about Canadian stocks.

One day, a broker from, I think, Arizona called to ask if Consolidated Moose Pasture qualified for margin. I said, no, penny stocks don't qualify (but he ought to have known that).

He replied that he believed the stock was trading at $30 and that he had bought a ton of share certificates directly from the Canadian promoter at a discount. He thought gold was going to the moon and so he hadn't really done any due diligence on the stock he bought. No, I had to explain, the Consolidated Moose Pasture was trading at 30 cents. Even stockbrokers are gullible, so don't feel bad.

The moral of these stories is that if you ever decide to speculate in gold or any other futures or commodity-related market, which are dominated by professionals, I implore you to fully understand what it is you are getting into.

You need to get competent advice from people who have experience, and then force yourself to take baby steps at the beginning. Then pray you don't lose your shirt.

After I completed the manuscript for this book, I decided on a new venture — to become, in addition to my other responsibilities, the Managing Director and investor in a Guyana gold operation called West Point Ventures Ltd (BVI), until then owned by a large insurance company, but not operated.

In private hands, West Point had invested several million dollars in acquiring claims for large-scale mining, plus 31 miles of the most productive placer mining concessions along the Mazaruni River deep in the rainforest interior, close to Venezuela. Diamonds and gold have been mined in the area for two hundred years.

Lessons from the Trader Wizard

The mines and dredge operations have until recently always been small and undercapitalized. Today there are several Canadian mining and exploration operations in Guyana, including IAMGOLD's Omai Mines, Guyana Goldfields, Aranka, and ValGold, among others. The excitement among those parties is obvious.

The Guiana Shield, stretching from Central America to Africa, is internationally known as one of the world's most productive areas for precious metals and diamonds. The epicenter is known to be in Venezuela, about 200 miles from the West Point property where all the Canadian operators are working.

Mining professionals have always believed that the physically challenging interior of Guyana holds the most promise for major new gold discoveries in the world. Recent changes in government and the development of some interior roads and airstrips alongside the rivers of the rainforest has served to open up the country somewhat to minerals exploration. The West Point-owned dredge is by far the largest and most modern in the country; it is featured in the Guyana Government Mining Commission brochure.

When the insurance company's manager showed me their purchase and plans for development, I expressed my interest, but only if the company would agree for me to finance additional dredges and acquire export licenses, a gold buying operation from the country's 100 or so small mining operators and a charter for a gold bullion bank in the capital city of Georgetown.

I then acquired a large number of shares in West Point from this insurance company in July 2007, and was appointed a Director as well as Managing Director of the Company.

Yes, I enjoy trading and everything about it, but I have always loved gold trading and gold mining operations. I am certain to want to write a book about this new chapter in my life.

Trading in oil and other energy futures

Petroleum futures have been around for some time, but with widespread fears of rising prices and temporary shortages, these contracts have become one of the most popular trading vehicles of speculators.

Energy futures involve trading in the following contract instruments:

* Brent Crude Oil (LO, IPE)
* Crude Oil (light, NYMEX)
* Gas-Oil (QS, IPE)

Specialties to Trade

- Heating Oil (NYMEX)
- Natural Gas (NG, NYMEX)
- Propane (NYMEX)
- Unleaded Gas (NYMEX)

Oil futures meet an essential need by establishing a mechanism to be used by commercial sellers and buyers to be sure of firm future prices, which they assure through hedging. Most of us, who put gasoline into our cars and fuel up our homes with oil, think we know a little about energy prices. But this is not a market for amateur speculators.

The base contract for heating oil futures is 42,000 US gallons (1,000 US barrels) of No. 2 heating oil with delivery at the Port of New York. Trading is on the New York Mercantile Exchange (NYMEX) (http://tfc-charts.com/chart/HO/W).

As with all futures contracts, the original margins for heating oil futures are low: 10% with a $3,375 minimum margin. That means that if the price of the contract rises 20%, the speculator (who takes the opposite side of what may be a professional's contract) will double his money. But if the price falls 30%, the speculator would be wiped out.

On August 1, 2007, Heating Oil on the NYMEX is trading at $2.10. To get the dollar equivalent, multiply 42 by the current. It is $88.20 a barrel.

Back on October 20, 2003, when I did this example, HO traded at 82.34¢ per gallon, or $34.58 per barrel. Contracts at that time were also sold on the New York Mercantile Exchange for delivery in the months of December 2003 @ 83.31¢ per gallon, January 2004 @ 83.91¢ per gallon, February 2004 @ 83.41¢ per gallon, March 2004 @ 81.56¢ per gallon and monthly through to August 2004 @ 72.41¢ per gallon.

Under exchange rules, the minimum daily price fluctuation is .01¢ per gallon ($4.20 per contract) to a maximum of 1¢ per gallon ($420 per contract). The margin can be put up in cash or collateral, such as a letter of credit or Treasury bills (up to 90% of the market value). When you use bills, you can apply the interest charges against the position cost.

In the market itself, the moving force is the professional. Let's say that, in October 2003, the purchasing agent of Smith Manufacturing Co. (SMC) was asked to order 10,000 barrels of No. 2 heating oil for December 2003 delivery at the then current market price of 82.34¢ per gallon.

If he bought that day, he would have had to put up $8,234 (the normal 10% margin), and arrange for storage of the heating oil that was purchased and pay interest on the money.

Lessons from the Trader Wizard

Instead, say SMC bought 10 December futures contracts at 83.68¢ per gallon (the .25¢ is added for all futures and the .12¢ reflects the costs of storage and financing). This requires a cash outlay of $8,368. In early December, say there is another price boost by OPEC for Crude Oil and the cash price of No. 2 oil is 88¢ per gallon. The purchasing agent buys 10,000 gallons for $88,000. This is $10,000 more than budgeted, but he sells his futures contracts for the same price. The small loss, $2,250, represents his insurance premium.

Role of the speculator

The speculator gets into the game in June when he thinks that, before December, there will be an over supply so that the price of the oil will drop a bit. He sells short December 10 futures contracts at $85.25 each. That means he does not own the oil, but merely agrees to make delivery in December. That's no fee and no interest.

The speculator is right, say. In November 2003, the price of the oil dips, so he buys back his contracts at 80.25¢ per gallon and chalks up a $5,000 gross profit on a margin of $8,525 in two months.

If he guesses wrong and the price of oil goes up, he will have to cover his position at a loss, and hope for a bigger profit on his next deal.

When he becomes experienced and has the aid of a knowledgeable broker-advisor, the venturesome speculator can use hedges of his own to protect some of his holdings. Or he can take advantage of unusual spreads between current and future prices: as much as 33¢ per gallon; 65¢ in the cash market, and 98¢ in the six-month futures market.

If he sells the 98¢ contract short and the spread narrows, he can buy back at a lower price for a profit. Or when the spread is narrow, he can buy long on one contract and sell short on the other. But he should always remember that about 70-90% of all futures contracts end up with a loss. You must make a big hit occasionally to win.

Specialties to Trade

3   Trading in foreign currencies

You need a plan and to stick to that plan. And I say you need to be patient and let markets come to you. If you want to play tennis with a pro, the only way to win is being on the defensive and hope the opponent makes unforced errors. You are trading against market pros (HB&Bs) and yet you can't wait to go on the offensive. That doesn't make sense. The object of the game is to win.

April 24, 2007

The Chicago Mercantile Exchange (CME) provides unusual speculative opportunities in the trading of foreign currencies. This is called the forex market. It is a market that trades over US$1 trillion a day, mostly by professionals.

Currencies futures involve trading in the following contract instruments:

* Australian Dollar (AD, CME)
* British Pound (BP, CME)
* Canadian Dollar (CME)
* E-Mini EuroFX (E7, CME)
* E-Mini Japanese Yen (J7, CME)
* Euro Dollar (CME)
* Euro Yen (CME)
* EuroFX (EC,CME)
* Japanese Yen (CME)
* Mexican Peso (MP,CME)
* New Zealand Dollar (CME)
* Swiss Franc (CME)
* US Dollar Index (CEC)

For good charts, see http://tfc-charts.com/currency_futures.

Just as with commodities futures, foreign currency speculators perform an essential function by taking opposite sides of contracts bought or sold by corporations and financial institutions to hedge their monetary-risk exposure around the world. Unlike other types of commodity trading, currency futures reflect reactions to what has already happened, rather than anticipation of what's ahead.

Specialties to Trade

For small margins of 1.5-4.2%, roughly $1,350 to $2,700, you can control large sums of money: 100,000 Canadian dollars; 125,000 euros; 62,500 British pounds; 12.5 million Japanese yen, etc.

The attraction is leverage. You can speculate that at a fixed date in the future the value of your contract will be greater (if you buy long) or less (if you sell short).

The daily fluctuations of each currency futures contract are limited by CME rules. A rise of $750 per day provides a 37.5% profit on a $2,000 position. That's a net gain of $705 ($750 less $45 in commissions). If the value declines, you are faced with a wipeout or, if you set a stop order, the loss of part of your security deposit. Vice versa when you sell short.

The CME provides a formal marketplace for hedging currencies of other nations as they relate to US dollars. Importers, exporters and multinational firms rely on forward contracts to protect their profits. They are willing to pay to reduce their foreign exchange risks.

The speculator takes the opposite side of the deal, or he can use spreads between the values of major currencies. Here is an example: As at August 1, 2007, the euro is quoted in US dollars at $1.371 and the British pound at $2.033. Each euro contract calls for 125,000 euros and the pound contract for 62,500 pounds. To get the dollar difference, multiply and subtract: (125,000 x $1.371) minus (62,500 x $2.033) gives $44,312. Since the trader believes (say) that the euro is more stable than the pound, he buys the euro and sells the pound. In a few months, say the spread widens to $50,000, he closes out the deal, pays a round-trip commission of $150 and takes his $5,538 profit. If the spread narrows, he's a loser.

Guidelines for successful currency speculation

(1) **Maintain a reserve**. If the market moves against you, you may have to cover as much as your original margin deposit. If you set aside $5,000 for speculation, keep $1,500 in reserve. Better yet, set stop-loss orders and keep your capital.

(2) **Become familiar with the world economic scene**. You should understand and regularly follow export-import imbalances, tariff changes, fluctuating interest rates, inflation interest rates, inflation, etc, in the US and in the nations whose currencies you hold.

(3) **Don't "day-trade"**. Getting in and out of a position in one trading day takes expertise and should be left to professionals. For the amateur, it's second-guessing. Chances are you will always be one step ahead or one step behind.

Lessons from the Trader Wizard

(4)   **If the price moves adversely, get out fast**. Don't sit on losses. Sour trades seldom sweeten. A drop of a few cents (or a rise if you're short) in this highly leveraged market can be costly. Set stop limits and hope you can get out in time.

(5)   **Don't open a discretionary account**. Your broker-advisor might know more than you do about currency, but don't look to him or her to make all the decisions. You can heed good advice, but it's your money!

(6)   **Concentrate on currencies that have a limited supply.** These are volatile and, therefore, present profit-making opportunities. There are only about $50 billion Swiss francs available compared to over $500 billion euros. Accordingly, the Swiss currency can move up or down more quickly.

As with all commodities and futures markets, you need to have a significant understanding of currency markets before participating.

Even then, you probably will end up a loser. One of the problems with trading these contract markets is that they are not as closely supervised as equity markets. Recently there was a case where US authorities arrested 47 individuals from their forex trading offices in the World Trade Centre in New York, involved in an apparent multi-firm currency scam trading operation that had been going on for over 20 years. Should anybody be surprised?

That incident is more evidence that US capital markets need to be re-organized so that the public has a fair opportunity to use and profit from these markets.

Specialties to Trade

4 Preferred, rights & warrants

Now, remember, this is not a system per se, but a disciplined approach to strategy where the time series analysis can help you track stocks of good quality companies into the AZ and DZ and to either make Buy or Sell decisions later. There are other factors involved in the actual buy and sell decisions, but these are nuances that depend on the individual's personality and resources (time, money, experience, info, etc). The key point I make to those who are interested in learning is that market prices move in trends and cycles and it is your job to buy at the beginning of a Bullish phase and to sell at the beginning of a Bearish phase. If you want to protect your wealth, with hopes of building it when times are good, there is no longer an opportunity of buying and holding forever the stocks of the best quality companies. These are merely prices and we trade prices.

May 25, 2007

Why some traders like preferred over common shares

I like preferred shares. I think there is a time and place for them in the portfolios of a great many more traders than actually hold them.

The InvestorGuide.com glossary defines preferred shares as:

"Capital stock which provides a specific dividend that is paid before any dividends are paid to common stock holders, and which takes precedence over common stock in the event of liquidation. Like common stock, preferred shares represent partial ownership in a company, although preferred stock shareholders do not enjoy any of the voting rights of common stockholders. Also, unlike common stock, a preferred share pays a fixed dividend that does not fluctuate, although the company does not have to pay this dividend if it lacks financial ability to do so.

The main benefit to owning preferred shares is that the owner has a higher level claim on the company's assets than common stockholders. Preferred shareholders always receive their dividends first and, in the event the company goes bankrupt, preferred shareholders are paid off before common stockholders. In general, there are four different types of preferred stock: cumulative preferred, non-cumulative, participating and convertible."

Specialties to Trade

Some advisors believe that preferred shares benefit corporations more than traders, but I don't agree. A preferred stock is just what the name states. It has features that take preference over the common. Typically, the preference is on all income available after payment of bond interest and amortization, but before dividend payments on the common stock.

For the most part, compared to common stock, preferred stock is safer. Therefore a preferred share is a "middle risk" security, about halfway between a bond and a common stock.

Like a security that pays fixed interest, most preferred dividend payments are fixed. But, not being as secure as a bond, when the corporation does not earn enough money, the dividends may be skipped but the bond interest is still paid. If dividends are missed, usually they are cumulative and would be paid when profits return, but you ought to check. A few preferred share issues are non-cumulative for missed dividends.

There may be traders who are seeking another particular preference, such as a feature that permits it to be converted to common stock.

Some traders are attracted to preferreds because of their low cost — typically $25 or $50 per share, compared to the $1,000 or $5,000 face value of bonds — and their more frequent payments, being quarterly dividends rather than semi-annual interest.

Also, in many jurisdictions, dividend income is taxed at a lower rate than interest income.

Above all, preferred shares are bought for the high dividend yield. It's almost always a higher dividend yield than offered by the common stock.

There is a downside to preferred stock. Unless it is also convertible into common, in the future this instrument will not provide a higher dividend yield as do most common stocks of seasoned, growing, profitable companies.

In addition, that fixed income is vulnerable to changes in the interest rate. When the cost of money goes up, the value of preferred stocks goes down.

Guidelines for trading in preferred shares

Preferred shares are very different to common shares. It pays to check into what you are buying. When selecting them, here is what you should look for:

Lessons from the Trader Wizard

Quality

Only consider preferreds that are S&P-rated BBB or better. The difference in yield between highly and poorly rated preferreds is seldom significant. The slightly lower dividend rate is more than offset by added safety.

Corporate debt

Since bond interest must be paid first, the lower the debt ratio, the safer will be your position in preferred stocks.

Sinking fund

This permits a corporation each year to buy up a portion of its issued and outstanding preferred shares so that the entire issue is retired before the stated maturity date, eg, starting five years after the original issue, the company buys back 5% of the shares annually for 20 years. Usually sinking fund preferred stock yields less than straight preferred, because it's a little safer.

Early redemption

Be sure there is nothing in the call provision that permits early redemption. Usually you're OK with preferred shares of large corporations.

Corporate surplus

When retained earnings are large, the board of directors might consider retiring some of the outstanding debt and preferred shares. For the common shareholder, this means less interest and dividends that must be paid to others and thus a chance for higher dividends on the common stock. For the preferred shareholder, if the stock is selling below par, any prospects of redemption tend to raise the market price.

Junior preference issues

Many of these allow refunding prior to the stated date through the issue of common shares. These carry a lower rating and tend to be more volatile than senior issues.

Marketability

Preferred shares of high-quality corporations listed on major exchanges are actively traded. Those of small companies, especially when sold OTC, may have thin markets and be subject to sharp price differentials. You can see this by the daily reports, where price changes can be as much as two points — far more than the swings of the common shares.

Voting rights

Most preferred shareholders are shut out from having any voice in company management unless the company gets into financial trouble. Even then, sometimes this is not a legal possibility.

Restrictions on common dividends

Adequate working capital and a satisfactory surplus should be required before dividends on the common stock can be paid. This helps protect you against a dip in earnings.

Restriction on subsequent issue of preferreds or bonds

There should be a provision — say two-thirds of the preferred shareholders — to limit management from issuing new preferred stock or bonds.

Premiums

Always consider the value of the preferred in relation to straight debt issues. As a rule of thumb, buy preferreds only when the yield is 25% greater than that of bonds of similar quality.

Interest rate trend

As five-year Treasury bonds moved up rapidly in price — meaning yields fell — from near year-end 1999 to a trend reversal in May 2003, the 2H03 was not the best time to be buying preferred shares. The best time was December 1999, when traders should have switched from common shares to preferreds, and held through to May 2003, when they should have switched back to common.

Experienced brokers

Many registered reps don't understand preferred stocks, so if you plan substantial holdings of them, deal with an experienced broker-dealer and a registered rep that has a lot of skill in trading them.

Trading preferred shares to maximize dividend income

One practice I used in my money management career many years ago was to try to get as many as 12 dividends a year by rolling over preferred shares. That can be done, but it's neither easy nor always advisable.

316

With a 6% dividend yield, a dozen dividend payouts a year would hypothetically total an 18% annual rate of return (before commissions), but it takes a lot of attention to the market to accomplish a result like that.

Realistically, you'll probably have to settle for about six to seven dividend payouts a year, which is still an 8–10% return from preferreds yielding 6%.

This extra income is possible because, unlike accrued interest on bonds, dividends on preferred stocks are not included in the sale price. By holding the shares on the dividend record date, you get full payout. After a record date, you sell and buy another preferred with an upcoming record date.

Timing is important because, after the record date, the price of the preferred will drop, typically from 25–50% of the dividend. Thus, a 6% preferred might trade at 102 before (quarterly) dividend and drop back to 101.25 or 101.50 in the next day or so. If you sell then, you will take a small capital loss, which will reduce your return from the dividend income. But, if you wait a week or so, you may not lose anything if the price comes back up. However, if you wait too long, you will not be able to roll over as often.

Because of full service commission costs, I would recommend dealing in units of 500 or 1000 shares or more in using this strategy.

All convertible securities (CVs) combine the fixed distribution feature of senior securities and the growth potential of common stocks. As the name implies, CVs can be converted into shares of the related common stock at specified ratios — usually until a specified date, but occasionally indefinitely.

Convertibles represent income plus potential appreciation. They can be in the form of preferreds or debentures. When the term "convertible/s" is used alone here, it refers to both preferred stocks and bonds.

Convertible preferred shares

Convertible preferred stocks are similar to, but not as secure as, convertible debentures as they are not as likely to be paid off in case of corporate liquidation.

CV preferreds have four main features or benefits:

*   **Income and growth.** A CV preferred is often issued in connection with an acquisition, where the dividend rate would be attractive to the selling stockholders who want income. The convertibility feature also provides them with the potential of some capital appreciation.

- **Tax advantage**. The dividend is taxed at a lower rate than the interest income of a debenture.

- **Continuity**. Preferred stock will remain outstanding until it becomes advantageous for holders to exercise their conversion privileges, whereas the debentures have a limited life.

- **Lower price.** They sell at $25 to $50 each (compared to a usual par value of $1,000 for CV debentures), which makes them attractive to small traders.

CV preferreds have many of the above advantages (except tax savings) for corporations, plus they carry no fixed obligation like a debt. Preferred stock is not a debt that may have to be repaid at a specific time or that may have to be retired by a fixed date — directly or through sinking fund provisions.

I have an associate who built his portfolio management business around convertibles. When it came to CVs, he was the go-to guy. While I'm not as enthused, I do think they have their place in the financial spectrum, particularly as a buy-out tool in corporate finance, and as a trading strategy for special situation holdings in promising but unseasoned companies.

In the latter case, it's nice to hold a little of the debt and to give the management team, who will take the risk, a little more upside on their holdings of the company's common shares.

Convertible debentures

Convertibles represent income plus potential appreciation. They can be in the form of preferreds or debentures. Convertible debentures are more complicated than convertible preferreds or straight debentures.

Convertible bonds (called debentures when there is no asset backing) represent a debt of the issuing company. They can be viewed as a debt with a warrant attached or as an issue of stock with a put option.

Definitions used with convertibles

Issue: This names the issuing company, the interest rate of the bonds and the date of maturity when the bond will be redeemed. Some securities have a deadline for conversion. After that date, you may get fewer shares of stock.

Rating: This is based on a company's financial strength, as considered by a service like Moody's or Standard & Poor's. The top Moody's rating is Aaa

318

(S&P is AAA), then Aa, A, Baa, etc. B ratings flash a warning signal. All C ratings apply to bonds of poor standing.

Amount outstanding: This is the dollar value of the bonds now outstanding. As a general rule, be wary of small issues, ie, less than $50 million. Their market will be limited, which means a wider than usual spread between bid and offer prices.

Call price: This is the price you receive if all or part of the bonds are redeemed in advance of the maturity date: 102.63 means you get $1,026.30 per bond.

Conversion price: To determine how many shares of stock your bond will convert to, divide the conversion price into the par value ($1,000). Thus, a conversion price of 50 equals 20 shares of common stock. Your broker's information will do the calculation.

Conversion premium. The percentage of difference between the conversion value and the market price of the CV. With ABC, each CV can be swapped for 47.8 shares of common stock. When the common is trading at $12.25, the conversion value is $585.55 ($12.25 x 47.8). Since the CV is selling at 61.50 ($615), the difference is about $30. Divide $30 by $615 to get a premium of 4.88%.

Yield of CV: The interest rate divided by the current price of the debenture. With ABC 6% trading at $800, this is a yield of 7.50%.

Yield of common: This is the dividend on the stock divided by the current price of the stock. With ABC, at $10.00 paying a dividend of 50¢ per share, the yield is 5.00%.

Note: This data, plus other information, such as the value of the CV based on the price of the common stock and the value of the common based on the price of the CV, are available in printed reports from Moody's, Standard & Poor's and Value Line. Ask your broker for a copy or check your local library.

Formula for the premium on new CVs

To calculate the premium on a new issue, use this formula:

Where
PC = the price of the common stock
SC = the number of shares by conversion
PV = the par value of the convertible
$P = the dollar premium you pay

CV = the present value of the convertible
P = the percentage of premium

$$CV = PC \times SC$$
$$PV - CV = \$P$$

Then:

$$P = \$P/CV$$

Example: ABC convertible debentures 8% due in 2010, rated A, are selling at 100. Each bond is convertible into 32.39 shares of common stock, which is trading at 29.

To find the percentage of premium:

$$CV = 29 \times 32.39 = 939.31$$
$$1000 - 939 = 61$$
$$61/939 = 6.5\%$$

This is a low premium for a CV of a high-quality company with a sound credit rating. If the corporate prospects are good and the stock is attracting trader interest, the ABC CVs could be worthwhile.

In most cases, both types of CVs (the bonds and the preferred shares) are callable prior to maturity, but not during the first few years after issue. This encourages the initial sale.

Over the years, a couple of my professional colleagues heavily promoted the features and benefits of CVs to their clients. However, despite what some brokers and advisors may tell you, CVs are no sure road to financial success.

What they are is a conservative way to play the equity market and an aggressive way to play the fixed-income market. Income-oriented traders like the comparatively high yields; speculators become excited about the possible gains from a rise in the price of the related common stock.

CVs are best in bull markets. With careful management, they can be profitable in bear markets. But, in flat markets, CVs are seldom worthwhile. The key is the corporation's ability to make more money, and pay higher dividends, which over time pushes up the value of the common stock, thereby making the CV more valuable. Otherwise, since you paid a premium for the conversion privilege, the losses can be substantial.

Usually CVs are protected against major dilutions (over 5%) of the related common stock (from stock splits or stock dividends) by appropriate adjustments of the conversion terms.

Lessons from the Trader Wizard

Value determinants

CVs are sold as securities that let traders "have their cake and eat it too". This optimism is based on the idea there are two value determinants:

Investment value: This is an estimated price, set by an analyst, at which the CV would be selling if it had no conversion feature. It is supposed to be a floor price under which the CV will not decline regardless of price action of the underlying common stock.

This "investment" value is always related to the prevailing interest rate, so it will fluctuate. Thus, when the stock is selling well below the conversion price, an 6% CV, issued at par, would trade at about 66 when the yield on straight bonds is about 9%.

Conversion value: This is the amount a CV would be worth if it were exchanged for shares of the common stock. It is almost always higher than the investment value. A bond convertible into 50 shares of common stock has a conversion value of $1,000 when the stock is at 20 per share. If the price of the stock rises to 30, the conversion value will be $1,500 — or probably more because of the ever-present element of hope.

The point of conversion depends on the yield, not the market prices of the securities. Example: ABC 6s, '08 entitle the holder to 30 shares of common, now selling at 36 and paying a dividend of $2 a year. The CV would probably be trading at around $1,100.

The yields of both the bond and common are the same: $60. If the stock's payout is raised to $2.25, the income will be $67.50 for the stock versus $60 for the bond. It's time to think about a swap.

Be mindful that: (i) there will be a constant yield on the CV as long as the corporation is solvent; and (ii) there may be a boost in the dividend of the common stock.

A CV will usually sell at the higher of its two current values and, in a strong market, at a premium. But don't let anyone kid you; CVs, by their nature, are typically speculative assets.

Summing up the positives and negatives about convertibles

Positives

Worthwhile financial instruments for children and grandchildren. While you are alive, the income from CVs is ample and after you've passed, your heirs can also hope for appreciation.

Specialties to Trade

Floor, but no ceiling. High-grade CVs do have some sort of price floor but almost no price ceiling. This applies to their common stocks, too. In bear markets, the values of CVs can fall just as fast, and far, as the common stock and, when interest rates rise, their declines are almost certain.

More favorable margin requirements. Usually brokers require less collateral for CVs than for common stocks and most banks will loan more: normally 80% of their value compared to 50% for stocks. Thus, there's greater leverage than with stocks. And when the yields are high, the income will reduce the net payment to the lender.

Some negatives

Specialized analysis: The profitable selection of CVs requires careful comparison and analysis. You have to study the CV instrument as well as the fundamentals of the issuer.

Limited marketability: CVs have less trader acceptance than common stock. Check the CV trading volume and price movements over a couple of months. With long-term investments, of course, temporary fluctuations are not important.

High premiums: The prices of both CV preferred shares and bonds are often overpriced because of their well-publicized advantages.

This is especially true with new issues in strong bull markets, because CVs are issued when the company and the underwriter feel they can command the maximum price.

Trading considerations for CVs

The common stock: The premium value of any CV lies in the worth of its related common stock. If a stock is speculative, the CV will be risky too. If it's a stock of a highly conservative company, the conversion privileges of the CV won't make the corporation grow faster or more profitably.

Buy CVs only of the companies whose common stocks you want to own on the basis of quality, value and prospects.

Trade-off: The trader faces a trade-off between the premium and the yield of CVs, which is the difference between the income of the convertible and the dividend on the related stock. Professionals look for issues where the spread can be made up in about three years.

Example: A $1,000 par value, 9% debenture of ABC can be exchanged for 20 shares of common stock. The stock is at 42, so the difference is $160

($1,000 – $840), which is a 19% premium. The stock pays a $2 dividend or a total of $40 if a swap were made. The difference between the $90 interest and the $40 dividends is $50 a year.

To calculate how long it will take for the extra income from the interest to make up the conversion premium, divide $160 by $50 to get 3.2 years. So, with a profitable and fast-growing company, that 19% premium on the ABC CV is acceptable.

Duration of the conversion privilege: If the conversion period is short, the company may not be able to show growth and profits fast enough for the common stock to appreciate to the point at which the option will be valuable.

Don't assume the conversion period runs for the life of the debenture. Sometimes, the convertibility of a debenture, preferred or related warrant lapses before the senior security matures. If you are looking for long-term gains, you may be better off with the common stock than with the CV, especially if there is a chance of an early call at a price that is well below the market value.

Often, too, in many CVs the conversion price rises over time, so that today's attractive option could be meaningless several years in the future.

Buying time: In weak stock markets and in the first phases of a business downturn, it's best to concentrate on CVs of companies in defensive industries, such as utilities, food processors, and food chains, etc. In strong markets and in the early stages of business recovery, maximum capital gains are generally found in CVs of companies in cyclical industries, such as machinery, aerospace, construction, etc.

Be wary in all bull markets: Be sure the related stock is not selling at or near its all-time high.

When stock prices are high, dealers float new issues of CVs to take advantage of trader optimism. If you buy new CV IPOs, you may pick up a few points quickly, but the long-term prospects are likely based on overly enthusiastic projections and expectations.

In bear markets, relax and be patient: Even in a bear market, if the company is a high quality growth company, the price of its common stock will, in a year or two, continue its rise with the up-move of the overall market. You'll get a good yield, but bear in mind that CVs are often issued by corporations that are not strong enough to float straight debt.

Specialties to Trade

Interest rates: The toughest time to own CVs is when the cost of money is rising. A small interest rate increase of 0.5% will cause a drop of 5 to 7 points in the investment value of a CV.

Comparable yields: As a rule of thumb, the yield of the CV should be no more than 25% below that of a non-convertible issue of comparable quality or the price of a non-convertible bond. If you find a bargain, be cautious. Usually there's a reason (logical or not) for the low price of any security. The capital markets offer no free lunch.

Timing: The trader should make the swap when the income from the dividends on the common stock is greater than the interest of the debentures or the dividends of the preferred.

Example: ABC $4.00 preferred is convertible to 1.05 shares of common stock. The owner of 100 shares of preferred is sure of $400 annual income. By converting, he can own 105 shares of common that, with a $5.00 per share dividend, brings in $525.

Guidelines for CV premiums

When the premium is under 15%, the capital risk is small with high-quality (ie, rated B or better) companies.

When the premium is 15-25%, the investment is fairly risky. The CV yield should be high enough to justify the risk or the prospects for the company should be very good.

When the premium exceeds 25%, the yield should be relatively high, but the corporate prospects should also be outstanding. Otherwise, face it, you're speculating.

How to project returns with CVs

Here's an example of how to guesstimate what your profits will be with a $1,000 debenture convertible to 25 shares of common stock, now trading at 32.

If the stock goes up

Say, by year two after issuing a CV, company ABC reports a hefty rise in profits and continuing good prospects. As a result, the price of the common stock jumps 25% to $40 per share. The CV goes up too, but at a slower rate, say 20%, from 100 to 120. There is a reason for this.

Lessons from the Trader Wizard

As the bond price increases, the CV acts more like a stock and less like a bond. Investment value is of diminishing importance, the risk increases and the yield declines, which are factors that tend to hold back the price of the senior security. Conversion is unrealistic, but some holders might want to sell the CV and take their profits.

ABC continues to do well, and with a buoyant stock market, the price of the common stock hits $60 per share (an 87% gain). But the CV price goes up only 50% to 150. At this point, the bond-like characteristics are lost and the CV is interchangeable with the stock, which is indicated by disappearance of the conversion premium.

Before deciding to convert, check the CV and stock comparative yields. Where interest is $50 per year, the stock dividend must be $2.00 per share to equal it.

When a CV's conversion value and market price become the same, the stock and the CV should move up and down together.

When a CV sells with a negative conversion premium (ie, below its conversion price), professional traders go for the arbitrage. They buy the CV and simultaneously sell the stock short. Converting the CVs lets them replace stock borrowed for the short sale.

Example: If the ABC CV is priced at 145 while the conversion value is $1,500, the trader will buy 10 bonds for $14,500. He will then sell short 250 shares of ABC common for $15,000 for a quick profit of $500.

If the stock goes down

The other possibility is that ABC runs into trouble and its profits decline so that the price of the common stock is cut in half to 16. The price of the CV will also fall, but the drop in price will be cushioned by its investment value of 75, which is a 25% drop. The price of the CV might go lower, as the investment value would have to be readjusted. If the interest rate rose sharply, the price of the CV would fall even further.

If the CV had started out with a high coupon, say 9%, and the prime interest rate declined substantially, the price of the CV would rise as a reflection of its investment value. The reverse would be true if the CV originally carried a low rate and the interest rate rose sharply.

Specialties to Trade

About the trading of rights and warrants

Trading rights

Corporations will issue rights when trying to raise equity capital quickly to restructure the balance sheet.

Rights are in common use in industries like public utilities where management seeks to counter the company's heavy debt obligations by issuing more common shares, but not do so immediately. So they sell the rights to shareholders.

To those shareholders who receive these rights, the securities are a form of option to buy common stock (usually) at a more favorable price ahead of the public, say at 17 when the stock is trading at 20.

The discount reflects the fact that the new shares will dilute the value of the outstanding stock since total assets and earnings of the company are now divided among a larger number of shares. However, there are no commissions and if the shareholder doesn't want to exercise any or all of his rights, he can sell them in the open market.

Because of the discount, some traders think rights are the same as warrants, but that's not entirely correct. Warrants are issued in combination with other securities as a kicker to interest the trader. Rights are used to raise quick cash on their own and they have a much shorter life than warrants, typically a month or less.

Benefits of rights to the corporation

Build shareholder goodwill: All shareholders like to acquire new stock at discount prices.

Lower costs of raising capital: Existing shareholders already like the corporation, so are likely to subscribe, especially if they feel that adding capital will create greater profits.

Broaden stock ownership at small cost: Because some shareholders will not exercise their rights, from lack of interest or money, they will sell them in the market to other traders, including new shareholders for the corporation.

Benefits of rights to the shareholders

Built-in profit: When ABC offered rights on 10 million shares at 17, the stock was trading at 20. If you owned 1000 shares, with one right for every

326

four shares, you could buy 250 more shares @17 and pay $4,250 for stock with a market value of about $5,000, a gain of $750. But note that, with the extra shares, the ABC stock price will drop on the market. That's because you could have also sold those rights on the market for their intrinsic value, which for ABC is $500 (ie, 1000 rights @ $0.50).

No commissions: When you exercise rights, there are no broker-dealer commissions involved. So don't worry about extra commission costs on odd lots.

Maintaining one's ownership position: If you like your position in a company, exercise your rights because, in a study by Barron's, 80% of stocks bought with rights outperformed the market in the year following the issue.

Calculating the values of rights

Shareholders who own a stock before it goes "ex-rights" are eligible for the rights. As rights have an intrinsic value, the price and value of the stock will decline after the "ex" date.

Rights also have speculative value because of their leverage. In this example, you'll see that a 10% rise in the stock price can mean a 25% jump in the price of the right. Or vice versa on the loss side.

To calculate the value of one right before the ex-date, add 1 to the number of rights, and use this formula:

$$VR = (MP - EP) / (NR + 1)$$
where
VR = value of right
MP = stock's market price
EP = exercise price
NR = number of rights needed to buy one share

Let's assume that ABC stock is trading at $20 per share; that shareholders get one right for every four shares; and that each right entitles the holder to buy one new share at $17 each.

$$VR = (20 - 17) / (4 + 1) = 3 / 6 = \$0.50$$

Thus, each right is worth $0.50 and the stock, at that point, is worth 20.

After ABC stock has gone ex-rights, there'll be no built-in bonus for shareholders, and the right will sell at its own value or possibly higher if the ABC share price rises, or lower if it declines.

Specialties to Trade

Shareholders should never let them lapse in the market. You lose not only the actual value of the right in the market, but you may also lose a tax benefit if you have a loss. You may have to decide quickly, because rights have a very short life, usually 30 days or less.

Guidelines for trading in rights

It's best to buy rights on the market soon after they are listed for trading and to sell a day or two before the lapse date.

Always look at the total costs including commissions and taxes on the rights and the future sale of the stock. In trading small numbers of odd lots, commission costs as a percentage of the transaction value can be significant.

Rights issued on foreign stocks may not be exercised by US residents except in the rare cases the issuer has registered the related securities with the SEC. So sell them.

Some shareholders will not exercise their rights so, after the expiration date, there may be an opportunity to buy these rights. You should give your broker an early indication of your desire to participate in the over-subscription.

About trading warrants

Warrants are like rights in that both represent an option to buy usually common stock. A warrant is an option to buy a stated number of shares of stock at a stipulated price during a specified period. But, whereas rights usually expire in a month or so, warrants have a long life: five, 10, 20 years or even unlimited life.

To the trader, warrants are speculations because they have no claim on the assets of the corporation, have no voting rights, and pay no dividends. They are generally issued in bearer form and are not registered with the company. If lost or stolen, there's almost no way for a broker-dealer or an exchange to "flag" them, so you keep these positions with your broker.

Warrants can be useful to corporations when issuing new senior securities such as bonds or preferred stocks. To the buyer, they are a "kicker", which is an inducement to purchase. The warrants give the bond or preferred stockholder an opportunity to make extra money if the price of the stock rises.

Corporations fix the price at which the warrant can be exercised to a level above the current market price of the stock at the time the warrant is issued. Thus, with ABC common stock at 20, the warrant might entitle the holder to buy one share at 30. Then, if ABC common stock goes from 20 to 40, the warrant holder will have an instant profit of $10 per share when he buys the stock at 30.

Warrants can be tricky to trade. As a rule, I think they should be bought only in bull markets and sold short only in bear markets. However, warrants are an attractive vehicle for speculation, if properly selected and carefully managed. They offer high leverage because of their relatively low cost and fast market movements.

Benefits of warrants to the corporations

Lower interest costs than would be needed to issue regular bonds: Typically, new issue bonds sold with warrants will have coupons as much as two points below the prevailing cost of money: say 6% vs. 8% for straight debt.

Tax benefits in that net costs are lower: With a $1,000, 7%, 25-year convertible bond with a warrant attached, the value, for tax purposes, would be $680 for the bond and $320 for the warrant.

The corporation can write off the $70 annual interest as an expense and amortize the $320 as a bond discount over the 25 years, thus creating an additional $13-per-year tax deduction. The after-tax cost of the bond/warrant would be $28.50 compared to $35 for straight debt or convertible.

Benefits of warrants to the owner

Compared to the related stock, the warrant is always lower-priced and more volatile. Since the two securities tend to move somewhat parallel to each other, an advance in stock price creates a higher percentage gain for the warrant than for the stock.

Example: Say a warrant to buy a stock at 20 has a price equal to its intrinsic (tangible) value of 5 when the stock is selling at 25. When the stock moves up to 35 and gain is 40%, the 10-point rise to 15 for the warrant is a 200% gain. That illustrates the leverage of warrants.

But the downside risk is also greater with warrants than with the stock. A 5-point drop for the stock, from 25 to 20, is a 20% decline, but a similar loss for the warrant, from 15 to 10, is a 33% decline.

Warrants do not always trade at intrinsic value. As a general rule, leverage is not advantageous when the warrant has little or no intrinsic value, such as happens when the stock is trading well below the exercise price. But, as with all speculations in an erratic market, I found there's little logic in the evaluation.

Factors to consider when trading in warrants

Like any speculation, warrants represent hope. When the price of the common stock with a related warrant is below the exercise price, the warrant has only speculative value. Thus, a warrant to buy a stock at 60 is intrinsically worthless when the stock is at 59.

In practice, however, a warrant has value that reflects the corporation's prospects, the stock market conditions at the time, and the remaining life of the warrant.

A while ago, ABC common stock was trading at 44 and the warrants, which were an option to buy the stock at 52, were selling at 7, which meant the buyer needed 59 plus commission costs to breakeven. That 34% speculative value seemed like quite a leap of faith at the time.

When the price of a stock rises above the specified exercise price, the warrants, in addition to intrinsic value, are often inflated by speculation. So, when ABC rose 18% to 52, the price of the warrant soared from 7 to 11.50, which was still a 22% premium, down from the earlier 34% premium. But those who bought ABC at 7 were up 57%.

Hopefully, now you see why warrants are speculations.

As with all time-based trading instruments, the closer a warrant gets to its expiration date, the smaller the speculative premium it commands. After expiration, the warrant is worthless. Conversely, if there is real hope that the price of the stock will rise, the longer the life of the warrant, the higher the percentage premium.

With perpetual warrants, no matter how seemingly remote the chances, a speculator's faith can pay off. *Forbes* magazine once described a classic example of blind faith. In 1942, Tri-Continental Corp., a closed-end investment company, with holdings in conservative stocks, was faring poorly. Its warrants were trading at $0.03 each and traded primarily for tax loss reasons. The warrant could buy 1.27 shares at $22.25, which was far above the stock price at that time.

But by 1969, the stock market was rising and the 1942 purchase had paid off in spectacular fashion. By then, a 1942 investment of $312 in common stock had grown to be worth $29,000, but over the same period a $312 purchase of the perpetual warrants would have been valued at $703,000. That's not bad if you could wait 27 years for the big pay off.

Lessons from the Trader Wizard

In today's normally volatile markets, the speculation in warrants can be remarkable, but only experienced speculators should be trading them. There are huge profits in bull markets, and disastrous losses in bear market conditions.

A guideline for maximum premiums in the warrant market

From this guideline (which I copied down years ago because it seemed reasonable), you will see that the maximum premium to pay for warrants with a few years of life, is 41% when the stock is trading at 100% of the exercise price of the warrants.

Stock price as % of exercise price	Warrant price as % of exercise price
80%	28%
90%	34%
100%	41%
110%	48%
120%	55%

The speculative value of a warrant is greatest when the warrant price is below the exercise price. If the stock moves up, the price of the warrant can jump fast.

In this case study, ABC could have been bought later at a 34% premium when the stock was 85% of the warrant exercise price. A while later, it was selling at a 22% premium when the stock was 100% of the warrant exercise price.

How to figure the value of a warrant

The easiest way to calculate the value of a warrant is by using one of the free software tools on the Internet (eg, http://numa.com/derivs/ref/calculat/warrant/calc-wta.htm).

I recommend you try to work out some calculations on your own beforehand if you intend to trade warrants in the market.

Keeping in mind that that market price of warrants is hard to predict, here are two guidelines:

- For volatile stocks, here's a rule of thumb used by some traders: a warrant is worth 40% of the exercise price plus or minus 50% of the difference between the market price and exercise price of the common stock.

Specialties to Trade

- If the current market price is higher than the exercise price, add half the difference. If it's lower, subtract half the difference.

Example: Say ABC common stock is trading at 50 and the warrant is exercisable at 60. The value of the warrant in this case is 40% of 60 (equals 24) less half of 10 (5) to get 19.

With the common stock at 70, and the warrant exercisable at 60, the formula would be 24 plus 5 for a value of 29.

This is a tricky calculation and may not be all that accurate, so if you are really interested in speculating in warrants, try a more sophisticated approach, as follows:

The current intrinsic value (CIV) of the warrant equals the sum of the stock price (SP) plus the number of shares per warrant (N) minus the exercise price (EP).

$$CIV = (SP + N) - EP$$

To determine the percentage of premium, where,
WP = warrant price

PP = percentage premium.

$$PP = ((WP - CIV) / (SP \times N)) \times 100\%$$

With the stock at 60, the 1-to-1 warrant is exercisable at 60, the intrinsic value is:

$$CIV = (60 + 1) - 70 = -9$$

And, where the warrant price is 25

$$PP = (25 - (-9)) / (60 \times 1) \times 100\% = 34 / 61 \times 100\% = 55.7\%$$

At a warrant price of 25, the percentage premium is 55.7%, so I wouldn't be interested in this warrant at this time. Why? The stock price at 60 was 86% of the 70 exercise price, so a 31% maximum premium is indicated as a guideline from our table.

Should the warrant price fall to 10 and the stock price remain at 60, let's re-do the calculations:

$$PP = (10 - (-9)) / (60 \times 1) \times 100\% = 19 / 61 \times 100\% = 31.1\%$$

Lessons from the Trader Wizard

From the table I showed as a guideline, this warrant price now qualifies as a reasonable price to pay in terms of its speculative value.

Of course, I still have to want to buy the stock on a quality basis before I'm prepared to speculate in the warrants. That is the bottom line: I'd never look at a warrant unless it was a security offered by a Cara 100 company.

How to pick warrants for capital gains

Every warrant speculator should follow a trading discipline. The Trader Wizard offers the following guidelines:

In a bull market:

- Always buy warrants to sell, not to exercise. Sell into strength of a bull market. Don't buy them in a bear market.

- Buy warrants of a common stock that you would buy anyway, like a Cara 100 company. If the common stock does not go up, there is little chance that the warrant's price will advance.

- Stick with warrants of fair-to-good quality corporations whose stocks are listed on major exchanges. They have broad markets. Only when you feel confident, seek out special situations in warrants of small, growing companies. Many of these young companies rely on warrants in their financing. The actual or anticipated growth of the common stock can boost the price of their warrants rapidly.

- Buy warrants of growing corporations that have actively traded stocks. The best profits come from warrants associated with stocks that have potential for strong earnings improvement, a prospective takeover, news-making products or services, etc.

- Be wary of warrants where the related stock is closely controlled or thinly traded. If someone decides to sell a large holding, the warrant values can fall fast.

- Buy warrants when they are selling at historic low prices, or in the Cara Accumulation Zone. The downside risks are small. But watch out for "super bargains" because commissions can weigh on your profit potential.

- Buy warrants when the stock price is not less than 80% of the exercise price and not more than 120% of it. Watch the premium percentage carefully.

Specialties to Trade

- Watch the expiration/change date or you could end up with a worthless expired contract. Premium percentages fall the closer it gets to expiry. After expiration a warrant has no value.

- Avoid short-life warrants. Inexperienced traders ought to avoid holding warrants with a lifespan of less than four years.

- Spread risk. If you lack warrants trading experience, but have sufficient capital, buy warrants in, say, three different companies. The odds are that you may hit big on one, break even on one and lose on the other. Your total gains may be less than if you had gambled on one warrant that proved a winner, but your losses will probably be much less if you're wrong. And you will have gained experience.

- Look for special opportunities. I have seen cases where warrants are part of a package with convertible bonds. Then both the warrants and the bonds may be used to acquire the stock. If you want to buy the stock, sell the warrants after a market rally, especially if the bonds trade at a bigger discount. Use the CV bonds to acquire the stock.

Short-selling warrants in a bear market

Do not buy warrants in a bear market, but consider short-selling them. In bear markets, the leverage of warrants can be profitable with short sales but added precautions are necessary. Basically, it's the opposite of buying long. You assume that the same relationship between the stock and warrants continues when their prices fall.

But short-selling is always tricky and, with warrants, you must watch for:

- thin markets with little volatility due to a lack of speculator interest;

- the possibility of a "short squeeze" — the inability to buy warrants to cover your short sales as the expiration date approaches the life of warrants. An expiration date may be extended. This pushes out the date when the warrants become worthless, but the stock might rise during that extra period, so a short-seller may not be able to cover his position at as low a price as anticipated;

- exchange regulations that could affect your plans, eg, a securities exchange may prohibit short-selling of listed warrants several months before expiration date.

5 Special situations

Anything goes these days. And what do we have to show for it? I'll tell you — because it concerns me. Nobody can be objective these days because, heaven forbid, the advice might be negative, and "negative" doesn't sell. The market is set up for people to buy. The market is marketing.

June 9, 2007

Buying micro-cap stock

While most of you have never traded instruments like options and futures, CVs, rights and warrants, I suspect many of you have traded in micro-cap stock at one point in your life.

Being an expert in this field, I can tell you there is only one guideline to trading success in a micro-cap stock: buy into a good stock promoter and sell any time you think he's selling. Little else matters, particularly in the case of very small companies.

How you can tell when the promoter is selling is difficult, but not impossible.

When current stock prices are fairly flat in the face of massive trading volume, following a period of strong promotion and rising share prices, I'm 98% certain the promoter is selling.

I've even experienced cases where the stock promoter himself called me in the Bahamas from afar to "find out" why his stock was trading so much volume. Then he pointed a finger at one of my friends in Europe.

Now that's called scouting. He's simply trying to determine if the word is out at that point that he is selling stock. So, he'll call various people close to the market to see the lay of the land. If he's confident that "the Street" doesn't suspect his selling, he'll continue to sell.

Stock promoters are truly wholesalers of stock. They are the dream merchants who pick up worthless or low-value stock and acquire some assets, put together a story and then go out to create interest. He'll go to the market letter writers, the broker-dealer RRs who play the penny-stock game, and the larger retail accounts on his "sucker's list".

If he does a good job as a promoter, the stock price goes up regardless of whether the asset performs as hoped.

That is not to say he has done a single thing wrong. In fact, I trust stock promoters about as much as I trust Wall Street. Some are trustworthy, but I presume they're all lying until I do my homework and prove otherwise. Many promoters, I've found, haven't conducted any nefarious business — *at least, no more than your average commercial or investment banker*.

But, if you're going to buy into micro-cap stocks, you have to understand *there is a good chance of misrepresentation to the corporate literature and the promoter's claims*. If you're that interested in the story — and they mostly sound very good — then you have to do your homework.

And you have to be prepared to sell on your own analysis, because nobody is going to present you with a good case for selling. At least, I haven't seen too many.

Consider the following: Say somebody tells you about a new process of producing gem-quality stones. As the story goes, the pebbles found at the bottom of a stream bed can be mined by the shovel full by a man and his spouse and put into a special furnace to harden them almost to diamond strength. With a little elbow grease buffing, the stones can be sold to gem merchants for very high prices. The financial analysts have looked at the numbers; the market advisory letter writers have salivated over the storyline; and all the visitors have returned home from the mountain stream with free "gems" for their spouses and to have the local gemologists examine.

All seems fine as a promoter visits the "mine site" and negotiates to buy the deal with a net profit royalty to the mountaineer and his spouse. While the production team is dreaming of their upcoming first trip to Paris and Milan, the promoter is readying the stock for sale to the public. As the story goes, everybody wants "in". The stock price zooms higher, from a few pennies to well over $10. Soon, the daily turnover grows to a huge number as the stock hangs in the $14 to $15 range. A couple of months go by before more than a few retail traders start to look into the deal. They find that sales are "OK" at an annualized rate of $2 million. Margins are good, and the bottom line could be as high as $1 million in the company's first year. That's after paying out the $250,000 royalty to Mountaineer (Offshore) Ltd, which its owners have rationalized as being "effective tax planning".

But then reality hits when the securities commission receives its first public filing, available for all to see on Edgar, the SEC public record system. It seems nobody read the fine print that the promoter had held an option on 20 million shares, which he was free to exercise if the stock advanced above $5 from its former base of five cents. The operative word here is "held" because the promoter has now exercised his option @ 1¢, putting $200,000 into the treasury, which keeps the promotion active. But, now there are 35 million shares outstanding and at a current price of $14, the market cap has grown to $490 million. The micro-cap-cum-small-cap stock is presently trading at 500 times earnings. At best, earnings for the next year are expected to grow by 25% to a net of possibly $1.25 million. Ouch!

Worse, there were 10 million shares traded in the past three months at between 12 and 15 (dollars of course) that the promoter has sold, which explains why he's now living in Panama, and no longer has the time to work on this deal. He's now busy looking for a shell public company where he can vend in a Belize lobster farming deal that he could build into the "next great" micro-cap stock.

Does this type of thing happen? All the time! Buyer beware. Do your homework. Sell your position as soon as volume increases start to jump well ahead of price increases. Enjoy a trip to Panama or Paris and Milan yourself. You've probably earned it.

If you want someone else to do your homework on micro-cap (and some small-cap I suppose) — which, in most cases, is wise until you get the hang of it — you could try a market advisory letter. Some appear to have good credentials and an enviable track record. I have never used one, however, because I do my own homework.

Every speculative trader who has learned to make good money in a special situation has also learned along the way to differentiate between speculation, promotion and scam. If you're new to the game, it pays to read up on case studies. They tell a story of fortune or misfortune, as the case may be. You can learn plenty from the stories of others.

Is a special situation a speculation, promotion or scam?

In this section I'll tell you about a great promotion that was "in play" as I took notes. But first, have a look into a scam. You'll spot the difference. Then in later sections, I'll get into what I think are good speculations, or valid special situations.

Specialties to Trade

A typical scam

Headline: "British court jails Canadian in huge bond fraud"

KEVIN WARD, ASSOCIATED PRESS
LONDON (October 31, 2003)

A Canadian man, who was part of an elaborate swindle involving fake 1930s bonds, supposedly worth US$2.5 trillion, was sentenced to six years in a British prison today. Michael Slamaj, who settled in Canada in 1973 after leaving his native Yugoslavia, showed no emotion when Judge William Britles passed sentence for a crime that he said was driven by "greed".

"These offences are so serious that only an immediate prison sentence is justified", Britles said in denying defense counsel's appeal for a suspended sentence. Slamaj, 52, and Briton, Graham Halksworth, 69, were found guilty of conspiracy to defraud. Slamaj was also convicted of possession of fake bonds and using them to obtain credit. He was sentenced to six years on each offence, to be served concurrently. Halksworth was also given a six-year prison sentence.

The con started to come undone when the men tried to cash $25 million of the US Treasury bonds at a bank in Toronto in 2001. An RCMP officer became suspicious because the high-denomination notes, dated 1934, were printed in "dollar", rather than "dollars". In addition to the spelling mistake, there were other errors, including the use of zip codes despite the fact the numbers used by the US postal service didn't come into use until the early 1960s. Further examination revealed they had been run off on an ink-jet printer, a curiosity given that the machine is a more modern invention.

The bonds had been authenticated by Halksworth, a widely experienced forensic scientist who has done work for a number of banks and helped introduce Scotland Yard's fingerprint system in the 1960s. The documents were stored by the men in safety deposit boxes at banks in London, which police raided. The scam further unraveled when Slamaj tried to enlist the help of a British lawyer in selling some of the bonds at a discounted rate, but the lawyer, Michael Segan, contacted the police instead. "As soon as they mentioned the figures involved I realized that this would have bought the planet twice over, and I knew they were con men," Segan told their trial in east London.

Slamaj, a self-confessed conspiracy theorist, claimed the case against him was part of a plot by the US Government, which wanted to make

338

sure it never had to pay out on the bonds. Like Slamaj, Halksworth also denied the charges against him, saying the bonds were sent by the US Government to China's anti-communist leader, Chiang Kai-shek, in the 1940s in exchange for 120 tonnes of gold. The men claimed the plane carrying them crashed in the Philippines where they remained undiscovered in the jungle for decades before they were found by locals. Slamaj, who is an engineer, said the bonds came into his possession during a visit to the Philippines when he was looking at building a factory to produce ethanol, a project he had been working on for years.

Police said the bonds were the work of a crime ring in the Philippines that Slamaj was involved with. The ring was trying to use the bonds to obtain credit.

About scams

In the mid-1980s, there was a high-flying stock on the Vancouver Stock Exchange (VSE) that had zoomed from a couple cents to over $10 in a matter of weeks. A fellow Dean Witter broker in New York City called me for my opinion on the company, which apparently sold auto insurance in California, so I did the research. It took me no more than five minutes to find a fraud.

As I encourage you to do with these small companies, I first read the auditor's opinion to the corporate financials. Amazingly, in this case, I saw that the auditor, a supposedly competent CPA firm, had referred to "Generally Accepted Accounting Principals".

Principles, yes. principals? ... (uh) No.

So I called the authorities and the stock was suspended, later delisted. Just like the auditing firm, it was all a fake. Unfortunately, that stock was one of the top two high-flyers on the VSE that year, growing to a market cap exceeding $100 million.

In another case, after I had moved to a new broker-dealer firm to become Executive VP, a former colleague brought around to my office a stock promoter who was a mutual acquaintance. The promoter immediately offered me, under the table, free bearer certificates he was carrying if I would put his stock on my firm's recommended list. (This happened a few times from different promoters.) I quickly handed back his stock, but did promise to look into his claims of hitting a big oil well in Illinois.

After they left my office, I picked up the phone and called the State of Illinois Securities Commission and asked to speak to somebody who could confirm a filing on a particular oil well. Soon after, I was reading to the state regulator from the promoter's literature, which had been filed with the exchange in Canada. In response, the regulator was saying that the story sounded doubtful because, apparently, Illinois only had 50-75-foot shallow wells and this report made claims of a deep-hole gusher, like in Texas.

When the Illinois regulator pulled out the filing, he then said that this particular well had been a dry hole. Nothing at all in the area. He also didn't know the name of the consulting geologist, so he presumed that too was a fraud.

I called the exchange to have the stock halted, pending investigation. Shortly after that, I met the same former broker associate and the promoter on the street. They were upset with me. The broker even said that he had personally traveled to Illinois and saw the oil being pumped and trucked from the well. I said, "You saw a lot of dirty water". A couple of years later, I read that the Mexican police had arrested that promoter and his wife.

It always pays to do your homework.

I could go on, because over the years I have spotted a considerable amount of fraud. Balance sheets that don't balance ... whatever. You simply have to be alert if you are being targeted with a "special situation". I've discovered that crooks are not the smartest or most competent people on earth.

Even my own dad said to me after I had represented the Ontario Securities Commission and the RCMP as a witness in a trial court against a group of scoundrels, "Those fellows seemed like such nice people." But the chief cop for the Law Society of Upper Canada (Ontario) had the final word to me, "Crooks never stamp the truth on their forehead".

A good promotion

The world is full of better mousetraps, encapsulated in drawings in patent offices, but never seeing the light of day. If products and services have any hope of success, they have to be marketed. Marketing is necessary; marketing is good.

At least, good marketing leads to a good promotion.

The first question I ask is: "Who are these people?" I have to know because in life, as in the market, past is prologue. People who are winners, stay winners, and vice versa.

A good promotion is run by a previously successful promoter. There is a track record and I want to see it. I want to know precisely with whom I'm possibly going to be dealing with — before I want to hear the "story". If I don't see a track record and, worse, I can't immediately see the details and contact details of the promoter, then I'm history. I go no further.

Assuming that first step goes well, I look at the product or service from the perspective of down-to-earth benefits rather than "pie-in-the-sky" features. I don't look at the trees, but study the forest. If the big picture doesn't make sense to me immediately, there is no appeal for me to go further.

Here's where you have to have common sense and a lot of it if you lack the experience of studying many of these so-called special opportunities. When, like me, you've looked at maybe five or 10 a day for 20 years, you can spot the good ones from the not-so-good and the bad.

Otherwise, you have to take your time, speak to as many people as possible and sleep overnight on your final decision.

A good promotion can be awfully convincing. A few years ago, two of my associates, shrewd people of immense wealth who have been written about in glossy magazines, fell prey to a good promotion. It was an advance-fee scam perpetrated, in this case, by the manager of a well-known Texas bank who conspired with the promoter to defraud more money than many people earn in a lifetime.

In that situation, the promotion was good enough to hide a scam but actually I've found that most scams are cheaply and poorly promoted. On the other hand, I've found that most good promotions are that way because it cost a lot of money to build them.

People who know that it costs money to make money will put it up if they believe they have a good product to sell. Thus, if I see a good promotion, I'll look further at the "opportunity".

A good speculation

If you can actually calculate a risk-adjusted return, and know how to manage the risk if you decide to take a speculative position, then you may be on to something special.

When you cross the spectrum of risk — from proven to probable to possible — you have to assign a different discount value. For example, if Consolidated Moose Pasture has staked some good-looking claims, anything's possible. The discount rate would be very high. If we're talking a proven gold mine, however, then I can discount my risk quite a bit less.

Specialties to Trade

What the speculator should be on the lookout for is a situation in the "probable" category — not yet fully proven and funded, but worthy of a risk based on discounted cash flow analysis using a reasonable discount factor.

This is how mining exploration companies are financed; the principles should apply to any special situation.

In the late-1990s billions of dollars were invested in dot-com speculations. Like 17th-century Dutch "tulip bulb mania", the vast majority of these situations were terrible speculations (http://prestigeadvisors.com/The_Tulip_Bulb_Mania.htm).

After you have read about tulip bulb mania, I ask you if there is any substantive difference between tulips of mid-17th-century Holland and the dot-com companies of 1998-2000?

In conclusion, you know it's a bad speculation when the key figures (ie, metrics) being relied upon have little or nothing to do with future cash flow. If cash flow is not part of a business plan, it is not a business model that makes sense. Full stop. End of discussion.

The principle of a good speculation is that you only put out money to make money. If you're guessing about if and when that money is coming back to you, then you're gambling.

There is nothing wrong with gambling, of course, if it's just a form of entertainment.

Discounted cash flow ... remember the term. It's all you need to know when considering a speculation in a special situation.

Guidelines for trading in special situations

You have to have a sense of humor if you expect to make any money in special situations, especially if you have seen them promoted on TV. Things are not always going to go your way.

Recall the dotcom IPO market of 1999-2000. Not a joke. The greed in everybody was the primary driver of that "hot" market.

The SEC regulators should have stepped in. There is a difference between a "special situation" and something ridiculous.

Here are a few "special situation" trading guidelines I recommend:

- Repeat to yourself what is so special about this situation. Can the big picture be described in simple-to-understand English? In the case of Ivanhoe Energy and Ivanhoe Mines, there is a single "special" element: that the promoter is Robert Friedland, arguably the world's greatest stock promoter. At least he is in my books.

- Review the promoter's calculations of discounted cash flow. Is the discount rate reasonable? Are the assumptions reasonable? Sometimes this data is not available, but if there is no cash flow at all, then you're dealing with a high-risk situation, which requires a very high discount factor in your calculations.

- What percentage of your assets are you prepared to commit to this holding? If its "fun money" then it shouldn't be more than 3-5% of your financial assets (excluding your home, car, etc). If you are a serious speculator, maybe 30-50% of your portfolio has been set aside for speculation, but never more than 10% of that amount should be invested in a single situation, and only then if you have done a lot of homework. Because so many of these trades go bad, you need to diversify.

- After your funds clear the bank, I urge you not to fall prey to the notion of "In for a dime, in for a dollar". If you decided to invest $2,000 or $22,000 up front, then that should be the limit. That simple rule stops you from getting loaded up. You know, some of these promoters recognize the live ones. Once you're hooked, they employ professional "loaders" who, believe me, can talk most people into pretty much anything.

  To illustrate my point, once a successful loader had come to my office for a job interview. I was, at that moment, having trouble getting through the nurse-receptionist to talk directly to my doctor. While on hold, I made the innocuous statement to my visitor that there ought to be a machine that cracks the code of the doctor's office protocol, and he quickly said to me: "Hand me the phone book and find the first number you find for any local doctor. If I get through, hire me."

  Not only did he get through to some unknown doctor on the first call, he then told me he could likely get immediately to eight out of 10 doctors who were at the office at that moment. Amazing. I later saw he could do it! He had been a "professional loader".

  So, when some of these people call, it's pretty hard to say "no", unless you have already set rules for yourself and follow them.

Specialties to Trade

- As many special situations are not widely marketed or publicly traded, at least not in large daily volumes, you have to stay in close contact. If results seem to be going astray, call more frequently. Call daily if you have to. At some point, you have to be realistic and sell at a loss. That's the one constant in dealing with special situations: the probability of losses. Get used to it if speculation is an activity in which you wish to participate. Remember, if trading ever makes you uncomfortable, close the position(s). You have already missed the time to have called for information. This is Cara Rule #1.

Guidelines for new issues (IPOs)

Like penny stocks, new issue equities are sold on the principle of greed. The corporation might very well be a mature and popular one, but the initial public offering (IPO) stock is unseasoned. The fact is that it might go quickly up — or quickly down — depending on the market environment at the time and the sizzle to the story.

In early 2007, for example, the IPO for Interactive Brokers failed to live up to expectations even though the corporation made it to the Cara 100 Global Best Companies list.

The sizzle, of course, is sold during what the broker-dealers call the "dog and pony show", which is when the underwriter drags the corporate executives around Wall Street to perform their dance, like a monkey on a chain. Or a dog and pony.

If the new-issue pitch goes well and the key accounts display sufficient greed, then the underwriter knows he has a hot new "pony" on his hands. He'll ride it until he gets that bonus money. Otherwise, it's a dog. Too many dogs and the underwriter is looking for a new job because his clients are definitely not looking for dogs.

The IPO story is written up in a remarkably conservative fashion by securities lawyers who desperately want to protect the dealers, the ones who create these products, from being subsequently sued for damages resulting from misrepresentation.

Since many clients do sue anyway, the lawyer basically writes in the securities prospectus some "full disclosure" nonsense like "Beware, this company is a dog". Then it's the underwriter's task to tell you "dog" really means "pony".

You get my point: it's like "hold" means "sell" and "buy" means "buy at your own risk because we're selling".

Lessons from the Trader Wizard

In the case of a seasoned stock, you might get me to sniff around if I see the words "strong buy", but only if I think the broker-dealer is not desperate to unload his position, which I automatically presume is the case if the stock is trading above its 200-day (40-week) moving average, when the new so-called "strong buy" recommendation is issued.

But that's the excitement of the new issue market. There is no price history. And the fact the underwriter is selling an IPO automatically means it is a "strong buy".

When you're in the securities sales business for a couple of years, you can read these new issue documents and just smell the prospects. Dog, pony, dog, pony ... dog.

On the buy side, what the prospective buyers of IPOs are hoping for is the good sense of the underwriter to underprice the issue so that it has a pop in the after-market. That built-in gain, although as yet unrealized, gives the "warm fuzzies" to the holder, and it also provides an opportunity for a quick profit to a "flipper".

A "flipper" is an account of a broker-dealer that expresses interest in buying a new issue as soon as it is announced. Then, if he is lucky enough to obtain an allotment, he is automatically a seller before he even has to pay for it. This isn't a tactic, it's a strategy. If a true flipper decides to hold an IPO stock long enough that he has to actually pay for it, I fall off my chair. Then I get up and find out why.

A flipper only wants a free option. If you've been around in business as much and as long as me, you'll hate being in a position where you have to give somebody a free ride. In fact it should be part of your daily mantra: always make the client pay for his option.

The new-issue game is not as easy as the media would have you believe. It's really tough to move $100 million of stock in some company most people had never heard of before seeing it on somebody's new issue list. A million is a lot of money, so 100 million is a hundred times a lot of money. To prove to the Street, you're good to do the job, you have to hand out these free options.

I have heard that in Hong Kong the buyers line up for blocks with dollars in their hands when new issues hit the streets. I always looked of course, but I never saw such good fortune at my office. If I could find a flipper, I made sure he got an allocation. Like chicken soup, it was good for the soul. Got me going, so when I had to call my tough accounts, I was emotionally high and ready to push paper.

Specialties to Trade

I once had a sophisticated retail client (his name is Joe, really) who had accounts with pretty much every broker-dealer on the Street. Constantly on the phone, he usually knew what was coming down from the IPO syndicates even before the dealer reps who had to sell these new issues.

He knew which issues would be hot and those that might be "dogs". Regardless, he would offer to buy them all — 1,000 shares as a minimum and 10,000 shares or more if he could, in the hot ones. With an average IPO price of $25, he was into the broker-dealer for at least $25,000 every time he saw an IPO on the Street. And, since he had accounts with many dealers, he often got to buy the same new issue from all of them in a particular IPO syndicate, on the same day, extending his financial commitment into the millions.

But, whenever he saw that picture of roses being painted, he would automatically try to scale back to maybe 100 or 200 shares from any one dealer — if we'd let him. Alternatively, when he received quick rejections from five or six broker-dealers for any size allocation, he would know the issue was really hot, so he would call the rest of them and squeeze hard for 10,000 shares each. Often, on the basis that the squeaky wheel gets oiled first, he would get 5,000 shares. He would then easily make a couple of points on the hot new issues — much more than would be needed to cover his fractional point losses on the dogs.

This client knew, of course, that every underwriter on the Street has a reputation to protect, so his biggest loss was usually an eighth, which on 1,000 shares (say $25,000) is just $125 plus commissions on the sale back since IPO sales have the selling commission included in the price. In the aggregate, he made a lot of money with this strategy.

To his credit, he never reneged on taking down a new issue even when he knew it would open at a discount. Even a flipper has to maintain his reputation.

We all knew his game, of course, but on the Street, information is power, so all his brokers continued to deal with him. If this particular client said that ABC was a dog, then you can be sure our best clients never saw ABC going into their accounts.

In my case, I'd simply say that I had it on good authority this was not the stock to buy at this particular time. I didn't even have to be in the dealer syndication meetings to know what was hot and what was not.

Stock prices, of course, move up and down long-term on the basis of fundamentals, but the truth is nobody wants to start below water.

Lessons from the Trader Wizard

The bottom line to the new-issue game is that retail traders ought to avoid it altogether, unless you are a sophisticated flipper. New issues are really best suited to the institutional buyer.

If you do get involved with IPOs and hear the words, as said on CNBC by Prudential's Larry Wachtel, "Priced at 30. First tick, 300. Talk about excess", don't talk, just sell. Flip the damn thing. It's only a paper gain as long as you hold and it could end up as wallpaper if you continue to hold it.

Do precisely what the underwriter does: he sells it all and cleans up his books within the month.

Another issue re the IPO game is the underwriter himself. At the peak of the market in late 1999, as Wall Street was pushing out one bad deal after another, an experienced IPO analyst spoke out on CNBC to tell the viewers that he would never consider an IPO that wasn't brought to the market by one of the leaders on Wall Street. Pure hog wash, but it's all part of the marketing game.

The professional arbitrage game

Although I served in many capacities in and out of the securities industry, I've never been a professional arbitrageur. Maybe because it's an insider's game. You're either privy to information that is not open to the world, or you are not. To get relevant information, you have to go looking for it, and there was always a cost I was not prepared to pay.

I was never part of the club — the type of club that would pass gossip from private secretaries, wives and lovers, business partners, lawyers and accountants, bankers and, I suppose, holy people. I prefer to do my business transparently.

That's not to say you can't deal honestly in the "arb" game (which isn't too far removed from the private equity business), I'm just too much a skeptic to go along with the crowd who actually believe in the "Chinese wall" concept where pending deal information is not leaked or shared by parties that are not essential to the deal. It usually is.

But, there is an arbitrage activity that I do find appealing and at the same time helpful to the capital markets. It's called inter-market trading arbitrage.

Many of the major stocks, say the Dow 30, are listed for trading on markets around the world. If you are in this game as a professional, you would have accounts set up for electronic trading at broker-dealers around the world. Some of these markets trade in the same time zone, like NYSE/NASDAQ and Toronto or London and Frankfurt. HSBC, for example, is listed on many markets (http://bigcharts.marketwatch.com).

In fact, on October 31, 2003, the NYSE lists 469 stocks from 51 countries. Many of these stocks trade in their own markets and markets like London, Hong Kong and Toronto. Others facilitate electronic trading via the Internet (http://nyse.com/pdfs/forlist031031.pdf).

Successful arbitrage trading would be to sell ABC on NYSE at say 50 and buy the equivalent number of shares on the TSX at (the CDN$ equivalent of) 49.75, at the same moment. The profit is usually not high per transaction, but if you have enough capital and make enough transactions, this can be an opportunity for quick profits.

The problem, of course, is that you have to stick to it, and it's costly to put these transaction systems in place. Like anything good, it's a business opportunity, not a one-time speculation.

Another type of arbitrage trading comes along at times when there are rights or warrants trading in a market that have not been issued to foreign shareholders or have not been registered for trading in foreign markets.

In one deal I did for a professional mutual funds manager who alerted me to the opportunity, I acquired control of US non-marketable securities that were legally traded in Canada, and used these rights to protect my short-selling in a stock that was part of a possible merger, where the company had to accept less than market value if the transaction went through. Rather than speculate on the merger actually happening, I shorted the stock, but held in reserve some rights to cover my risk.

Sometimes these arbitrage situations return quick profits, but you always have to commit resources and focus, which may distract you from more important (and profitable) trading in the few stocks you usually trade. And that is the point I make repeatedly here. To be a good trader, to be good at anything, you must focus on what you are good at, and have the time and money to accomplish your goals.

As I spent more time in the securities business, I found that my time became more valuable and my mind-set increasingly focused. I stopped trading "special situations" like arbitrage.

About stock splits

At times a corporation will declare a stock split. Before I get into it, I want to say there is no empirical evidence that a stock split is: (1) a special situation; (2) an indicator of future growth in corporate earnings or stock price changes; or (3) whatever. No proof at all.

The best way to explain what happens is through an example. Assume ABC Corporation has 5,000,000 shares of $1.00 par common stock outstanding. Further, assume that at the time the stock splits, the price of the stock is $60.00 per share and that the company is splitting its stock two for one.

After the split, ABC Corporation will have 10,000,000 shares of stock outstanding, at a par value of .50 (per share), and the stock price will be $30. Remember that par value has nothing to do with the market price of a stock.

How does this impact the individual trader? Let's say a person owned 500 shares of ABC common stock prior to the split. Before the split he had stock worth $30,000 (500 shares x $60 per share). After the split he owns 1,000 share of ABC stock at $30 per share. He still owns $30,000 worth of stock. Only now, he has twice as many shares at half the price.

It's the same principle as making change. Assume I have a $20 bill and ask someone for two $10 dollar bills. After this person makes change for me I have twice as many bills, but they still add up to $20. The other person still has $20, but he has half as many bills. Although some people like to say you are better off (whether it's stock or money or anything else) after the split, you're no better off.

Generally, the reason a company decides to split their stock is to make it more attractive for retail traders to purchase. The reasoning is that more people will want to buy the stock at $30 rather than $60. It's mostly psychological.

Further, if more people buy the stock at the lower price, the stock will rise in price, but there is no guarantee that the stock will continue to rise in price after the stock split. If there were, traders would profit handsomely by buying the stock on the day it splits and selling afterward at a higher price.

Unfortunately, because the stock splits, it does not mean that the lower priced-shares will rise in price after the split. Many times a stock declines in price after a split.

This reminds me of the time my dad's banker called to see if he wanted to borrow some money to invest in the bank's stock because the banker claimed to have heard some scuttlebutt about his company's stock going to split two for one. This was unusual because it wasn't his broker calling, but his commercial banker.

Specialties to Trade

I told my dad to call the banker back to see if he would guarantee any loss. You see, even if you know for sure there's going to be a split, there is no assurance the stock price will go up.

Stock splits are not special situations for traders, but just something the corporation's management would elect to do to make round lots of 100 shares of their stock easier to buy by the small trader.

American depository receipts (ADRs)

An American depository receipt (ADR) is a US-listed security that mirrors a foreign-listed security. There may be legal reasons that the actual stock cannot be listed for trading in the US market, but this factor should not concern you. If the underlying corporation and its share price represents a good value to you, then buy.

JP Morgan has a particularly good daily review of foreign markets, which you can access prior to the market open in North America. They also have the most extensive listing and research that I have found on the foreign issues called ADRs. It's a free service but you have to agree to their terms of use (http://www.adr.com).

Although many people look at the ADR market as a special situation, I see it a different way. Moreover, I use the JP Morgan web service as a standard research tool. Under the tab called ADR Universe, you can analyze ADRs by region, by country and by industry sector. When you have located a target, you can immediately call up a plethora of financial data.

With a single click, you can even have this service provide you the list by cross-listed market, such as if you wish to confine your search to NYSE-, NASDAQ- or AMEX-listed stocks.

With another click, you can see a listing of the major institutional traders and mutual fund owners and their holdings. In fact, there is such a large amount of information available; I give this website a five-star rating.

Believe me, you too will find this website to be invaluable when seeking out internationally listed securities that are commonly affected by changes in global interest rates, commodity prices and economic factors. The airline industry is an excellent example.

You know that I say that the financial services industry has turned the capital markets into a marketing game. Wall Street and its counterparts across the globe like to keep their stories straight for maximum impact. Stocks in industry groups tend to move up and down in tandem because analysts and

Lessons from the Trader Wizard

money managers like to follow one another. Few people find comfort in working outside the box.

Maybe its safety in numbers. Who knows? But, much trading is clearly people acting in concert.

Sometimes the "talking heads" just repeat the script without thinking of what it is they are actually saying.

Over 20 years ago, I recall my mentor and technical wizard Ian Notley, who in my mind is unquestionably the world's leading trend and cycles analyst, tell me a story about Foster's Brewery.

A local TV talking head had gone on what I call "financial entertainment television" to say that he was buying brewery stocks because he heard weather forecasters predicting a particularly hot summer in the US. Ian said: "Rubbish! Look at Foster's Brewery and see the same move. But they are in Australia, in the southern hemisphere, where the seasons are opposite. It'll be winter there soon."

The lights started going on. Immediately I could see that it would be important to know how traders in foreign markets were acting on stocks in the same industry group. Three years later, I was founding the eastern Canada operations of Canaccord Capital, the dominant independent full-service broker-dealer based in Vancouver. So, without a word to Ian, I designed a suite of offices I knew he'd like when I leased half the Toronto Exchange tower penthouse.

With construction underway, I called him in Connecticut to dine with me in Toronto where I popped the question. Although it was a shocker to the financial world, Notley joined me, and then, at the total cost of about $1 million, I had his old Trend & Cycle Department re-designed and built for him. That way, I could see for myself what he was seeing in the market.

Nobody is better at his game. Directly or indirectly, he taught me probably 80% of what I know about capital markets that is important, particularly to look to the world instead of your local market to see what's going on in the world.

Ian taught a lot of others too, like Martin Pring and Larry Berman, and has followers worldwide. I recall several years ago, a popular analyst by the name of Joe Granville wrote about Notley in his book, calling him the world's greatest living market technician. In this case, Granville was right. Twenty years later, Notley's still a friend. His Notley Group, based in Connecticut, is now independent, serving hundreds of institutional clients from offices around the world.

Specialties to Trade

This background will illustrate why I devote so much time to the study of sector rotation and international stocks, and, in particular, ADRs that are traded mostly in their domestic markets. It's my window into somebody else's world.

One other thing: an ADR might not trade in a one-to-one ratio with the underlying stock. It could be that the ADR represents 10 shares or 100 shares or half a share, and so forth. You have to check. Otherwise, you'll be confused when seeing an entirely different price in the foreign market, even after adjusting for foreign exchange.

Speculating in collectibles

I like to track the collectibles market only as an indicator of inflation, but I understand that many people, alarmed at inflation prospects, prefer to own something tangible, such as diamonds, art, antiques, stamps and so forth. If you enjoy these, that's great. While I would not consider them as worthwhile portfolio holdings (ie, for trading), your knowledge of collectibles markets can also help your prospects for successful trading in securities.

At up to 15% (or possibly more) on each side of a collectibles transaction, the commission costs are high. That would mean paying 30% plus taxes, if you sell for a profit. Therefore, collectibles are seldom traded.

Diamonds are advertised as "being forever" and there's no money in them until they are sold. Then your profit depends on the size of the dealer's commission. You are always buying at retail and selling at wholesale. It is true that the values of many of these items have risen sharply during some years, but you get no income and if you have to sell in a hurry, you will seldom get "your" price.

To illustrate the potential profits and real perils, let's discuss diamonds. Their values soared during the inflationary 1970s culminating with the peak price in 1980: for a one-carat quality stone in 1976: $6,700; 1977: $7,700; 1978: $18,000; 1979: $22,000; 1980: $50,000. After the inflation cycle broke, the price started to decline. In 1981, it had fallen to $44,000 and, by 2003, it was down to $12,800.

As with all collectibles bought for "investment" purposes, make sure that you deal with a reliable organization, insist on double certification and when you buy or sell, make certain that the certificate matches the stone.

6
The mechanics of buying and selling:
the Trader Wizard's "How To" guidelines

All the time, longer-term, I am weighing today's risk versus tomorrow's potential reward. Moreover, I am always trying to assess where prices are with respect to trends and cycles, and the causes of that. Since nobody on the sell-side is likely to tell me, and I am trading in competition with both the sell-side and the buy-side (ie, to out-perform the market indexes), I have to look for the leading indicators (bellwethers) of probable future price motion. As I say, there is a rhythm to all prices. The market is a dance.

July 25, 2007

The more actively you trade the market, the more important it is to understand the most simple orders and techniques of buying and selling.

You will find numerous types of orders that assure flexibility and/or protection against unexpected price fluctuations. Some of them can also be money savers. All are governed by strict industry regulations.

Definitions of the most widely used
market and limit orders

Although the information is available practically anywhere, I couldn't complete a book on trading without describing the most commonly used trading orders.

Market order. This specifies that the broker must buy or sell at the best price obtainable. If the order is to buy, he must keep bidding at advancing prices until he finds a willing seller. Vice versa if it's to sell. The customer is certain that a market order will be completed.

When you buy at market, you may make or lose a fraction of a point over a day's trading, but when you are shooting for say a 25% profit, that's not important. In selling, with a market order you may have to accept a loss greater than anticipated; but, you'll be sure of making the sale. Unless I'm involved in fast markets where prices are fluctuating by the second, however, I prefer limit orders.

Specialties to Trade

Contingent order. This specifies the purchase of new securities at a given price, after the prior sale of other securities at some other stated price. Various time limits can be set for the prior sale. Usually, this means that you want to be sure to dispose of old holdings before you make new commitments.

Good-till-canceled order (GTC). This is good until the last trading day of each month. At that time, if it has not been executed, it is automatically canceled.

Open order. This is also known as a GTC order. To buy or sell at a set price until the order is either executed or canceled.

Time order. This is usually associated with a limit order. It can be for a day, a week, a month or, occasionally, GTC; eg, a good-this-week (GTW) order which holds for one week and expires at the end of the last trading day.

Fill-or-kill (FOK) order. This is for immediate action. If it cannot be filled at once, in its entirety, at the stipulated price, it is canceled and a fresh quote is given from the floor.

Stop order, to sell. The sell price is placed below the current price. It becomes a market order when the price of the stock is at, or below, the stop sell price.

Stop order, to buy. This is placed above the current market price. It becomes a market order when the stock trades at, or above, the stop buy price.

Stop limit order. For a purchase, it is placed above the current market price. It becomes a market limit order when the price of the stock trades at or above the stop limit price. To sell, it is placed below the current price. It specifies a price below which the order must not be executed.

Example: If the price of ABC is 50 and you enter a limit order to sell a round lot (100 shares) at 52, the limit order becomes effective only when the stock price rises to 52. Vice versa for selling at a limit of, say, 48.

Now, you can see that some limit orders may never be completed even if the stock is trading around the price you want. Limit orders are typically best, but there's always the danger that your order may miss being executed by a fraction of a point and you will have to start over again.

How to use stop orders

Stop orders are valuable tools in trading, especially in selling. They can cut losses short and can also be used to acquire a security at the lowest price if and when the stock price rises to or above a set price.

When setting a stop price for selling, it's wise to enter the order at a fraction above a round figure: at 50.15, for example. Hopefully, your order will be executed before the stock drops to a round figure (50) that most other traders will designate.

Remember, there is no guarantee that your stock will be sold at the exact stop price. In a fast-moving market, the stock may drop rapidly, skip the stop price and thus the sale will be at a lower-than-anticipated figure.

Stop orders are useful for several reasons.

1. **Limit losses on stocks you own**. You buy 100 shares of ABC at 50 in hopes of a quick gain. You are a bit queasy about the market so, at the same time, you enter an order to sell the stock at 48 stop. If ABC drops to 48, your stop order becomes a market order and you've limited your loss to two points per share.

    As all traders know, the problem is where to set the stop. Unless you plan to hold a quality stock for years for your children or in your retirement-plan portfolio, always set stop prices that will keep your losses low. The trigger point depends on the type of stock, the market conditions and the percentage of loss you are willing to accept. Always be ready to take quick, small losses if the stock, or market, does not do what you expected.

    Generally traders set their loss target at about 10% below cost or the recent high. Traders who are concerned with long-term gains, are more cautious and prefer a loss figure of about 12-14%, which for a stock bought at 50 is 43-45. For best results, set stop prices on the downside and have courage enough to back up your decisions.

    Once any stock starts to fall, there's no telling how far down it will go. And if you are like most people, you will hang on in hope (and embarrassment). Only rarely will such a loser bounce back within the next six to 12 months. So cut your losses short and let your profits run.

2. **Limit losses when you sell short**. In anticipation of a bear market, you sell short 100 shares of ABC at 50. To reduce your risk if you are wrong and the market rises, you enter an order to buy 100 shares of

ABC at 52 stop. If the stock price advances that high, you'll limit your loss to $200 (plus commissions).

With a stop-limit price, you specify a price below which the order must not be executed. This is useful with a volatile stock in an erratic market. If the price of the stock slips past the stop price, you won't be sold out.

You enter an order to sell 100 ABC at 50 stop-50 limit. The price declines from 50.50 to 50. At that point, your order becomes a limit order at 50, not a market order. Your stock will not be sold at 49.90, as can happen with a stop order at 50.

Traders also use a variation of this technique by specifying two different prices, one for the stop and one for the limit. You tell your broker to sell 100 shares of ABC at 50 stop, limit 48. Thus, if ABC falls to 50 or below, your order to sell at 48 takes over. The broker will sell, hopefully at a price above 48, but if the decline continues, the stock will not be sold.

3.   **Assure a profit**. A year ago, you bought 100 shares of ABC at 50 and it is now 65. You are planning a vacation and do not want to lose too much of your gain (ie, your unrealized profit), so you give your broker an order to sell at 60 stop, good until canceled. If the market declines and the sale is made, you are sure of a 10-point-per-share gain, which is still a 20% return on your cost of 50.

Similarly, the stop order can protect an unrealized profit on a short sale. This time, you sell ABC short at 55. The price falls to 40 so you have a $15-per-share gain. You look for a further price decline, but want protection while you're away. You enter a buy order at 45 stop. If the stock price does jump to 45, you will buy 100 shares, cover your short position and have a $1,000 real profit (assuming the broker is able to make the buy right at 45).

4.   **Touch off predetermined buy, sell and sell-short orders.** If you rely on technical analysis and want to buy only when a stock breaks through a trend line on the upside and sell, or sell short when it breaks out on the downside, you can place advance orders to "buy on stop", "sell on stop" or "sell short on stop." These become market orders when the price of the securities hits the designated figure.

Example: ABC stock has been bottoming at 48.50 and now appears ready to move up. But you want to be sure that the rise is genuine because in the past there's been resistance at just about 50 whereupon the stock falls back down again. You set a buy stop order at 51. This becomes a market order if ABC hits that peak.

Guidelines for maximizing trading profits

As the Trader Wizard, I offer you these hints to help you maximize your trading profits.

1. Have a system and stick to it. Presumably, you will have selected a system after a certain amount of study and expert recommendations. Follow the same approach closely until there are strong, logical reasons to change. Learn to become a "mechanic" in your method of operating; that way you'll avoid playing "pin the tail on the donkey". Success while jumping around is a matter of luck, not skill. Be patient. Even in trading, profits usually take time to develop.

2. Anticipate, don't follow. The value of a technical approach to trading is its ability to anticipate trend reversals. On its own, trend following (commonly used by market technicians) can get you into trouble. Leaders anticipate. Learn to be a leader. Study the inter-relationships in markets if you think there is a trend reversal developing.

3. Concentrate on industries, not stocks alone. Every day, I hear Wall Streeters say "buy stocks, don't buy the market". But the market is not a vacuum. Nothing in the market moves on its own. Stocks tend to move together. Sometimes counter-cyclically. First action in an industry group is with the leaders (because of big-money institutional buying), then the public moves in, often with secondary stocks.

4. Trade with the trend. Strategically, the "trend is your friend". In a rising market, be a buyer. Vice versa on the downside. Really, it's that simple. For tactical execution, however, you have to do just the opposite. Say you want to buy GE and it has been trading in the 27-29 range after a bottom at 22. Say there is some short-term market selling and the price drops to 26. That's the time to buy, if you're intending to buy at all.

5. Watch low-priced stocks more carefully. A new trend is more likely to continue on for high-priced stocks than to reverse itself, so, if you're about to buy into low-priced stocks, be sure that the direction of the price trend is clearly established. Think about the cruise ship's turning radius versus the tack of a sail boat. Same for stocks. Be aware that low-priced stocks tend to move up and down at a relatively faster rate. If the price of a stock selling under -10 rises quickly, and you're assured a trend reversal has occurred, then double your position and then watch its action twice as carefully.

6. Act promptly. Successful trading can be a matter of hours or days. If you cannot keep close watch, don't trade for the short-term.

7. Watch the volume. All things being equal, bullish price movements display expanding volume on rallies, while trading volume usually declines in sell-offs and consolidation areas. But not always. Don't short a quiet market; it could be basing for a rally.

8. Be mindful of whole numbers. A trader is more likely to give his broker an order to buy at a whole number (40, 45, 50) than at a fraction (40.25, 44.95). When the price of the stock hits that round number, usually there will be a flood of orders that will create a support or resistance level. Not always, but often enough for you to be mindful of the possibility.

9. Check the technical pattern. Too many chartists are revisionists. They keep changing their interpretations. I usually don't like trading by patterns, even though I know that certain ones (like "head and shoulders") make sense, so make sure that the pattern is clear-cut.

Investopedia uses "head-and-shoulders" to describe a chart formation in which a stock's price:

1. Rises to a peak and subsequently declines.
2. Then, the price rises above the former peak and again declines.
3. And finally, rises again, but not to the second peak, and declines once more.

The first and third peaks are shoulders, and the second peak forms the head.

The right shoulder is created when the bulls try to push prices higher after a pull-back (ie, pressure from the bears), but are unable to do so. If the pattern is a long-term one, this signifies the end of the up-trend. Confirmation of a new down-trend occurs when the "neckline" is penetrated.

As I see it, there's a lot of tea-leaf reading in pattern trading. However, the closer the chart action resembles a theoretical textbook pattern, the more likely your chances of success if you use the knowledge in your decision-making.

StockCharts.com has a good introduction to understanding chart patterns. http://stockcharts.com/school/doku.php?id=chart_school:chart_analysis: introduction_to_char.

Lessons from the Trader Wizard

Once you've mastered a few common patterns, you will spot them quickly and they can help you in your task of maximizing trading profits, just like an understanding of the other points here will help.

Understand how leverage works before you use margin

Leveraging your portfolio involves using the current value of your stocks or bonds as collateral for a loan from your broker or banker, which is then used to invest in a bigger portfolio. The margin represents the amount you can borrow at any point.

You should only borrow money if: (a) you are reasonably sure you can extend your profits with a bigger portfolio; and (b) you can afford to take the losses if the leverage works against you. For sure, your risk is bigger.

Buying on margin is most appropriate in periods of low-to-moderate interest rates, as the income from additional dividends/interest may offset the cost of the loan. But even when money is expensive, using leverage can be effective for aggressive traders who have the temperament and financial resources to assume the added risk.

With securities, the margin regulations and minimum requirements are set in each country by the local monetary authority. In the US it is the Federal Reserve Board. However, your broker-dealer or bank may set higher limits.

I believe you should borrow only when you have at least $5,000 in cash or securities. The margin requirements are 50% initially and 25% for maintenance. So, with $5,000 you can borrow $2,500 and you must maintain $1,250 in equity, which is the difference between the market value of your portfolio and the amount you owe the lender.

The upside of leverage

Like much of what happens in the stock market, using leverage is most effective when stock prices rise.

With $5,000 cash in your account, you can buy 100 shares of a stock at $50 each. By using margin, you will have $7,500, so you can buy 150 shares.

If, in our example, the stock moves to 55, you will have a 10% appreciation ($500) in your cash account or 15% ($750) appreciation in your margin account. At this point, your cash account assets (ie, your equity) will be $5,500, whereas the margin account assets will be $8,250. In the margin account, the equity will be $5,750 ($8,250 value minus $2,500 loan). Since this equity will be above the maintenance minimum of $1,375, you can now increase your loan.

The downside of leverage

But leverage can work both ways. If your stock declines in price, you will lose money much faster in a margined account than in a cash account.

With a five-point drop in the price of the stock, the cash-account loss will be $500 whereas the decline in the margin account is $750. If the decline is substantial so your equity falls below 25%, your broker will issue a margin call. You will have to come up with more cash or other collateral.

Typically, brokers charge interest on the margin loan that is at least 1% above that of the current call money rate at which brokers borrow from banks. In recent years, with nominal interest rates, there is a relatively small spread between the income from the portfolio dividends and/or interest and the interest paid on the margin debt, which makes margin attractive.

As margin interest is tax deductible in many countries, the use of leverage is more beneficial to those in the highest tax bracket. For a trader who pays 50% tax, he could deduct $250, which is half of the interest, but for those paying taxes at a lower rate the tax benefits may not be much.

Under-margined accounts

If the value of your margin account falls below minimum maintenance requirements, it becomes under-margined and, even if the deficit is only $10, there will be a margin call. To check when you're approaching this 25% level, divide the amount of your debit balance by three and add the result to your net loan. Thus, one-third of $5,000 is $1,666, plus $5,000 equals $6,666. If the portfolio value is less, your account becomes restricted and your ability to make withdrawals is affected.

If you use margin, don't let your equity fall below 60%, because in a volatile market, it's easy to get a margin call.

Margin rules

The first rule of margin is that the broker-dealer must protect his own capital which, in turn, protects the capital of the industry and keeps the capital markets strong.

Rules of the Federal Reserve Board apply to all publicly traded stocks whether they are listed or not. Over and above Fed requirements, a stock exchange sets special margin requirements on individual issues that show a pattern of volume and/or price fluctuations that are extraordinary. These requirements are intended to discourage the use of leverage in certain issues, possibly only at certain times, because of undue speculation.

The broker-dealer, of course, can apply its own policy on margin credit for all or some of its accounts. Brokers are not permitted to margin some publicly traded stocks; however, you can probably use unlisted or foreign issues to borrow from your bank. On some high-quality, actively traded OTC stocks, banks have been known to lend substantially more than brokers are permitted for listed stocks.

While shares of most mutual funds are unlisted, their portfolios contain stocks and bonds listed on major exchanges. Therefore, mutual fund shares are subject to Fed margin requirements.

In addition, Americans whose accounts show a pattern of "day trading" (ie, purchasing and selling the same marginable issues on the same day) are required to have the SEC-mandated margin in their accounts before trading.

Margin account rules are explained in detail on the broker-dealer's account application. It pays to read the fine print before you get into a deficit margin position and the broker has to sell out your portfolio. I've had to sell out client holdings before. It's a thankless task to use the rules to effect a decision the client could not force himself to take.

How to effectively use margin

People say that it's bad to be in debt. Not always true.

It's not true if you have "good debt" on your books. Good debt is margin loans on your core securities holdings, and bad debt would be a bank loan to finance physical assets that are wanted and not needed.

Margin debt is "money earning money". That debt (which is your liability) is offset with an asset that has enterprise value, and if the asset is appreciating in value (either its going-concern value or its price in the market) faster than your associated liability, then you are growing wealth.

So "good debt" is a capital builder. It's one good thing a bank does for you.

The country's national debt is, of course, a different story. What I don't understand is how our elected representatives ever got the power to spend more than we give them directly through taxation.

There ought to be a law against writing checks you can't cash.

Specialties to Trade

Well, there is, but there ought to be a law for today's legislators to stop stealing from the future, from our kids and grandkids and even from their kids.

Most of this government debt is, of course, bad debt. Dropping bombs in far-away war theaters serves to create inflation, not wealth. Inflation destroys wealth.

How margin affects yield

For effective use of margin, you ought to know how it can affect your yield.

The cash-yield per cent (CY%) is the return on securities you bought and paid for outright. But if you buy on margin, in order to determine precisely what yield you get, you have to figure the real return on your capital. I call that the margin equivalent yield (MEY).

But MEY is two-way. Remember that.

You can calculate a MEY from this formula:

MEY = ((100 / %M) x CY%) – ((100 / %M) – 1) x DI%
where %M = % Margin and where DI% = Debit Interest %.

Assume there is no price appreciation, and the total return (TR) is from interest earned.

Example 1: You are on a 50% margin base, receive 4% cash yield from stock dividends and pay 7% interest on your debit balance.

MEY = 100 / 50 x 4% – (100 / 50) – 1 x 7%
MEY = 2 x 4 = 8% – (2 – 1 x 7%)
MEY = 8% – 7% = 1%

Thus, the 4% return drops to 1% with use of margin. Ouch!

Example 2: You are on a 50% margin base, but receive 12% cash yield (from distributions of an income trust, say) and your cost of margin is, say, 5% interest on your debit balance.

MEY = 100 / 50 x 12% – (100 / 50) – 1 x 5%
MEY = 2 x 12 (= 24%) – (2-1 x 7%)
MEY = 24% – 7% = 17%

Thus, the 12% return is increased to 17% with use of margin. Terrific!

Lessons from the Trader Wizard

What you can buy on margin

Check with your broker to find out what securities they permit you to buy on margin. Some securities are not marginable. Sometimes it's a regulatory rule, sometimes a house rule. Many brokers will not margin stocks under $5 or $3, even if the companies happen to be large-cap, like Nortel.

With stocks, the margin formula is: add two zeros and divide by the margin requirement (typically 50%). This gives you the dollar amount of stocks you can buy with the cash you have available (except in restricted accounts). Thus, if you put $10,000 cash into a margin account to buy marginable stocks where the broker's requirement is 50% margin, you could buy up to $10,000/0.50 = $20,000 worth.

As already mentioned, use of margin can lead to problems in falling markets. In evaluating margin, when the price of a stock falls below a round dollar price, the next lower round-dollar figure is used.

Thus, when a stock drops from 100 to 99.90, its new marginable value is 99, which is a loss of 1% of its worth. But a stock selling at 10 that falls to 9.99 is valued at 9, which is a 10% loss.

Bonds have different margin requirements

With most brokers, $10,000 cash to buy bonds, on margin, you can buy:

- $20,000 worth of listed convertible bonds;
- $40,000 worth of non-listed convertible bonds;
- $100,000 face value of municipal bonds; or
- $200,000 face value of government bonds.

That's a lot of government bonds to control with $10,000 cash!

How to get extra leverage

Many traders, including professional capital managers, buy a corporation's convertible securities on margin rather than the common stock.

With convertibles (assuming a purchase price reasonably close to investment and conversion value), the risk is substantially reduced on the downside due to the price resistance encountered as the CV nears the floor provided by its intrinsic value. On the upside, there's no such resistance and the full benefits of leverage are attained.

With a margined position in CVs, the risk may be no greater (and can be less) than would be incurred by non-leveraged ownership of the common stock of the same company, while the appreciation potential may be substantially greater.

Here's an example, based on an actual situation. It compares a leveraged holding in ABC 6.5% convertible bonds with a $10,000 holding in the common stock of the same company. The CV was at par and the common stock at 8.

To buy 20 CVs, the trader put up $10,000 and margined the balance. At the same time he bought 1,250 common shares for $10,000 cash. The stock declined 25% to 6. Due to its inherent investment value and adequate interest coverage, the CV, reflecting the stock decline, dropped 7% to $930 per bond (a 14% loss on the $20,000 fully margined holding).

In a few months, both securities were back to their original level. In the next 18 months, the bonds rose 80%, so their value was $36,000, which was a gain of $16,000 from the bottom. But the stock went up 50% to 12, or $15,000, which was a gain of just $5,000.

The leveraged position in the CVs produced both superior protection on the downside and superior capital appreciation on the upside.

Furthermore, over a year, the bond interest of $1,300 would have easily covered the $700 cost of carrying the margin account at 7%.

Note that if you had margined the stock, your risk would have been greater and your offsetting income less, but you would have done better. But if the prime interest rate had risen sharply during that period, the price of the CVs would have dropped further.

About short-selling stocks

I believe short-selling is an essential trading strategy for every trader.

Selling short means selling a stock you don't own, hence it is considered a speculative practice. Worse, there is an aura of fear and suspicion surrounding this type of trading, and it is seldom recommended by advisors (most of whom have never sold short in their careers).

The requirements for short-selling

Margin. All short-sales must be made in a margin account, usually with stock borrowed from another customer of the brokerage firm under an agreement signed when the margin account was established.

Collateral: As a minimum, collateral must be the greater of $2,000 or 50% of the market value of the shorted stock, but not less than $5 per share on issues selling at $5 or more, nor less than either $2.50 per share or 100% of market for stocks trading under $5 per share. These provisions take care of any dividends or rights due to the lender of the stock.

For inexperienced and impatient short-sellers, it's best to maintain a margin balance equal to 70-80% of the short-sale commitment. This should eliminate the need to come up with more collateral during extra volatile markets.

Commissions: You pay regular commission, taxes and fees on the initial short sale and subsequent purchase of the stock.

Premiums: You may have to pay your broker a premium for his borrowing the stock to make settlement on the original short sale, usually $1 per 100 shares per business day.

Dividends: All dividends on shorted stock must be paid to the owner. That's why it's best to concentrate on warrants or small-cap stocks that pay low or no dividends.

Rights/stock dividends: Because you are borrowing the stock, you are not entitled to the use of rights or the receipt of stock dividends. If you know or suspect a company might cut its dividend, you can do well by selling short as the stock price is almost sure to drop. But the decline, if it occurs, may be too small to offset the commission costs.

Sales price: For stocks, short sales must be made on the up-tick or zero up-tick, ie, the last price of the stock must be higher than that of the previous sale. If the stock is quoted at 80, you cannot sell short when it drops to 79.90, but must wait for it to come back to 80 or better. Or, with a zero up-tick, the last two sales must be at the same price.

Taxes: Gains or losses on short sales are short-term and thus, taxable at the highest income-tax rate.

Misunderstandings regarding short-sales

Since it is the most misunderstood of all securities transactions, I'd like to address several misunderstandings about short-sales.

Most traders buy stocks long, which means they purchase at what they believe to be a low price — say at 40 — and hope to sell at a higher price — say 50. Short-selling is just the opposite. The trader sells high, at 50, and hopes to buy low, at 40 or less.

Think about why you buy a stock: you believe there is unrecognized value, which the market price will soon catch up to, or you believe the current market price is well below its norm, based on long-term metrics like PE and so forth, and that the price will eventually revert to its mean.

Well, what's wrong with believing the opposite and short-selling in those instances?

For every transaction there is a buyer and a seller. Why should the sellers be typically only wholesaling insiders peddling stock at inflated prices to the unsuspecting public?

There's nothing to stop a shrewd trader from first taking the sell side and then later buying back his short position.

I think doing so helps keep the market honest.

Since over the long term, the stock market is down one-quarter to one-third of the time, short-selling can be a profitable trading strategy during bear phases. And as stock prices fall faster than they rise, since fear is a greater motivator than greed, a short position is usually quicker to produce profits than a long position.

I happen to believe that short-selling can be profitable at almost any time.

While most short sales are made with borrowed stock, some people (for tax purposes) sell short with stock they own (that is, they sell against the box).

Professionals prefer to make their short sales with warrants, which never pay dividends, or with stocks that pay little or no dividends. (As long as you control the stock, you are responsible for paying to the real owner the dividends you receive.)

Since these professionals do not have to pay commissions, they can afford to take greater risks and sell short in buoyant markets to take advantage of the almost inevitable temporary declines.

Amateurs, on the other hand, will make more money and sleep easier if they sell short only in primary bear markets, along with the trend.

Example: After watching the Dow drop weekly during 2001, you become convinced that there's a bear market. Your research shows that fund favorites like GE are trading at high PEs of well above 40, which is clearly outside any normal range.

Lessons from the Trader Wizard

So you take the following action:

1. In May 2001, you arrange with your broker to borrow 100 shares of GE.

2. You sell short at 51 and, to boost your profits, do so on a 50% margin so you're putting $2,550 of your capital at risk.

3. A year later, GE is down to 31. You cover your short position by buying back the stock for $3,100. After deducting commissions and fees, your pre-tax profit is about $1,900, which was a neat 75% annual return on your capital — at a time when Wall Street professionals were giving a bath to your friends.

The speed of the stock's fall depends on bull market or bear (prices fall faster in bear markets than corrections in bull markets), the extent of the overvaluation of the stock and whether large selling institutions have been unloading blocks of stock. Selling short, for the first time especially, takes courage, particularly with a good quality stock.

If you're going to do it, use technical analysis to set target prices. Review the long-term charts to find the obvious points of resistance in the past. And, if you're not successful three times in a row, quit until you figure out the problem.

There are, at present, and over the years, many regulatory issues with short-selling that you ought to be aware of. The literature is easy to find.

In one complaint, surrounding the filing of a class action lawsuit in Florida against Eckard Drug Stores, the plaintiffs alleged that lawyers who filed the suit may have been part of a scheme to manipulate the stock price of Eckard's parent corporation, for the purpose of making money from selling the stock "short" prior to filing suit. It has been argued that such manipulation appears to be rampant among some members of the bar.

The SEC, which is responsible for new rules for trading, has a difficult task. The public is watching closely to see if new short-selling rules are really meant to help or to hurt the public. By "hurt" I mean to discourage the individual trader from using the same practices as traders who work for financial institutions.

Personally, I'd like to see the SEC loosening the short-sale rules for highly liquid mid- and large-cap stocks, while tightening the rules for smaller-cap issues that are more vulnerable to market manipulation, including via "naked" shorting.

Specialties to Trade

I do not agree with the perception that, in my view, has been caused by the sell-side that short-sellers, day traders and hedge funds are the bad guys. The bad guys are the rule breakers.

Shorts and their defenders argue that shorting plays a key role in restraining over-heated markets. Had shorts been freer to ply their trade, some say the 1999-2000 tech and telecom stock bubble might not have swelled to such an extent before bursting.

When properly executed, selling stocks short can preserve capital, turn losses into gains and, under some conditions, defer or minimize taxes. With few exceptions, the only people who made a lot of money in the bear markets of the 1970s, 1981-82, 1987 and 2000-2002 were those who sold short at one time or another.

When you sell short, think of these examples and scoff at ridiculous notions such as (i) selling short is anti-American, or (ii) will result in unlimited losses.

With stock you own, the maximum loss will be 100% if the stock becomes worthless. But with a short sale, if your projections are wrong and the price of the stock, instead of going down, moves up, say from 50 to 500, you could lose 1000% of your portfolio. But you would have to be mighty foolish to let this happen.

Short-selling is not for the faint of heart or for those who rely on tips instead of research. You may have nervous moments if your timing is poor and the price of the stock jumps right after you sold short. But if your projections are correct, the price of that stock will fall eventually.

In summary, short sales are made when traders sell stocks (usually borrowed) in the hopes of buying back at lower prices. These traders might be conservative, enterprising or speculative, depending on how they approach the market. By now you are aware of that.

Regardless of the type of trader you are, if and when you decide to sell short, you must have the courage of your convictions and be willing to hang in there for months, even years. I recommend that inexperienced traders who want to go short deal with a brokerage firm that offers experienced counsel and a list of stocks to borrow.

Factors to understand when selecting stocks for short sales

Obviously, in opening a short position, short-sellers anticipate a decline in the value of the shorted stocks and, usually, a drop of the overall market. It hurts to be wrong. So short-sellers go looking for indicators that help them be right more often than they're wrong.

In choosing stocks for short-selling, professionals use computers to analyze economic, industry and corporate factors. Others, like myself, rely mostly on an interpretation of a stock's trend and cycle price data.

Information regarding short sales is widely available in many financial publications like *Barron's*, *Investors Business Daily* and *Wall Street Journal*.

This information may possibly be useful in timing your buying and selling, but I believe it is not easy to interpret correctly. However, for those who are interested in selecting stocks for short sales, here are the most widely used information sources and how I believe short-sellers interpret them:

1.   **Total short sales:** Short-interest figures are published in *Barron's*, *Investor's Business Daily* and *Wall Street Journal*. These figures show stocks in which: (a) 5,000 or more shares have been sold short; or (b) there has been a month-to-month change of at least 2,000 shares sold short.

       The data also reports the total number of the company's outstanding common shares, the short interest of the previous month and those stocks that are involved in arbitrage because of a merger or acquisition.

       According to technical theory, a large short interest is bullish because this provides a cushion for the market. Eventually, short-sellers will have to cover their positions. This demand will boost volume and prices. Stocks with large short positions often show the greatest gains.

       Similarly, a low and shrinking short interest warns that speculators are becoming bullish and that a market top may be approaching. Maybe so, but traders have different objectives, and the major institutional traders, who dominate trading in managing their mutual funds, seldom sell short. So, in effect, short-selling represents the action of a relatively small group of individuals and hedge fund managers and their interpretation of the industry short-sales data is not always accurate.

       Yet, when enough people believe something, it becomes self-fulfilling.

2.   **Short-interest ratio (SIR):** This shows the short interest as a percentage of average trading volume for the preceding month. The potency of any short-interest total depends on how it compares with

the total volume of trading. If the average volume is 30 million shares daily and the short interest is 30 million shares, the ratio is 1.00. Generally, it takes a ratio of 1.70 or higher to act as a bull-market prop.

When the ratio falls below 1.00, it's usually a bear-market signal. In most cases, a falling ratio is unfavorable and bull markets often start when the ratio is 2.00 or higher. Many technicians start buying when the SIR hits 1.7 because since 1932, no sustained market rise has taken place without the short-interest ratio moving above 1.7.

3.   **Specialist short sales**: These are made by professionals who have intimate knowledge of the market and specific stocks. When they risk their own funds to go short, they believe that the prices of certain stocks are going to decline. When their short sales are high (over 67%), it's a bearish indicator. When they reduce their short positions (under 40%), an improved market can be expected. These data are widely reported. These are thought to be reliable for timing both sales and purchases, but they must be followed carefully and interpreted correctly. They should never be used alone.

4.   **Insider transactions**: Insider trading reports disclose the number of corporate officers, directors and major shareholders who bought or sold stock in the previous few months. The assumption is that when the number of insiders who are selling exceeds the number buying and the stock is at a high level, then these knowledgeable people believe a decline is due. I question this logic, because most insider selling is for legitimate personal financial planning purposes. Simply put, it's not wise to have all your eggs in one basket.

In any event, one quarter year of data such as this does not make a trend. Try to wait for at least two quarters of reports to confirm the trend.

5.   **Volatility**: Some trading advisory letters measure volatility by beta, which is the historical relationship between the price movement of the stock and the overall market and interest rates.

Each stock has a beta number: 1.0 moves with the market; 1.5 is highly volatile; and 0.7 is stable. In the Dow 30 index, Disney (DIS) has a beta of 1.20, United Technologies (UTX) is 1.15, Microsoft (MSFT) is 1.15, and Merck (MRK) is 0.95.

Betas change, however, as General Motors (GM) 20 years ago had a beta of 0.70 and now it is 1.20. So beta is not likely to be helpful in selecting stocks to short-sell.

6. **Comparative relative strength (RS):** this is a technical calculation that compares a stock's recent price movement to an index, but also can be a calculation that takes into account the consistency and growth of earnings and whether the last quarterly earnings were lower or higher than anticipated by Wall Street.

This data is available from statistical services such as Investor's Business Daily, Value Line and Standard & Poor's Earnings Forecast, which reports earnings estimates made by analysts of brokerage firms and advisory services.

Some traders say that when corporate earnings are lower than the estimates, the stock is a candidate for short-selling, and when they are higher than projected, you should not be considering selling short. These are usually better theories than practice.

Studies show that: (a) the short position must be of some magnitude to have any effect on the price action of the stock; (b) certain stocks seldom attract much short-selling even after massive moves; and (c) some short-sales are artificial in that they represent arbitrage, because of a proposed merger when the shorted shares will never be repurchased.

Summing up:

There is some evidence that the short-interest theory affects the overall market, but there are doubts as to its validity with individual stocks. Well-known analyst Barton Biggs says, "Read the short-interest tables to find out what the volatile stocks are. They do not prove anything else". Hear! Hear!

One analyst found that a high and rising short interest does not have an upward impact on a specific stock. But these same stocks do show greater volatility both up and down than the overall market. So, the short interest information might be useful to you.

Why and when you should consider shorting

I believe very much in a concept called "reversion to the mean". I recommend the application of trend and cycles analysis to the timing of buying and selling a long position, but also to the opening and closing of short positions.

Every trader has to get in sync with the rhythm of the market. When you get good at it, you'll look at the markets as a living organism, breathing in, breathing out. There is a repetition in the price patterns of stocks as traders go through the cycle of greed to fear.

Specialties to Trade

The further a stock gets outside its normal trading pattern, the more I believe it will swing back. This oscillation can be charted around a zero line, which is simply the long-term trend or norm. At the upper peak of this oscillation, I'm a seller (or short-seller as the case may be), and at the apparent low point in the cycle, I'm a buyer (or short-coverer).

If the long-term trend is up (ie, bullish), then I tend not to short-sell, but if I do I would be quick to cover and I would look for a smaller profit on the trade (than shorting in a bear phase). Sometimes it's not so easy to determine whether the market is, on balance, bullish or bearish; but you can easily tell when a stock is trading out of its normal trading range.

Clearly, a bear phase represents the best time for short-selling. You don't have to be so quick to cover and you would look for higher average profit on each trade.

But whether I'm taking long or short positions, there are more factors involved than simply an analysis of a single price series. Many market inter-relations must be studied; these include economic, industry and corporate factors. Even the long-term, intermediate-term and short-term price data must be analyzed together. Equity prices must be reviewed against prices of bonds, commodities and currencies and, in some cases, even collectibles.

In the beginning you will find decision science to be a bit like rocket science, but I assure you that in time you'll get the hang of it. The whole process will become quite natural.

Like I say, it's just like breathing. Interest rates up. Bond prices down. Prices of financial and insurance companies down. Utilities and consumer non-discretionary stocks down. Commodity-sensitive stock prices up (eg, oils, metals, papers, gold, etc). Asset-backed currencies (eg, Swiss francs) up and debt-backed currencies (eg, US$) down. Collectibles up. Real estate up. And so on. You start with the most simple market inter-relationships and you look for confirming trends.

Look for the weight of the evidence. If I think GE is ready to sell or to sell short, I want to see the same indications for stocks that GE trades like. Since GE is mostly a financial services company and a company financed largely by debt, I want to see a topping phase in Citigroup, for example. If I see a lot of upward price potential in the banks, insurance companies, brokers, etc, then I'm not going to be too comfortable shorting GE.

In time, you can become quite skilled at this, but at the end of the day, you must recognize that you are dealing in probabilities. When the probabilities are strongly in your favor, you make the decision. If you are wrong, you close the position. You try to be right more than you're wrong and you try to have higher average gains than average losses.

In fact, as a trader, I try to be right 70% or more of the time and I try for 7% or higher average gains on winning trades within an average seven-week holding period and a 4% or lower average loss on losing trades within an average four-week holding period. These numbers work.

It needs to be said that in dealing in probabilities you cannot also be trying to get the maximum possible profit on trades. You must set reasonable goals and stick to them.

List of "Try tos" and "Try not tos" when short-selling

Every student of the market sticks to a discipline of using proven tactics, especially when short-selling, which carries a higher-than-average risk element. Here is a list of guidelines for short-sellers:

- **DO** your homework first and make certain you understand the risks and rewards.

- **DO** short well-known stocks that are becoming unpopular. When institutions sour on a company, they get out at almost any price. This constant pressure sparks more selling and you'll be sure of your profit. Choose industries and companies whose charts show a downtrend, especially those with past histories of sharp, long swings up and down.

- **DO** check the volatility. The best stocks to short are those that move widely and, at the time of the sale, are trending down quickly.

- **DO** cover short sales on weakness. And always cover when you feel the most bearish news is out and your stocks are down to a reasonable price level.

- **DO** set protective prices. On the upside, 10% or more above the sale price, with flexibility for volatile stocks; with a stock bought at 50, at 55. On the downside, below your sale price: 8% if you are aggressive, 14% if you are conservative (46 and 43, respectively). Be careful with stop orders. The more aggressive you are, you may be picked off if the stock rises to the precise point of the stop order and then declines, and vice versa. To maximize your profits, move that stop price with the price change.

- **DO** rely on the 10-day moving average of the odd-lot selling indicator ratio obtained by dividing Odd Lot short sales by total odd-lot sales, using New York Stock Exchange (NYSE) statistics. According to the

Specialties to Trade

Financial & Investment Dictionary of Barron's, historically, odd-lot investors — those who buy and sell in less than 100-share round lots — react to market highs and lows; when the market reaches a low point, odd-lot short sales reach a high point, and vice versa. When the indicator has been below 1.0 for several months, sell short. When it's down to .50, the odds are even more favorable for a short sale. But do not sell short when the indicator rises above 1.0, and cover all shorts when the one-day reading bounces above 3.0.

- **DO** look for warrants for short-selling. They are volatile, low-priced and never pay dividends.

- **DON'T** fight the trend. Avoid short sales unless both the major and intermediate trends are down. If it's a bull market, why try to buck optimism? You may be convinced that a stock is vastly overpriced, but unless you have great patience, don't sell short until there is clear evidence of a decline in the market generally and your stock specifically.

- **DON'T** be impatient. Stay in there for longer than you'd like, say three to six months or even a year, if you are still convinced that your analysis is correct. Forget about short-term, two- and three-day market rallies. Use charts and trend lines. As long as the major trend and the intermediate trend are down, hold your short position. Cover when there's a reversal into a confirmed up trend (eg, a crossover of the three-week (15-day) versus the 10-week (50-day) moving average).

- **DON'T** put up more money when you get a margin call. You guessed wrong so have the discipline to get out fast. Remember the importance of being a "mechanic".

- **DON'T** short issues with thin capitalization. With a limited number of shares, trading volume will be small. If large blocks of stock are closely held, you could be caught in a squeeze and have to pay a large premium to borrow the stock or to flatten your short position in the market.

My advice (repeated): Stay away from shorting a stock with a small and thin capitalization. You don't know who is behind the trading. I once watched a short syndicate get squeezed from about $3 to over $11 — even though the company itself was probably worth under a buck. In fact in that case, the company CEO and the employees' pension plan were clients of mine, and I was not comfortable. The short syndicate turned to issuing mob-backed death threats against the CEO, so I immediately had the company's lawyer call in the RCMP. Then the mob started calling me, which as it turned out was also the case with the chief compliance officer of the TSX, who told me, "These people call me routinely from New York to tell me they're going to kill me. I stopped counting at about 60 death threats."

- **DON'T** short big dividend payers. You have to turn the dividends over to the owner of the stock. This can be expensive and, to an extent, it provides a floor for the price of the stock.

- **DON'T** short stocks with a large short interest (equal to three days of normal trading). Short sellers have already made their move and now every short seller is a potential buyer. Think about it. If there are already too many shorts, the stock can rally sharply when short sellers start to cover their positions. A relatively high (compared to past cycles) and rising short interest usually indicates that trader bearishness is being overdone and that the market is ready for a rise. If and when short sellers fear higher prices, they'll quickly run for cover and buy heavily, thus boosting the market. On the other hand, a relatively low and shrinking short interest in a high-priced stock warns that trader bullishness is excessive and that a market top is approaching.

Selling against the box

Selling against your box is what we used to call a technique for freezing paper profits or postponing taxes by using your own holdings and putting positions simultaneously into long and short accounts with brokers.

Here's how it works:

On March 1, Mr. Smith buys 100 shares of ABC stock at 40. By September, the stock has zoomed to 60 and still looks good, but the overall market is weakening and Mr. Smith gets nervous. In a different account, he sells short 100 shares of ABC with his own shares as collateral.

- If the price of ABC stays around 60, he will lock in his gains minus commissions. He will sell the stock at 60 for a $20 per-share profit, which is the 60-sale price minus the 40-cost.

- If the price of ABC rises to 70, he'll still do OK. He delivers his own stock. He won't make that extra 10-point profit (from 60 to 70), but he will still have a $2,000 gain, which is the difference between his 40-cost and the 60-sale price.

Specialties to Trade

- If the price of ABC drops to 50, Mr. Smith has two choices:

  - To cover his short position by purchasing new shares. He will break even, because his 10-point profit on the short sale will be offset by a 10-point loss on the value of the stock. Commissions will reduce his net.

  - To cover his short position with the shares he owns. He makes $1,000 profit on the short sale, but has a smaller profit on the stocks he owns: $1,000 versus the $2,000 gain he had before.

Selling against the box is a favorite year-end tactic. The short sale brings in immediate cash, and the profit (or loss) is deferred until the short position is covered the following year or even two or three years hence.

But be careful:

- Once the trend of the stock turns up, it is more likely to continue to rise than to fall. You may postpone some taxes, but you may also find that your year-end profit, from a lower-than-sold price, will be narrowed or eliminated.

- Under the wash sale rule, there will be no tax loss if the short sale is covered by buying the same or identical securities within 31 days after the date of the original short sale.

- With gains, the taxes can be long-term when the shares are held for more than 12 months. This can be tricky so check with your broker. The holding period for the owned stock stops when the short sale is made and begins again when the short sale is covered by a stock purchase. Thus, to qualify for long-term capital gains, a stock must be held for one year, ie, nine months before the short sale is made plus 91 days after the short position is covered.

- Commissions can eat away at profits.

Automatic (formula) trading by dollar cost averaging plans

With formula-based trading plans, trades are made automatically at pre-set intervals or according to pre-designed ratios.

On the surface, this could be an effective personal planning strategy. But you should read what I really think before venturing into this kind of strategy.

Formula plans fall into two broad categories:

- Plans where investments are made with fixed dollars and/or fixed time periods.

- Ratio plans where action is based on pre-determined criteria to buy, sell or revise holdings.

Formula plans average out, missing maximum profits and skipping big losses. There's no system that can guarantee that a fool cannot lose money, but if and when effectively carried out, formula plans can avoid the two most common trading mistakes: buying too high and selling too low.
Automatic trading plans are always better than a "buy, hold and wait to get wealthy" approach. They are usually superior to random, impulsive choices. But they are never as effective as thoughtful, well-planned, well-timed trading.

In my opinion, automatic trading — while it certainly has merit for the average trader — is a purchase strategy promoted by many advisors as a way to keep their client in the stable of a particular advisor or mutual fund distributor.

Plan trading is kind of like your local bank that would like to see you deposit all your weekly or monthly savings. Once you commit, they get your money, but they don't have to continue to do a lot to service your account. Their fees and commissions then are automatic. Maybe that's the plan!

If you require that much self-discipline to be a trader, I suggest you will not be a successful one anyway. A forced saving is no replacement for the application of the tools I teach. Besides, your forced saving just might be going into a bad investment. Good money after bad?

On the other hand, there is some merit to some traders of such plans. All traders should at least understand them.

Dollar cost averaging (DCA)

Dollar cost averaging is the most widely used direct-trading formula plan. DCA plans (which is trading in fixed dollars and/or at fixed times) rely on consistency and, in most cases, prompt reinvestment of all income from dividends or interest. You invest a fixed amount of dollars at specific time intervals: one month, three months or whatever time span meets your savings schedule. Your average cost will always be lower than the average market price during the accumulation period.

Specialties to Trade

These plans must be maintained for years to be truly worthwhile, because the markets are volatile and the same dollars buy more shares at low prices than at high. You wouldn't want to dollar cost average only at the peak of market cycles.

These plans have extra appeal for long-term traders because they eliminate the difficult problem of timing.

The following table illustrates how DCA works, ie, what happens when you invest $1000 regularly, regardless of the price of the stock. The lower the market value, the more shares you buy.

Average Share Price vs Average Share Cost

Quarter	Amount Invested	Share Price	Shares Purchased	Cumulative Average Share Cost
1	$1,000	$40.00	25	$40.00
2	$1,000	$25.00	40	$30.77
3	$1,000	$25.00	40	$28.57
4	$1,000	$10.00	100	$19.51
Year 1	$4,000 (total)	$25.00 (average)	205 (total year 1)	$19.51
5	$1,000	$20.00	50	$19.61
6	$1,000	$25.00	40	$20.34
7	$1,000	$40.00	25	$21.88
8	$1,000	$50.00	20	$25.53
Year 2	$4,000 (total)	$33.75 (average)	135 (total year 2)	$25.53
Final	$8,000	$50	340 (total)	$25.53

Carried out consistently, most formula plans buy relatively cheap and sell relatively dear. They would produce flat returns if the market were flat. Because they require rising markets, which over the long-run are typical, they are presumed safe and, if you are patient and persistent, can provide you better-than-average profits.

But, in my view, they remove the pride and skill sets developed in judgment-based trading.

Unfortunately, with most systems, consistency of implementation rarely happens. These days, when the stock market is so volatile, with the Dow moving up and down as much as 100 points in a few hours, traders tend to get overly excited and decide to buy more at the tops of market cycles and, of course, less when the markets are depressed.

That's just the opposite to what they ought to be doing.

I find some mechanical systems for dollar cost averaging to be worthless; others may seem to have certain limited usefulness; and others show flashes of brilliant success at times, perhaps giving the illusion that they are the answers to the mystique of the stock market.

Forget the mystique of the "black box". The difficulty always comes when, flushed with success, a trader begins to believe he has found a magic formula and neglects to apply the required homework and use of common sense.

How to improve dollar cost averaging plan results

The essence of all trading success to buy high-quality stocks as bear markets bottom and to sell high-quality stocks as bull markets peak. Since you are operating under a formula, you cannot use judgment in deciding the quality of a company whose stock you may want to trade and whether a bull or bear market will continue.

Here are some supplementary techniques that can help improve your profits:

• Once the formula has given a signal, wait for confirmation of this trend. Wait 30 to 60 days before buying or selling. You will have to develop your own timing schedule, but a month is minimal and two months may be too long.

• Act only at the midpoint of the zone. This is another delaying tactic. It shifts the action point up or down.

• Use stop orders. When your formula stock-selling point is reached in a rising market, place stop orders to sell a few points below the current market level. If the up trend continues, you will not sell your stocks too soon. In the opposite direction, when your formula buying point is reached in a declining market, put in an order to buy at a few points above the current market. If the downtrend continues, you will not buy too soon.

• Change ratios or zone. When you find that the formula plan is out of step with reality, you probably have been too conservative. Any change at or near the top of a bull market will not be effective. You will be almost out of stocks anyway. This is the wrong time to invest more heavily in stocks. It is probably more effective to make a zoning change at the time when the market drops into the middle or lower ranges. You will hold more stocks, so your profits should increase as the prices rise.

Automatic (formula plan) trading by ratio plans

Ratio plans compel caution in bull markets and bravery in bear markets. They force purchases as prices rise and they force switches or sales as prices decline. They are best for cyclical stocks in cyclical markets and require frequent attention.

Here are the ratio plan methods most widely acclaimed by professionals in this field:

- **Percentage of stocks.** With this plan, you decide what percentage of your portfolio funds should be in stocks: 25%, 50%, 75%, etc. At convenient time intervals, you sell or buy stocks to restore or maintain the set ratio regardless of the level of stock prices.

  Example: You start with $20,000 and plan to have 80% in good-quality common stocks and the remaining 20% in bonds or a savings account. You buy $16,000 worth of stocks. After six months, you find that the stock market has risen, so that the total value of your holdings is now $23,000. The stocks are now worth $19,000, or approximately 83% of the total $23,000. Therefore, you must sell $600 worth of stocks to reduce these holdings to $18,400 (that is, to the pre-determined 80% of the total $23,000). You then add the $600 (less commissions and taxes) to your savings account.

  If the stock market declines in the next half year, so that your total holdings are worth only $18,000, with your stocks valued at $14,000, you buy more stocks. Because the stocks are now only 77% of the total, you shift $400 from your savings to buy more stocks to reach that 80% mark.

  You obey the formula no matter how scared you are that the market is going to drop more. With all formula plans, you must learn to regard falling prices as a chance to buy more stocks at lower prices to help make up for paper losses. That's not easy, but it's essential.

- **Percentage changes.** With this type of formula plan, actions are taken when the value of the portfolio increases or decreases by a set percentage. You start with $2,000, equally divided between stocks and bonds.

Lessons from the Trader Wizard

The change can be the same each way or varied, eg, you sell when the value of the portfolio goes up 25% and you buy when it drops 20%.

When you have a 25% gain, you sell some stocks and you buy bonds. Or when the value dips 20%, you sell some bonds and you buy stocks to get back to the original balance.

Compared to a buy-and-hold strategy, this plan provides a 5% gain. With wider swings, the profits can be greater.

For most people, this is more interesting than practical. Most of us are unwilling to accept such discipline, because we believe that a rising stock (and market) will continue to go up and that a falling stock (or market) will somehow reverse its trend. But, statistically, over several market cycles, this plan will work out well.

A variation is the 10% approach. There are no value judgments or complicated calculations. Each week, you add up the worth of your portfolio based on the closing prices. Then, you set up a 50-day moving average (MA). As long as the MA continues to rise or hold steady, you maintain a fully invested position.

When there's a dip of 10% or more below the previous high, sell out or, if you're cautious, sell the losers. Don't start buying again until the MA rises 10% above the monthly low point. Then, go back to a fully invested position.

This sounds better for short-term trading than for long-term trading, but, surprisingly, it doesn't work out that way. Most trends continue longer than anticipated and, with a diversified portfolio of quality stocks, that 10% decline will not come as quickly and as often as you may think. Vice versa for that 10% upswing. Of course, with volatile holdings, you can be whipsawed and hurt by too many commissions.

Variable ratios: These apply primarily to mixed portfolios. The key is the percentage of stocks held: up as stock prices decline, down as they rise. It's a defensive plan that works best when the market moves within a fairly limited range. In a bull market, the percentage of stocks might drop from 75% to 50% or less. Toward the end of a bear market, the buying starts again. In each case, the shift is from stocks to fixed-income holdings.

The objective is to find an average that calls for half weighting of stocks and half in bonds, eg, when the DJIA is 13000. You buy more stocks at low prices, ie, at or below Dow 12000, and sell more at high prices, ie, at or above Dow 14000. Proceeds of sales would be put into fixed income securities.

Specialties to Trade

The problem with this system is to determine that central price average of the equity market trading range. If stock prices zoom up past your selected median, you'll be almost out of stocks and miss maximum appreciation. On the downside, however, you will always build a measure of protection, but you will not get back into stocks at the right time — unless you're lucky.

A compromise is to tie the central zone to some outside-the-market criterion such as: (1) growth of gross national product (this is hard to follow, and you will miss sharp, temporary rallies, still — that's the idea of formula plans — you act on rote, not judgment); or (2) determinants of stock prices rather than the stock prices themselves.

Thus, if the PE ratio of the DJIA is between 14 and 18, the ratio might be 50% stocks, 50% bonds. When the multiple falls below 14, the percentage of stocks might rise to 60%, and so on.

The difficulty is that there is no way of knowing how long the new base will continue. In the late 1960s, a PE of 14 was low; by the late 1970s, it was high. From the mid-1980s through 2000, it has been low again. In fact in 2000, it was extremely low. It's really a question of inflation: when inflation is above average, the PE ratio of the DJIA is relatively low, and vice versa.

Tax write-offs are not the key to successful trading

Never buy or sell a security without the transaction being part of a trading plan, not a tax plan.

If the failed Enron Corporation taught the world one thing, it was that tax-driven trading decisions usually don't build wealth. And protecting and creating wealth should be the foundation of every trader's mission statement.

If your goal is to beat the tax man, it's going to be tough to also succeed in the capital markets. To me, it's a mug's game, analogous to the motorist who will drive three extra miles to buy cheaper gasoline for his car. He ends up buying 20 gallons of gas five cents cheaper for a savings of $1.00 but it cost him 50 cents in gas, 20 cents in wear and tear on his car and 10 extra minutes of precious time. But he'll say he got a deal.

If you ask the same man if he'd go stand in the corner for three cents a minute, or flip burgers at McDonalds for 10 cents a minute, he'd think you were nuts. Go figure.

In the same vein, why would you seek a lower payout on any trade just for the satisfaction of saying you beat the tax man?

Lessons from the Trader Wizard

The key to successful trading is to find the highest risk-adjusted returns. There is no other personal objective as important. Taxes don't come even a close second.

Having said that, Americans know that long-term gains are defined as profits on securities held for more than a year, and short-term gains are where they are held a year or less. Since short-term gains are taxed at the trader's income rate (as high as 40%) and long-term gains are taxed at a fixed 20%, it is obviously tax efficient to sell for a gain after holding a stock for more than a year (long-term), and to sell for a loss when holding a stock for a year or less (short-term). Traders, then, try before year's end to offset short-term gains with short-term losses. But that is not a trading plan.

Also, investment bankers, cognizant of the high tax rate of certain traders, have created financial products that take advantage of the Income Tax Act. Products like Canadian labor-sponsored funds, business trusts, mining flow-throughs and movie deals abound. I don't know why, because they seldom ever result in good portfolio returns. I learned that from experience.

Twenty years ago, I "invested" over $100,000 in a movie deal and 100 cents on the dollar went to "money heaven". Results like that don't happen with high-quality (Cara 100) securities. Maybe at the time I was looking for entertainment. If so, I should have bought myself a book of 10,000 tickets to the movies. There sure have been a lot of good ones over the years.

Wrap-up

Do you recall the 1994 Oscar-winning movie *Forrest Gump*: "I am so simple I am special. Simple is as special does"?

We probably all agree that simple is best, especially as simple works. I know it does in capital markets trading.

The object of the trading game is to win, which you do through sticking with what works, keeping things trouble-free, and not trying to look like a genius.

That was one of Forrest Gump's endearing qualities. And through his perseverance as a shrimp farmer, Gump became "as rich as a gazillionaire!"

"Mama said there's only so much fortune a man really needs, and
the rest is just for showing off ...
So I gave a whole bunch of it to the Four Square Gospel Church.
And a whole bunch to the Bayou La Batre Fishing Hospital ...
And even though Bubba was dead, and Lt. Dan said I was nuts,

Specialties to Trade

I gave Bubba's Mama Bubba's share ...
And 'cause I was as rich as a gazillionaire, and I liked doin' it so
much, I cut the grass for free."

- Forrest Gump

I don't need to remind you of the expression "time is money". The focus on time and money today is the reason that the Trader Wizard exists.

Like Gump, I'm here for those of you who don't have the time to cut the grass. I'm hoping you are investing most of your time seeking to make and protect your fortune and that this book has helped.

In case you are left wondering, unlike Gump, I'm not "as rich as a gazillionaire" because "I liked doin' it so much, I cut the grass for free" from 4Q2000 to 4Q2007. Still, I made it to paradise where I now offer my services through Cara Trading Advisors (Bahamas) Limited.

Afterword

For some of you, this book will evoke as many questions as I provided answers. That's fine by me. I feel my role as a writer of "Lessons" is to get people to think.

One task I had hoped to accomplish was to explain in greater detail the companies I selected for my Cara Global Best 100 Companies list, but that will have to be for another book. So too, I had wanted to explain in depth the Cara Accumulation/Distribution methodology and my Buy/Sell Alert system. That will need a third book.

In reviewing this book, however, I can say that I believe there is something of value for everybody who has an interest in capital markets. For the newbie trader, you will probably feel the material is too advanced. For the seasoned pro, you will chuckle that most of the material is common knowledge. However, based on some 50,000 letters received directly and through my blog in the past four years, I feel I hit the target in the middle. That was my objective — to serve as many readers with as much valuable information that I, a seasoned professional trader, could pass along.

Yes, much of this material is well covered in other books, but in this book I bring my experiences and judgments into everything I laid out for you in the form of lessons. This was a very personal book. I hope you appreciate the hard work that went into it.

The Cara 100

Please note this list is as of January 8, 2008.
For a current list, please visit BillCara.com.

Name	Symbol	Country
Aetna Inc.	AET	USA
ABB Ltd (ADR)	ABB	Switzerland
Companhia de Bebidas das Americas (ADR)	ABV	Brazil
Barrick Gold	ABX	Canada
Adobe Systems Incorporated	ADBE	USA
Applied Materials, Inc.	AMAT	USA
Activision, Inc.	ATVI	USA
The Boeing Company	BA	USA
Bed Bath & Beyond Inc.	BBBY	USA
Banco Bradesco S.A. (ADR)	BBD	Brazil
Brunswick Corporation	BC	USA
The Black & Decker Corporation	BDK	USA
BHP Billiton Limited (ADR)	BHP	Australia
Bristol Myers Squibb Co.	BMY	USA
Cameco Corporation (USA)	CCJ	Canada
Carnival Corporation	CCL	USA
CNOOC Limited (ADR)	CEO	China
China Telecom Corporation Limited (ADR)	CHA	China
China Mobile Ltd. (ADR)	CHL	China
C.H. Robinson Worldwide, Inc.	CHRW	USA
Costco Wholesale Corporation	COST	USA
Cisco Systems, Inc.	CSCO	USA
Cognizant Technology Solutions Corp.	CTSH	USA
Chevron Corporation	CVX	USA
Deutsche Bank AG (USA)	DB	Germany
Dell Inc.	DELL	USA
Diageo plc (ADR)	DEO	UK
The Walt Disney Company	DIS	USA
The Dow Chemical Company	DOW	USA
Genentech, Inc.	DNA	USA
EnCana Corporation (USA)	ECA	Canada
Embraer-Empresa Brasileir de Aero (ADR)	ERJ	Brazil
Electronic Arts Inc.	ERTS	USA
Exelon Corporation	EXC	USA
General Electric Company	GE	USA
Gold Fields Limited (ADR)	GFI	South Africa
Goldcorp Inc.	GG	Canada
Gerdau S.A. (ADR)	GGB	Brazil

GOL Linhas Aereas Inteligentes SA (ADR)	GOL	Brazil
Google Inc.	GOOG	USA
Garmin Ltd.	GRMN	Cayman Islands
Goldman Sachs Group, Inc.	GS	USA
GlaxoSmithKline plc (ADR)	GSK	UK
HSBC Holdings plc (ADR)	HBC	UK
HDFC Bank Limited (ADR)	HDB	USA
Interactive Brokers Group, Inc.	IBKR	USA
ICICI Bank Limited (ADR)	IBN	India
Imperial Oil Limited (USA)	IMO	Canada
Infosys Technologies Limited (ADR)	INFY	India
Intel Corporation	INTC	USA
J.C. Penney Company, Inc.	JCP	USA
Johnson & Johnson	JNJ	USA
Kookmin Bank (ADR)	KB	Korea
The Coca-Cola Company	KO	USA
Kohl's Corporation	KSS	USA
Lehman Brothers Holdings Inc.	LEH	USA
Linear Technology Corporation	LLTC	USA
Mobile TeleSystems OJSC (ADR)	MBT	Russia
Manulife Financial Corporation (USA)	MFC	Canada
Millicom International Cellular SA (USA)	MICC	Luxembourg
NIKE, Inc.	NKE	USA
Nokia Corp.	NOK	Finland
NetEase.com, Inc. (ADR)	NTES	China
Nucor Corporation	NUE	USA
Oracle Corporation	ORCL	USA
optionsXpress Holdings, Inc.	OXPS	USA
Paychex, Inc.	PAYX	USA
Petroleo Brasileiro S.A. (ADR)	PBR	Brazil
Perdigão S.A.	PDA	Brazil
The Procter & Gamble Company	PG	USA
PetroChina Company Limited (ADR)	PTR	China
QUALCOMM, Inc.	QCOM	USA
Companhia Vale do Rio Doce (ADR)	RIO	Brazil
Research In Motion Limited (USA)	RIMM	Canada
Royal Bank of Canada (USA)	RY	Canada
Starbucks Corporation	SBUX	USA
Silver Wheaton Corp. (USA)	SLW	Canada
SanDisk Corporation	SNDK	USA
StatoilHydro ASA (ADR)	STO	Norway
Suncor Energy Inc. (USA)	SU	Canada
The Stanley Works	SWK	USA
Teck Cominco Limited (USA)	TCK	Canada
Telefonica SA	TEF	Spain
Teekay LNG Partners L.P.	TGP	Bahamas

Target Corporation	TGT	USA
Toyota Motor Corporation (ADR)	TM	Japan
TOTAL S.A. (ADR)	TOT	France
Tenaris S.A. (ADR)	TS	Argentina
Trane Inc.	TT	USA
UBS AG (USA)	UBS	Switzerland
United Technologies Corporation	UTX	USA
Votorantim Celulose e Papel S.A (ADR)	VCP	Brazil
Vimpel-Communications (ADR)	VIP	Russia
Walgreen Company	WAG	USA
Westpac Banking Corporation (ADR)	WBK	Australia
Whole Foods Market, Inc.	WFMI	USA
Whirlpool Corporation	WHR	USA
Wal-Mart Stores, Inc.	WMT	USA
Exxon Mobil Corporation	XOM	USA
Yahoo! Inc.	YHOO	USA

Glossary of Terms

A note to readers:

While many of these definitions are meant as a reference section for readers, some definitions are a reflection of my blog, and are, therefore, tongue-in-cheek.

alternate PPT: in China known as the Pork Protection Team similar in concept to the US Strategic Petroleum Reserve, but focuses on hog reserves to control pork prices from escalating out of control.

American depository receipts (ADRs): a negotiable certificate issued by a US bank representing a specified number of shares (or one share) in a foreign stock that is traded on a US exchange. ADRs are denominated in US dollars, with the underlying security held by a US financial institution overseas. ADRs help to reduce administration and duty costs that would otherwise be levied on each transaction.

arbitrage: the simultaneous purchase and sale of an asset in order to profit from a difference in the price. This usually takes place on different exchanges or marketplaces. Also known as a "riskless profit".

arbitrageur: a type of investor who attempts to profit from price inefficiencies in the market by making simultaneous trades that offset each other and capture risk-free profits.

backwardation: a downward sloping forward curve (as in an inverted yield curve); one says that the forward curve is in backwardation. The opposite market condition is known as contango.

basis: 1. The variation between the spot price of a deliverable commodity and the relative price of the futures contract for the same actual that has the shortest duration until maturity. **2.** A security's basis is the purchase price after commissions or other expenses. Also known as "cost basis" or "tax basis". **3.** In the context of IRAs, basis is the after-tax balance in the IRA, which originates from non-deductible IRA contributions and rollover of after-tax amounts. Earnings on these amounts are tax-deferred, similar to earnings on deductible contributions and rollover of pre-tax amounts.

basis point (bp): a unit that is equal to 1/100th of 1%, and is used to denote the change in a financial instrument. The basis point is commonly used for calculating changes in interest rates, equity indexes and the yield of a fixed-income security. The relationship between percentage changes and basis points can be summarized as follows: 1% change = 100 basis points and 0.01% = 1 basis point.

bear market: a prolonged period in which investment prices fall, accompanied by widespread pessimism. If the period of falling stock prices is short and immediately follows a period of rising stock prices, it is instead called a correction. Bear markets usually occur when the economy is in a recession and unemployment is high, or when inflation is rising quickly.

bear spread: 1. An option strategy seeking maximum profit when the price of the underlying security declines. The strategy involves the simultaneous purchase and sale of options; puts or calls can be used. A higher strike price is purchased and a lower strike price is sold. The options should have the same expiration date. **2.** A trading strategy used by futures traders who intend to profit from the decline in commodity prices while limiting potentially damaging losses.

book value: 1. The value at which an asset is carried on a balance sheet. In other words, the cost of an asset minus accumulated depreciation. **2.** The net asset value of a company, calculated by total assets minus intangible assets (patents, goodwill) and liabilities. **3.** The initial outlay for an investment. This number may be net or gross of expenses such as trading costs, sales taxes, service charges and so on. In the UK, book value is known as "net asset value".

BRIC: an acronym for the economies of Brazil, Russia, India and China combined. The general consensus is that the term was first prominently used in a Goldman Sachs report from 2003, which speculated that by 2050 these four economies would be wealthier than most of the current major economic powers.

bull market: a prolonged period in which investment prices rise faster than their historical average. Bull markets can happen as a result of an economic recovery, an economic boom, or investor psychology.

call: 1. The period of time between the opening and closing of some future markets wherein the prices are established through an auction process. **2.** An option contract giving the owner the right (but not the obligation) to buy a specified amount of an underlying security at a specified price within a specified time.

CAPEX (Capital Expenditure): funds used by a company to acquire or upgrade physical assets such as property, industrial buildings or equipment. This type of outlay is made by companies to maintain or increase the scope of their operation. These expenditures can include everything from repairing a roof to building a brand new factory.

certificate of deposit (CD): a savings certificate entitling the bearer to receive interest. A CD bears a maturity date, a specified fixed interest rate and can be issued in any denomination. CDs are generally issued by commercial banks and are insured by the FDIC. The term of a CD generally ranges from one month to five years.

cheapest to deliver: the least expensive underlying product that can be delivered upon expiry to satisfy the requirements of a derivative contract.

Chinese Wall concept: the ethical (not physical) barrier between different divisions of a financial (or other) institution to avoid conflict of interest. A Chinese Wall is said to exist, for example, between the corporate-advisory area and the brokering department to separate those giving corporate advice on takeovers from those advising clients about buying shares. The "wall" is thrown up to prevent leaks of corporate inside information, which could influence the advice given to clients making investments, and allow staff to take advantage of facts that are not yet known to the general public.

closed-end funds: a mutual fund that has been closed – either temporarily or permanently – to new investors because the investment advisor has determined that the fund's asset base is getting too large to effectively execute its investing style.

combination: when an investor holds a position in both call and put options on the same asset.

commercial paper: an unsecured obligation issued by a corporation or bank to finance its short-term credit needs, such as accounts receivable and inventory. Maturities typically range from two to 270 days. Commercial paper is available in a wide range of denominations, can be either discounted or interest-bearing, and usually have a limited or nonexistent secondary market.

Commodity Research Bureau (CRB Index): an index that measures the overall direction of commodity sectors. The CRB was designed to isolate and reveal the directional movement of prices in overall commodity trades.

compound annual growth rate (CAGR): the year-over-year growth rate of an investment over a specified period of time. The compound annual growth rate is calculated by taking the nth root of the total percentage growth rate, where n is the number of years in the period being considered.

contract for difference (CFD): an arrangement made in a futures contract whereby differences in settlement are made through cash payments, rather than the delivery of physical goods or securities.

Glossary of Terms

convertible bonds: a bond that can be converted into a predetermined amount of the company's equity at certain times during its life, usually at the discretion of the bondholder. Convertibles are sometimes called "CVs".

convertible securities (CVs): a debt instrument that combines a coupon paying bond with the option to convert the bond into common stock at a set price. These are frequently described as hybrid securities because they combine features of debt and equity, converting to ordinary shares at a set date based on a pre-determined ratio.

counter-cyclical stock: a type of stock in which the underlying company belongs to an industry or niche with financial performance that is negatively correlated to the overall state of the economy. As a result, the stock's price will also tend to move in a direction that is opposite to the general economic trend, meaning appreciation occurs during times of recession and depreciation in value occur in times of economic expansion.

covered call: an options strategy whereby an investor holds a long position in an asset and writes (sells) call options on that same asset in an attempt to generate increased income from the asset. This is often employed when an investor has a short-term neutral view on the asset and for this reason holds the asset long and simultaneously has a short position via the option to generate income from the option premium. This is also known as a "buy-write".

debenture: unsecured debt backed only by the integrity of the borrower, not by collateral, and documented by an agreement called an indenture. One example is an unsecured bond.

debt instrument: a paper or electronic obligation that enables the issuing party to raise funds by promising to repay a lender in accordance with terms of a contract. Types of debt instruments include notes, bonds, certificates, mortgages, leases or other agreements between a lender and a borrower.

discretionary or free cash flow: measure of financial performance calculated as operating cash flow minus capital expenditures. In other words, free cash flow (FCF) represents the cash that a company is able to generate after laying out the money required to maintain or expand its asset base. Free cash flow is important because it allows a company to pursue opportunities that enhance shareholder value. Without cash, it's tough to develop new products, make acquisitions, pay dividends and reduce debt.

disinflation: a drop in the inflation rate, ie, a reduction in the rate at which prices rise.

Dow Jones Industrial Average (DJIA): the most widely used indicator of the overall condition of the stock market, a price-weighted average of 30 actively traded blue chip stocks, primarily industrials. The 30 stocks are chosen by the editors of the *Wall Street Journal* (which is published by Dow Jones & Company), a practice that dates back over 100 years. The Dow is computed using a price-weighted indexing system, rather than the more common market cap-weighted indexing system.

Dow 30 Industrials Index: the Dow Jones Industrial Index top 30 companies.

equity, debt, commodity or currency derivative: a derivative instrument with underlying assets based on equity securities. An equity derivative's value will fluctuate with changes in its underlying asset's equity, which is usually measured by share price.

exchange-traded funds (ETFs): a fund that tracks an index, but can be traded like a stock. ETFs always bundle together the securities that are in an index; they never track actively managed mutual fund portfolios (because most actively managed funds only disclose their holdings a few times a year, so the ETF would not know when to adjust its holdings most of the time). Investors can do just about anything with an ETF that they can do with a normal stock, such as short selling. Because ETFs are traded on stock exchanges, they can be bought and sold at any time during the day (unlike most mutual funds).

the Fed: the Federal Reserve Bank. These are banks that carry out federal operations, including controlling the money supply and regulating member banks. There are 12 district Feds, headquartered in Boston, New York, Philadelphia, Cleveland, St. Louis, San Francisco, Richmond, Atlanta, Chicago, Minneapolis, Kansas City and Dallas.

FETV: financial entertainment television. Also known as CNBC.

Financial Accounting Standards Board (FASB): a seven-member independent board consisting of accounting professionals who establish and communicate standards of financial accounting and reporting in the United States. FASB standards, known as generally accepted accounting principles (GAAP), govern the preparation of corporate financial reports and are recognized as authoritative by the Securities and Exchange Commission.

Forex: an over-the-counter market where buyers and sellers conduct foreign exchange transactions. It is also called the foreign exchange market.

generally accepted accounting principles (GAAP): the common set of accounting principles, standards and procedures that companies use to compile their financial statements. GAAP are a combination of authoritative standards (set by policy boards) and simply the commonly accepted ways of recording and reporting accounting information.

greater fool theory: belief held by one who makes a questionable investment, with the assumption that he/she will be able to sell it later to a bigger fool.

Global Industry Classification Standard (GICS®): a standardized classification system for equities developed jointly by Morgan Stanley Capital International (MSCI) and Standard & Poor's. The GICS methodology is used by the MSCI indexes, which include domestic and international stocks, as well as by a large portion of the professional investment management community. The GICS hierarchy begins with 10 sectors and is followed by 24 industry groups, 67 industries and 147 sub-industries. Each stock that is classified will have a coding at all four of these levels.

gnomes: the movers and shakers of capital markets who control HB&B, mainstream media, the largest corporations and, some say, Presidents and Prime Ministers.

going concern value (sometimes called enterprise value, fair value or equity value): the value of a company as an ongoing entity. This value differs from the value of a liquidated company's assets, because an ongoing operation has the ability to continue to earn profit, while a liquidated company does not.

goldilocks: term used to describe the US economy, implying that it is "not too hot, not too cold", an optimal environment for equity prices to rise. This term is used extensively by Larry Kudlow and his cohorts at CNBC.

HB&Bs: humungous banks and brokers, the Goldman Sachs and Lehman Bros of the world. The HB&B control large amounts of capital that can be used to manipulate market prices.

HBOP: humungous bail-out package.

hedging: making an investment to reduce the risk of adverse price movements in an asset. Normally, a hedge consists of taking an offsetting position in a related security, such as a futures contract.

high-yield bonds or junk bonds: a high-paying bond with a lower credit rating than investment-grade corporate bonds, Treasury bonds and municipal bonds. Because of the higher risk of default, these bonds pay a higher yield than investment-grade bonds. Based on the two main credit rating agencies, high-yield bonds carry a rating of 'BBB' or lower from S&P, and 'Baa' or lower from Moody's. Bonds with ratings above these levels are considered investment grade.Credit ratings can be as low as 'D' (currently in default), and most bonds with 'C' ratings or lower carry a high risk of default; to compensate for this risk, yields will typically be very high.

hold: be in possession of or have in one's portfolio; or an analyst's rating which (paradoxically) usually means don't hold.

HPEC: humungous private equity corporation.

initial public offering (IPO): the first sale of stock by a private company to the public. IPOs are often issued by smaller, younger companies seeking capital to expand, but can also be done by large privately-owned companies looking to become publicly traded. Also referred to as a "public offering".

J6P: Joe 6-pack.

junior issues: generally speaking, any issue that ranks lower in claim to another issue in terms of dividends, interest, principal, etc.

kicker: a right, warrant or some other feature added to a debt instrument to make it more desirable to potential investors.

law of large numbers: in statistical terms, a rule that assumes that as the number of samples increases, the average of these samples is likely to reach the mean of the whole population. When relating this concept to finance, it suggests that as a company grows, its chances of sustaining a large percentage in growth diminish. This is because as a company continues to expand, it must grow more and more just to maintain a constant percentage of growth.

Lehman Brothers US Aggregate Index: an index used by bond funds as a benchmark to measure their relative performance. It includes government securities, mortgage-backed securities, asset-backed securities and corporate securities to simulate the universe of bonds in the market. The maturities of the bonds in the index are more than one year.

limit order: an order placed with a brokerage to buy or sell a set number of shares at a specified price or better. Limit orders also allow an investor to limit the length of time an order can be outstanding before being cancelled.

London Interbank Offered Rate (LIBOR): an interest rate at which banks can borrow funds, in marketable size, from other banks in the London interbank market. The LIBOR is fixed on a daily basis by the British Bankers' Association. The LIBOR is derived from a filtered average of the world's most creditworthy banks' interbank deposit rates for larger loans with maturities between overnight and one full year.

Glossary of Terms

long-term MA: an indicator frequently used in technical analysis showing the average value of a security's price over a set period. Moving averages are generally used to measure momentum and define areas of possible support and resistance.

market order: an order to buy or sell a stock immediately at the best available current price. A market order is sometimes referred to as an "unrestricted order".

mini-bubble: 1. An economic cycle characterized by rapid expansion followed by a contraction. **2.** A surge in equity prices, often more than warranted by the fundamentals and usually in a particular sector, followed by a drastic drop in prices as a massive sell off occurs. **3.** A theory that security prices rise above their true value and will continue to do so until prices go into freefall and the bubble bursts. A mini-bubble has these characteristics, but on a shorter, smaller scale.

Morgan Stanley Capital International (MSCI): a leading provider of equity, fixed-income and hedge fund indexes. MSCI has been providing global equity indexes for more than 30 years. In 2003, it launched a new family of US equity indexes. Morgan Stanley's global equity benchmarks have become the most widely used international indices by institutional investors across 23 developed and 27 emerging markets.

moving average convergence divergence (MACD) or moving average departure analysis: a trend-following momentum indicator that shows the relationship between two moving averages of prices. The MACD is calculated by subtracting the 26-day exponential moving average (EMA) from the 12-day EMA. A nine-day EMA of the MACD, called the "signal line", is then plotted on top of the MACD, functioning as a trigger for buy and sell signals.

naked call: an options strategy in which an investor writes (sells) call options on the open market without owning the underlying security. This stands in contrast to a covered call strategy, where the investor owns the security shares that are eligible to be exercised under the options contract. This strategy is sometimes referred to as an "uncovered call" or a "short call".

naked shorting: the illegal practice of short selling shares that have not been affirmatively determined to exist. Ordinarily, traders must borrow a stock, or determine that it can be borrowed, before they sell it short. However, some professional investors and hedge funds take advantage of loopholes in the rules to sell shares without making any attempt to borrow the stock.

net asset value (NAV): the dollar value of a single mutual fund share, based on the value of the underlying assets of the fund minus its liabilities, divided by the number of shares outstanding. NAVs are calculated at the end of each business day.

New York Stock Exchange (NYSE): the largest stock exchange in the US, located on Wall Street in New York City. The NYSE is responsible for setting policy, supervising member activities, listing securities, overseeing the transfer of member seats, and evaluating applicants. Of the exchanges, the NYSE has the most stringent set of requirements in place for the companies whose stocks it lists, and even meeting these requirements is not a guarantee that the NYSE will list the company.

open-end fund: a type of mutual fund where there are no restrictions on the amount of shares the fund will issue. If demand is high enough, the fund will continue to issue shares no matter how many investors there are. Open-end funds also buy back shares when investors wish to sell.

OPM: other peoples' money.

organic growth: the growth rate that a company can achieve by increasing output and enhancing sales. This excludes any profits or growth acquired from takeovers, acquisitions or mergers. Takeovers, acquisitions and mergers do not bring about profits generated within the company, and therefore, are not considered organic.

Organisation for Economic Co-operation and Development (OECD): the OECD is a group of 30 member countries who discuss and develop economic and social policy.

par: 1. The face value of a bond. Generally $1,000 for corporate issues, with higher denominations such as $10,000 for many government issues. **2.** A dollar amount assigned to a security when first issued.

penny dreadful: a negative cash-flow development company (always with a great story to hook the punters!).

PE ratio: a valuation ratio of a company's current share price compared to its per-share earnings. Also sometimes known as "price multiple" or "earnings multiple".

Plunge Protection Team (PPT): created in 1989 as an outgrowth of the President's Working Group on Financial Markets, this group of government agencies, stock exchanges and HB&Bs are primarily responsible for preventing destabilizing stock market declines. Their footprints can be regularly seen in market manipulations.

POG: price of gold.

Glossary of Terms

preferred stock: a class of ownership in a corporation that has a higher claim on the assets and earnings than common stock. Preferred stock generally has a dividend that must be paid out before dividends to common stockholders and the shares usually do not have voting rights. The precise details as to the structure of preferred stock is specific to each corporation.

premium: 1. The total cost of an option. **2.** The difference between the higher price paid for a fixed-income security and the security's face amount at issue. **3.** The specified amount of payment required periodically by an insurer to provide coverage under a given insurance plan for a defined period of time. The premium is paid by the insured party to the insurer, and primarily compensates the insurer for bearing the risk of a payout should the insurance agreement's coverage be required.

Producer Price Index (PPI): a family of indexes that measures the average change in selling prices received by domestic producers of goods and services over time. PPIs measure price change from the perspective of the seller.

profit margin (PM): a ratio of profitability calculated as net income divided by revenues, or net profits divided by sales. It measures how much out of every dollar of sales a company actually keeps in earnings. Profit margin is very useful when comparing companies in similar industries. A higher profit margin indicates a more profitable company that has better control over its costs compared to its competitors. Profit margin is displayed as a percentage; a 20% profit margin, for example, means the company has a net income of $0.20 for each dollar of sales.

punter: a risk-taker who trades the penny dreadfuls.

put: an option contract giving the owner the right, but not the obligation, to sell a specified amount of an underlying asset at a set price within a specified time. The buyer of a put option estimates that the underlying asset will drop below the exercise price before the expiration date.

range-bound (ie, side-tracking) trading: a trading strategy that identifies stocks trading in channels. By finding major support and resistance levels with technical analysis, a trend trader buys stocks at the lower level of support (bottom of the channel) and sells them near resistance (top of the channel).

registered representative (RR): an individual who is licensed to sell securities and has the legal power of an agent, having passed the Series 7 and Series 63 examinations. In Canada and other countries, these numbers are different.

relative strength: a measure of price trend that indicates how a stock is performing relative to other stocks in its industry.

relative strength index (RSI): a technical momentum indicator that compares the magnitude of recent gains to recent losses in an attempt to determine overbought and oversold conditions of an asset. RSI 7, 14 and 28 can be seen on some charting services versus RSI 7 Daily, Weekly and Monthly.

restructuring: a significant modification made to the debt, operations or structure of a company. This type of corporate action is usually made when there are significant problems in a company, which are causing some form of financial harm and putting the overall business in jeopardy.

rights: a security giving stockholders entitlement to purchase new shares issued by the corporation at a predetermined price (normally less than the current market price) in proportion to the number of shares already owned. Rights are issued only for a short period of time, after which they expire.

rule of 72: the estimation of doubling time on an investment, for which the compounded annual rate of return times the number of years must equal roughly 72 for the investment to double in value.

Standard & Poor's 500 (S&P 500): a basket of 500 stocks that are considered to be widely held. The S&P 500 Index is weighted by market value, and its performance is thought to be representative of the stock market as a whole. It provides a broad snapshot of the overall US equity market, over 70% of all US equity is tracked by the S&P 500. The Index selects its companies based upon their market size, liquidity, and sector. Most of the companies in the Index are solid mid-cap or large-cap corporations.

US Securities and Exchange Commission (SEC): a government commission created by Congress to regulate the securities markets and protect investors. In addition to regulation and protection, it also monitors the corporate takeovers in the US. The SEC is composed of five commissioners appointed by the US President and approved by the Senate. The statutes administered by the SEC are designed to promote full public disclosure and to protect the investing public against fraudulent and manipulative practices in the securities markets.

Sharpe Ratio: a risk-adjusted measure developed by William F. Sharpe, calculated using standard deviation and excess return to determine reward per unit of risk. The higher the Sharpe Ratio, the better the fund's historical risk-adjusted performance.

short-interest ratio (SIR): a sentiment indicator that is derived by dividing the short interest by the average daily volume for a stock. This indicator is used by both fundamental and technical traders to identify the prevailing sentiment the market has for a specific stock. Also known as the "short ratio".

sinking fund: a means of repaying funds that were borrowed through a bond issue. The issuer makes periodic payments to a trustee who retires part of the issue by purchasing the bonds in the open market.

spread: 1. The difference between the bid and the ask price of a security or asset. **2.** An options position established by purchasing one option and selling another option of the same class but of a different series.

stop order: an order to buy or sell a security when its price surpasses a particular point, thus ensuring a greater probability of achieving a predetermined entry or exit price, limiting the investor's loss or locking in his or her profit. Once the price surpasses the predefined entry/exit point, the stop order becomes a market order. Also referred to as a "stop" and/or "stop-loss order".

straddle: an options strategy with which the investor holds a position in both a call and put with the same strike price and expiration date.

strap: an options strategy created by being long in one put and two call options, all with the exact same strike price, maturity and underlying asset. Also referred to as a "triple option".

strip: 1. For bonds, the process of removing coupons from a bond and then selling the separate parts as a zero-coupon bond and interest paying coupons. Also known as a stripped bond or zero-coupon bond. **2.** In options, a strategy created by being long in one call and two put options, all with the exact same strike price.

Subchapter S Corporations: a form of corporation, allowed by the IRS for most companies with 75 or fewer shareholders, which enables the company to enjoy the benefits of incorporation, but be taxed as if it were a partnership.

swap: traditionally, the exchange of one security for another to change the maturity (bonds), quality of issues (stocks or bonds), or because investment objectives have changed. Recently, swaps have grown to include currency swaps and interest rate swaps.

switch: a futures-trading strategy involving the offset of one contract with entry into another position that has nearly identical details but a longer expiration. Commonly referred to as a "roll forward".

synthetic put: an investment strategy of short selling a security and entering a long position on its call.

T-bill rate: a negotiable debt obligation issued by the US Government and backed by its full faith and credit, having a maturity of one year or less. US Treasury Bills are exempt from state and local taxes. These securities do not pay a coupon rate of interest, and the interest earned is estimated by taking the difference between the price paid and the par value of the bond, and calculating that rate of return on an annual basis.

Temporary Open Market Injections (TOMOs): trillions of Federal Reserve bank monies that are "loaned" to the HB&B, who in turn use the funds to manipulate prices, up or down, in various market sectors.

tickee: consumer's money for discretionary spending.

Treasury Bills (T-bills): a short-term debt obligation backed by the US Government with a maturity of less than one year. T-bills are sold in denominations of $1,000 up to a maximum purchase of $5 million and commonly have maturities of one month (four weeks), three months (13 weeks) or six months (26 weeks). T-bills are issued through a competitive bidding process at a discount from par, which means that rather than paying fixed interest payments like conventional bonds, the appreciation of the bond provides the return to the holder.

Federal Funds Rate: the interest rate at which a depository institution lends immediately available funds (balances at the Federal Reserve) to another depository institution overnight.

trend trading: a trading strategy that attempts to capture gains through the analysis of an asset's momentum in a particular direction. The trend trader enters into a long position when a stock is trending upward (successively higher highs). Conversely, a short position is taken when the stock is in a down trend (successively lower highs).

warrant: a derivative security that gives the holder the right to purchase securities (usually equity) from the issuer at a specific price within a certain time frame. Warrants are often included in a new debt issue as a "sweetener" to entice investors.

year-over-year: compared to the same time period in the previous year.

yield: the annual rate of return on an investment, expressed as a percentage.

Glossary of Terms

yield curve: a line that plots the interest rates, at a set point in time, of bonds having equal credit quality, but differing maturity dates. The most frequently reported yield curve compares the three-month, two-year, five-year and 30-year US Treasury debt. This yield curve is used as a benchmark for other debt in the market, such as mortgage rates or bank lending rates. The curve is also used to predict changes in economic output and growth. It can be positive, negative, normal, steep, inverted or flat.

zero-sum game: a situation in which one participant's gains result only from another participant's equivalent losses. The net change in total wealth among participants is zero; the wealth is just shifted from one to another.